Handbook of Canadian Higher Education Law

Theresa Shanahan, Michelle Nilson, Li-Jeen Broshko

Editors

Queen's Policy Studies Series
School of Policy Studies, Queen's University
McGill-Queen's University Press
Montreal & Kingston • London • Ithaca

Queen's | Policy Studies

Publications Unit
Robert Sutherland Hall
138 Union Street
Kingston, ON, Canada
K7L 3N6
www.queensu.ca/sps/

Library and Archives Canada Cataloguing in Publication

Handbook of Canadian higher education law / Theresa Shanahan, Michelle Nilson, Li-Jeen Broshko, editors.

(Queen's policy studies series)
Includes bibliographical references.
Issued in print and electronic formats.
ISBN 978-1-55339-442-6 (paperback),—ISBN 978-1-55339-500-3 (epub).
—ISBN 978-1-55339-501-0 (pdf)

1. Education, Higher—Law and legislation—Canada. 2. Universities and colleges—Law and legislation—Canada. I. Shanahan, Theresa, 1963-, editor II. Nilson, Michelle, 1970-, editor III. Broshko, Li-Jeen, 1974-, editor IV. Series: Queen's policy studies series

KE3904.H35 2015   344.71'074   C2015-902891-4
KF4225.H35 2015   C2015-905076-6

TABLE OF CONTENTS

INTRODUCTION/PREFACE

PETER MERCER

I have been asked by the editors of this extremely valuable handbook to provide a brief introduction to it. This may seem counterintuitive given that I have served since 2005 as the President of Ramapo College, designated as New Jersey's Public Liberal Arts College. However, I had previously taught for several years at the University of Windsor and University of Calgary law schools before spending 20 years in a variety of administrative roles at the University of Western Ontario, including dean of law and vice-president administration and general counsel. I have also continued as one of the instructors in the Senior University Administrators Course, which has enabled me to stay abreast of Canadian higher education.

Only a couple of generations ago, senior administrators and trustees of Canadian colleges and universities held office for terms – 20 or 30 years was not uncommon – that would be unthinkable today. The sheer operational complexity and the intense regulatory and political scrutiny to which institutions are subject has meant that the average term of office of a dean or a president or a board chair has significantly and steadily declined. Today's university is engaged with many more external constituencies, particularly in its research operations, and these engagements often feature separate structures that can sometimes behave as if they are autonomous. Faculty members, as well, more frequently engage in research and other academic projects beyond the boundaries of their home institution.

Virtually all these changes increasingly raise the spectre of potential legal action on any number of grounds, and in a way that is menacing to the layperson. Degree programs in education administration and other sorts of training and education workshops typically include a legal component, but there are few accessible resources available. In-house counsel, where they exist, are obviously a valuable resource but only if they are approached to give advice. In that respect, there is one other factor at play in higher education institutions that must be acknowledged. In my experience, those involved in the workings of universities are often attracted to them because of the intellectual environment and the opportunity to work more or less independently. They have flourished in their individual careers from the beginning and have become accustomed to resolving problems themselves as they arise.

This proclivity can cause problems in two ways. First, the situation may have legal components that the decision maker may not recognize. Second, even where it is recognized that there are legal issues, the tendency to want to fix the problem without help often means that the situation has grown worse by the time it lands on the in-house counsel's desk.

All those involved in the workings of Canadian institutions of higher learning – the board, the president and senior administration, the faculty, staff, and students – should therefore welcome the appearance of the *Handbook of Canadian Higher Education Law*. Its twelve chapters cover important topics in a way that can be readily understood by non-lawyers, thus enabling them to make informed decisions that minimize the prospect of legal challenge. In the increasingly complex world of higher education, it is not enough to have in-house counsel with primary responsibility for legal matters. Too often, situations with significant legal implications are brought to their attention too late in the day because administrators at the centre of the problem do not realize potential bases of liability. This handbook will go a long way to developing the antennae necessary to recognize that legal advice needs to be sought.

The various topics covered in the *Handbook*'s early chapters illustrate a dominant underlying theme: in a professional domain such as higher education, where we expect individuals to exercise their discretion relying on their skills, training, and experience, what limits on the exercise of that discretion are properly to be imposed by the legal system? Generally speaking, the courts are not inclined to second-guess decision makers in higher education. Indeed, the clearest cases of judicial intervention tend to be where the higher education system has failed to follow its own prescribed rules. Ironically, this failure tends to occur, at a procedural level, when the individual case's resolution seems clearest on its merits. The lesson to be learned can be stated as Rule #1: Follow your own prescribed rules and procedures, and Rule #2: Follow Rule #1. Formalities cannot be dispensed with just because the substantive result seems obvious.

The *Handbook* sensibly moves from the general, beginning with a legal overview of higher education, to the particular, with individual chapters focusing on the legal context of the various actors in the system – faculty, students, government, and particular communities of interest. This makes it particularly useful as a reference and guidance source for them.

From my perspective as someone who is about to enter a tenth year as president of a public liberal arts college in the United States after

spending over 25 years in the Canadian higher educ?
theme of accountability continues to occupy the spotl₁₃
of the border. In both countries, this is evidenced by a renew∪
on accreditation standards, a dynamic tension between the pro∿
states and the federal branch with the latter using research funds a∵
lever, and a focus on outcomes measures across institutions. A cynic
might note that a principle of inverse proportion is operating in both
countries as each demands increasing accountability even as their fiscal
support for higher education is reduced.

One thing that a handbook such as this cannot do is account for the
political dimension of higher education administration. As I write this,
events that began unfolding at the University of Saskatchewan in May
2014 remain a hot topic of conversation. The provost, who appears to have
exceeded his authority by purporting to strip a dissident dean not only
of his administrative position as dean but also, *inter alia*, of his tenured
faculty position, resigned. The president, who described the provost's action as a "blunder" and reinstated the former dean to his tenured faculty
position, was shortly thereafter fired by the board of governors without
cause and to prevent further damage to the reputation of the university.

This termination of a university president is but one example of several
that have occurred at Canadian universities in the last decade. In such
a volatile environment, the *Handbook of Canadian Higher Education Law*
should make a valuable companion.

Peter P. Mercer, LL.B.
President of Ramapo College of New Jersey

ACKNOWLEDGEMENTS

We would like to thank Simon Fraser University for their generous financial support of this work through the University Publications Fund, Single Publication Grant program. We would also like to thank York University for their financial support of this publication. We thank Keith Banting and Kim Nossal of the School of Policy Studies, Queen's University, for their support of this project; Valerie Jarus and Mark Howes from the Publications Unit, who undertook the production of this publication; and Ellie Barton, our copy editor, for her patience and exceptional editorial assistance. Finally, we thank each of the chapter contributors for their expertise, patience, and wisdom.

Theresa: To Michelle Nilson for her initiative and inspiration, and for getting this project off the ground. And to Li-Jeen Broshko for her enthusiasm for keeping it going. It has been an honour to work with such good colleagues. I am grateful to my colleagues and to Dean Ron Owston of the Faculty of Education at York University for providing me time and support to complete this project.

Michelle: Book ideas that fill a large gap such as this one are rarely the inspiration of one individual, and this text is no exception. Thank you to the students of my spring 2011 Ethics, Law, and Professional Leadership (EDUC 960) course. Preparations for the course and subsequent discussions with students about the limitations and opportunities within Canadian higher education law served as the inspiration for this project. I am forever grateful for the opportunity to work with and learn from them. I am also grateful to my colleagues and Dean Magnusson in the Faculty of Education at Simon Fraser University for their encouragement and support. Finally, and most importantly, I am grateful to Theresa Shanahan for her thoughtfulness and her diligence in bringing this project to fruition and to Li-Jeen Broshko for her ability to make connections and her constant enthusiasm.

Li-Jeen: To Simon Fraser University for the learning opportunities that it has afforded to me over the years, both theoretical and applied. Also, to my wonderful co-editors and the authors who made this book possible.

PART I
Overview of Postsecondary Education in Canada

Chapter 1

THE LEGISLATIVE FRAMEWORK OF POSTSECONDARY EDUCATION IN CANADA

THERESA SHANAHAN

OVERVIEW OF POSTSECONDARY EDUCATION IN CANADA: THE LEGISLATIVE FRAMEWORK

The purpose of this introductory chapter is to provide a historical and contextual overview of postsecondary education in Canada, describe the legislative framework of Canadian postsecondary education, set out the constitutional structure and coordination, identify the sources of postsecondary education law, and discuss the implications of the distinct Canadian constitutional features on postsecondary education.

Canadian higher education has been shaped by many factors including federalism, regionalism, language, religion, culture, and geography.[1] Embedded in a broader social, economic, bureaucratic, and political context, Canadian higher education has evolved in response to distinct structural features of Canadian society including our parliamentary system and Constitution, the diverse identities and values across the country, and material regional disparities especially around resources and the economy.[2]

---

[1] For reviews of each provincial higher education system in Canada see Jones, *Higher Education in Canada*.

[2] For a thorough examination of the workings of Canadian federalism, see Bakvis and Skogstad, *Canadian Federalism*.

Handbook of Canadian Higher Education Law, edited by Theresa Shanahan, Michelle Nilson, and Li-Jeen Broshko. Montreal and Kingston: McGill-Queen's University Press, Queen's Policy Studies Series.

EVOLUTION OF POSTSECONDARY EDUCATION IN CANADA

Evidence of postsecondary education can be traced to the first French settlements in Canada, in the 1600s, mainly church-affiliated through the Jesuit priests and Ursuline nuns. Laval University traces its roots back to the establishment of the Grand Séminaire de Québec in 1663, one of the earliest documented Canadian postsecondary institutions. Well before Confederation in 1867 the first organized universities emerged with British colonialism in Lower Canada (Quebec) and Upper Canada (Ontario) as well as Nova Scotia and New Brunswick.[3] By Confederation there were 18 universities and additional classical colleges across Canada.[4]

Reasons for contemporary legislative arrangements in education in Canada are historically embedded in the story of Confederation. Education developed in Canada starting in communities often initiated by local religious groups who gathered together and organized and ran schools, decided the curriculum, and hired the teachers. These education arrangements predated compulsory schooling legislation by government. Education in Canada was driven by public demand and not government laws. By the time of Confederation in 1867, each of the four original provinces (Ontario, Quebec, Nova Scotia, and New Brunswick) had its own education systems in place organized along religious (denominational) and language lines. Lower Canada (Quebec) was strongly French-speaking and Catholic (with a large English-speaking and Protestant minority) while Upper Canada (Ontario) was strongly English-speaking and Anglican (with a large Catholic and French-speaking minority). The cultural diversity between the colonial regions was sufficiently entrenched as to represent an obstacle to Confederation. Federalism provided the solution allowing the coexistence of the two cultures – English and French. Federalism protects the geographically based cultural minorities in Canada. Historically, federalism enabled governments to administer a geographically large area by allowing regional government to administer local issues, balancing federal and provincial rights and interests.

In order for Confederation to occur, "the Fathers of Confederation" conceded to colonial leaders the preservation of the existing provincial education systems. This principle of provincial control over education became enshrined in the Canadian Constitution uniting the colonies.[5]

---

[3] For a full history see Harris, *History of Higher Education in Canada 1663–1960*.

[4] CMEC, *Postsecondary Education Systems in Canada: An Overview* (2009).

[5] The *British North America Act, 1867* created the new country and set out the principles of federalism. In 1982 it was renamed the *Constitution Act, 1867*, which incorporated amendments since its enactment and other constitutional legislation. These were subsumed into the repatriated *Constitution Act, 1982*, which also includes the *Canadian Charter of Rights and Freedoms*.

Minority religious and language rights were a major issue in negotiations leading up to Confederation. Catholics were a powerful minority in Ontario while Protestants were a powerful minority in Quebec. Both groups had established school systems and fought to preserve them. By Confederation in 1867, education had sufficiently evolved locally and regionally for it to remain in the hands of the provincial governments who were best positioned to respond to the distinct constituents of each province. The Constitution preserves this arrangement and also protects the two official languages of the country, French and English. As additional colonies joined the federation and became new provinces of Canada, these constitutional arrangements remained in place.

Pre-confederation colonial legislatures established universities through royal charter along with land endowments from the Crown with leadership assigned to the local Anglican (Church of England) clerics. In response other Protestant denominations began organizing and establishing colleges and seeking royal charters. Thus from the mid-1880s a modest higher education expansion occurred in Canada via the church. This denominational influence and character of Canadian higher education shifted after Confederation. The university infrastructure that was in place at the time of federation was subsumed by the new provinces. Disputes around state support of certain denominational colleges over others by way of Crown endowments became a thorny issue in some provinces, such as Ontario, while in others higher education was a small enterprise and not seen as a state priority, and had little state financial support in any event. At this point in history we see the move toward state support of secular provincial institutions to avoid denominational controversies in Ontario, and eventually this publicly funded but secular feature would become a dominant feature of Canadian higher education.[6]

Thus, these two features of our contemporary higher education systems in Canada, namely, state (provincial government) control over degree granting and the principle of state funding for secular institutions, became central to provincial law and policy in higher education.[7] The

---

[6] As a result, denominational universities either became independent secular universities or affiliated with public universities. In the latter instance, the denominational university retained control over administration, hiring, admissions, and its religious character but within a wider secular university that provided the degree-granting authority. We see this particularly in Ontario's postsecondary system with the University of St. Michael's College, the University of Trinity College, and Victoria University – each originally established by religious groups – suspending their degree-granting powers and making various affiliation arrangements with the University of Toronto. Similarly, Huron University College, Brescia University College, and Kings University College affiliated with Western University in London, Ontario.

[7] Skolnik, "State Control of Degree Granting."

four western provinces – British Columbia, Alberta, Saskatchewan, and
Manitoba – each created one secular provincial university after join-
ing the federation, influenced by the American state university model.
By contrast, other parts of the country were being influenced by the
American research university (based on the German research university
model), as well as the Anglo Oxford and Cambridge models. Eventually
the one provincial university model was abandoned in the four western
provinces, but conversely adopted in two eastern Maritime provinces of
Prince Edward Island and Newfoundland and Labrador.[8]

In 1906 the Flavelle Commission[9] established the principle of university
independence from the state and recommended bicameral university
governance, which was gradually adopted by most English-speaking
universities in Canada.[10] But Canadian higher education was not a high
public or government policy priority up until World War II.

After the war this changed with the federal government's decision to
pay the tuition of qualified veterans, a policy that resulted in a dramatic
expansion of university enrolments in Canadian higher education and
a movement toward more access to what was once an elite institution.[11]
Three national reports came out in the 1950s and 1960s that cemented the
importance of universities in economic, cultural, and personal development, further influencing government and public perspectives. The Royal
Commission on National Development in the Arts, Letters and Sciences,
known as the Massey Commission, released its report in 1951. The report
highlighted the role of universities in nurturing Canadian culture and
intellectual identity, as well as in training individuals for the labour market to enhance economic growth. It recommended federal government
support for university science and medical research, and development
of a council for the support of the arts, humanities, and social sciences.[12]

---

[8] Jones, "Canada" (2011). Manitoba joined the federation in 1871, and the University of Manitoba was founded in 1877 as an examining body and then with a
formal charter in 1917; British Columbia joined the federation in 1871 and made
a few unsuccessful attempts to start a university, but it was not until 1908 that
the University of British Columbia was founded; Alberta joined the federation in
1905 and created the University of Alberta in 1906; likewise Saskatchewan joined
the federation in 1905 and established the University of Saskatchewan in 1907.
See Harris, *History of Higher Education in Canada 1663–1960*.

[9] Government of Ontario, *Royal Commission*. It was known as the Flavelle Commission after its chair, Joseph Flavelle.

[10] The legislative framework of institutional university governance in Canada
is the subject of chapter 4. For a review of the evolution of university governance,
see Jones, Shanahan, and Goyan, "University Governance."

[11] Cameron, *More Than an Academic Question*. See also Fisher et al., *Canadian
Federal Policy and Postsecondary Education*, 18–19.

[12] See Government of Canada, *Report of the Royal Commission on National Development in the Arts, Letters and Sciences*, 161, 377.

This influential report set the stage for the federal government's financial support of higher education via direct unconditional grants to universities for research in 1957 through the establishment of a funding council under the *Canada Council Act*.[13] The Royal Commission on Canada's Economic Prospects, known as the Gordon Commission, followed in 1957, and also linked the universities as essential to a developed economy.[14] The third report, *Financing Higher Education in Canada*, emanated in 1965 from the Canadian Universities Foundation (now the Association of Universities and Colleges of Canada [AUCC]).[15] Known as the report of the Bladen Commission, it recommended substantial increase to funding of university education.[16] These three reports reflected the prevailing views and influenced the direction both provincial and federal governments were to take in support of universities. New institutions were created to meet the general public's demand for postsecondary education, which led to increased enrolments.

With the expansion and demands for access came discussion about funding. The federal and provincial governments agreed that expansion and a significant federal investment was needed to sustain higher education growth; however, finding a mechanism that satisfied both governments proved elusive. Although the provinces at this point had jurisdiction over postsecondary education, the federal government retained an interest in sustaining enrolment levels as government policy, and was increasingly viewing higher education as good for the country's economic prospects. When the veterans' benefits program wound up, the federal government continued to direct grants to universities based on enrolments but not without provincial objections over the federal intrusions into provincial authority, especially in Ontario and Quebec. Over the next four decades (1950–1990) higher education in Canada would continue to expand and the federal government's financial support of postsecondary education would continue to evolve into a patchwork of federal granting programs. This expansion was fuelled by the federal government's desire to increase access to Canadian postsecondary education within the context of the central constitutional role of the provinces in providing postsecondary education.[17]

---

[13] Now known as the *Canada Council for the Arts Act*, RSC 1985, c C-2.

[14] Government of Canada, *Royal Commission on Canada's Economic Prospects*.

[15] During the publication process AUCC changed its name to Universities Canada (UC) so all subsequent references in the book to AUCC refer to the body now known as UC.

[16] Canadian Universities Foundation, *Financing Higher Education in Canada*, 14.

[17] Chapter 2 of this book takes up the role of the federal government in postsecondary education in more detail. See also Fisher et al., *Canadian Federal Policy and Postsecondary Education*.

One of the most sweeping reorganizations of higher education in the country occurred in the province of Quebec within the social context of the "quiet revolution" and rising Quebec nationalism. The Royal Commission of Inquiry on Education, known as the Parent Commission after its chair, was struck in in 1963. The commission produced a five-volume report published between the years 1963 and 1966 that proposed a sweeping reform of the existing elitist, Catholic Church-dominated education system from elementary through to postsecondary education.[18] Up to that point the Quebec system had been based on a classical curriculum, which by the 1960s was being widely criticized for its social, economic, cultural (language), and gender inequities, for its conservative views, and for the low level of formal schooling in the province. In the mid-1960s the Quebec government began to implement many of the Parent Commission's recommendations. It established a Ministry of Education in 1964,[19] began to secularize education throughout the province, standardize curriculum, ended secondary school at Grade 11, and abolished or reconstituted 200 classical colleges into junior general colleges and vocational colleges (non-degree institutions) called CEGEPs (collège d'enseignment général et professionnel). The CEGEPs offered a two-year, pre-university program, as well as three-year vocational programs. To increase participation rates in higher education, the Quebec government established free tuition for the CEGEPs for Quebec residents, introduced a robust system of bursaries and loans for universities, and created the Université du Québec network in 1969 whereby autonomously governed campuses of one university were located in different regions through the province.[20] The resulting structure of education in Quebec has been described as unique in North America.[21] The Université du Québec, with a network of six university institutions, specialized schools, and research centres throughout the province, is the largest university in Canada and constitutes a province-wide system similar to some US state universities. These principles of access and affordability are reflected in Quebec's

---

[18] *Report of the Royal Commission of Inquiry on Education.*

[19] Up to that point, the province had a Department of Public Instructions, which had a Catholic committee and a Protestant committee. Quebec first established a formal Ministry of Public Instruction in 1868 but abolished it in 1875 under pressure from the Catholic Church.

[20] For a history of Quebec's postsecondary education, see CMEC, *Postsecondary Education Systems in Canada: Provinces and Territories* (2013); Donald, "Higher Education in Quebec: 1945–1995"; Magnusson, *Brief History of Québec Education;* Edwards, *English Language CEGEPs of Quebec;* Henchey and Burgess, *Quebec Education in Transition.*

[21] Skolnik, *Community College Baccalaureate,* 2.

current postsecondary education system, which still enjoys some of the lowest tuition fees across Canada.[22]

As higher education systems across Canada expanded in the 1960s and 1970s, provincial governments began to focus on issues of access, funding, and coordination. Publicly funded, *non-degree* institutions were emerging in the 1960s in the other Canadian provinces as well as Quebec to respond to the increasing demands for access to postsecondary education. Provinces began to establish new types of non-degree institutions generally referred to as colleges. Their structure and function varied by province. In the western provinces the colleges fed universities with transfer functions whereas in Ontario the colleges ran parallel to the universities without an explicit transfer function. These institutions were intended to increase access, were more tightly regulated by provincial governments than universities, and had a more vocation and technical orientation than universities.

Over the next twenty years provincial governments began experimenting with coordinating structures to assist them in managing the expanding higher education systems. These bodies varied across the provinces in their form, function, and scope. Some were advisory bodies only, while others had more decision-making powers. Some focused only on the university sector, while others focused on the whole provincial postsecondary system. Ultimately, provinces would go in different directions: some abandoned coordinating bodies and then recreated a new form, while others transformed their coordinating bodies into postsecondary councils. Some Maritime provinces have come together to create a regional coordinating body. Notwithstanding these various provincial initiatives, Canadian higher education remained quite stable and system level arrangements remained generally unchanged through to the mid-1990s.[23] Contemporary provincial legislative arrangements are taken up in chapter 3 of this book.

THE LEGISLATIVE FRAMEWORK OF EDUCATION IN CANADA

Canada is a federal system of government, a constitutional monarchy with a democratic parliamentary government based on the British system. Although it began as a classical, centralized federation, it has become increasingly decentralized in its governance. Canada is divided

---

[22] Undergraduate students in Newfoundland and Labrador and in Quebec have the lowest average tuition rates in Canada (NL $2,649 and Quebec $2,774); the rate in Quebec includes the recent (2012) 10 percent increase in tuition fees that sparked widespread student protests. See Statistics Canada, *University Tuition Fees, 2012/2013*.

[23] Jones, "Canada" (2011).

into two constitutionally autonomous levels of government – federal and provincial.[24] Each level of government has its own sphere of power and jurisdiction. The country is made up of ten provinces and three semi-autonomous territories. The head of state for both the federal and provincial governments is the monarchy or its representatives (the governor general at the federal level and the lieutenant-governor at the provincial level). Currently this role is largely ceremonial in Canada. Parliament is composed of two legislative chambers at the federal level, the House of Commons and the Senate, whereas there is only one legislature chamber at the provincial level. At both the federal and provincial levels, members of parliament are elected to the legislature by citizens and represent defined geographical areas. By contrast, federal senators are appointed by the federal government, and unlike other federal states,[25] do not provide direct representation for the provinces. The Canadian Senate has less power and is more constrained in its ability to represent provincial interests in federal policy-making.[26] Elected representatives in the federal and provincial legislatures are usually associated with a particular political party, and the leader of the winning party after an election is asked by the Crown's representative to form a government. The leader of the party becomes the prime minister at the federal level, or the premier at the provincial level. The prime minister or premier and their cabinet form the executive council.

The judicial branch of power at the federal level is made up of the Supreme Court of Canada, the Federal Court, the Federal Court of Appeal, the Tax Court, the Court Martial Court, and the Court Martial Appeal Court. Each province also has its own court system that includes provincial trial courts and courts of appeal. Most of the country follows the British common-law tradition[27] except the province of Quebec where the legal system has its roots in civil law and the Napoleonic Code from France, albeit significantly penetrated by the common law.[28] The coexist-

---

[24] The territorial and local municipal governments do not have constitutional status.

[25] For example, Germany, Australia, and the United States are federations with upper houses that provide direct representation for citizens of their constituent states/provinces.

[26] There is ongoing debate in Canada about the relevance and utility of the Senate given its limited function in government and concerns that Senate appointments are motivated by patronage.

[27] Common law is judge-made law based on decisions of the court that become precedents.

[28] The common law has found its way into the current Quebec legal system, which reflects both codified civil law and the judge-made common law. For provincial issues in Quebec the civil law prevails, but where the federal government has jurisdiction over the issue the common law prevails. Quebec, like the rest of

ence of common law and civil law in Canada is known as legislative "bijuralism," whereby two different legal traditions interact within one jurisdiction, both equally authoritative and legitimate sources of law.[29]

The *Constitution Act, 1867*[30] sets out the division of powers between the federal and provincial government. Section 93 of the *Constitution Act, 1867* gives *exclusive* jurisdiction over all levels of education to the provinces, stating that "[in] and for each Province the Legislature may exclusively make Laws in relation to Education."[31] This combined with section 92, which provides exclusive provincial jurisdiction over "the Establishment, Maintenance, and Management of Hospitals, Asylums, Charities, and Eleemosynary Institutions in and for the Province, other than Marine Hospitals," grounds provincial authority over postsecondary education.[32] The federal government has no legal jurisdiction to make laws pertaining to education and plays no direct regulatory role in the ten provincial systems of education. There is no federal department of education, and no minister of education in the cabinet at the national level. Postsecondary education is under the responsibility of a provincial or territorial minister of education. Some smaller provinces have all levels of education (K–12 and postsecondary education) under one ministry. Larger provinces tend to have elementary and secondary education under one Ministry of Education while higher education is under a separate ministry.[33]

Unlike the federal government, under the Canadian Constitution the provinces have limited financial powers to raise revenues through the power of taxation. Section 92 confines the provinces to direct taxation to raise revenue for provincial purposes.[34] Consequently, the provinces

---

the Canadian provinces, is bound by Canadian federal laws. Quebec is also subject to the constitutional division of powers. For a full discussion of the history of Canada's legal system, and Quebec's hybrid system in particular, see McCormack and Bueckert, *Introduction to the Law and Legal System of Canada*.

[29] McCormack and Bueckert, *Introduction*, 61.

[30] *The Constitution Act, 1867*, (30 & 31 Victoria) c 3. Section 92 enumerates 16 areas where the provinces have sole legislative power. Section 95 provides for two concurrent areas of jurisdiction shared between the federal and provincial governments (agriculture and immigration).

[31] *The Constitution Act, 1867*, (30 & 31 Victoria) c 3, s 93.

[32] *The Constitution Act, 1867*, (30 & 31 Victoria) c 3, s 92.

[33] For example, currently Ontario has two ministries: the Ministry of Education, responsible for K–12, and the Ministry of Training, Colleges and Universities, responsible for postsecondary education. However, Ontario had collapsed all levels of education from kindergarten through postsecondary into one ministry from 1993 to 2002.

[34] The definition of "direct taxation" has been contentious and has been reviewed by the Supreme Court of Canada many times. Currently it includes personal income and corporate tax, sales tax on goods and services, and rev-

rely considerably on the federal government taxation powers for federal transfer payments into the provincial general revenue coffers to fund postsecondary education.

SOURCES OF EDUCATION LAW

There are a number of sources of provincial and federal law influencing the governance of postsecondary education. These include both education statutes and non-education statues that intersect with, and apply to the employment workplace or the administrative features of postsecondary institutions, or to the provision of education as a service.

Postsecondary Education Statutes, Regulations, Policies, and Case Law

Each province has postsecondary education legislation that sets out the governance of the system of postsecondary education, provides degree-granting powers to postsecondary institutions, and sets out quality assurance arrangements. The provincial postsecondary education statutes are passed by the provincial legislature; these statutes codify the law and set out the powers and responsibilities of the minister responsible for postsecondary education. In some provinces these organization and degree-granting statutes are system-wide and cover all institutional types (for example Alberta); in other provinces the array of legislation governing the system is broken down by group of institutions, by sectors (university or college), by degree-granting status, or along public and private lines.

There are a myriad of regulatory arrangements for postsecondary education across the provinces. These diverse and distinct provincial legislative arrangements inevitably shape provincial governments' coordination, management, and policy-making in higher education. Although provincial approaches to and arrangements for higher education law and policy vary, there is evidence of both divergence and convergence in higher education law and policy-making for a complex Canadian higher education system.

In addition to postsecondary education statutes, there are postsecondary education regulations attached to each piece of education legislation. These regulations are passed by the minister or cabinet but not the legislature. They are subordinate pieces of legislation that flow from

---

enues from licensing and other fees. See, for example, *Royal Bank of Canada v Workmen's Compensation Board of Nova Scotia*, [1936] SCR 560, 1936 CanLII 39 (SCC) – 1936-06-17; *CPR v AG for Saskatchewan*, [1952] 2 SCR 231, 1952 CanLII 39 (SCC) – 1952-06-30; *Ontario Home Builders' Association v York Region Board of Education*, [1996] 2 SCR 929, 1996 CanLII 164 (SCC) –1996-08-22.

the parent statute. Regulations have the same legal force as the parent statute except they are more detailed and technical, and usually focus on operationalizing the parent statute. In the event of a conflict between the regulations and the parent statute, the parent statute will usually prevail.

Postsecondary education ministry guidelines and policies may also influence the shape of postsecondary education and may have the force and effect of law when they emanate from a parent statute and where the minister has been given the legal authority to create the guidelines or policies. These guidelines must be tied to a statutory source of law to have the legal force of the statute. Finally, postsecondary education case law comes from decided cases on legal issues. It is made by judge's decisions on cases and evolves as new cases are decided.

Non-Education Statutes, Regulations, Policies, and Case Law

There are other sources of *non-education* law that intersect with and dramatically affect the structure and function of postsecondary education. These can be provincial statutes or federal statutes. For example, provincial and federal labour relations law governs collective bargaining; workplace and employment statutes set out laws relating to employment standards; human rights legislation protects individuals from discrimination in public and private sector employment and in the provisions of services such as education; freedom of information legislation captures universities and colleges and governs the release of personal information; occupational health and safety laws govern all working conditions of staff and faculty; copyright, patent, and trademark laws protect intellectual property of faculty and also govern the distribution of protected material. Property law governs the universities and colleges' conveyance of real property. Contract, tort, criminal as well as constitutional law statutes are all relevant to the workings of governments and institutions in postsecondary education. All of these non-education statutes have a direct impact on the day-to-day administration and management of postsecondary institutions.

THE CONSTITUTION AND EDUCATION

The *Constitution Act, 1982* is the supreme law in Canada. The *Constitution Act, 1982* includes the *British North America Act (BNA) 1867* (renamed the *Constitution Act, 1867*) and all the various statutes enacted in between 1867 (Confederation) and 1982 (repatriation). It governs and binds federal and provincial legislatures and their agencies and persons acting for the state. It is the ultimate source of legal authority in Canada conferring on legislatures the power to pass statutes (such as education statutes) and limiting the exercise of legal authority. Statutes in turn confer power on the executive, cabinet, and ministers. The legislature delegates power to the cabinet and ministers to make regulations connected to statutes, and it gives certain bodies/agencies powers within the education system. All other provincial and federal laws must be consistent with the Constitution or else they will be struck down as "unconstitutional."

Scope and Authority of the Charter of Rights and Freedoms

The *Canadian Charter of Rights and Freedoms* has had a major impact on provincial education since its creation and entrenchment in the *Constitution Act* in 1982. The *Canadian Charter of Rights and Freedoms*, as part of the Constitution, enjoys its supremacy. Section 32 (1) (b) states that the *Charter* applies to the "legislature and government of each province in respect of all matters within the authority of the legislature of each province." The Supreme Court has interpreted this section as capturing government action and the actions of their agents. The *Charter* does not apply to the private sector or to private relationships.[35]

It is less clear what constitutes "government action." The *Charter* addresses violations of civil liberties by provincial (and territorial) and federal governments. Certainly the *Charter* applies to provincial government law-making and thus to provincial education legislation.[36] While government action may include the activities of public school boards and their employees in certain instances,[37] the application of the *Charter* to public universities is another matter. In a series of cases dealing with mandatory retirement, the Supreme Court of Canada has considered the application of the *Charter* to universities and other postsecondary institutions.[38] The issue at hand was whether the publicly funded institution was independent from government or whether its employees were indeed government actors. Although universities operate in an environment regulated by provincial governments and receive public funds, they have considerable autonomy over their activities. In *McKinney v University of Guelph*, the court found that there was insufficient control by government to justify the application of the *Charter* to publicly funded universities on the employment matters before the court. Justice La Forest commented that "though the legislature may determine much of the environment in which universities operate, the reality is that they function as autonomous

---

[35] See *RWDSU v Dolphin Delivery Ltd.*, [1986] 2 SCR 573.

[36] *Mahe et al. v Alberta* (1990), 105 NR 321(SCC).

[37] The Supreme Court has applied the Charter to some of the activities of school boards that constitute government action in a number of cases: *R v M (MR)*, [1998] 3 SCR 393; also *Chamberlain v Surrey School District No. 36*, [2002] 4 SCR 710.

[38] See *McKinney v University of Guelph et al.*, [1990] 3 SCR 229; *Harrison v University of British Columbia*, [1991] 1WWR 681(SCC); *Stoffman v Vancouver General Hospital*, [1991] 1WWR 577 (SCR); *Douglas/Kwantlen Faculty Association v Douglas College*, [1991] 1WWR 643 (SCC).

bodies within that environment."[39] The court took into consideration the collective bargaining agreement that the university employer and employees had entered into that set out employment terms, and they decided imposing the *Charter* would distort the collective bargaining process. The court did not view the internal labour relations process within publicly funded universities as "government action" and would not apply the *Charter* to it. However, they left open the possibility that in other situations publicly funded universities in Canada may be found subject to the *Charter*, especially in instances where universities are carrying out government policy or programs, and depending on the regulatory environment of the postsecondary system within the province that shapes universities' organization and governance independence from government.

Recent cases suggest that courts are finding, in their daily operations, that publicly funded universities are not creatures of government and hence not subject to the *Charter*. However, when universities are carrying out government policy or legislation they may be considered as government agents, and these actions may attract *Charter* scrutiny.[40] The case law suggests that the critical focus is on the relationship of the institution to government (as government actors or "organs of government"[41]) and on the nature of the offending activities in question (as government actions). That the institution is subject to government regulation and public funding, and/or that the institution is created by government legislation, is not sufficient to attract *Charter* scrutiny. Justice La Forest in *McKinney* clarified this point:

> It is evident from what has been recounted that the universities' fate is largely in the hands of government and that the universities are subjected to important limitations on what they can do, either by regulation or because of their dependence on government funds. It by no means follows, however, that the universities are organs of government.[42]

The same analysis cannot be made of publicly funded colleges, however, as they are more tightly controlled by provincial governments and would easily attract *Charter* scrutiny. In *Douglas/Kwantlen Faculty Association v Douglas College*, the Supreme Court considered the status of a community college and distinguished the regulatory structure and independence of the publicly funded colleges from publicly funded universities. They

---

[39] *McKinney* at 274.

[40] A detailed discussion of the Charter and universities follows in later chapters. For this line of cases see *Eldridge v British Columbia (Attorney General)* 1997 CanLII 327 (SCC); *Pridgen v University of Calgary*, [2012] ABQB 139 Can LII).

[41] *McKinney v University of Guelph et al.*, [1990] 3 SCR at 272.

[42] Ibid.

found that the community college was a Crown agent, substantially controlled by government, with a specific mandate to implement government policy. The board of a community college is appointed and can be removed by government. Consequently, the court found the publicly funded colleges to be government actors and hence their dealings with employees were subject to *Charter* scrutiny.[43] Subsequent chapters in this book revisit this issue of the applicability of the *Charter* to colleges and universities across various legal areas in more detail.

IMPLICATIONS

The absence of a federal department or ministry of education in Canada that would coordinate and make laws about education across the country is a significant feature shaping Canadian higher education. There is no national decision-making authority or mechanism for national postsecondary policy development. The Council of Ministers of Education (CMEC), which consists of the provincial and territorial minsters of education, acts as a national forum for discussions on education matters, but it has no executive decision-making authority over Canadian education and it only acts upon consensus. Consequently, the CMEC has had limited influence on education across the country. The constitutional division of powers in Canada means that the historical development of education has been province specific. Higher education governance is highly decentralized in Canada. Each provincial government makes laws regarding education, regulates and organizes public education, and provides operating funds at all levels. Each provincial system of education is distinct in each Canadian province. Therefore in Canada there is not one "system" of education but rather ten provincial and three territorial "systems" with unique features. This makes examinations of Canadian postsecondary education complex, and any discussions inevitably lead to provincial distinctions. The following chapters discuss in more depth the federal government's role in postsecondary education (chapter 2) and specific provincial governance arrangements in postsecondary education (chapter 3).

---

[43] *Douglas/Kwantlen Faculty Association v Douglas College*, [1991] 1 WWR 643 (SCC) 584-585.

Chapter 2

THE ROLE OF THE FEDERAL
GOVERNMENT IN POSTSECONDARY
EDUCATION

THERESA SHANAHAN

INTRODUCTION

The federal government has a wide variety of powers in areas that intersect with postsecondary education. The powers of the federal government
are set out in section 91 of the *Constitution Act, 1867*. Section 91 states:

> **91.** It shall be lawful for the Queen, by and with the Advice and Consent of
> the Senate and House of Commons, to make Laws for the Peace, Order, and
> good Government of Canada, in relation to all Matters not coming within
> the Classes of Subjects by this Act assigned exclusively to the Legislatures
> of the Provinces.[1]

In addition to the power to legislate around issues pertaining to "peace,
order and good government," the federal government has the power to
legislate in any area *not* explicitly given to the provincial governments
under the *Constitution Act*. This section goes further and annunciates
specific areas of federal power as well as providing the federal government with wide powers of taxation to raise revenue by any system of

---

[1] *The Constitution Act*, 1867, (30 & 31 Victoria) c 3, s 91.

Handbook of Canadian Higher Education Law, edited by Theresa Shanahan, Michelle Nilson, and Li-Jeen Broshko.
Montreal and Kingston: McGill-Queen's University Press, Queen's Policy Studies Series.
© 2015 The School of Policy Studies, Queen's University at Kingston. All rights reserved.

taxation.[2] Taxation powers give the federal government considerable financial powers to raise revenues. Furthermore, the federal government has spending powers, and although not enshrined explicitly in the Constitution, the federal government has the right to spend money outside its areas of constitutional jurisdiction – the Constitution forbids the federal government from passing laws or regulations in certain areas but does not explicitly forbid federal spending in those areas. This spending power allows the federal government to spend money in postsecondary education as long as it does not attempt to legislate or regulate postsecondary education. Spending power can have an enormous influence on shaping components of postsecondary education.

Moreover, the federal government *does* have education responsibilities that emerge from other areas of federal jurisdiction outlined in Section 91 of the *Constitution Act, 1867,* and these responsibilities make federal government activity legitimate in all levels of education.[3] The federal government is responsible for national defence, which includes the education of military personnel and their children. For example, the federal government operates the Royal Military College of Canada, a federal institution under a federal charter that offers university degrees. National security including crime and prisons gives the federal government some authority over education in Canadian prisons and youth detention centres. The responsibility for external affairs allows the federal government to fund international education programs and international scholarships through the Department of Foreign Affairs, Trade and Development.[4] The federal government is responsible for economic development and consequently funds postsecondary vocational training programs, apprenticeship programs, student financial assistance programs, and graduate scholarship programs under this area of jurisdiction. It is under this responsibility for the economy that the federal government is a major funder of postsecondary research that is seen as contributing to the economy. Section 91 also allows the federal government jurisdiction over any other area of "national interest," which has justified its funding of bilingual language education programs in the country.

---

[2] Including direct taxation, corporate tax, personal income tax, and duties and fees.

[3] *The Constitution Act, 1867,* (30 & 31 Victoria) c 3.

[4] And previously through Canadian International Development Agency (CIDA), which has been merged into the Department of Foreign Affairs, Trade and Development.

THE FEDERAL GOVERNMENT AND TERRITORIAL HIGHER EDUCATION

The federal government does play a role in supporting the education system in the three northern territories: the Northwest Territories, the Yukon, and Nunavut. Constitutionally, the three Canadian territories do not have the same autonomous status and powers as the provinces.[5] Thus, under the Constitution, the territories fall under the legislative jurisdiction of the federal government. As such they are subject to direct control from the federal government. However, the federal government has delegated many of its legislative powers to the territories, including responsibility for education. In practice, therefore, the territorial governments have many of the same powers as provincial governments. They have an elected legislative assembly, and like their provincial counterparts, they are allowed to enact laws for their territorial area, but they work with the federal government to create the basic framework. The head of state is a territorial commissioner who performs the same role as the provincial lieutenant governor as the Crown's representative. The premier and the cabinet form the executive branch of government. Each territory has a court system, albeit sometimes shared with a neighbouring territory. Under delegated federal power, the territorial governments are responsible for education. Each territorial government has a department responsible for the organization and regulation of all levels of education within the territory.

FIRST NATIONS POSTSECONDARY EDUCATION

The federal government has constitutional jurisdiction over "Indians, and Lands reserved for Indians" under section 91 of the *Constitution Act*.[6] The *Indian Act, 1985* also gives the federal government responsibility over "Indian affairs" but only for "registered (status) Indians," that is, Aboriginal peoples who ordinarily reside on a reserve or on lands belonging to government (Crown land as opposed to private property). The numbered treaties concluded between 1871 and 1921 also commit the federal government to providing schools and educational services to signatory First Nations as part of ongoing treaty obligations. However, the Métis and Inuit are not recognized under the *Indian Act* and did not sign the subsequent treaties, nor did most of the Aboriginal peoples in British

---

[5] The territories do not have the legal status to vote on constitutional amendments of federal and provincial powers, but in practice they are included in intergovernmental meetings and decision-making.

[6] *The Constitution Act, 1867*, (30 & 31 Victoria) c 3, s 91(24).

Columbia.[7] Despite their being indigenous to Canada and participating in Canadian nation building, the federal government's commitment under the treaties does not extend to them.[8]

Taken together these sections allow the federal government to exercise jurisdiction over the education of *some* of Canada's Aboriginal peoples who live on reserves or on Crown land. The *Indian Act*, particularly sections 114–122, sets out the powers of the federal minister of Indian Affairs and Northern Development to arrange for the education of "Indian" children age 6 to 16 years. The federal Department of Indian Affairs and Northern Development[9] provides funding for band councils or other First Nations educational authorities to support instructional services for status Indians *residing on-reserve*. The federal government also operates on-reserve schools, but the majority of these have been handed over to the bands themselves. Aboriginal children who live on reserves may also attend an off-reserve school operated by a local provincial school board under an agreement with the board and the band.[10] In this case the federal government reimburses the band council for the provincial school board's fees.[11] If Aboriginal peoples do not reside on reserves or on federal or provincial Crown land (i.e., they are not "registered or status Indians" as defined by the *Indian Act*), the federal government has no jurisdiction over them. In this instance the education laws of the province apply to them, and their education becomes the responsibility of the provincial

---

[7] By contrast, the Canadian Constitution does recognize Indian, Métis, and Inuit peoples as Indigenous peoples, and under section 35 protects the rights of all three groups. However, Métis peoples are not named as being under federal responsibility. Consequently, federal government support for Métis education has not been historically consistent or stable. Section 4 (3) of the *Indian Act*, RSC 1985, c I-5.

[8] For examples of treaty wording on education, see the Standing Senate Committee on Aboriginal Peoples, *Reforming First Nations Education*, 10. For more on Acts, Agreements, land claims, and treaties, see Aboriginal Affairs and Northern Development Canada, https:// www. aadnc-aandc.gc. ca / eng / 1100100028568 / 11 00100028572. See also the Indigenous Foundations project, an information resource on key topics relating to the histories, politics, and cultures of the Aboriginal peoples of Canada, at http:/ /indigenousfoundations.arts.ubc.ca/home. html.

[9] The federal government changed the name of the department to Aboriginal Affairs and Northern Development Canada effective June 2011. The mandate for the department and the minister's statutory authority remained unchanged, but the new title better reflected the minister's responsibilities with respect to First Nations peoples.

[10] See for example in Ontario under the *Education Act*, s 188.

[11] The federal government also provides funding for the provision of student support services such as transportation, counselling, accommodation, and financial assistance.

government. In practice the federal government has limited its role to one of funding schooling for Aboriginal children.[12]

However, there is no similar direct provision under the *Indian Act* that pertains to the federal government's responsibility over *postsecondary* education. Consequently, federal government support for Aboriginal postsecondary education is less systematically articulated and uneven. Moreover, support for non-First Nations (such as the Métis) or unregistered "Indians" living off reserve has largely been left to the provincial government.

At the postsecondary level, the federal department of Aboriginal Affairs and Northern Development Canada provides two main kinds of funding for Aboriginal postsecondary education: support to postsecondary institutions provided through the Post-Secondary Partnerships Program; and individual student financial support provided through the Post-Secondary Student Support Program and the University and College Entrance Preparation program.

The latter programs support "status Indian" and Inuit students who are enrolled in eligible postsecondary programs. These include community college and CEGEP diploma or certificate programs, undergraduate programs, and advanced or professional degree programs.[13] Student funding supports only "status Indians" (as defined by the *Indian Act*) living on and off reserve, and Inuit, and includes funding for tuition, books, and living allowances to attend a postsecondary institution (Aboriginal or non-Aboriginal institutions). The funding also covers travel when a student must leave his or her permanent residence to attend college or university. Other Aboriginal students and Métis are not eligible for these programs. Administration of the program is done through the First Nations bands, which determine the amount of funding per student and the selection criteria in accordance with national guidelines. First Nations students who want to pursue postsecondary studies and access available funding programs must apply through their local band.

Federal student funding of status Indians has evolved from a system based on estimates of need to a priority system that requires First Nations bands to determine which priority students will receive funding. This means that instead of the federal government funding all qualified, status Indian students who are in in need and seeking to attend postsecondary education, the federal government sets national guidelines and gives a limited pot of funds to the First Nations bands. Each band then ranks

---

[12] Standing Senate Committee on Aboriginal Peoples, *Reforming First Nations Education*, 10–11.

[13] See Aboriginal Affairs and Northern Development Canada, "Post-Secondary Student Support Program (PSSSP)," https://www.aadnc-aandc.gc.ca/eng/1100100033682/1100100033683.

the order in which students will get support to attend postsecondary education and decides which students will not get funds. This approach allows each band to decide the specific criteria of the priority ranking while following the national guidelines. It can also be seen as devolution of decision-making to the First Nations bands themselves. However, the federal government sets the size of the funding pot, effectively limiting the number of students who will get to participate. Without government financial support, qualified Aboriginal students are unlikely to be able to afford postsecondary education.

Aboriginal Affairs and Northern Development Canada also provides support directly to postsecondary institutions to develop and deliver college- and university-level programming and services aimed at increasing the participation and graduation achievements of Aboriginal students through the Post-Secondary Partnerships Program. The federal government sets the criteria for the funding. The program is proposal-driven, and the level of funding is determined by a national selection process that allocates resources based on the merit of the institutions' proposals. Available funding is limited. The program does not provide a stable stream of ongoing core operational funding to institutions. Many of these institutional funding programs are also aimed at "registered Indians" (as defined by the *Indian Act*), who are a subset of a larger First Nations people. The Métis and Inuit are not captured by this definition and so do not qualify for these services and support programs in the institutions.[14]

In Canada there are both publicly funded and private or independent postsecondary institutions – sometimes referred to as Indigenous Institutes of Higher Learning – established to serve First Nations and Métis peoples, although there is no specific legislative framework supporting these Aboriginal-controlled and focused postsecondary institutions. Some Aboriginal-controlled colleges partner with provincial postsecondary institutions to offer educational programming for Aboriginal peoples. Vocational adult learning programs, both credit and non-credit, are offered by Aboriginal learning centres, in some cases delivered by larger, mainstream institutions. Finally, Canada has one First Nations University of Canada. Located in Saskatchewan, it offers undergraduate and graduate degrees accredited through the University of Regina in an environment of First Nations culture. It is independently administered and controlled by First Nations, although funded by both the province of Saskatchewan and the federal government of Canada. The First Nations

---

[14] Standing Senate Committee on Social Affairs, Science and Technology, *Opening the Door*, 48.

University of Canada is a full member of the Association of Universities and Colleges of Canada (AUCC).[15]

The relationship between the federal government and Canada's Aboriginal people is complex. Aboriginal self-governance presents challenges to the institutions of Canadian federalism.[16] The status of Aboriginal peoples within Canada, their rights and responsibilities and the federal government's responsibilities to them, are defined by the Constitution, legislation, litigation, treaties, case law, and history.[17] There are many challenges and issues associated with Aboriginal education not the least of which is governance and regulation. Many Aboriginal people see postsecondary education as an inherent Aboriginal or treaty right enshrined in section 35 of the Constitution, which states:

RIGHTS OF THE ABORIGINAL PEOPLES OF CANADA

35. (1) The existing aboriginal and treaty rights of the aboriginal peoples of Canada are hereby recognized and affirmed.

(2) In this Act, "aboriginal peoples of Canada" includes the Indian, Inuit, and Métis peoples of Canada.

(3) For greater certainty, in subsection (1) "treaty rights" includes rights that now exist by way of land claims agreements or may be so acquired.

(4) Notwithstanding any other provision of this Act, the aboriginal and treaty rights referred to in subsection (1) are guaranteed equally to male and female persons.

In the cases of *R v Calder* and *R v Sparrow*, the Supreme Court sought to define Aboriginal rights under this section and interpreted them to include cultural, social, political, and economic rights including the right to have land, to fish and hunt, and to establish treaties.[18] In *R v Sparrow*, the Supreme Court of Canada said that these rights must be existing rights in 1982 when the Constitution was repatriated, and that the section could

---

[15] For more on Aboriginal education, see Fisher et al., *Canadian Federal Policy and Postsecondary Education*; and Stonechild, "Pursuing the New Buffalo." The evolution of federal government support of Aboriginal postsecondary education can be found the Assembly of First Nations' report issued in 2000, *First Nations PSE Review*. For a more recent study (2006) on postsecondary attainment of Aboriginal peoples, see Mendelson, *Aboriginal Peoples and Postsecondary Education in Canada*.

[16] For a discussion of Canadian federalism and Aboriginal governance, see Papillon, "Canadian Federalism."

[17] Fisher et al., *Canadian Federal Policy and Postsecondary Education*, 110.

[18] *R. v. Calder*, [1996] 1 SCR 660; *R v Sparrow*, [1990] 1 SCR 1075.

not be used to revive extinguished rights. Since section 35 falls outside the *Charter of Rights and Freedoms*, it is exempt from the notwithstanding federal government override clause in section 33 of the *Charter*. Nevertheless, a broad and liberal interpretation of treaty education clauses would be needed to include a postsecondary education federal guarantee, and the extent of cultural content in that postsecondary education would be a critical determinant for the guarantee to apply.[19] Moreover, the scope of what the guarantee would cover remains undetermined: complete, full funding for *all* First Nations students by the federal government in *all* postsecondary programs? or something less than full funding?[20]

Significantly, the federal government interprets its role in funding Aboriginal postsecondary education as a matter of *social* policy and not a legal obligation pursuant to a statutory duty, a treaty, or a constitutional or fiduciary obligation under either the *Constitution Act* or the *Indian Act*. This perspective shapes, and effectively limits, the federal government's role in supporting Aboriginal postsecondary education. The difference in position of the federal government's obligation as social policy or legal duty plays out in a number of ways but is especially apparent in eligibility for student funding for federal student loans. Aboriginal students are eligible for federal government student assistance on the same terms and repayment conditions as all other students. The question arises whether Aboriginal students should be entitled to additional support or separate support programs if postsecondary education was viewed as a treaty or inherent Aboriginal right.[21]

In summary, federal funding and eligibility restrictions for Aboriginal students in general have persisted despite increasing demand for Aboriginal postsecondary education. Support for particular subgroups within the Aboriginal population, such as Métis students, is especially lacking and readily apparent in Métis students' access to and participation in postsecondary education.[22] Federal funding of Aboriginal postsecond-

---

[19] See the Supreme Court's interpretation of Aboriginal rights and "integral cultural" in *Delgamuukw v The Queen in Right of BC*, [1997] 3 SCL 1010 and in *Van der Peet v the Queen*, [1996] 2 SCR 507.

[20] For a discussion of Aboriginal treaty and inherent rights as they apply to postsecondary education, see Paquette and Fallon, *First Nations Education Policy in Canada*; and Papillon, "Canadian Federalism."

[21] See Paquette and Fallon, *First Nations Education Policy in Canada*, 140.

[22] For an analysis of postsecondary participation rates of Aboriginal peoples and barriers to PSE, see Canadian Millennium Scholarship Foundation, "Changing Course"; Malatest & Associates, *Best Practices*; and Usher, *The Postsecondary Student Support Program*.

ary education remains a barrier, and without clear federal government legislative responsibility this is unlikely to change.[23]

FEDERAL SPENDING POWER

Government spending powers are not explicitly dealt with under the Constitution; however, these powers are a significant feature of Canadian federalism and allow the federal government to spend money outside its areas of constitutional jurisdiction. This means that while the federal government cannot make laws or regulate education in Canada, it can spend money on education. Although the federal government does not have any direct constitutional law-making authority over education, it can spend money on education programs at all levels – and it does so.

Both the federal and provincial governments have spending powers that have become one of the most powerful government tools employed in policy implementation. However, the federal government has a larger financial capacity than the provincial governments, and so it can use its spending power in highly influential ways. Federal spending powers have impacted federal-provincial relations especially on matters of public health care, public education, and social welfare.[24] Although these areas fall under provincial jurisdiction, the federal government has created national policies and programs within these provincial jurisdictions and has attached funding to them, in some cases causing tension with the provincial governments.

FEDERAL EQUALIZATION PAYMENTS

Section 36 of the *Constitution Act, 1982* commits the federal and provincial governments to reducing regional disparities and unequal access to public services across the nation. Flowing from this, the Constitution also

---

[23] For actual rates of postsecondary attainment levels, see Statistics Canada, National Household Survey, Table 2, "Proportion of First Nations People, Métis and Inuit Aged 25 to 64 by Selected Levels of Educational Attainment and Sex, Canada, 2011," http://www12. statcan.gc.ca/nhs-enm/2011/as-sa/99-012-x/2011003/tbl/tbl2-eng.cfm.

[24] In 1999 the federal government and the provinces (except Quebec) entered into the Social Union Framework Agreement (SUFA), which set out principles for federal government spending in areas of provincial constitutional jurisdiction. Of particular concern were unilateral actions by the federal government in areas of provincial jurisdiction. The SUFA does not change the constitutional powers of governments nor is it legally binding, but rather sets out intergovernmental process with rules on conflict and cooperation in the area of social policy. For a comprehensive analysis of issues emerging from the social union framework, see Lazar, "The Social Union Framework Agreement."

includes a commitment from the federal government to the principle of "equalization payments," that is, the transfers of funds to the provinces from the federal government, to ensure provincial governments have comparable revenues to provide comparable levels of public services regardless of their population or revenue base. Equalization payments have become a system of unconditional grants by the federal government to provinces based on need. At various times depending on their economic situation, provinces may qualify for equalization payments from the federal government to ensure a standardized quality of delivery of public services. These payments will form part of the provincial general revenue, which then will go to support postsecondary education.

FEDERAL TRANSFER PAYMENTS

The federal government has an influential, albeit indirect, role in education by contributing funds through transfer payments to the provinces for health care, education, and social welfare. These funds find their way into the provinces' general revenue, which ultimately funds the provincial education system. Historically, these grants may be conditional or block. When the funds are conditional, the provincial governments must meet conditions to receive the money. Conditional grants allow the federal government to steer provincial spending in areas of federal priority. By contrast, block grants are unconditional and allow the provincial government a high level of autonomy in how they use the funds.

These transfer payments have evolved over time but were drastically reduced and significantly restructured in 1995, becoming one block fund known as the Canada Health and Social Transfer (or CHST). These payments to the provinces were based on tax transfer and cash transfer, and were allocated on an equal per capita basis. In 2003, to improve accountability and transparency, as well as strengthen health care across the nation, the Government of Canada and the provincial and territorial governments agreed to restructure and create two new separate transfer payments, one for health (the Canada Health Transfer, or CHT) and one for postsecondary education, programs for children, and other social programs (the Canada Social Transfer, or CST). Approximately 62 percent of the original CSHT was allocated to health care and the remaining 38 percent to postsecondary education, programs for children and social programs. In 2007 the Government of Canada restructured the Canada Social Transfer again, and the CST support to the provinces and territories is now calculated on a per capita basis. Total CST levels were set in legislation at that time, and growth of the CST transfer was set at 3 percent annually.[25]

---

[25] The 2007 federal budget committed $800 million a year toward the postsecondary education component of the CST subject to discussions with the provinces

Arrangements for accountability have evolved over the years along with the transfers themselves. Federal transfers began as conditional cost-sharing grants set up to encourage the establishment of national programming of comparable quality across the country. Once programming and priorities were established and shared between the two levels of government, the federal approach to accountability shifted and the transfers became unconditional block funding based on mutually agreed principles. The block funding gave provinces and territories more latitude in planning and administering programs. The current model of accountability for the transfers focuses on outcomes and reporting on spending. However, the provincial governments are free to use the funds as they see fit.

The federal withdrawal from funding postsecondary education through transfer payments can be seen in the creation of the Canada Health and Social Transfer (1995), which collapsed all the transfer payments for health, postsecondary education, and social welfare into one payment and then reduced the overall transfer. The postsecondary education and welfare portion of the transfer took the brunt of the reductions as health-care concerns dominated the policy agenda. The transfer cuts dramatically and negatively impacted provincial general revenue. Already in the midst of a recession, Canadian provincial governments responded in various ways. Many immediately cut postsecondary operating budgets. Significant differences in tuition policy across the provinces began to emerge at this time with some provinces freezing tuition and other provinces allowing postsecondary institutions to raise their tuition fees to make up for the loss of provincial revenue.[26] The consequences of the federal government's cut to transfer payments were felt across Canadian higher education as university students' tuition fees on average doubled in five years across programs.[27] When calculating the decrease in the transfer payments to postsecondary education against the increase in student enrolments between 1994/95 and 2004/05, per student funding in Canadian postsecondary education decreased by almost 50 percent

---

on best use and appropriate reporting and accountability, and also ensured that no province or territory would receive less under the new system than they had received previously. For a full description of the current system in place, see Government of Canada, *Budget* (2007); and Government of Canada, "History of Health and Social Transfers."

[26] Other provinces such as Quebec and British Columbia immediately froze tuition fees, which put revenue pressure on their postsecondary institutions.

[27] This phenomenon is well documented. Statistics Canada estimated that even undergraduate fees, where increases were capped by most provinces, rose 34 percent between1995/96 and 2001/02. Tuition increases in professional programs, which were deregulated, were substantially higher. See McMullen, "Tuition Fee Deregulation."

during this time period.[28] Notwithstanding the second restructuring of the transfer payments in 2003 and the subsequent investments in the new CST, according to one Senate Committee "the federal government's contribution to funding PSE through transfer payments is lower than it was in 1994."[29]

FEDERAL STUDENT ASSISTANCE PROGRAMS

To alleviate some of the pressure on students' tuition increases, the federal government has enhanced its student support mechanisms over the last two decades. The federal government has played an important role in student financial assistance since 1964 through the Canada Student Loans Program administered in collaboration with the provinces.[30] In 1994 a new *Canada Student Financial Assistance Act*,[31] which governs the provisions of loans issued to students, was passed by the federal government. The new legislation enhanced loan provisions, alleviated repayment provisions, created new mechanisms for assessing student need and financing loans through the private sector, and created a special fund for students with disabilities, part-time students, and women in certain programs. In 1998 additional financial support programs were created by the federal government under the Canadian Opportunities Strategy,[32] and subsequently the Canadian Education Savings Grant program under the *Canada Education Savings Act* was created, which set up a registered education savings program (RESP) to encourage families to save for their children's postsecondary education.[33]

---

[28] Bakvis, "The Knowledge Economy," 207; Shanahan and Jones, "Shifting Roles and Approaches"; Fisher et al., *Canadian Federal Policy and Postsecondary Education*.

[29] Standing Senate Committee on Social Affairs, Science and Technology, *Opening the Door*, 100.

[30] Quebec, Northwest Territories, and Nunavut do not participate in the Canada Student Loans Program and offer their own student assistance program.

[31] *Canada Student Financial Assistance Act*, SC 1994, c 28; see also *Canada Student Financial Assistance Regulations, 1994*.

[32] Government of Canada, *Canadian Opportunities Strategy*. The strategy was wide reaching and unfolded over several years. It provided financial support for students with disabilities and for part-time students, offered tax relief for student loan interest, inaugurated the Canadian Education Savings Grant, created RESPs, announced the creation of the Canadian Millennium Scholarship Foundation, created Canada study grants, improved student loan provisions, increased funding to the research granting councils, created the education credit and child-care expense deduction, and provided funding for at-risk youth education programs and job skills training that would lead to youth employment.

[33] See the *Canada Education Savings Act*, 2004 SC 2004, c 26 and the *Canada Education Savings Regulations, 2004*, which shelter interest on contributions from tax

Using their spending power and taking advantage of a budgetary surplus, the federal government also created, by an Act of the federal Parliament, and endowed for ten years, the Canadian Millennium Scholarship Foundation as a private, not-for-profit, corporate entity to provide need-based grants and merit-based scholarships to postsecondary students across Canada.[34] The program caused tensions with the provinces, especially in Quebec. It was viewed by the provinces as unilateral federal spending in an area of provincial jurisdiction and as violating the principles of the *Social Union Framework Agreement* (*SUFA*), which required consultation and collaboration when the federal government was spending money in provincial areas of constitutional jurisdictions. Moreover, the provincial governments already had student assistance programming in place, and they started to threaten to reduce it so that the federal funds would simply displace provincial funds, thereby thwarting the objective of the federal program to put additional funding in the hands of students.[35] Over the next decade the federal government would replace the Millennium Scholarship Foundation with a revamped Canada Student Loans Program (2008/09) and introduce the Repayment Assistance Plan (2009), a loan forgiveness program that aims to ensure no student debt remains after fifteen years of completing studies.[36] In the 2008 federal budget, the Government of Canada announced the consolidation of all federal student grants into a single program to augment the loans program.[37]

---

and provide government matching funds through the Canada Education Saving Grant of 20 percent, up to $500 on annual contributions and defers tax on income.

[34] The Canadian Millennium Scholarship Foundation was established by section 3 of the *Budget Implementation Act, 1998*. It was not well received by the provinces, and the Conservative federal government did not renew it at the end of the program's mandate in 2008. Instead the new federal government created a Canada Student Loans Program with the same money. This program reaches more students but offers less money per student.

[35] See Axelrod et al., "The Politics of Policy-Making"; Shanahan and Jones, "Shifting Roles and Approaches"; Wellen et al., "The Making of a Policy Regime"; Axelrod et al., "People, Processes and Policy-Making."

[36] Government of Canada, "CanLearn," accessed July 31, 2013, http://www.canlearn.ca.

[37] For details on the Canada Student Loans Program, see Human Resources and Skills Development Canada, "Canada Student Grants Program," accessed July 31, 2013, http://www.hrsdc.gc.ca/eng/learning/canada_student_loan/cgsp.html.

FEDERAL GOVERNMENT SUPPORT OF POSTSECONDARY RESEARCH

In the area of research the federal government has been equally active and strategic, investing in research granting agencies and Canada Research Chairs, supporting the indirect costs of research, funding research infrastructure through the Canada Foundation for Innovation, and supporting graduate and postdoctoral scholarships.[38]

Research Granting Agencies

Historically the federal government has been a major financial support for Canadian postsecondary research and development through three research granting councils that support investigator-initiated research programs by providing money directly to postsecondary institutions in the form of research grants.[39] Grants are awarded on a competitive, peer-reviewed basis. Currently the federal government is the primary external investor in university research.[40] During the last two decades, the federal government has increased and targeted research funding to advance its innovation strategy.[41] In 1998 the federal government began a 60 percent increase, over five years, to the funding of the three research councils. In 1999 the federal government reorganized one of the research councils, the Medical Research Council, into a multidisciplinary Canadian Institutes of Health Research and doubled its funding.[42] In addition, it expanded its National Centres of Excellence program, which supports applied and strategic science research networks that link researchers across the country in both the public and private sectors, focusing on the commercialization

---

[38] For a full review and analysis of the federal government's efforts in postsecondary research, see Fisher et al., *Canadian Federal Policy and Postsecondary Education*; Axelrod et al., "The Politics of Policy-Making"; Shanahan and Jones, "Shifting Roles and Approaches," Axelrod et al., "People, Processes and Policy-Making"; Bakvis, "The Knowledge Economy."

[39] See the Government of Canada, *Royal Commission on the National Development of the Arts, Letters and Science, 1949–1951*. Known as the Massey Commission after its chair, the report recommended direct investment in university research and eventually led to the establishment of the research funding councils in the 1970s.

[40] AUCC, *Momentum*, 13.

[41] Federal spending on research and development activities at universities and colleges increased from less than $800 million in 1997/98 to almost $3 billion in 2008/09. Standing Senate Committee on Social Affairs, Science and Technology, *Opening the Door*, 82.

[42] The three councils include the Social Science and Humanities Research Council of Canada (SSHRC), the Natural Science and Engineering Research Council of Canada (NSERC), and the Medical Research Council.

of research, increasing knowledge transfer, and generally advancing the federal government's economic agenda.[43]

Research Infrastructure

In 1997 the Canadian federal government created an independent, arm's-length foundation to fund research infrastructure – the Canada Foundation for Innovation (CFI)[44] – through public, private, and government partnerships, leveraging matching financial contributions from the private sector and provincial governments. The CFI is aimed at supporting research in universities, colleges, hospitals, and other not-for-profit institutions, but it has become a major source of funding for research in Canadian higher education. It funds up to 40 percent of infrastructure costs for research projects. By employing an arm's-length foundation to channel the money, the federal government sought to avoid criticism from the provinces over interference.

Canada Research Chairs

In 2000, the federal government created the Canada Research Chairs (CRC) program, creating 2,000 permanent, government-supported university research professorships to retain and attract the best research scholars to Canadian postsecondary education.[45] The program was expanded in 2008, and again in 2011 when ten new chairs were announced in the federal budget along with thirty new Industrial Research Chairs at Canadian colleges.[46] In 2011, the federal government took this trajectory further and created the Canada Excellence Research Chairs (CERC) program to support universities in building their research programming by awarding world-class researchers and their teams $10 million over seven years to establish research programs at universities.[47]

---

[43] See Networks of Centres of Excellence of Canada, http://www.nce-rce.gc.ca/Index_eng.asp.

[44] See http://www.innovation.ca/.

[45] See http://www.chairs-chaires.gc.ca.

[46] Government of Canada, *Next Phase of Canada's Action Plan*; Government of Canada, *Budget* (2011).

[47] The chairs are awarded to align with the federal government's science and technology strategy in five research areas: environmental sciences and technologies, natural resources and energy, health and related life sciences and technologies, information and communications technologies, and the digital economy. The 46 Canada Excellence Research Chairs have been awarded. Ten more awards have been created for the second phase, announced in the June 2011 budget. CERC is advertised by the Canadian federal government as the most prestigious and generous research program available globally. The funds come

Indirect Research Costs Program

The federal government has also moved to support the indirect costs (overhead) of research through the Indirect Costs Program established in 2003.[48] These costs include operating and maintaining research laboratories, improving safety standards, and managing intellectual property.

Graduate and Postdoctoral Research Scholarships

Finally, the federal government increased its investment in the number and amount of graduate scholarships awarded in the Canada Graduate Scholarships Program administered by the research councils. Income from some general scholarships and postsecondary scholarships was given tax exemption in 2006. New doctoral and postdoctoral scholarships were created in 2008 and 2010 federal budgets, respectively.[49]

Across these research initiatives, we see evidence of direct federal government intervention into the hiring practices of Canadian postsecondary institutions through major investments in human resources. Although the grants went directly to universities, the eligibility requirements stipulated in the applications process enabled the federal government to exert its influence. In some cases the application process involved postsecondary institutions submitting an institutional strategic research plan and aligning institutional proposals with government priorities, which magnified the steering effect of the program on postsecondary research. Significantly, all of these federal government research initiatives have put funds into the hands of postsecondary institutions and individual postsecondary researchers, effectively bypassing provincial oversight. The overall amount of federal government support of research through the granting councils and the new CRC and CFI programs is comparable to the amounts the provinces received for postsecondary education under the Canada Social Transfer. Given the magnitude of research funding, and its gravitational pull on postsecondary institutions, the federal government's spending power in this area cannot be overlooked when discussing the federal government's role and power in shaping Canadian postsecondary education within the larger legislative framework of postsecondary education and of intergovernmental relations in Canada.

---

from the three granting councils, and Social Sciences and Humanities Research Council administers and houses the secretariat of the program on behalf of the three councils. See Government of Canada, *Canada Excellence Research Chairs*, www.cerc.gc.ca.

[48] See http://www.indirectcosts.gc.ca/home-accueil-eng.aspx.

[49] Standing Senate Committee on Social Affairs, Science and Technology, *Opening the Door*, 83–85. Note that as of 2010, postdoctoral research fellowships are taxable.

FEDERAL SUPPORT OF APPRENTICESHIP AND VOCATIONAL/LABOUR MARKET PROGRAMS

The federal government has historically invested in labour market skills training and apprenticeship programs in Canadian postsecondary education, in particular with colleges, and in partnership with other government institutions and industry. In the mid-1980s, however, under the Canadian Jobs Strategy, the federal government began to retrench, moving away from public provision of training in colleges and government institutions and toward private provision of training in the workplace and industry. In the 1990s the federal government devolved the responsibility of funding and administering training programs to the provinces through Labour Market and Development Agreements but retained responsibility for labour mobility across the country. These changes in the delivery of labour market training signalled the federal government's retreat from directly providing skills training through publicly funded postsecondary institutions; at the same time, these changes increased private sector, industry, and regional provincial government involvement and influence in the sector. Although the federal government has retained some funding of apprenticeship programs, it has delegated delivery to the provinces and private sector.

IMPLICATIONS: FISCAL FEDERALISM AND HIGHER EDUCATION

Federal spending power as exercised through an assortment of transfer and equalization payments as well as through direct funding of various programs is known as "fiscal federalism" and is part of the complicated business of intergovernmental relations in Canada.[50] Together with the constitutional legislative framework, these transfers and payments determine how the federal system works. Stevenson characterizes fiscal federalism as a system that has evolved through incremental changes even in the face of massive social and economic change; it is asymmetrical in that the federal government does not treat all the provinces alike, nor does it have a fixed set of principles to do so. It is complex and marked by an elaborate structure of intergovernmental consultations, negotiations, and agreements. It is fraught with short-termism without long-term goals or outcomes, whereby changes made solve one problem

---

[50] See Brown, "Fiscal Federalism." Brown defines fiscal federalism as "the evolving system of financial arrangements between the federal and provincial orders of government," and adds that "it is an essential part of the discussion of how Canada's federal system works" (63). See also Stevenson, "Fiscal Federalism and the Burden of History."

but create another.[51] Finally, there is a high degree of federal penetration into provincial jurisdiction.[52]

Fiscal federalism functions as an important feature of Canadian higher education. A portion of the Canada Social Transfer (CST) is notionally intended for postsecondary education and is nominally earmarked by the federal government to support provincially funded postsecondary education. But as the CST is a block, unconditional transfer payment, the provinces are not legally required to allocate the specified sum to postsecondary education. Federal funds for the Canada Social Transfer go into the provinces' general revenue fund which will, in turn, be used to fund any provincial priorities. Often the reality is that much less than the amount earmarked by the federal government finds its way into postsecondary education depending on the fiscal situation and other pressing policy priorities of the provinces.[53]

Nevertheless, the federal government's influence over postsecondary education through transfers and its spending power is readily apparent in Canadian postsecondary education over the last two decades (1993–2013), especially in four key areas: federal-provincial transfer payments and their impact on tuition, student financial assistance, research and development, and vocational skills development/labour market training. Notwithstanding constitutional arrangements that give exclusive jurisdiction over education to the provinces, Canadian postsecondary education has changed significantly through the unilateral spending efforts of the federal government in these four areas – efforts that have been largely uncontested, if not resisted, by provincial governments.

This period in Canadian postsecondary education is referred to by Tupper as the federal government's "Quiet Revolution";[54] in the mid-1990s, the federal government appeared to be withdrawing from funding Canadian postsecondary education through transfer payments to the provinces, but it ended up exerting stronger influence over postsecondary education by directly funding students, faculty, and institutions. This was accomplished through the use of fiscal policy and investments in areas of legitimate federal constitutional authority that intersect with postsecondary education, namely, research, student assistance, and tax incentives.

The federal government's modification to provincial transfer payments in the mid-1990s, generally seen as a retreat from funding postsecondary education through provincial transfers, dramatically altered postsecondary tuition fees across the country. The resulting trajectory of

---

[51] Stevenson, "Fiscal Federalism and the Burden of History," 6.
[52] McRoberts, "Federal Structures."
[53] See Bakvis, "The Knowledge Economy."
[54] Tupper, "The Chrétien Government and Higher Education."

tuition increases in most provincial postsecondary systems has not been reversed, notwithstanding the federal government's assertion that the value of recent transfer payments has increased considerably.[55] Although postsecondary tuition policy is squarely provincial jurisdiction, the federal government's constitutionally legitimate modification of the transfer payments influenced tuition direction across the country. At the same time the federal government's approach to student assistance shifted the cost of postsecondary education in Canada toward students and their families (private resources) and away from the state (public resources) through the adroit use of treasury-based tax subsidies, tax incentives, grants, and loans as well as authority-based policy instruments in the form of legislation and regulation to achieve its aims.[56] This approach to student assistance put federal funding directly into the hands of individual students, and did so in a targeted manner to improve postsecondary access and participation of underrepresented Canadians. The federal government's approach to vocational and apprenticeship training has had the effect of increasing private sector presence and influence in this area.

The federal government's massive reinvestment in postsecondary research may have altered the research culture and organization of postsecondary systems in Canada. Arguably, federal investment has introduced stratification and differentiation in terms of research intensity into what historically was a relatively flat and homogenized provincial postsecondary system. For example, one of the consequences of this period was the creation of the U-15 universities,[57] the major research-intensive medical-doctoral universities that purport to be the top tier of the postsecondary education ladder in Canada and whose presidents meet on a regular basis to strategize and lobby around common concerns. There has also been a skewing of research resources into the top research universities, which has led to disparities across the country based on gender, discipline, and region. At the same time, when funding is scarce in the postsecondary system, as it may be during recessions, postsecondary institutions have a tendency to seek out other revenue sources. Evidence of institutional "mission creep" can also be seen in the Canadian higher education landscape around research culture and institutional research mandates. Canadian higher education is currently very dynamic and tensions exist between stratification, differentiation, and academic drift. In this respect the federal government's massive funding of research over the last two

---

[55] See Government of Canada, "History of Health and Social Transfers."

[56] Some provincial governments also adopted polices to shift the cost of postsecondary education onto families away from public resources, which accelerated this trend.

[57] Formerly known as the G10 then the G13 and presently as the U-15 universities in Canada.

decades has altered institutional behaviour and has begun to influence system organization.

The federal government's approach to postsecondary education has been to retreat in some areas while advancing in others. Notwithstanding the complex federal-provincial constitutional arrangements and the tension-filled intergovernmental dance, the federal government has managed to increase its activity in, and influence on, Canadian postsecondary education.

Chapter 3

THE ROLE OF THE PROVINCIAL GOVERNMENT IN POSTSECONDARY EDUCATION

Theresa Shanahan

COMPONENTS OF THE PROVINCIAL POSTSECONDARY SYSTEMS

Canadian higher education systems are dominated by publicly funded and secular universities and colleges. Historically, Canadian higher education was broken down along degree-granting lines with two dominant institutional types: university degree-granting institutions, and non-degree postsecondary institutions commonly referred to as community colleges. In the past Canada's postsecondary system of education has been described as "among the most pure and unambiguous binary systems in the world."[1]

In Canada, postsecondary institutions were divided into two sets with distinct mandates, funding, and governance arrangements. One was the universities, and the other was what Statistics Canada, the national statistical agency, refers to as Non-University Postsecondary Institutions (NUPS). What determined which set an institution belonged to was whether it had the authority to grant a baccalaureate degree. In Canada, with almost no exception, all institutions

---

[1] Skolnik, *Community College Baccalaureate*, 2. See also Skolnik, *Postsecondary Education in Canada*.

Handbook of Canadian Higher Education Law, edited by Theresa Shanahan, Michelle Nilson, and Li-Jeen Broshko. Montreal and Kingston: McGill-Queen's University Press, Queen's Policy Studies Series.

which had that authority have been called universities. And in fact, in Canada, the majority of institutions which can grant a baccalaureate – until recently – have fit the commonly held notion of a university. They have graduate programs and at least one professional school.[2]

Universities typically provided the academic (doctoral, masters, baccalaureate, and professional) degrees, whereas non-university postsecondary institutions (colleges) provided diplomas and certificates in more vocational and technical programs. As Skolnik himself notes, this is no longer an apt description of the Canadian postsecondary landscape. This distinction by institutional type and degree-granting authority has become blurred over the last two decades as the expansion of higher education in Canada and the expansion of degree-granting status to the non-university postsecondary institutions (NUPS) have given rise to a range and diversity of postsecondary institutions, structures, programs, and degree types that are not so neatly captured by the traditional categorization. Universities continue to grant degrees, but increasingly colleges and other non-university postsecondary institutions are offering applied and associate degrees.[3]

There are various terminologies applied to the regulation of postsecondary institutions by provincial governments, which contribute to complexity and even confusion over system organization and institution types. Across Canadian provinces, public and private postsecondary institutions may be "recognized," "authorized," "registered," or "licensed" by government, or they may be completely unregulated in Canada. If they are "recognized" or "authorized" postsecondary institutions, they have been given authority to grant academic credentials by the provincial or territorial government, usually through charters or legislation, and they are captured within provincial or territorial mechanisms for program and institutional quality. If they are "registered" or "licensed" institutions, they are monitored by government for consumer protection purposes but not for institutional or program quality. If institutions are not registered or licensed, they may still operate as private commercial enterprises, and their programs are unregulated and unmonitored by government.[4]

In terms of size, Canada's higher education landscape includes 163 provincially "recognized" public and private universities (including theological schools) with degree-granting status authorized by a provincial government. Canada has 183 provincially "recognized" public

[2] Skolnik, *Community College Baccalaureate*, 2.

[3] For a detailed discussion of degree expansion in Canada and the implications on system design, see Marshall, "Differentiation by Degree."

[4] For further information on these distinctions see CMEC, *Postsecondary Education Systems in Canada: An Overview* (2009); see also Canada Council on Learning, *Navigating Post-secondary Education*.

colleges and institutes, some of which also offer applied and bachelor's degrees authorized by a provincial government. In addition there are 68 university-level institutions and 51 college-level institutions operating as "authorized" institutions that have selected programs approved under provincial authority.[5] The Association of Universities and Colleges of Canada recognizes 98 of these public and private universities as members.[6] There are hundreds of private career colleges across the country. Some are licensed by provincial governments and others operate as unlicensed entities that are not regulated in any way.[7]

Postsecondary institutions are not distributed equally across the regions or provinces. The greatest concentration of public universities and colleges is found in the provinces of Ontario and Quebec and roughly aligns with the greatest population density.[8] In 2011, undergraduate full-time and part-time enrolment in postsecondary education exceeded 1 million and graduate student enrolment reached approximately 148,000.[9] Recent data from Statistics Canada place the total number of students enrolled in Canadian universities and colleges (2012/13) at just over 2 million (see Table 3.1).[10] The overwhelming majority of students are enrolled in *publicly funded* postsecondary education institutions in Canada. The publicly funded postsecondary system dominates our higher education landscape and consequently dominates higher education system planning, law, and policy-making. This is one of the distinguishing contextual features of Canadian higher education, setting it apart from neighbouring

---

[5] CMEC, *Education in Canada: An Overview* (2008).

[6] AUCC, *Our Universities*. AUCC changed its name in 2015 to Universities Canada. The numbers vary depending on source and who is recognizing the institutions. Provincial and CMEC figures do not correspond with AUCC figures. Approximately 98 public and private degree-granting institutions with university status are members of the Association of Universities and Colleges of Canada – the closest thing Canada has to institutional accreditation. Some of these degree-granting institutions have federated or affiliated with one another and put their degree-granting authority in abeyance, thus reducing the number to approximately 90 AUCC-recognized institutions offering degrees across Canada. The majority of AUCC members are publicly funded universities, which also contributes to the discrepancy between AUCC and provincial government numbers.

[7] The National Association of Career Colleges (http://www.nacc.ca), a national body advocating for career colleges, is attempting to promote quality assurance; however, it is not an accreditation body and membership is voluntary.

[8] Standing Senate Committee on Social Affairs, Science and Technology, *Opening the Door*, figure 2, p. 7.

[9] AUCC, "Back to School – Quick Facts."

[10] Statistics Canada, Table 477-0019, "Postsecondary Enrolments, by Registration Status, Pan-Canadian Standard Classification of Education (PCSCE), Classification of Instructional Programs, Primary Grouping (CIP_PG), Sex and Immigration status."

jurisdictions such as the United States. Another feature is the (aggregate) high participation rates. Canada has one of the most educated populations in the world. Since 2000 Canada has ranked first among the 37 OECD and G20 countries with available data in the proportion of 25- to 64-year-olds (51 percent in 2012/13) with a tertiary education (completed degree from a college, university, or polytechnic). This participation rate is well above the OECD average.[11]

TABLE 3.1
Postsecondary Enrolments, by Registration Status, Pan-Canadian Standard Classification of Education (PCSCE), Classification of Instructional Programs, Primary Grouping (CIP_PG), Both Sexes, 2012/13

	Total	University	College
Canada	2,023,191	1,283,229	739,959
Full-time	1,489,536	956,154	533,385
Part-time	533,652	327,078	206,574

Source: Adapted from Statistics Canada, Table 477-0019, "Postsecondary Enrolments, by Registration Status, Pan-Canadian Standard Classification of Education (PCSCE), Classification of Instructional Programs, Primary Grouping (CIP_PG), Sex and Immigration Status."

Publicly Funded Postsecondary Education

The Canadian postsecondary system comprises publicly funded post-secondary institutions and privately funded postsecondary institutions. Publicly funded institutions rely largely (but not solely) upon the provincial government for operating funds. Publicly funded postsecondary institutions in Canada may be universities or non-university institutions; they may be degree-granting or non-degree granting institutions. Degree-granting schools generally include universities, colleges, institutes, institutes of technology and advanced learning, and polytechnics. Public non-degree granting institutions may be called colleges, centres, colleges of applied arts and technology, community colleges, institutes, or CEGEPs.

---

[11] Canada's high postsecondary participation rate is widely reported in various places. For example, OECD, *Country Note: Canada*, 1; Science, Technology and Innovation Council, *State of the Nation*, 79–80.

Universities

There are four categories of public universities within Canada. Large *medical-doctoral research intensive universities* offer a wide array of PhD doctoral programs as well as other professional, graduate, and undergraduate programs. *Comprehensive teaching and research universities* offer a broad range of research and programs at the undergraduate and graduate level and may include professional degrees. Small *liberal arts universities* focus primarily on undergraduate education. *Special purpose universities* offer university degrees in specialized fields.[12]

In Canada, publicly funded universities are not generally considered arms of the government;[13] they are not state universities and they are not state controlled. Canadian publicly funded universities are constituted as not-for-profit, independent corporate entities by an Act of the Legislature (provincial or federal) or by royal charter or royal proclamation.[14] Although most Canadian universities derive their degree-granting

---

[12] See Canada Council on Learning, *Navigating Post-secondary Education.*

[13] Legally there are certain exceptions delineated in a small number of *Charter* cases, which I will refer to later in this chapter. Subsequent chapters also refer to various cases in which the *Charter of Rights and Freedoms* has been found to apply to publicly funded universities in a certain range of actions under certain circumstances.

[14] The Royal Military College of Canada, located in Ontario, was established in 1874 by the federal government by an Act of the Canadian Parliament. It is the only federally established institution in Canada with degree-granting powers. See http://www.royalmilitarycollege.ca/.

Royal charters came from the Crown in England and usually predated Confederation in 1867, after which universities were generally (re)established and governance was continued as a corporation by an Act of the Legislature. A number of universities in Canada trace their foundations back to a royal charter, including University of King's College in Nova Scotia, 1802, http://www.ukings.ca/history; McGill University in Montreal, founded as the Royal Institution for the Advancement of Learning in 1821 by King George III and reconstituted as McGill by royal charter in 1852 by Queen Victoria, http://www.archives.mcgill.ca/public/exhibits/installation/main/gallery-1852.htm; King's College, the precursor to the University of Toronto, established by royal proclamation in 1827 by King George IV, http://utarms.library.utoronto.ca/researchers/the-universitys-original-charter; University of Laval, in 1852 by Queen Victoria, although it traces its roots back to New France and the Jesuits and Ursuline nuns in 1663, http://faculty.marianopolis.edu/c.belanger/quebechistory/encyclopedia/LavalUniversity-QuebecHistory.htm; Queen's University, in 1841 by Queen Victoria, http://www.queensu.ca/secretariat/index/RoyalCharter2011.pdf; University of Trinity College, now federated with University of Toronto, in 1852 by Queen Victoria, http://www.trinity.utoronto.ca/about/governance/statutes.html; Bishop's University, in 1853 by Queen Victoria, http://www.ubishops.ca/?id=1663 (Bishop's was originally established as a college by an Act of the federal government but

authority from provincial legislation, they are independent legal corporate entities. Government involvement in universities comes through the passing of the statute creating the university, funding the system, creating laws and regulations governing the system, and developing postsecondary policy. The main areas of provincial government intrusion into publicly funded universities concern funding and accounting for funds. Traditionally there have been four fundamental freedoms allowed to universities: the setting of curriculum and evaluations, the hiring of faculty, the admissions of students, and the pursuit of research. These freedoms are not set in any statute but arise historically and are observed in practice, contributing to high levels of university institutional autonomy in Canada.[15]

Non-University Postsecondary Institutions

Non-university postsecondary institutions (NUPS) across Canada are a diverse and evolving sector that varies by province in form, function, and programming. This sector includes public colleges, specialized institutes, community colleges, institutes of technology, colleges of applied arts and technology, CEGEPs, and career colleges. While previously offering certificates or diplomas, with an applied focus in a wide range of fields, many now offer applied or associate degrees or have a liberal arts focus. The public colleges emerged later in Canada and are a considerably younger sector than the Canadian universities. In general the colleges were created to increase access and to respond to the growing demand for postsecondary education in Canada as well as to respond to labour market needs. In some provinces the colleges feed into the university system (Quebec) or have a transfer function into universities (British Columbia and Alberta). In other provinces, they were created as a separate and parallel system to universities with no explicit transfer function (Ontario). Across Canada institutes and polytechnics, another type of NUPS, emerged out of the college sector. They often have broader

---

subsequently raised to the status of a university with the royal charter); and the University of Ottawa, which was given a royal charter from Queen Victoria in 1866 and granted a pontifical charter by Pope Leo XIII in 1889, http://www.archives.uottawa.ca/eng/history.html.

[15] The findings of the Flavelle Commission contributed significantly to the historical practice of university independence from government and are taken up in later chapters. See Government of Ontario, *Royal Commission on the University of Toronto, 1905-06* (known as the Flavelle Commission after its chair, Joseph Flavelle).

For discussions on Canadian institutional autonomy, see Winchester, "An Anachronism?"; Arthurs, "Question of Legitimacy"; Boggs, "Ontario's Royal Commission."

programming than community colleges, offering technical vocational programing as well as trade licensure and applied degrees.[16]

Privately Funded Postsecondary Education

Private postsecondary institutions rely upon their own source revenue. They may receive some public funds through government student assistance programs if they qualify, or they may receive funds through government research grants. But primarily their revenue is made up of tuition, other fees and private donations.[17] Privately funded postsecondary intuitions in Canada include private (for-profit and not-for-profit) career colleges and institutions (called colleges, schools, academies, or institutes), secular private universities, faith-based denominational institutions, and international institutions operating within Canada. In general the private postsecondary sector in Canada has more limited degree-granting authority and is less regulated by government. Some private colleges may be licensed or registered by government, or they may operate as unlicensed entities. This sector is more fluid, stratified, and susceptible to market pressures.

Within this privately funded postsecondary sector, the private career college (PCC), known as the shadow or phantom sector, is one of the fastest-growing sectors by institutional numbers, although not by student enrolment. However, it receives much less attention from provincial government law, regulation, and policy compared to the public sector. The regulatory context of PCCs across Canada varies but typically includes registration with the provincial government for consumer protection purposes but not for programmatic purposes. For example, conditions of registration will often include meeting the requirements for liability insurance, establishing trust funds for international student fees, complying with criteria for tuition rebates and student eligibility for government financial assistance, meeting provisions for record keeping such as student transcriptions, having minimum qualifications for instructors, and submitting detailed program descriptions. Internally, the relationship between the institution and the student is governed by contract law that sets out student rights and complaints procedures. In

---

[16] In Ontario, colleges in this category are called Institutes of Technology and Applied Learning (ITALs). In other provinces, they are simply referred to as Institutes of Technology.

[17] The province of Manitoba provides some government grants to four private theological institutions in the province through the Advanced Learning Division. Similarly, some private colleges in Quebec accredited with the government receive public funds. The province of Alberta provides operating grants to five not-for-profit private university colleges for delivery of approved, credit degree programs. See the appendix for more details on provincial profiles.

some provinces the PCCs have created membership organizations that have set up arm's-length, third-party quality assessment procedures.[18]

CREDENTIALS

There are a range of credentials offered in Canadian postsecondary education institutions. Some credentials are controlled by government and restricted by legislation, and others are unrestricted. The "degree" credential is restricted. Among institutions that have legislative or governmental ministerial authority to offer degrees, there are a number of levels of restricted degree credentials granted in Canada: doctoral degrees, master's degrees, professional degrees, baccalaureate degrees, applied degrees, and associate degrees (two-year degrees available only in British Columbia for college transfers to university). Trades certificates (apprenticeships) required for licensing are also restricted. In addition, postsecondary institutions may offer unrestricted credentials including certificates (one year or less) and diplomas and attestations (CEGEPs).[19]

SYSTEM-LEVEL ARRANGEMENTS: ORGANIZATION, GOVERNANCE, AND THE REGULATORY ENVIRONMENT

The provincial governments have exclusive constitutional authority to legislate, regulate, and coordinate postsecondary education within their territory under Section 93 of the *Constitution Act*. They are also the primary funders of public postsecondary education.[20] Each province and territory has a ministry or department responsible for postsecondary education. This may be a dedicated ministry for higher education or it may be grouped with elementary and secondary education. Higher education decision-making is typically centralized in the assigned ministry; however, the minister of finance and the premier of the province have considerable power and influence.[21] Law, policy, and government decision-making and planning can be systemwide, sector-specific, or less commonly by individual institution.[22] Some provinces do not have the overarching structural component or legislative framework to allow for

---

[18] See, for example, Government of Ontario, *Private Career Colleges*. For a detailed analysis of PCCs, see Milan and Hicks, *Ontario Private Career Colleges*.

[19] The Canadian Degree Qualification Framework outlines degree levels in Canadian postsecondary institutions in detail. See CMEC, *Ministerial Statement*.

[20] Subject to the caveat that the federal government indirectly funds postsecondary education in a number of influential ways, as described in chapter 2.

[21] For a thorough examination of decision-making in postsecondary education, see Trilokekar et al., "Making Postsecondary Education Policy."

[22] Prior to the 1960s, provinces tended to take an institutional approach to coordination of the postsecondary system, which meant provincial governments dealt

a systemwide approach to policy and decision-making in higher education; consequently, each sector is dealt with individually in legislation and policy.

Provincial organization and legislative arrangements for postsecondary education vary across the Canadian provinces. There is no one dominant approach. Each province has legislation that organizes the system and/or sectors; legislation that constitutes the institutions and gives them power to operate; legislation that provides for degree-granting authority; and arrangements for quality assurance sometimes enshrined in legislation or in a quality or accountability assurance framework. In some provinces all of these powers may be found in one omnibus statute, and in other provinces there are several pieces of legislation and policy documents covering a range of responsibilities.

System Coordinating Bodies

Unlike the United States, Canada does not have a long history of using intermediary bodies to organize and govern the postsecondary system. Those provinces that did create intermediary bodies did not give them executive decision-making authority over the provincial system; rather, they were advisory bodies that assisted provincial governments and made recommendations.[23] The coordinating structures and their powers that do currently exist vary by province. British Columbia, Alberta, and Saskatchewan have moved away from a provincial coordinating structure but do have bodies responsible for quality assurance and credit transfer in the system. Ontario and Quebec have advisory councils. Manitoba recently dissolved its council, which had been unique in Canada as an intermediary agency that not only coordinated programs and advised institutions and government, but also made decisions about distributing funding. These functions are now the responsibility of the Manitoba government.[24] Prince Edward Island, Nova Scotia, and New Brunswick have created a regional coordinating agency that plays an advisory role, the Maritime Provinces Higher Education Commission. Newfoundland

---

with institutions on an individual basis. This is no longer the case. See Skolnik and Jones, "Coordination between University and College Sectors."

[23] Jones, "Brief Introduction." According to Jones, no structures or mechanisms of this sort existed at all before 1950.

[24] The Government of Manitoba dissolved the Council on Post-Secondary Education (COPSE) in 2014 and replaced it with an education advisory council, an arm of the Department of Education and Advanced Learning. Now the Manitoba government, through its Advanced Learning Division within the department, is directly responsible for system planning, funding allocations, programs of study, tuition and fees, and quality assurance of colleges and universities in the province. For more information, see http://www.edu.gov.mb.ca/ald/index.html.

and Labrador has an advisory council that promotes cooperation and transfer between the province's university and college.

University Institutional Autonomy

University structural arrangements have been characterized in Canadian postsecondary education by a high level of institutional autonomy for universities and strict control of degree granting by provincial governments.[25] Historically universities have not been heavily regulated by government, nor has the market or private sector played a large role in their historical evolution. While the government provides universities with degree-granting authority through legislation, it does not direct programming or directly monitor internal governance. Government intervention is usually around funding, fee/tuition structure, and quality assurance especially related to the introduction of new degree programs. Provincial governments may require universities to have internal quality assurance processes for programs, especially degree-level programs. They may also set up mechanisms for review of programs leading to degrees as part of their degree-granting regulations. Universities operate independently and control their own academic, admissions, and standards policies as well as degree requirements, program offerings, and staff appointments. Universities have considerable independence in managing their own financial affairs, albeit subject to financial audits and other accountability and reporting exercises.[26] Minimal intrusions associated with the accreditation of professional schools and programs from professional governing bodies for the purposes of licensure have been reasonably tolerated by Canadian universities. Most Canadian universities have an academic senate responsible for academic planning, and a board of governors responsible for financial and operating policies.

College Governance Arrangements

The structure, function, programming, and governing arrangements between provincial governments and Canadian colleges varies by province. In some provinces colleges are tightly controlled by provincial legislation (for example, the Colleges of Applied Arts and Technology, or CAATs, in Ontario). In other provinces colleges have more independence from government. In some provinces the colleges have an explicit feeder function for the universities (such as Quebec). By contrast, in Ontario the university and college sectors have operated in silos, and credit transfer has

---

[25] This section sets out the basic structural arrangements. Legislation and case law associated with university governance are detailed in chapter 4.

[26] CMEC, *Education in Canada.*

been an ongoing issue between the sectors.[27] In general, publicly funded colleges and institutes experience more government involvement in admissions policies, program approvals, curricula, institutional planning, and working conditions. Members of publicly funded college governing boards are appointed by provincial or territorial governments albeit with representation from students, faculty, and the public. Program planning committees involve business and industry representatives.

Quality Assurance in Canadian Higher Education

Canadian higher-education quality assurance focuses on the offering of restricted credentials, namely, degree granting. The regulatory framework addresses university degree granting (and university-level degree-granting institutions), and more recently publicly funded colleges seeking to offer applied or associate degrees. There is less quality assurance regulation for the offering of diplomas and certificates. Furthermore, Canadian higher-education quality assurance focuses primarily on programs leading to degrees and takes the form of cyclical programmatic reviews. It has not taken the form of institutional accreditation of universities.[28]

Historically, the Canadian system of postsecondary education has been considered relatively homogeneous, and lacking in institutional diversity at the university level. Degree-granting powers were strictly controlled by provincial governments, usually through legislation. Universities dominated the higher education system and had a monopoly on degree granting. Although Canadian higher education spans a large geographical area with wide regional differences, it is a smaller system compared with other jurisdictions.[29] Given these characteristics it is perhaps not surprising that postsecondary quality assurance in general did not emerge until recently as a national priority. And when it did emerge, it was as much driven by external forces – such as the European Bologna process,[30] globalization, internationalization, and the global mobility of people and

---

[27] For a full discussion of the emergence of colleges, see Dennison and Gallagher, *Canada's Community Colleges*.

[28] The same is not true of the college sector as there is evidence of institutional accreditation in some provinces. See, for example, quality assurance processes for colleges in Ontario in the appendix.

[29] For example, the higher education system in the United States has over 4,500 degree-granting institutions and over 1,000 community colleges that offer certificate and associate degrees. See http://www.nsf.gov/statistics/seind12/c2/c2s1.htm.

[30] The Bologna Process created the European Higher Education Area (EHEA) comprising 47 states that voluntarily agreed to comparable standards and quality for higher education qualifications in order to facilitate credential recognition and mobility among the participating states.

students, all of which required the recognition of credentials – as it was internally driven by public demands for accountability.

Unlike other jurisdictions, Canada does not have a formal, national, higher education institutional accreditation system, or an organization whose legal mandate is to accredit universities. Part of the reason for the lack of a national institutional accreditation system in Canadian higher education has to do with the small size, the relatively small number of institutions awarding degrees in Canada compared to other jurisdictions (such as, for example, the United States that has a massive higher education system). Historically, provincial governments have tightly controlled degree granting, and so private degree-granting institutions were few in number. The Canadian system of higher education lacked stratification, and degrees from universities across the country were seen as roughly comparable in quality. In essence a national accreditation system was not needed.[31] Some scholars have described the situation as "accreditation by legislation," meaning that if an institution had approval by a provincial government to offer a degree, it was considered accredited in Canada.[32]

The Association of Universities and Colleges of Canada (AUCC) provides an alternative to institutional accreditation. While the AUCC is *not* a national accreditation body, and does not advertise itself as such, it does maintain that "membership in the AUCC, held in conjunction with an appropriate provincial legislation or charter, may be accepted in lieu of institutional accreditation."[33] Membership in the AUCC ensures that the institution's degrees will be recognized across Canada. In this regard, AUCC membership has been described as "*de facto* accreditation" for universities in Canada.[34]

Historically, quality assurance in Canadian higher education has been largely conducted as an internal institutional matter. Given that each Canadian university is autonomous and responsible for academic matters, each university determines its own quality assurance practices. Colleges, on the other hand, have more government and industry input. However, this characteristic of quality assurance in Canadian postsecondary education is starting to change. The Association of Universities and Colleges of Canada (AUCC) and the Association of Canadian Community Colleges (ACCC) both have established frameworks and commitment to

---

[31] This historical context is now changing.

[32] Marshall, "Differentiation by Degree"; Marshall, "Degree Accreditation in Canada."

[33] AUCC, "About Quality Assurance." Note that AUCC changed its name to Universities Canada in 2015.

[34] For more on the nuances of degree accreditation in Canada and the role of the AUCC in particular see Dave Marshall's work in this area, including "Differentiation by Degree" and "Degree Accreditation in Canada."

principles of quality assurance for member institutions.[35] In addition, in 2007 the Council of Ministers of Education, Canada (CMEC) issued a degree qualifications framework that describes degree categories, sets out degree-level standards, and establishes procedures for assessing new degree programs and new degree-granting institutions.[36] Although the framework was adopted by the territorial and provincial ministers responsible for postsecondary education, the framework is not legally binding on any institution or province.[37] Legally postsecondary institutions must operate within their provincial or territorial governments' legislative or policy frameworks. And some provincial governments have established their own provincial quality and accountability frameworks. There is also evidence of a movement toward establishing credential and qualification frameworks[38] as an extra feature of provincial quality assurance frameworks (for example, in Ontario and the three Maritime provinces). Most provinces have created organizations to assist with the quality assurance process. In many provinces, the quality assurance regime is government led and systemwide (in Alberta, British Columbia, Saskatchewan, Manitoba, and the three Maritime provinces). By contrast, Ontario's and Quebec's university sectors have created independent councils that audit the university-led quality assurance processes around degree granting, while the college sectors have separate quality assurance bodies.[39]

Most provincial governments employ legal and/or treasury policy implementation mechanisms attached to quality goals. For example, some of the provincial frameworks are enshrined in legislation or in the shape of contracts and agreements between the provincial government and institutions. These agreements require institutions to put quality assurance policies and practices in place. Other features of provincial

---

[35] These organizations do not conduct quality assurance audits, though. And not all Canadian universities and colleges are members of the AUCC or ACCC.

[36] CMEC, *Ministerial Statement*.

[37] The CMEC framework provides guidance for provincial frameworks but is not binding on provinces. According to the Canadian Information Centre for International Credentials, "This framework provides a context for identifying how degree credentials compare in level and standard among jurisdictions, with a view to facilitating continuous improvement, the education and training of an internationally competitive workforce, and international recognition of the quality of Canadian credentials." http://www.cicic.ca/1270/Issues-in-quality-assurance/index.canada.

[38] Qualifications frameworks place a qualification and its outcomes within the larger education system within a jurisdiction.

[39] For a discussion of recent trends in quality assurance practices for degree granting across Alberta, British Columbia, Quebec, and Ontario, see Weinrib and Jones, "Largely a Matter of Degrees" and Klassen, "Quality Assurance."

quality assurance frameworks include mechanisms for reporting on key performance indicators with funding attached.[40] (See the appendix for a table of specific regulatory frameworks and quality assurance processes for each province.) While institutions continue to create and control the internal quality assurance process in Canadian postsecondary education, provincial governments are, at the same time, employing a range of mechanisms (including policies, legislation, regulations, institutional contracts and agreements, and the creation of infrastructure and organizations) to steer system-level quality assurance activities, using funding as a leverage. In addition, in Canada a recognized, public or private, in-province or out-of-province, postsecondary institution may be given the authority to grant degrees or other credentials through a provincial-government-mandated quality assurance mechanism or process.[41] At the same time, the regulated professions in Canada have associations that conduct accreditation reviews of university programs where degrees lead to professional licensing. Again, these are at the programmatic level and are not institutional accreditations. These reviews involve teams of experts who conduct on-site visits and report back to the professional association.

With the expansion of higher education systems in Canada and with the expansion of degree-granting to non-university postsecondary institutions, new kinds of institutions are emerging, and new kinds of arrangements between institutions are occurring. Quality assurance and accountability is growing as a postsecondary issue. In response, provincial governments are employing new kinds of frameworks and legislation, and are creating organizations to assist government with managing an increasingly complex postsecondary environment.

---

[40] For a review of the evolution of accountability policies and mechanisms in Canadian higher education, see Fisher et al., *Development of Postsecondary Education Systems in Canada*.

[41] For example, in Ontario, the Postsecondary Education Quality Assessment Board is "an arm's-length advisory agency that makes recommendations to the Minister of Training, Colleges and Universities of Ontario on applications for ministerial consent under the terms of the *Post-secondary Education Choice and Excellence Act, 2000*. Ministerial consent is required by all public or private degree-granting organizations, either for profit or non-profit, based outside the province to offer all or part of a degree program in Ontario. It is also required by all private organizations in Ontario, either for profit or non-profit, and by all Ontario public organizations not empowered to grant degrees by Ontario statute to offer all or part of degree programs. Consent is also required to use the word 'university' relating to an educational institution in Ontario." See "About Us," http://www.peqab.ca/about.html. Boards, councils, or commissions providing similar functions can be found in most of the other provinces. See the appendix for details in each province.

PROVINCIAL FISCAL ARRANGEMENTS

Provincial government funding has become part of the regulatory arrangements in Canadian higher education.[42] Increasingly, provincial governments use funding mechanisms as a policy lever to regulate and steer the system. Operating funding for publicly funded postsecondary systems comes from the provincial general revenue coffers, which are made up of provincial taxation revenue as well as federal government transfer payments to the province (as described in chapter 2). Institutional operating budgets for publicly funded postsecondary education consist of provincial government operating grants, student tuition fees, and an assortment of other funds (such as private sector donations, endowments, ancillary fees, other government grants, sale of products, investment income, federal government research grants, municipal government funding, and other miscellaneous funds). The largest source of revenue for the public postsecondary system comes from provincial government operating grants, followed by student tuition. In Canada, private-source funding for postsecondary education comes primarily from individuals, through tuition fees for example, but also includes some revenue from businesses and other private sources.[43]

Across the country tuition fees for publicly funded postsecondary education are more or less controlled by provincial government policy and tuition frameworks. Operating grants are based on formulas that link government funding to student enrolments. In order for publicly funded institutions to receive government funding for full-time enrolled students, they must follow the provincial tuition framework. Provincial government tuition policy, and hence institutional ability to generate revenue from tuition fees, varies by province. Canadian provinces have gone in different directions regarding tuition fees. In some provinces government policy has allowed some professional and graduate programs to deregulate their tuition fees. This policy allows institutions, in accordance with criteria and conditions within a tuition framework, to set their own fees in certain disciplines such as business, law, medicine, and dentistry. Other tuition fees, such as for undergraduate programs in Ontario universities, are strictly capped. Some provinces have frozen tuition fees (for example, Newfoundland). Previously, Quebec froze university tuition, which was the lowest in the country for the past three decades, but the province lifted the freeze in 2007 and has begun to

---

[42] For an in-depth discussion of government funding of Canada's colleges and universities, see Snowdon, *Without a Road Map*.

[43] For more information on the patterns of Canadian spending on higher education and comparisons to other international jurisdictions, see OECD, *Education at a Glance: OECD Indicators, 2012*.

increase university tuition rapidly.[44] However, Quebec residents do not pay tuition for college (CEGEPs).[45]

Another historical feature of provincial funding of postsecondary education has been the roughly equal treatment of institutions by governments regarding the distribution of operating grants. Over the past two decades, provincial governments in Canada have utilized various mechanisms to determine operating grants to fund the postsecondary system. In addition to block operating grants, special purpose grants and enrolment-based funding formulas have been employed across the provinces. Envelopes of funding have been tied to or targeted for certain purposes, and matched-funding mechanisms have been introduced to leverage government funding and draw external sources of revenue into the systems. Performance funding – that is, funding attached to performance indicators that may or may not be nested within an intuitional contract – although small in amount, has been introduced in some provinces (for example in Ontario) and abandoned and then reintroduced in others (for example in Quebec).[46] The provincial government also provides funding for capital projects at publicly funded universities and colleges.

While part of the annual provincial government's budget is set aside for education and postsecondary education, other provincial ministries – such as the ministry responsible for immigration, health, or labour market training – have, on occasion, been involved in initiatives that have benefited postsecondary education institutions. Consequently, provincial funds for postsecondary initiatives may come from other ministries outside the ministry responsible for postsecondary education.

IMPLICATIONS FOR GOVERNANCE AND REGULATION OF PROVINCIAL POSTSECONDARY EDUCATION

Higher education system growth and degree-granting expansion has blurred boundaries between the university and non-university sectors and has led to changes in the organization and regulation of provincial systems of higher education in Canada. System regulation is being challenged by both the convergence and the divergence of institutional missions (differentiation and homogenization are occurring at the same time, albeit slowly), and by transfer arrangements between new kinds of institutions and between sectors. In part in response to these local challenges and in part in response to international forces, quality assurance

---

[44] Tuition increases for undergraduate students in Quebec were the highest in the country in 2012/13, at 10.1 percent. They were the lowest for British Columbia undergraduate students at 2 percent. Statistics Canada, *University Tuition Fees, 2012/2013*.

[45] CMEC, *Education in Canada*.

[46] Fisher et al., *Development of Postsecondary Education Systems in Canada*.

and accountability have emerged as clear government priorities in post-secondary education. Provincial governments are responding to these challenges by creating new bodies tasked with quality assurance and articulating credit transfer pathways through the systems. At the same time increased involvement of industry and the private sector in higher education has shifted the relationship among the institutions, the state, and the market. Canadian higher education has become a more complex policy and regulatory environment. Provincial government can be seen as expanding control, exerting stronger influence, and using regulation and fiscal policy to shape the system. These intrusions are challenging university autonomy. Remarkably, these changes in postsecondary education system organization and regulation have occurred without a massive overhaul to the provincial legislative framework in most provinces.[47] Instead, a combination of laws and policies have incrementally altered the regulation of Canada's provincial postsecondary systems. The chart in the appendix provides the details on the legal and regulatory arrangements broken down by provinces and territories.

---

[47] See Shanahan and Jones, "Shifting Roles and Approaches," for a full discussion of the nature of changing governance approaches.

PART II
Institutional Governance

Chapter 4

GOVERNANCE AND ADMINISTRATION OF POSTSECONDARY INSTITUTIONS IN CANADA

BRENT DAVIS

INTRODUCTION

Universities are rife with paradoxes. Their mission is to pursue innovative ideas, but universities themselves are often resistant to change. Universities are provided significant operational funds from the public purse but will accept no direct government oversight. Canadian universities have cloaked themselves in charitable status, but governments encourage their pursuit of profits through commercialization of their technologies. From a corporate governance perspective, the central paradox is that the core component of all universities in Canada – the education of students – is not governed by the supreme governing board of the university but by a separate and subordinate academic board or senate. These paradoxes can make university governance a difficult proposition. This chapter will examine the legal framework within which Canadian universities seek to govern themselves amid these inconsistencies.

Persons charged with the governance of universities must account for academic culture and freedom; the multiple interests of students, faculty, staff, and governments; the inbuilt fragmentation of faculties and administration; and the distinct role universities play in Canadian society. If governance of an institution can be said to comprise the establishment of

Handbook of Canadian Higher Education Law, edited by Theresa Shanahan, Michelle Nilson, and Li-Jeen Broshko. Montreal and Kingston: McGill-Queen's University Press, Queen's Policy Studies Series.

checks and balances to ensure proper management,[1] then the predominant goal of a university would have to be, as stated by Mr. Justice Powell in *NLRB v Yeshiva University*,[2] to operate a quality institution of higher learning that will accomplish broadly defined educational goals within the limits of its financial resources.[3] But the mechanism employed in Canadian universities to achieve this policy – governance shared between a senate and a board of governors – has engineered conflict by entrusting the senate with defining educational goals and the board with ensuring such goals are financially sustainable. If good governance is not achieved, the university risks headlines such as "Independent Panel to Be Struck to Review Concordia Governance."[4] Understanding the governance of universities, the roles of the board of governors, the senate, and the various offices and how they interact is not only a valuable endeavour to ensure good governance but can provide significant benefits if conflicts, with their attendant costs and reputational risks, are avoided.

SOURCES OF UNIVERSITY GOVERNANCE LAW IN CANADA

The framework of university governance law in Canada is extremely complex. A significant amount of legislation – from *The Constitution Act, 1867* and the *Canadian Charter of Rights and Freedoms* (hereafter the *Charter*) to individual and provincial enabling statutes – impacts the governance of Canadian universities. Moreover, universities can be subject to academic customs and policies that are often, but not always, enshrined in faculty employment contracts or collective agreements. These legal sources address a staggeringly large array of university powers and responsibilities.

The Constitution Act, 1867

Although not specifically mentioning universities, the provinces were granted the power by section 93 of *The Constitution Act, 1867* to make all laws in relation to education.[5] The provinces also received the right in section 92(7) of *The Constitution Act, 1867* to legislate over the establishment, maintenance, and management of hospitals, asylums, charities, and eleemosynary[6] institutions in and for the province. By obtaining jurisdiction over education, charities, and eleemosynary institutions,

---

[1] Farrington and Palfreyman, *Law of Higher Education*, 91.
[2] 444 US 672 (USSC 1980).
[3] Ibid., 688.
[4] Bradshaw, *Globe and Mail*, February 22, 2011, A4.
[5] *The Constitution Act, 1867* (UK), 30 & 31 Victoria, c 3.
[6] Eleemosynary institutions are a medieval concept and were organizations created as a way of distributing charity. Such corporations, usually hospitals, schools, or colleges, were established by a private founder and were subject to

the provinces were granted the right to legislate over both the form of universities (eleemosynary or charitable corporations[7]) and their primary function (education). Paradoxically considering the provisions of the Act, postsecondary education in Canada is largely funded by federal government money passed through the provinces.[8] As a result, universities must take into account both federal and provincial postsecondary priorities in their strategies and activities. Today, the creation and organization of a university is akin to the establishment of not-for-profit corporations in that their creation is closely regulated by the provincial government but, once created, the organization is granted the power to govern itself.[9] The importance placed on a university's ability to self-govern by the provinces can be viewed as a concrete expression of government's respect for the doctrine of academic freedom.

University Incorporating and Enabling Statutes

Each university is authorized to exercise the specific powers granted by its incorporating document. In some provinces, each university is established by and subject to its own Act of Legislature (or royal charter[10]), while in other provinces, all universities are established and governed by a single Act of Legislature.[11] Depending upon the jurisdiction in which the university is incorporated, it may be given all the powers of a "natural person"[12] and may or may not be subject to the applicable provincial not-for-profit *Corporations Act*.[13]

---

the oversight or visitation of the founder, his heirs, or a person appointed by the founder. This person was known as the visitor.

[7] Universities are normally registered as charities in Canada. The oldest universities have been registered since January 1, 1967, when the federal government required all entities requesting charitable status to register.

[8] Boychuk, "Differences of Degrees," 456. The federal government also contributes significant sums through its programs sponsoring university research.

[9] For the most part anyway – see discussion on the *Charter* below.

[10] Canadian universities created by royal charter include the University of Toronto, McGill University, Queen's University, Université Laval, and Bishop's University.

[11] In Alberta, the *Post-secondary Learning Act*, 2003, c P-19-5 governs the creation and governance of universities. In British Columbia, the *University Act*, RSBC 1996, c 468 continues those universities already in existence and governs their administration.

[12] *University Act*, RSBC 1996, s 46.1.

[13] *University of Toronto Act*, ss 1(2), 1(3) (subject to the *Corporations Act*, RSO 1970, c 89); *University Act*, RSBC, s 3(4). The *Business Corporations Act*, SBC 2002, c 57 does not apply to a university, but on the recommendation of the minister, the Crown may declare that all or part of the Act applies.

The Acts of the Legislature creating and managing universities have interesting features with respect to the powers of the Crown in post-secondary education. Such features, in particular the degree to which the government is viewed as delivering specific policies through the university, can become critical when considering whether the *Charter* applies to the university's activities. The relevant statutes in Ontario, British Columbia, and Alberta all reserve to the Crown the authority to establish a university and use of the name "University,"[14] and only those institutions authorized by the minister have the power to grant degrees. The enabling Acts of the Universities of Toronto and Ottawa, as well as the Alberta *Post-secondary Learning Act* and British Columbia *University Act*, provide that a university must present to the responsible government minister an annual report that includes financial matters.[15] The British Columbia legislation reflects a strong respect for academic freedom by specifically preventing the minister from interfering in the universities' exercise of powers respecting academic policies and standards, admission and graduation standards, and selection and appointment of staff.[16] However, the government's relaxed approach does not extend to the establishment of new degree programs, which requires ministerial approval.[17] Statutes in other provinces respect the concept of an autonomous postsecondary sector by not reserving any specific rights to the Crown other than the right to compel the university to produce a financial report. In contrast, Alberta reserves to itself the widest scope of powers in overseeing its universities. The *Post-secondary Learning Act* allows the minister to restrict, prohibit, and impose conditions on university powers and rights.[18] It also grants approval power to the minister for borrowing[19] and the issuance of guarantees by universities,[20] as well as the incorporation and dissolution of subsidiaries.[21] These differences indicate that the scope of powers capable of being exercised by universities in various jurisdictions in Canada may vary widely depending on the applicable legislation.

---

[14] *Post-Secondary Education Choice and Excellence Act*, 2000, SO 2000, c 36, s 3; *University Act*, RSBC 1996, c 468, s 67(1); *Post-secondary Learning Act*, s 3.

[15] *University of Toronto Act*, s 19(1); *University of Ottawa Act*, s 27; *University Act*, RSBC 1996, s 49; *Post-secondary Learning Act*, s 79.

[16] *University Act*, RSBC 1996, s 48(1).

[17] Ibid., s 48(2).

[18] *Post-secondary Learning Act*, s 59(2).

[19] Ibid., s 73(1).

[20] Ibid., s 74(2).

[21] Ibid., s 77.

The *Canadian Charter of Rights and Freedoms*

Universities have been described as quasi-public institutions,[22] which, one supposes, must indicate that they exist uncertainly on the line between a public and private institution. In Canada, this paradox has caused controversy in light of the *Charter* responsibilities imposed on public institutions. Section 32(1)(b) of the *Charter* provides that it applies to "the legislature and government of each province in respect of all matters within the authority of the legislature of each province." The Supreme Court of Canada has interpreted this to mean that the *Charter* applies only to government action and not to private activity.[23] It would be reasonable to conclude that universities, as incorporated and autonomous entities, are engaged in purely private activity. However, as discussed above, *The Constitution Act, 1867* allocated to provincial governments the authority over universities' core mission of public education which, at the postsecondary level, is delivered partially through universities.

Two cases have provided the foundation for the analysis of the application of the *Charter* to universities' activities. The first case is *McKinney v University of Guelph*, which considered whether the university had infringed the *Charter* rights of its employees through its mandatory retirement policy. Five of the seven justices at the Supreme Court of Canada confirmed that the human resource policy-making activities of the university were not governmental and therefore were not subject to the *Charter*. Justice La Forest conceded that in the course of a university carrying out its functions, there may be "situations in respect of specific activities where it can fairly be said that the decision is that of the government, or that the government sufficiently partakes in the decision as to make it an act of government."[24] In her dissent, Justice Wilson found that the *Charter* did apply to the university because universities are regulated and funded by government, and they deliver a traditional government function pursuant to statutory authority.

In the second key decision, *Eldridge v British Columbia (Attorney General)*, the Supreme Court of Canada considered whether the *Charter* applied to a hospital when it decided not to provide sign language interpreters for deaf patients in the course of providing a publicly funded health scheme. In concluding that the *Charter* did apply in this instance, Justice La Forest confirmed that

---

[22] Farrington and Palfreyman, *Law of Higher Education*, 92. However, Alberta's *Post-secondary Learning Act* includes "university" in the definition of "public postsecondary institution" making, in the eyes of at least one commentator, Alberta's universities public institutions. See Ross, "University Technology Transfer."

[23] *RWSDU v Dolphin Delivery Ltd.*, [1986] 2 SCR 578.

[24] *McKinney v University of Guelph et al.*, [1990] 3 SCR 229, para 42.

an entity may be found to attract *Charter* scrutiny with respect to a particular activity that can be ascribed to government.... If the act is truly "governmental" in nature – for example, the implementation of a specific statutory scheme or a government program – the entity performing it will be subject to review under the *Charter* only in respect of that act, and not its other, private activities.[25]

Eldridge provided later courts with a concrete example of an autonomous entity delivering a specific government program and requiring related decisions to comply with the *Charter*. The differing outcomes in *McKinney* and *Eldridge* are based on the activities at issue; the implementation of mandatory retirement policies was classified as an internal management issue to which the *Charter* did not apply, whereas the scope and quality of medical services were characterized as a governmental activity very much subject to the *Charter*.

In *Pridgen v University of Calgary*, two brothers were suspended following public criticism of their professor on Facebook. When the brothers appealed their sanctions to the Faculty Review Committee, they were unsuccessful and were instead provided with six- and four-month probations. The issue before the Alberta Court of Queen's Bench was whether in disciplining students under the authority of the *Post-secondary Learning Act*, the university had to comply with the *Charter*. In answering in the affirmative, and quashing the university's disciplinary decision, the court stated:

> The University is the vehicle through which the government offers individuals the opportunity to participate in the post-secondary educational system. When a university committee renders decisions which may impact, curtail or prevent participation in the post-secondary system ... it directly impacts the stated policy of providing an accessible educational system as entrusted to it under the *Post-secondary Learning Act*. The nature of these activities attracts *Charter* scrutiny.[26]

In dismissing the university's appeal, Justice Paperny concluded that the *Charter* was applicable to the university's disciplinary processes,

> because the statutory authority includes the power to impose serious sanctions that go beyond the authority held by private individuals or organizations including the power to fine, suspend or expel students. Accordingly, *Charter* protection for students' fundamental freedoms, including freedom of expression, applies in these circumstances.[27]

---

[25] *Eldridge v British Columbia (Attorney General)*, [1997] 3 SCR 624, para 44.
[26] *Pridgen v University of Calgary*, [2010] AJ No 1181, para 67.
[27] *Pridgen v University of Calgary*, [2012] AJ No 443, para 105.

Although concurring in the result, the two remaining appeal justices declined to address the *Charter* issue.

Since *Pridgen*, the application of the *Charter* to university activities has been further refined by a number of cases brought to the courts by student groups. In *Lobo v. Carleton University*, the student group objected to the university's refusal to allocate it space for non-academic extra-curricular activities. In concluding that the *Charter* did not apply to the case at hand, Justice Roccamo distinguished the *Pridgen* decisions by referencing the differences between the statutes at issue in the two cases. While the *Post-secondary Learning Act* made Alberta universities subject to significant government involvement, the *Carleton University Act, 1952* "created an autonomous entity whose structure and governance is in no way prescribed by the government."[28] Further, there was no evidence of Carleton University providing a specific government program or statutory scheme.[29] The Ontario Court of Appeal agreed, stating: "when the University books space for non-academic extra-curricular use, it is not implementing a specific government policy or program as contemplated in *Eldridge*."[30]

In *Wilson v University of Calgary (Board of Governors)*, the university requested a registered campus club to arrange posters containing graphic pro-life photos in such a way as to not be visible from public walkways. In allowing the students' application for judicial review of the university's decision, the court reinforced the requirement placed on university decision-makers in *Pridgen* that they undertake a consideration of the effect of disciplinary action on a student's *Charter*-protected rights, in this case freedom of expression.[31]

Finally, in *British Columbia Civil Liberties Association v University of Victoria*, the court again had the opportunity to consider a university's decision regarding the approval of use of university property for anti-abortion activist activities. Following *Eldridge*, the court held that if the "impugned activity or decision falls within the University's sphere of autonomous, operational decision-making, the *Charter* will not apply to such a decision."[32]

---

[28] *Lobo v Carleton University*, 2012 ONSC 254, para 14.

[29] Ibid., para 17.

[30] *Lobo v Carleton University*, 2012 ONCA 498. See also *R v Whatcott*, 2012 ABQB 231 where the court held that, in using provincial trespass legislation to prevent Mr. Whatcott from disseminating anti-abortion material, the university could not act contrary to the *Charter* any more than the Alberta legislature could when it enacted the legislation.

[31] *Wilson v University of Calgary (Board of Governors)*, 2014 ABQB 190, para 148.

[32] *British Columbia Civil Liberties Association v University of Victoria*, 2015 BCSC 39, para 48.

These cases clarify that not all university activities or decisions will attract *Charter* scrutiny. Nevertheless, university decision-makers are left to struggle with trying to understand where a court will draw the line between their university's core public functions and its private activities. The answer may be clearer in those provinces, such as Alberta, with more recent postsecondary education legislation that delineates the government activities that are specifically delegated to universities. In such cases, decisions of the university that limit a student's ability to pursue an education will very likely be subject to *Charter* considerations. In provinces with legislation lacking specifics, such as Ontario, the situation will remain uncertain. The Court of Appeal in *Lobo* endorsed the approach taken in *Eldridge* and left the door open to finding that the *Charter* would apply to an Ontario university that was implementing a specific government policy or program.

Academic Policies, Custom, and Usage

In addition to statutory sources of law, universities are subject to their own internal policies and customs, and in certain circumstances, these academic customs may apply to the entire higher education community. As part of its normal governance function, each university will have created written policies with respect to employment practices, utilization of space, conflicts of interest, intellectual property, and many other areas that faculty, staff, and students encounter every day. Individual universities may also have unwritten customs specific to them that supplement written policies and, having been in effect for a significant period of time, become part of the established conduct of the business of the university.[33] Examples of academic custom and usage at specific universities include notification during the tenure review process[34] and whether closing a downtown campus is considered to be an issue upon which the board of governors must consult the senate.[35] Academic customs and usage that extend to the entire higher education sector as a whole include the well-known concept of academic freedom and, by extension, faculty members' expectation of ownership of the fruits of their "academic work." In determining disputes at a university, the applicable policies and customs will play a significant role.

---

[33] Kaplin and Lee, *The Law of Higher Education*, 28–30.
[34] *Bason v American University*, 414 A.2d 522 (DC 1980) 525.
[35] *Kulchyski v Trent University*, 2001 CarswellOnt 2759 20–23, paras 91–107.

EVOLUTION OF UNIVERSITY GOVERNANCE IN CANADA

Prior to 1905, provincial governments in Ontario were accused of directly interfering with the operations of the University of Toronto, even to the extent of political involvement in faculty appointments.[36] This interference resulted in the appointment of the Flavelle Commission in 1906 to review the governance of the University of Toronto against other leading universities of the day. The commission concluded that the governance processes of the university should be autonomous from the political whims of government.[37] To achieve this end, a corporate board of governors was recommended consisting of respected citizens appointed by government with the mandate to manage the administrative affairs of the university without outside interference.[38] To provide balance to the proposed governance structure, the commission argued that an academic senate, comprising senior scholars and academic administrators, should be created to manage the academic affairs of the university. The *University of Toronto Act* was amended to reflect the commission's conclusions, which were used as a model for the enabling statutes of newly created universities in Western Canada.[39] With these proposals, the commission provided a clear framework for the bicameral governance structure common to Canadian universities today.

Unfortunately, bicameralism is not a perfect solution for the ills of governing a university. In the words of Sharpe J.A. in *Kulchyski v Trent University* 95 years after the Flavelle Commission:

> Bicameralism has both advantages and disadvantages. On the positive side, it provides a system of governance that distinguishes management issues from issues of educational policy and allocates responsibility for each to specialized governing bodies capable of reflecting the interests and concerns bearing upon the matters assigned. On the negative side, by dividing governing authority, bicameralism may complicate decision-making and ... result in deadlock.[40]

By the 1960s, the bicameral governance model was subject to increasing criticism that certain constituencies were not adequately represented in either the board or the senate. A national study published by Sir James Duff and Robert Berdahl proposed that reform of university governance was needed but that it could be accomplished within the bicameral model. Their report placed responsibility for the disharmony and tension that existed at some Canadian universities to the ineffectiveness of

---

[36] Boggs, *Ontario's Royal Commission on the University of Toronto, 1905–06*, 18–19.
[37] Royal Commission on the University of Toronto, *Report*, xxi.
[38] Jones, Shanahan, and Goyan, "Traditional Governance Structures," 30.
[39] Ibid. The government adopted the new legislation on April 16, 1906.
[40] 2001 CarswellOnt 2759 16.

their senates.[41] Their solution was to increase the representativeness of boards to include faculty and of senates to include students. Moreover, increases in governance transparency and in the interactions between boards and senates were to be encouraged. The recommendations also included cooperation between the board and senate in both long-term academic planning and the university budgeting process.[42] The scope of the changes varied depending on the particular university, but by the 1970s increased faculty and student representation had been implemented along the recommended lines.

Commentators have argued that the ineffectiveness of senates remains an issue today. In a 2002 study, Glen Jones argued that senates face a disparity between the roles its members feel it should play and its actual roles in practice. In areas such as determining research policies, strategic research directions, priorities for fundraising and development, and future directions of the institution, Jones's study concludes that the senate is subservient to the board of governors and senior administrators.[43] Other commentators have suggested that senates have lost their decision-making power for reasons related to the increasing complexity of the task of managing a university or where the roles of the Board and Senate have become intertwined on questions that combine academic and financial matters.[44] Regardless of the cause, disempowerment of senates seems to be an active and current issue on campuses of Canadian universities.

GOVERNANCE STRUCTURES AND PRACTICE

In an environment as fraught with history and tradition as a university, proper nomenclature is important. The incorporating statutes of Canadian universities may refer to the various university bodies as a governing council, board of governors, board of trustees, senate, academic council, convocation,[45] or other such variation. Regardless, universities are for the most part structured so as to create the division of powers prescribed

---

[41] Jones, Shanahan, and Goyan, "Traditional Governance Structures," 30.

[42] Ibid., 30, 31.

[43] Ibid., 41, 42.

[44] Berkowitz, "University Senate – Is It Still Useful?"

[45] Convocation in the Canadian context usually involves the entire university community including the chancellor, president, senate, all faculty, all graduates (and others as specified). A gathering of the convocation is typically required to confer degrees, including honorary degrees, and to award diplomas. See for example sections 5 and 6 of the *University Act*, RSBC 1996. It may have other functions depending on the institution, such as appointing the president, but convocation does not otherwise take part in the administration of the university.

in bicameralism[46]: the management, administration, and control of the property, revenue, business, and affairs of the university are vested in the board of governors (or equivalent), and the regulation of the system of education and ancillary matters are vested in the senate (or equivalent). The division imposed by bicameralism remains a source of tension in Canadian universities as decisions made by one body can significantly impact the decisions required to be made by the other. Exacerbating the tension is that university bodies are designed, unlike boards of private corporations, for representation rather than for strategic management.[47] The efficiency and effectiveness of decision-making will depend on the particular university. According to Farrington and Palfreyman, effective university decision-making is encouraged by eschewing "command and control" management in favour of strategic planning developed with input from all constituencies; striking the right balance of experience, skills, and expertise on the governing body, including lay members with appropriate experience and understanding of their roles and public sector values; establishing governing bodies at a size that promotes active involvement in decision-making while reducing the number of committees and increasing the role of full-time managers; and adopting a regular and self-critical approach to review of the governing bodies' effectiveness.[48] While these recommendations strive to strike a balance between corporate governing principles and the needs of a "community of scholars," the recommendations themselves may cause tension between administration and faculty, particularly the de-emphasis on faculty administration and heavier reliance on non-faculty managers.

The good governance of Canadian universities is not just in the interest of their close constituents. Because of the significant amount of public funds provided for their operations, well-governed universities are in the interests of the public as well. The importance of safeguarding against impropriety and misapplication of funds has been demonstrated in the last 15 years by various institutional failings in the United Kingdom that have been the subject of internal and external reports. Failings have taken the form of inappropriate severance payments to staff, the improper conduct of business, irregularities in governance and management of overseas courses, and expenses fraud.[49] Adherence to clear lines of accountability in both financial and academic matters thus ensures not only good governance but bolsters the case of universities in main-

---

[46] Jones and Skolnik, "Governing Boards in Canadian Universities." Of the 45 Canadian universities surveyed by the authors, 39 self-identified as bicameral institutions, five identified themselves as unicameral, and one as tricameral. The University of Toronto is an example of a unicameral governance structure.

[47] Farrington and Palfreyman, *Law of Higher Education*, 92.

[48] Ibid., 93.

[49] Hodges, "Fear Is the Key."

taining their much cherished self-governance. In order to achieve these ends, Canadian universities have generally organized themselves along the lines discussed below.

Board of Governors

The board of governors is the executive governing body of the university and is composed of lay, faculty, and student members as prescribed by the incorporating statute of the university.[50] It is important to note that the board of governors is not necessarily the corporate body that constitutes the university, and that exists before any professors are appointed, although it is in some cases.[51] The board has ultimate responsibility for the university and is therefore the most important governing body in the legal sense. Members are appointed through a variety of methods – ex officio; by the province, the board itself, or the senate; or elected by a constituent group such as alumni or students.[52] Boards tend to include at least 50 percent lay members and their average size, in Canadian universities, is 27 members.[53] University statutes contain numerous powers that are wielded by boards, including the general management and operation of the university; appointing the officers of the university, deans, and professors; adopting a budget; confirming tuition fees; managing university real and intellectual property; and making regulations, rules, and policies regarding all these matters. As the highest authority, the board has formal responsibility for contracts and disciplinary power over staff and students.[54] Board members are not normally compensated for financial loss or travel expenses necessitated by their positions.[55]

Although the board is the supreme university governing body of a self-governing institution, it is not immune from scrutiny. As an entity created by statute, the board is subject to the *Judicial Review Procedure Act*[56] in circumstances where it exercises a statutory power of decision. In *Hancock v Algonquin College of Applied Arts and Technology*,[57] the court considered whether the statutory duty of the college to submit annual estimates to the body overseeing all colleges in the province was exercising a statutory power of decision capable of judicial review pursuant to the

---

[50] See, for example, section 16(3) of the *Post-secondary Learning Act*.

[51] See, for example, section 16(2) of the *Post-secondary Learning Act*.

[52] See, for example, section 9 of the *University of Ottawa Act*.

[53] Jones et al., "University Governance," 142.

[54] Farrington and Palfreyman, *Law of Higher Education*, 115.

[55] Ibid; see also the Ontario Public Appointments Secretariat website, http://www.pas.gov on.ca/scripts/en /home.asp, for remuneration of provincial appointees.

[56] RSO 1990, c J.1.

[57] (1981), 33 OR (2d) 257.

Judicial Review Procedure Act. The court concluded that the statute imposed an administrative duty on the board to provide a budget forecast rather than any power or discretion. As suggested by the *Hancock* and *Pridgen* decisions, universities can be subject to judicial review of their decisions taken in exercising a statutory power or discretion and, in some cases, can have them weighed against the fundamental rights of the *Charter.*

Senate

The senate is vested with the academic governance of the university, and the power of the board in academic matters is severely limited. Faculty form the largest group of members of Canadian university senates with students, university officers, administrators, non-academic staff, board members, alumni, and government appointees making up the remaining numbers in varying degrees depending on the particular institution. Senates have an average voting-member number of 61.[58] Senates are not usually incorporated as separate corporations by their statutes although an exception to this is the *Post-secondary Learning Act* which, as is the case with boards created by the *Post-secondary Learning Act*, specifically creates each senate as a corporation. The resulting effect is that each senate subject to the *Post-secondary Learning Act* is capable of individual corporate action such as contracting and litigation.

Powers of the senate can vary widely but usually comprise determining questions relating to academic qualifications for admission; determining examination conditions; approving courses of study; awarding fellowships and scholarships; overseeing the library; preparing the university calendar; addressing matters reported by the faculties; addressing student academic appeals; establishing terms of institutional affiliation; and creating regulations, rules, and policies regarding all of these matters. In some statutes,[59] there are also a considerable number of areas in which the board and senate must liaise or obtain consent from the other. In British Columbia, the board must consult the senate on matters related to the real property and structures of the university[60] as well as any heritage properties the university may administer.[61] The board must obtain the

---

[58] Jones, Shanahan, and Goyan, "Traditional Governance Structures," 32.

[59] Certain statutes, tending to be older in origin than the *Post-secondary Learning Act* such as the *University of Ottawa Act*, envision little overlap of jurisdiction. Section 17 of the *University of Ottawa Act* states: "[t]he Senate is responsible for the educational policy of the University and, subject to the approval of the Board in so far as the expenditure of funds is concerned, may create, maintain and discontinue such faculties, departments, schools or institutes or establish such chairs as it may determine."

[60] *University Act*, RSBC 1996, s 27(2)(d).

[61] Ibid., s 27(2)(e).

senate's approval for the procedures to appoint candidates for president, deans, librarians, registrar, and other senior administrators[62] and must also obtain approval from the senate before determining the number of students that may be accommodated by the university or any faculty.[63] Senates may also be entitled to create a standing committee to assist the president with preparation of the annual budget.[64] The senate is usually entitled to recommend to the board the establishment or discontinuance of any faculty, department, course, chair, fellowship, or scholarship.[65] Conversely, the senate must obtain the permission of the board before entering into any agreements for entrance examinations to a corporation or society of British Columbia.[66]

The diminishing role of senates in Canadian universities has been lamented at least since the Duff-Berdahl report. Explanations for the diminishment range from the unionization of faculty to the increased reliance on government grants and the resulting external government priority-setting to the increasing importance of the university president and senior administrators in setting the direction of the university. A significant issue is the budgetary process. In one study, a significant majority of faculty (67.3 percent) supported a budget role for the senate whereas only 37.1 percent of administration supported such a role.[67] This study indicated that academic decision-making in the context of fiscal restraint is one of the greatest challenges facing modern Canadian senates.[68] The general lack of direction provided in incorporating statutes regarding the consultations required between the board and senate on budget matters may be a contributing factor to conflict.

Faculties

Faculties (also referred to as Schools in some universities) are subordinate to the senate and are charged with organizing the academic mission of their particular discipline. Canadian university statutes do not generally include language regarding the power and duties of faculties. Those statutes that do so include such powers and duties as making rules for the government, direction, and management of the faculty and its affairs and business; appointing examiners for examinations in the faculty; determining courses of instruction; and prohibiting the teaching in the

[62] Ibid., s 27(2)(f).
[63] Ibid., s 27(2)(r).
[64] Ibid., s 37(1)(e).
[65] Ibid., s 37(1)(i).
[66] Ibid., s 37(1)(r).
[67] Jones, Shanahan, and Goyan, "Traditional Governance Structures," 35.
[68] Ibid., 36.

faculty by other than properly appointed members of the teaching staff.[69] The dean is the head of the faculty and has general supervision over and direction of the academic work and instructional staff of the faculty.[70] The dean has the power to summon a meeting of the faculty and may appoint or delegate his or her powers to supporting academic officers within the faculty.[71] While the faculties are subordinate to the senate, there is often an implied expectation of dialogue between the faculties and the senate regarding academic and student matters. Faculties carry out much of the day-to-day academic decision-making and express opinions on university-wide issues under discussion by senior bodies, acting in some cases as a brake on rapid decision-making.[72] Since faculties have the closest connection to students, they are often where decisions of the board and senate are most deeply felt.

Officers of the University

Chancellor

In medieval English universities, it was the chancellor who, together with the masters, formed the corporation with the chancellor as the chief executive. The incumbent was originally appointed by the bishop, since the corporation was originally ecclesiastical.[73] Prior to the sixteenth century when the statues were changed, the chancellor was normally required to be resident.[74] The chancellorship later became an elected office and most of the functions, other than awarding degrees, were handed over to a subordinate officer, the vice-chancellor. In modern Canada, the office of chancellor is usually established by the relevant university statute and is a ceremonial role that consists of leading convocation and conferring degrees.[75] The chancellor is sometimes referred to as the titular head of the university[76] and is a position that has been held to be analogous to that of a director of a company.[77] A chancellor holds office for an initial

---

[69] *University Act*, RSBC 1996, s 40.

[70] *Post-secondary Learning Act*, s 21(1)(b).

[71] Ibid., ss 21(4) and 29(2).

[72] Farrington and Palfreyman, *Law of Higher Education*, 123.

[73] Ibid., 127.

[74] University of Cambridge, "Vice-Chancellor's Office," accessed March 3, 2011, http://www.admin.cam.ac.uk/offices/v-c/role/previous-vcs.html.

[75] See, for example, *University of Toronto Act*, ss 4(3) and 4(4).

[76] *University of Ottawa Act*, s 12(2).

[77] *Trinity College v Levinter* (1923), 54 OR 290 (Ont. CA). In the case, the chancellor acted as a member of a committee of the corporation entrusted with the management of lands and funds, and was held to be examinable for discovery as an officer of the corporation.

term of three or four years depending on the statute. Some statutes require that the chancellor hold Canadian citizenship or be a permanent resident.[78] Apart from the aforementioned ceremonial duties, the role of the chancellor is to generally represent the public interest of the university. The position is often held by a person with a significant public profile,[79] preferably with a substantial connection to the university.

Vice-Chancellor and President

In the modern Canadian university, the role of vice-chancellor has merged with that of the president.[80] It is the most important office in the university and the focal point of legal concern given the wide range of responsibilities and powers accorded to the president. A president has day-to-day supervision over and direction of the operation of the university, and the role is most closely akin to a chief executive officer.[81] Other powers may include recommending appointments, promotions, and removal of members of the teaching and administrative staffs; summoning a meeting of a faculty; establishing any committees the president thinks necessary; and preparing and presenting an annual report and budget to the board. The president is sometimes required to take responsibility as signatory for certain critical contracts signed by the university – such as funding memoranda or regulatory licenses – and is often the chief government lobbyist of the university requiring registration pursuant to the *Lobbying Act*.[82]

In British Columbia, appeals from decisions of the president regarding suspension of teaching or administrative staff or students are heard by the board. In cases of discipline, the president should apply rules of natural justice; that is, the nature of the charge to which the staff member or student is subject should be known to the accused and the staff member or student should have the opportunity to answer the charge before any decision is taken.[83] In 2006, the Ontario Court of Appeal considered the exercise of a university president's statutory discretion in disciplining a student in *Freeman-Maloy v York University*.[84] The court confirmed that,

---

[78] See, for example, the *Post-secondary Learning Act*, s 6(2).

[79] Such as Mike Lazaridis at University of Waterloo and David Peterson at University of Toronto.

[80] See, for example, *Post-secondary Learning Act*, s 10, *University Act*, RSBC 1996, s 13, and *University of Ottawa Act*, s 13(3) where the rector, the equivalent of the president, is the vice-chancellor.

[81] Some university statutes actually equate the two offices. See, for example, the *University of Toronto Act*, s 5(1).

[82] *Lobbying Act*, 1985, c 44 (4th Supp).

[83] Farrington and Palfreyman, *Law of Higher Education*, 131.

[84] (2006) 79 OR (3d) 401.

although a university president is not subject to governmental control, he or she is in other respects subject to the regime of public law. In particular, university presidents have been previously found to be "public officers,"[85] and the exercise of a power of decision granted to a university president by statute is subject to judicial review.[86] Therefore, presidents must take care to exercise their statutory powers in a manner that is consistent, transparent, and fair.

Other Senior Offices

The offices that exist in a particular university that are subordinate to the president will vary, and most such offices are not referenced in the university's statute. The most frequently cited office in the governing statutes is the secretary or registrar. A secretary's statutory duties may include being secretary to the board and senate; maintaining the rolls of graduates and honorary graduates of the university; signing diplomas; and other duties as assigned by the president or board.[87] In practice, the secretary of the university is a key member of the executive group, and his or her office is the repository of the official university legal documents, regulations, and policies. The secretary's office is often also responsible for maintaining compliance with privacy legislation. This critical role is reflected in a significant number of large Canadian universities merging the office of secretary with that of the university general counsel.[88] A registrar may also be charged with the secretarial functions noted above, as is the case in the *University Act*.[89] More typically, the registrar is not a statutory office and is responsible for managing the student enrolment function of the university. Vice-presidents are also not normally statutory officers. In cases where they are, they are appointed by the board and assigned their powers, duties, and functions by the board on the recommendation of the president. In the Canadian university, the administration, advancement, research, and academic (often referred to as the provost) functions are normally led by a vice-president who reports to the president. The provost is sometimes considered the first among equals of the vice-presidents. Larger universities have also appointed vice-presidents of human resources and of university relations. Where the university is affiliated with a large faculty of health sciences, the dean

---

[85] Ibid. This characterization suggests, together with the disposition of the Freeman-Moloy matter, that presidents may, given the proper circumstances, be subject the tort of misfeasance of public office.

[86] Ibid.

[87] *University of Ottawa Act*, s 14.

[88] See for example York University, University of Calgary, and University of Ottawa.

[89] RSBC 1996, ss 64(1) and 64(2).

of health sciences can also hold a vice-president office.[90] The exact config-
uration of the university's senior offices is not the chief concern, rather
it is the importance of having qualified and experienced administrative
officers who can ensure that the board, senate, and subordinate bodies or
offices act within their authority and in the best interests of the university.

Liability of University Officers and Directors

The size, variety, and complexity of the operations, and the corresponding
legal issues, of a modern university expose its officers and directors to a
scope of liability issues not normally faced by other not-for-profit or charitable organizations.[91] University officers and directors have responsibilities
to their institution, employees, faculty, students, alumni, and the public.
There is some confusion regarding the proper standard of care applicable
to university officers and directors. The situation is complicated by the
fact that officers and directors of business corporations, not-for-profit
corporations, and charitable corporations may have different standards
of care.[92] However, it is suggested that since universities are almost always charities, in addition to being akin to not-for-profit corporations,
the standard of care of their officers and directors is most appropriately
addressed by charities law. In Ontario, the standard of care of officers
and directors of charities is governed by the *Charities Accounting Act*,
which applies to "any corporation incorporated for religious, educational,
charitable or public purpose."[93] The *Charities Accounting Act* deems the
corporation to be a trustee of the property held in trust for charitable purposes. The officers and directors have fiduciary duties to the corporation
to ensure it fulfills its duty as a trustee.[94] As fiduciaries, the officers and
directors must subordinate their own interests to those of the university,
avoid any conflict, and conduct their duties with honesty, due care, and

---

[90] See, for example, the vice-president and dean of health sciences, McMaster
University.

[91] There are approximately 100 federal and Ontario statutes that impose some
variety of statutory duties on the officers and directors of a university. These
duties arise in three main areas: employees and the workplace, taxation, and
environmental/facilities compliance.

[92] In Ontario, officers and directors of business corporations must satisfy an
objective test imposed by statute by exercising the care, diligence, and skill that a
reasonably prudent person would exercise in comparable circumstances. Officers
and directors of not-for-profit corporations must meet a common-law subjective
test (the British Columbia *Society Act*, RSBC 1979, c 390 and the new *Ontario Not-
for-Profit Corporations Act*, Bill 65 being the exceptions) by exercising the degree of
skill reasonably expected from a person of his or her knowledge and experience.

[93] *Charities Accounting Act*, RSO 1990, c C.10, s 1(2).

[94] Bourgeois, *Law of Charitable and Not-for-Profit Organizations*, 226.

attention.[95] Provided that the directors have diligently exercised their decision-making responsibilities and scrutinized the issues before them in good faith, they may be able to rely on the "business judgment rule" to insulate them from liability.[96]

CONFLICT IN UNIVERSITY GOVERNANCE

As alluded to earlier in this chapter, the bicameral system can lead to conflict. Two recent decisions of Canadian courts have addressed the relationship between university boards and senates in decision-making.

Paramountcy: *Kulchyski v Trent University*

In *Kulchyski v Trent University*, the court considered a situation in which the president established a task force charged with reviewing space planning and capital needs in the context of current provincial infrastructure funding proposals. The task force recommended that Trent University's downtown facilities be closed and sold. The university's board approved the plan, but the senate did not and sought judicial review of the board's endorsement. The divisional court held that the board was authorized by section 10 of the *Trent University Act* to pass the resolution directing the closure of the downtown facilities. This decision was appealed to the Ontario Court of Appeal which, in a split decision, endorsed the divisional court's ruling.[97] The majority found no legal requirement that the senate had to approve the board's decision before the university proceeded with the closure, given the language in section 10 of the *Trent University Act*. The decision to close the downtown facilities was not, in the view of the majority, an educational policy decision but rather a pragmatic decision by the board, in that the board had no obligation to indefinitely provide financial support to any policy, educational or otherwise, that was draining the coffers of the university.[98] It is interesting to note that the Attorney General of Ontario was granted intervenor status and supported the board position. In the Attorney General's view, the board would be

---

[95] Ibid., 40.

[96] *Hadjor v Homes First Society*, [2010] OJ No 4079. The "business judgment rule" states that a director will not be held liable for mistakes that had been made after an honest and good faith evaluation of the decision: Burke-Robertson, *Primer for Directors*.

[97] *Trent University Act*, SO 1962-63, c 192. Section 10 reads, in part, "[e]xcept as to such matters specifically assigned by this Act to the Senate or the councils of the faculties, as hereinafter referred to, the government, conduct, management and control of the University, and of its property, revenues, expenditures, business and affairs are vested in the Board."

[98] *Kulchyski, supra* note 35 at 11, para 32.

unable to discharge the duties imposed on it by the *Trent University Act* if it required the concurrence of the senate for any decision viewed by the senate as having an impact on educational policy.[99] It is clear that the majority concluded that section 10 of the *Trent University Act* conferred on the board the power to break a deadlock since it related to the board's supreme and exclusive jurisdiction over financial issues.

The minority supported the view that bicameralism establishes two governing bodies, each with its own areas of responsibility, but that not all issues fall neatly within one of these areas. Justice Sharpe referred to some of the provisions providing for overlap and stated:

> Quite apart from these specific provisions, it seems to me that a power-sharing between the Board and the Senate is implicit in the bicameral scheme of governance created by the *Trent University Act*. Where an issue gives rise to aspects falling within the powers of both the Board and the Senate, bicameralism requires the concurrence of both bodies. While each body has exclusive authority to decide that aspect of the decision which falls within its powers, neither body has exclusive or paramount authority over the entire question.[100]

Therefore, in the minority's view, the board cannot decide where to spend the university's resources without the senate's determination of educational policy, and the senate cannot implement educational policy without the board's agreement to make available the required resources.[101] In the view of the minority, any deadlock created by the bicameral mechanism cannot be broken by unilateral action by the board but only through debate, discussion, negotiation, compromise and, if all else fails, legislation. The minority also noted that the issue of the downtown facilities was a long-standing issue at Trent, and it had been customary over the long history of the issue for the entire campus to consider it a matter of educational policy. Taken together with the mechanics of the bicameral model at Trent, past practice at the university supported the need for the concurrence of both the board and the senate on the question of closure.[102]

---

[99] Ibid., 12, para 38. The Attorney General of Ontario noted that requiring the concurrence of the senate on a decision of the board that had an impact on educational policy would be the equivalent of a veto over all board decisions.

[100] Ibid., 16, para 62.

[101] Ibid., 17, para 66.

[102] Ibid., 23, para 107.

Clarity of Mandate: *UBC Faculty Association v UBC*

In *University of British Columbia Faculty Association v University of British Columbia*,[103] the British Columbia Court of Appeal considered a number of aspects of the bicameral governance model. The UBC senate had passed an education policy addressing student evaluation of teaching. Amid a series of complicated labour issues, the court addressed whether the collective agreement, concluded between the board and the faculty, binds the senate to follow its terms if they conflict with a policy introduced by the senate. The Court of Appeal concluded that the enabling statute created separate jurisdictions for the board and senate, and that there was no intersection or overlapping.[104] The *University Act* does not contain paramountcy language that would allow the board, using its power to enter into collective agreements, to usurp the statutory power of the senate to set educational policy. If the board had such power, the court stated, it would effectively be able to dictate aspects of academic policy through the collective bargaining process. If the senate oversteps its mandate, it can be held accountable through judicial review. If the application of the policy unfairly affects an employee, he or she can submit a grievance to an arbitrator.[105] Thus, the senate's statutory mandate over educational policy is respected despite the faculty association's argument that such mandate is limited by collective agreement.

Case Analysis

The judgments in *Kulchyski* and *UBCFA* provide important judicial assessments of the legal issues involved in bicameralism at modern Canadian universities. Where financial and educational policy issues can easily be kept separate, or the enabling statute clearly requires the board and senate to jointly approve the decision, bicameralism works well. But where there is overlap of jurisdiction, and no direction provided by the enabling statutes, difficulties can arise.[106] On the surface it may seem that the two decisions reflect a differing amount of respect for the mission of the university senate, but the source for the disparate decisions lies in the interpretation of the two statutes at issue and the fact that the *UBCFA* decision did not involve conflict between the powers of the board and senate. The majority in *Kulchyski* found that the operative provision of

---

[103] 2010 BCCA 189 (Canlii). Leave to appeal refused [2010] SCCA No. 232.

[104] Ibid., 16, para 66.

[105] Ibid., 29, para 79.

[106] For an example of a decision discussing application of an enabling statute requiring the board of governors to seek advice from the senate of a special purpose, teaching university, please see *Capilano University Faculty Association v Capilano University*, 2014 BCSC 712.

the *Trent University Act* accorded the board with the exclusive and paramount jurisdiction to determine financial issues that affect the university. In other words, despite the ramifications of the board's decision to close the downtown facilities – that is, the negative impact on the educational experience at Trent University – the majority construed the statutory language to give the board ultimate authority in the circumstances. The minority did not support the majority's interpretation of the *Trent University Act* raising financial issues above educational issues. Instead, they weighed university past practice together with the language of the enabling statute to conclude that senate consultation was required and that any ensuing deadlock could be broken only by legislation. The court in *UBCFA* assessed the two approaches in the *Kulchyski* decision and concluded that while the minority's viewpoint is attractive, it would cause more problems in practice than it would solve. Moreover, the *University Act* did not share, in the view of the court, the same legislative intent of board paramountcy as the Ontario Court of Appeal found in the *Trent University Act*.

CONCLUSION

Amid the various paradoxes that comprise the modern Canadian university, positive university governance strives to strike the proper balance between a university's various components. If one component falters, or acts in a manner beyond its station, the equilibrium can be negatively affected. This chapter examined the legal framework within which such balance is sought. The Canadian university landscape is not as regulated or litigious as our British or American counterparts, but analogies can be drawn where necessary. Canada has its own unique university governance structure and practice that maintains British and American influences. The governance structures and practices of Canadian universities are also informed by uniquely Canadian features such as the *Charter* and the various commissions that sought improvement in the operation of universities. The governance of Canadian universities today is not an exercise in eliminating uncomfortable or seemingly unworkable paradoxes, but a matter of creating a well-ordered environment in which the paradoxes can co-exist, however disharmoniously.

Chapter 5

HUMAN RIGHTS ISSUES IN POSTSECONDARY EDUCATION

Lou Poskitt and Magdalena Wojda

INTRODUCTION

Developments in human rights law have a significant impact on post-secondary institutions, as both employers and providers of educational services and facilities. Human rights tribunals, boards of arbitration and courts, in all Canadian jurisdictions, have continued to develop key components of human rights law. Therefore, it is prudent for the administrators of postsecondary institutions to be familiar with the fundamentals and direction of human rights law, particularly in terms of defining "discrimination," "disability," and the "duty to accommodate" as these concepts apply to the workplace and to the provision of services and facilities to students.

This chapter provides an overview of human rights law in Canada as it applies to postsecondary institutions as employers and providers of educational services and facilities. Specifically, this chapter provides an overview of the grounds for human rights complaints and the potential remedies, as well as summaries of key cases involving postsecondary institutions. Finally, the chapter introduces strategies for defending against human rights complaints.

Handbook of Canadian Higher Education Law, edited by Theresa Shanahan, Michelle Nilson, and Li-Jeen Broshko. Montreal and Kingston: McGill-Queen's University Press, Queen's Policy Studies Series.

HUMAN RIGHTS JURISDICTION

The human rights obligations of postsecondary institutions may arise from not only provincial and territorial human rights statutes, but also the *Canadian Charter of Rights and Freedoms*. However, a substantive analysis of the *Charter* and its application in the field of human rights is beyond the scope of this chapter. Accordingly, this chapter deals exclusively with human rights issues arising under provincial and territorial human rights statutes.

We note that the types of bodies with decision-making authority under human rights legislation vary from jurisdiction to jurisdiction. For ease of reference, we refer to these bodies generically as "tribunals" throughout this chapter. It is also important to note that, in addition to specialized human rights tribunals, both the courts and collective agreement arbitrators have jurisdiction to deal with human rights matters.[1] Arbitrators, like human rights tribunals, have the power not only to interpret and apply human rights legislation, but also to fashion appropriate remedies.[2] Therefore, postsecondary institutions must look to human rights tribunal decisions, arbitration awards, and decisions of the courts to understand their human rights obligations.

This chapter provides a general overview of human rights principles as they apply to postsecondary institutions as employers and service providers. While these principles provide general guidance to postsecondary institutions across Canada about their human rights obligations, the specific language in provincial/territorial human rights statutes varies from jurisdiction to jurisdiction, and the human rights tribunal in each jurisdiction has developed its own policies, procedures and jurisprudence. Therefore, postsecondary institutions are advised to consult the legislation and case law arising in their jurisdiction to determine the specific rules that apply to their organizations. For ease of reference, Table 5.1 lists the human rights statutes in Canadian provinces and territories.

---

[1] *Douglas/Kwantlen Faculty Assn. v Douglas College*, [1990] 3 SCR 570; *Parry Sound (District) Social Services Administration Board v OPSEU, Local 34*, [2003] SCJ No 42.

[2] *Canpar v I.U.O.E., Local 115*, 2003 BCCA 609 at para 9.

TABLE 5.1
Human Rights Legislation

Province/Territory	Legislation
Alberta:	*Alberta Human Rights Act*, RSA 2000, c A-25.5
British Columbia:	*Human Rights Code*, RSBC 1996, c 210
Manitoba:	*Human Rights Code*, SM 1987-88, c 45
New Brunswick:	*Human Rights Act*, RSNB 1973, c H-11
Newfoundland and Labrador:	*Human Rights Code*, RSN 1990, c H-14
Northwest Territories:	*Human Rights Act*, SNWT 2002, c 18
Nova Scotia:	*Human Rights Act*, amended SN 1991, c 12
Nunavut:	*Human Rights Act*, S Nu 2003, c 12
Ontario:	*Human Rights Code*, RSO 1990, c H.19
Prince Edward Island:	*Human Rights Act*, RSPEI 1988, c H-12
Quebec:	Charter of Human Rights and Freedoms *(Charte des Droits et Libertés de la Personne)* SQ 1990, c 4
Saskatchewan:	*The Saskatchewan Human Rights Code*, SS 1979, c S-24.1
Yukon Territory:	*Human Rights Act*, RSY 2002, c 116

OVERVIEW OF DISCRIMINATION

What Is Discrimination?

"Discrimination" is a fluid concept,[3] and the human rights legislation in most provinces and territories does not define this term.[4] The meaning typically attributed to this term has developed through human rights jurisprudence, that is, in decisions issued by human rights tribunals, arbitrators, and the courts. In general terms, discrimination prohibited by a particular human rights statute encompasses any adverse treatment of an individual or group of individuals on the basis of a characteristic that is protected by that statute.[5]

---

[3] In Zinn, *Human Rights in Canada*, c 1, p 3, the author states, "The concept of discrimination is dependent on the societal values at any given time and, as such, is a fluid and ever-changing concept."

[4] The only jurisdictions in which "discrimination" is defined under human rights legislation are Nova Scotia, Quebec, and Manitoba.

[5] For an example of this type of definition, see *Andrews v Law Society of British Columbia*, [1989] SCJ No 6 at para 37.

The prohibition against discrimination does not, however, apply to every relationship that a postsecondary institution may have with an individual or group. The human rights legislation in each jurisdiction sets out specific fields of activity in which discrimination based on a protected ground is prohibited. These areas include employment; the provision of services, goods, or facilities; membership in a trade union; and accommodation (i.e., commercial and residential premises). As this chapter centres on issues arising for postsecondary institutions in relation to their faculty, staff, and students, our discussion focuses on the issues of discrimination in employment and in the provision of services and facilities.

Prima Facie *Case of Discrimination*

In general, a complainant alleging discrimination bears the onus of establishing a *"prima facie* case of discrimination." A *prima facie* case of discrimination is one where the allegations, if proven, are sufficient to justify a finding in the complainant's favour, absent an answer or justification from the respondent.[6]

In complaints alleging discrimination in employment or the provision of services and facilities, establishing a *prima facie* case requires the complainant to prove that

1. he or she is, or is perceived to be, a member of a group possessing a characteristic or characteristics protected under the legislation in question;
2. he or she experienced adverse treatment; and
3. the protected characteristic was at least a factor in the adverse treatment.[7]

What is specifically required to meet each of these elements will vary depending on the circumstances. For example, what constitutes "adverse treatment" in a given case will depend on the protected ground in issue (e.g., family status) and the relationship between the complainant and the respondent (e.g., employer/employee, or university/student).

In addition, the complainant may be required to establish that the area in which he or she alleges discrimination is one that is regulated by human rights legislation. In the context of a discrimination in employment complaint, for example, the complainant may be required to establish that he or she is actually an employee of the respondent. In the context

---

[6] See, for example, *Ontario (Human Rights Commission) v Simpsons Sears Ltd.*, [1985] 2 SCR 536 [*Simpsons Sears Ltd.*] at 558.

[7] See, for example, *Moore v British Columbia (Education)*, 2012 SCC 61.

of a denial of services complaint, the complainant may be required to establish that the respondent serves "the public" in order to fall within the protection against discrimination in the provision of services. The latter issue, however, is not typically contentious in cases involving postsecondary institutions since the Supreme Court of Canada has found that, in serving students, postsecondary institutions serve "the public."[8] The granting of bursaries and scholarships has also been deemed to be a service within the meaning of human rights legislation.[9]

An entity may be found to have violated a complainant's human rights even if it did not intend to discriminate against the complainant. It is the discriminatory result of the respondent's actions that is prohibited by human rights legislation. A respondent's intent – or lack thereof – in this respect is not determinative.[10]

Importantly, the protection afforded to an individual by human rights legislation encompasses not only discrimination based on the individual's membership in a protected group, but also discrimination based on the perception that the individual belongs to a protected group.[11] This means that, for example, adverse treatment based on the perception of a disability may amount to discrimination on the basis of disability even if the complainant is not in fact disabled.

If a complainant establishes a *prima facie* case of discrimination, the onus shifts to the respondent to justify the allegedly discriminatory conduct. We discuss the defences available to respondents in greater detail later in this chapter. First, however, we provide an overview of the grounds most commonly protected by human rights legislation across Canada.

Prohibited Grounds of Discrimination

While every Canadian jurisdiction has human rights legislation that prohibits discrimination that is based on certain proscribed grounds, those "prohibited grounds" vary to some extent from jurisdiction to jurisdiction. There are, though, certain grounds that are protected in most jurisdictions. We discuss these grounds below.

Physical or Mental Disability

While every human rights statute in Canada prohibits discrimination on the basis of "disability" in the context of employment and provision of

---

[8] *University of British Columbia v Berg,* [1993] 2 SCR 353.
[9] *Fisher v York University,* 2011 HRTO 1229.
[10] See, for example, *Simpsons Sears Ltd., supra* note 6 at 329 and 331.
[11] See, for example, *Jubran v North Vancouver School District No. 44,* 2002 BCHRT 10; judicial review allowed 2003 BCSC 6; reversed 2005 BCCA 201.

services and facilities, only certain statutes define this term. In general, however, the concept of disability for human rights purposes means a physical or mental condition that is involuntary, has some degree of permanence, and impairs the person's ability, in some measure, to carry out the normal functions of life.[12] Conditions that have been deemed to be disabilities include any degree of paralysis, amputation, lack of physical coordination, blindness or visual impairment, hearing impairment, muteness or speech impediment, physical reliance on a service animal or on a wheelchair or other remedial appliance or device, mental disorders, conditions of mental impairment or developmental disability, and learning disabilities.[13] Other conditions that have been found to be disabilities for the purpose of human rights protection include diabetes;[14] allergies and asthma;[15] chronic fatigue syndrome;[16] alcohol or drug dependence,[17] including nicotine dependence;[18] depression;[19] panic disorder, depressive disorder, and generalized anxiety disorder;[20] hysterectomy;[21] knee pain;[22]

---

[12] For example, *Tervit v Canadian College of English Language*, 2014 BCHRT 53 at para 20.

[13] For example, *Human Rights Code*, RSO 1990, c H.19, s 1; *Alberta Human Rights Act*, RSA 2000, c A-25.5, s 44(1)(l); *The Saskatchewan Human Rights Code*, SS 1979, c S-24.1, s 2(1)(d.1); *Human Rights Code*, SM 1987-88, c 45, CCSM, c H175, s 9(1).

[14] For example, *Human Rights Code*, RSO 1990, c H.19, s 1.

[15] For example, *Morgogh v Ottawa (City)* (1980) 11 CHRR D/80 (Ont. Bd. Inq.); *Legge v Princess Auto and Machinery Ltd.* (1983), 4 CHRR D/1339 (Man. Bd. Adj.); *Konieczna v Owners Strata Plan NW 2489 (No. 2)* (2003), 47 CHRR D/144 (BCHRT).

[16] For example, *Brimacombe v Northland Road Services Ltd.* (1998), 33 CHRR D/53 (BCHRC).

[17] For example, *Entrop v Imperial Oil Ltd.*, [1996] OHRBID No 30 (Ont. Bd. Inq.), affd [1998] OJ No 422 (Ont. Div. Ct.), affd on this point [2000] OJ No 2689 (ONCA).

[18] For example, *Cominco Ltd. v U.S.W.A., Local 9705*, [2000] BCCAAA No 62 at para 181 (BC Arb.).

[19] For example, *Mager v Louisiana-Pacific Canada Ltd.* (1998), 33 CHRR D/457 (BCHRT); *Miller v 409205 Alberta Ltd.* (2001), 42 CHRR D/311 (Alta HRP); *Sylvester v British Columbia Society of Male Survivors of Sexual Abuse*, 2002 BCHRT 14; *Oak Bay Marina Ltd. v British Columbia (Human Rights Commission)* (2002), 217 DLR (4th) 747 (BCCA).

[20] For example, *Senyck v WFG Agency Network (No.2)*, 2008 BCHRT 376.

[21] For example, *Wilson v Douglas Care Manor Ltd.* (1992), 21 CHRR D/74 (BC-CHR).

[22] For example, *Boyce v Westminster (City)* (1994) 24 CHRR D/441 (BCCHR).

colour blindness;[23] dyslexia;[24] gambling;[25] narcolepsy;[26] acne;[27] height;[28] HIV-positive without impairment;[29] fibromyalgia;[30] and sensitivity to scents and perfumes.[31]

By contrast, the flu, a temporary period of sciatica, and alcohol consumption that is not due to an alcohol addiction have been held, respectively,[32] not to be disabilities for the purposes of human rights legislation.[33]

One of the most common reasons for employee or student absenteeism is "stress." In and of itself, stress is not a disability.[34] However, if a person is affected so acutely by stress that it causes ongoing mental or physical symptoms, then it may qualify as a disability and trigger the duty to accommodate.

Race, Colour, or Place of Origin

Human rights legislation in every Canadian jurisdiction prohibits discrimination in employment and the provision of services and facilities on the basis of race, colour, or place of origin. Many jurisdictions also prohibit differential treatment on the basis of ancestry. Race and ancestry typically refer to an individual's ancestral history. Colour refers in general

---

[23] For example, *Bicknell v Air Canada* (1984), 5 CHRR D/1992 (Can. Trib.).

[24] For example, *Moore v British Columbia (Ministry of Education)*, 2005 BCHRT 580.

[25] For example, *Retail, Wholesale and Department Store Union v Canada Safeway Ltd.* (1999), 82 LAC (4th) 1 (Sask. Arb. Bd.; aff'd 1999 SKQB 81; rev'd on other grounds 2000 SKCA 119.

[26] For example, *Bubb-Clarke v Toronto Transit Commission* (2002), 42 CHRR D/326 (Ont. Bd. Inq.).

[27] For example, *De Jong v Horlacher Holdings Ltd.* (1989), 10 CHRR D/6283 (BCHRC).

[28] For example, *Fiset v Gamble* (1992), 18 CHRR D/81 (BCHRC).

[29] For example, *Biggs v Hudson* (1988), 9 CHRR D/5391 (BCHRC).

[30] For example, *Ketabchi v Future Shop Ltd.*, 2002 BCHRT 39.

[31] For example, *Brewer v Fraser Milner Casgrain LLP*, 2006 ABQB 258; appeal by Commission quashed 2008 ABCA 160; rev'd on other grounds 2008 ABCA 435; leave to appeal to SCC ref'd [2008] SCCA No 290.

[32] For example, *Ouimette v Lily Cups Ltd.* (1990), 12 CHRR D/19 (Ont. Bd. Inq.); *Neilson v Sandman Four Limited* (1986), 7 CHRR D-3329 (BCCHR); *Tanchak v Locke Property Management Ltd.*, [1997] BCHRTD No 27.

[33] See discussion in Zinn, *Human Rights in Canada*, c 5, pp 10.1–13.

[34] See, for example, *Matheson v School District No. 53 (Okanagan Similkameen) and Collis*, 2009 BCHRT 112 at para 14.

to one's skin tone, and place of origin typically refers to one's birthplace or place of training.[35]

It has been held that if a person's place of education is sufficiently correlated to his or her place of origin, differential treatment on the basis of the location of the university where the person obtained his or her credentials may amount to discrimination based on place of origin.[36] However, it has also been held that place of origin cannot be interpreted to include the place where an individual undertakes schooling when that place is not the country of his or her birth.[37]

Religion or Creed

Discrimination in employment and the provision of services and facilities on the basis of religion or creed is directly or indirectly prohibited in every Canadian jurisdiction.[38] The rationale for this prohibition is that individuals should be free to abide by legitimate faith-based rules or tenets, or the mandated practices of any religion, without detrimental repercussions. In the context of a postsecondary learning environment, this prohibition limits the circumstances in which employees or students may be forced to choose between their religious observances and their employment or academic obligations.

Religion or creed has been broadly defined for the purposes of human rights legislation and has been held to include both religious beliefs and religious practices, such as prayer, dietary and clothing requirements, and holy days. In general, any sincerely held belief that falls under a broadly defined interpretation of "religion" is a protected right.[39] When it comes to religious practices, the test is whether the complainant holds sincere convictions regarding the particular religious practice, rather than whether the religious order requires adherence to the practice.[40] In Canadian human rights legislation, the terms "creed," "religion," and "religious belief" are in general used synonymously and are distinguished from the term "political belief."[41]

---

[35] See, for example, *Bitonti v British Columbia (Ministry of Health No. 3)* (1999), 36 CHRR D/263 (BCHRT).

[36] *Agduma-Silongan v University of British Columbia*, 2003 BCHRT 22 [*Agduma-Silongan*] at 5.

[37] *Grosz v University of British Columbia*, 2005 BCHRT 70 at paras 67–68.

[38] See Zinn, *Human Rights in Canada*, c 9, p 1.

[39] Zinn, *Human Rights in Canada*, c 9, pp 10–11.

[40] See, for example, *Ryder v Cooper Market Ltd.* (1990), 13 CHRR D/38 (BCCHR). See also discussion in Zinn, *Human Rights in Canada*, chap. 9, pp 12–14.

[41] *Jazairi v Ontario (Human Rights Commission)*, [1997] OJ No 1526 (Ct. Jus. Gen. Div.) at para 40; affd [1999] OJ No 2474; leave to appeal to SCC refused [1999] SCCA No 448.

The most common form of discrimination based on religion or creed is "adverse effect discrimination," which arises where an otherwise neutral requirement or rule conflicts with an individual's religious practice.[42] These situations may arise when, for example, a work or class schedule conflicts with the observance of a holy day, the rules about personal appearance conflict with religious clothing requirements, or an employment or academic obligation is prohibited by an individual's faith.

Sex Discrimination

The human rights legislation in every Canadian jurisdiction prohibits discrimination in employment and the provision of services and facilities on the basis of sex. The protection against sex discrimination includes discrimination based on gender (e.g., male, female, transgendered, transsexual, intersex), as well as characteristics related to gender such as pregnancy, breastfeeding, and gender identity. The prohibition against sex discrimination also encompasses the protection against sexual harassment and discrimination based on sexual orientation, which we discuss in greater detail in the following sections.

Much of the litigation about this ground of discrimination has arisen from the denial of equal employment opportunities and benefits to women. These cases have involved issues like adverse treatment because of pregnancy and inequitable job requirements. In one leading case on human rights, *British Columbia (Public Service Employee Relations Commission) v British Columbia Government Service Employees' Union*,[43] for example, a minimum aerobic standard for forest firefighters that did not account for the physiological differences between men and women was found to be discriminatory.

Circumstances that would trigger issues relating to sex discrimination for postsecondary institutions in relation to the provision of services and facilities include, for example, a request from a student to breast-feed in class or for a leave related to her pregnancy, or a request from a transgendered student for access to separate change-room facilities. In many situations, such requests would trigger the institution's duty to accommodate the student's needs. We discuss the duty to accommodate in greater detail later in this chapter.

Sexual Harassment

Sexual harassment in employment and the provision of services and facilities is prohibited in all Canadian jurisdictions. Where the applicable

---

[42] See discussion in Zinn, *Human Rights in Canada*, c 9, pp 1–2.
[43] [1999] 3 SCR 3 [*Meiorin*].

human rights legislation does not explicitly provide for protection against sexual harassment, the jurisprudence recognizes this conduct as a form of sex discrimination.[44]

Sexual harassment may be broadly defined as unwelcome conduct of a sexual nature that detrimentally affects the work, facilities, or academic environment or leads to adverse consequences for the victims of the harassment.[45] The requirement that the conduct be sexual in nature has been interpreted broadly.[46] For instance, demeaning terms and language that seek to draw attention to someone who does not fit stereotypical norms of attractiveness have been found to be "sexual conduct."[47] Accordingly, terms such as "fattie" and "cow" have been held to be sexual in nature.

In addition, allowing or promoting the existence of an environment that has become sexualized constitutes "sexual conduct." For example, in *Mahmoodi v University of British Columbia*,[48] a professor invited a student into his home, where he lit candles and played romantic music. This was found to create a sexualized environment sufficient to meet the first element of the test. A more obvious example of a sexualized environment would be a workplace in which sexual jokes, comments, and pictures are prevalent.[49] As with other forms of discrimination, the intent or motivation of the respondent is not determinative.[50]

A complainant alleging sexual harassment must also prove that the conduct was "unwelcome." This standard is based on what a reasonable person would consider to be unwelcome. Importantly, it does not require knowledge on the part of the respondent that the conduct was unwelcome or an express rejection of the conduct by the complainant,[51] particularly when there is an imbalance of power or influence in the relationship, such as between a professor and student or a supervisor and subordinate.[52] It has been held that even when the complainant engaged voluntarily in a

---

[44] Zinn, *Human Rights in Canada*, c 11, p 1.

[45] *Janzen v Platy Enterprises Ltd.*, [1989] 1 SCR 1252 at para 56.

[46] See discussion in Zinn, *Human Rights in Canada*, c 11, pp 11–12.

[47] See, for example, *Fornwald v Astrographic Industries Ltd.* (1996), 27 CHRR D/317 (BCCHR).

[48] [1999] BCHRTD No 52.

[49] See, for example, *Burton v Chalifour Bros. Construction Ltd.* (1994), 21 CHRR D/501 (BCCHR).

[50] For example, see discussion in Zinn, *Human Rights in Canada*, c 11, pp 19–20.

[51] See, for example, *McNulty v G.N.F. Holdings Ltd.* (1992), 16 CHRR D/418 (BCCHR). See also Zinn, *Human Rights in Canada*, c 11, pp 15–18.

[52] See, for example, *Québec (Commission des droits de la personne) v Habachi* (1992), 18 CHRR D/485 (Que. Trib.).

physical act with the respondent, this was not an indication that the act was welcome.[53]

Sexual harassment tends to fall into two categories: (a) quid pro quo, where sexual acts are requested or encouraged in exchange for continued employment or advantages; or (b) conduct that leads to a hostile or toxic environment.[54] A hostile or toxic environment is created when an individual is subjected to ongoing unwanted sexual remarks or behaviour of others.[55]

An employer may be found liable for the wrongdoing of its agents and employees, whether or not the employer had direct knowledge of such misconduct.[56] It is, therefore, imperative that all allegations of sexual harassment be taken seriously, and investigated and addressed in a prompt manner. Firm and swift action to remedy sexual harassment may limit an institution's liability.

Sexual Orientation

Every Canadian jurisdiction prohibits discrimination in employment and the provision of services and facilities based on sexual orientation. While no provincial or territorial human rights legislation defines "sexual orientation," courts and tribunals have interpreted it broadly to include protection for gay men, lesbians, and bisexual and heterosexual men and women.[57]

The prohibition against discrimination based on sexual orientation protects individuals' sexual preferences and the legal rights that flow from their spousal relationships, such as the entitlement to spousal benefits.[58] Accordingly, there is significant overlap between sexual orientation and family or marital status. In general, treatment of an individual in relation to his or her spousal rights and benefits must not depend on a particular sexual orientation.

The protection against discrimination based on sexual orientation may also extend to businesses that serve the lesbian, gay, bisexual, trans (transgender, transsexual, trans-identified), two-spirit, queer, questioning,

---

[53] See, for example, *Dupuis v British Columbia (Ministry of Forests)* (1993), 20 CHRR D/87 (BCCHR).

[54] See discussion in Zinn, *Human Rights in Canada*, c 11, p 20.

[55] See, for example, *Shaw v Levac Supply Ltd.* (1990), 14 CHRR D/36 (Ont. Bd. Inq.).

[56] *Robichaud v Canada (Treasury Board)*, [1987] 2 SCR 84. See also discussion in Zinn, *Human Rights in Canada*, c 11, pp 29–36.

[57] Zinn, *Human Rights in Canada*, c 12, pp 2–3.

[58] Ibid., c 12, pp 4–8.

intersex and asexual (LGBT*TQIA+) communities.[59] In *Brillinger v Brockie*,[60] for example, the Ontario Human Rights Board of Inquiry ruled that a printing company discriminated against an organization mandated to disseminate information about gay, lesbian, bisexual, and transgender issues when the company refused to print stationery for the organization.

The issue of discrimination on the basis of sexual orientation could arise for a postsecondary institution in relation to its dealings with, for example, on-campus interest groups serving LGBT*TQIA+ students.

Marital or Family Status

Discrimination in employment or the provision of services based on both marital and family status is prohibited in every Canadian jurisdiction except New Brunswick. In New Brunswick, marital status is a protected ground but family status is not. In Quebec, marital and family status are protected by prohibition against discrimination on the basis of "civil status." Not all human rights statutes define "marital status," and those that do are not all consistent. Nevertheless, it is generally accepted that this term encompasses the status of being single, in a common-law marital relationship, married, separated, divorced, or widowed. Same-sex couples are afforded the same protections as opposite sex couples.[61]

Similarly, "family status" is defined by human rights legislation in a number of provinces, but the definitions differ. In Ontario, for instance, family status is defined as "the status of being in a parent/child relationship." The definition in the Alberta *Human Rights Act* defines family status more broadly as "the status of being related to another person by blood, marriage or adoption."

There have been important recent developments in the principles of discrimination based on marital or family status, which have resulted in jurisprudence that varies across jurisdictions. Specifically, two conflicting approaches to accommodating family caregiving obligations have emerged from recent case law.

One approach was established by the British Columbia Court of Appeal in *British Columbia, Campbell River and North Island Transition Society*,[62] which set a high threshold to establish a *prima facie* case of discrimination. Under the test articulated by the Court of Appeal, an employee claiming discrimination must establish two things: (a) the employer must have changed a term or condition of employment impacting the employee; and

---

[59] I am using the terminology from the University of British Columbia's "Positive Space Campaign," http://positivespace.ubc.ca/home/.

[60] [1999] OHRBID No. 12.

[61] Zinn, *Human Rights in Canada*, c 6, p 2.

[62] 2004 BCCA 260 [*Campbell River*].

(b) that change must cause "serious interference" with a "substantial" parental or other family obligation. The other approach, which has been adopted by the Canadian Human Rights Tribunal and endorsed by the Federal Court of Canada, treats family status discrimination claims in the same way as claims based on other protected grounds of discrimination: there is no initial weighing of the significance of the breach of the employee's rights in order to determine whether the employee has established a *prima facie* case.[63] Further, under the federal approach, discrimination may be established even in the absence of a change imposed by the employer (i.e., a change in the employee's family situation may be sufficient to trigger the duty to accommodate).

In general, courts and tribunals in British Columbia have accepted *Campbell River* as the correct approach for interpreting family status accommodation claims; however, some recent case law may signal a shift in the BC Human Rights Tribunal's approach in this context.[64] Courts and tribunals in other Canadian jurisdictions, on the other hand, have rejected *Campbell River* as too restrictive,[65] or they have settled on a middle ground between the two approaches. As a result, this area of the law remains in flux.

In general, family status cases are highly fact-specific and the results vary widely. For example, in *McDonald v Mid-Huron Roofing*,[66] the Ontario Human Rights Tribunal found that an employer breached its duty to accommodate family status by dismissing an employee who required further time off to attend the weekly hospital appointments of his wife who was experiencing complications related to her pregnancy. By contrast, in *Palik v Lloydminster Public School Div. No. 99*,[67] the Saskatchewan Human Rights Tribunal rejected a claim for accommodation that called for granting a teacher's assistant two days' special leave to attend the provincial hockey tournament of her 14-year-old diabetic son who, the complainant argued, required constant monitoring.

Political Belief or Activity

Political belief or activity is a protected ground in all of the provinces and territories except Alberta, Ontario, Saskatchewan, and Nunavut. Most of the jurisdictions that protect this ground do so in relation to employment

---

[63] See *Attorney General of Canada v Fiona Ann Johnstone and Canadian Human Rights Commission*, 2013 FC 113.

[64] See *Kovacs v John's Bedrooms Barn and Foam Warehouse and others*, 2013 BCHRT 31.

[65] See for example, *Communications, Energy and Paperworkers Union, Local 707 v SMS Equipment Inc. (Cahill-Saunders Grievance)*, [2013] AGAA No 41.

[66] 2009 HRTO 1306.

[67] (2006), 58 CHRR D/149.

and provision of services and facilities, with the exception of British Columbia, which prohibits discrimination on the basis of political belief only in respect of employment.

The prohibitions against discrimination based on political belief or activity vary from jurisdiction to jurisdiction. Prince Edward Island's *Human Rights Act* protects political belief narrowly, tying it to belief in the tenets of a political party. The legislation in other jurisdictions, such as British Columbia and New Brunswick, does not define political belief at all. Where political belief has not been defined, courts and tribunals have interpreted this term broadly to include any manner of political or civic opinion, affiliation or participation.[68]

Complaints of discrimination based on political belief are relatively rare. Typically, the only employers interested in an employee's political beliefs are political parties, where the party, as the employer, may have a bona fide reason to discriminate on the basis of an applicant's or incumbent's political affiliation.

Age Discrimination

Age is a protected ground in every Canadian province and territory. The extent of this protection, however, varies from jurisdiction to jurisdiction. For example, while age is a protected ground in all provinces and territories in relation to employment, it is not protected in Alberta in relation to the provision of services and facilities. In addition, the "age" that is protected may differ from one jurisdiction to the next: in certain jurisdictions, only individuals above a certain age are protected, while in others, discrimination on the basis of any age is prohibited.[69]

The issue of age discrimination often arises in cases involving policies which require employees to retire at a certain age (e.g., 65 years). Since compulsory retirement based solely on an individual's age easily meets the test of *prima facie* discrimination, the central issue in these cases is typically whether the impugned policy is a "bona fide occupational requirement." We discuss bona fide occupational requirements in greater detail later in this chapter.

Determining whether a mandatory retirement policy constitutes a bona fide occupational requirement is a very fact-specific exercise.[70] In general, tribunals, arbitrators, and courts have not been sympathetic to employers wishing to enforce blanket policies requiring retirement on the basis of assumptions or stereotypical views about aging workers.

---

[68] See, for example, *Re Jamieson and Victoria Native Friendship Centre* (1994), 22 CHRR D/250 (BCCHR).

[69] See discussion in Zinn, *Human Rights in Canada*, c 3, pp 1–2.

[70] Ibid., c 3, pp 31–36.

Instead, employers must approach the issue of age restrictions as a bona fide occupational requirement on a more individualized basis by conducting individualized testing and assessments of ability. Employers must also meet their accommodation obligations. Therefore, even if an employee demonstrates an age-based limitation, the employer will be required to accommodate that individual's restrictions or limitations to the point of undue hardship.

Criminal Conviction

Alberta, Manitoba, New Brunswick, Nova Scotia, and Saskatchewan do not offer protection against discrimination against persons convicted of or charged with a criminal offence. The provinces and territories that do offer this type of protection do so to varying degrees, with the greatest protection found in the BC *Human Rights Code*. As a result, the majority of case law about this kind of discrimination arises in British Columbia.

While all of the jurisdictions that prohibit discrimination on the basis of a criminal conviction protect against such discrimination in employment, only the territories extend this protection to the provision of facilities or services. Most commonly, human rights legislation protects individuals from discrimination in employment based on a criminal conviction for which a pardon has been granted. The second most common form of protection is a prohibition against discrimination in employment based on a conviction for an unrelated criminal offence. In some jurisdictions, such as British Columbia, this protection extends to "perceived convictions," where a person has been arrested or charged but not convicted.

In general, based on the decision in *Woodward Stores (British Columbia) Ltd. v McCartney*,[71] in determining whether a criminal act relates to a person's job or prospective job, an employer should consider the following factors:

1. Does the behaviour for which the charge was laid, if repeated, pose any threat to the employer's ability to carry on business safely and efficiently?
2. What were the circumstances of the charge and the particulars of the offense involved? For example, how old was the individual when the events in questions occurred, and were there any mitigating or extenuating factors?
3. How much time has elapsed between the charge and the employment decision? What has the individual done during that period of time? Has he or she shown any tendencies to repeat the sort of behaviour

---

[71] (1982) 3 CHRR D/1113.

for which he or she was charged? Has he or she shown an intention to rehabilitate himself or herself?

Only when the employer can demonstrate a degree of "relatedness" between the criminal act and the work to be performed may the employer lawfully discriminate on this basis.

Defences

As noted earlier, if a human rights complaint establishes a *prima facie* case of discrimination, the onus shifts to the respondent to justify the allegedly discriminatory conduct. If the respondent establishes that it was justified in its conduct, the complaint will be dismissed.

The respondent may justify discriminatory treatment in employment by proving that the treatment was a bona fide occupational requirement. Similarly, the respondent may justify discriminatory treatment in the provision of services or facilities by proving that it had a bona fide and reasonable justification for the treatment.

Bona Fide Occupational Requirement and Reasonable Justification

Whether through the operation of express human rights provisions or the applicable jurisprudence, discrimination in employment or the provision of services or facilities may, in general, be justified if it can be shown that the impugned treatment was based on bona fide and reasonable grounds.

The approach to justifying discriminatory treatment on these grounds was set out in *Meiorin*.[72] When a standard (e.g., rule, requirement, qualification, instrument) discriminates against an individual on a prohibited ground (e.g., disability), that standard will violate human rights legislation unless the institution imposing that standard can establish that the standard is a bona fide occupational requirement, or that the institution has a bona fide and reasonable justification for implementing that standard. In order to establish such a defence, the respondent must prove that

1. it adopted the standard for a purpose or goal rationally connected to the function being performed;
2. it adopted the standard in good faith, in the belief that it is necessary for the fulfillment of the purpose or goal; and
3. the standard is reasonably necessary to accomplish its purpose or goal, because the respondent cannot accommodate persons with the characteristics of the complainant without incurring undue hardship.

---

[72] *British Columbia (Public Service Employee Relations Commission) v BC Government Service Employees' Union*, [1999] 3 SCR 3.

In order to establish that a standard is "reasonably necessary" for the fulfillment of a legitimate purpose, the respondent must demonstrate that it cannot reasonably accommodate an individual (e.g., employee or student) who is unable to meet the standard without suffering undue hardship. This gives rise to the "duty to accommodate."

Duty to Accommodate

Not every human rights statute in Canada explicitly requires entities to accommodate individuals in protected groups to the point of undue hardship, but this duty is implied in every jurisdiction by virtue of human rights jurisprudence.

The "duty to accommodate" is a legal duty arising when an individual suffers from a limitation or impairment based on a protected ground. The law regarding the duty to accommodate is complex and constantly evolving. The essence of the duty is that parties involved in protected activities (e.g., employment or provision of services or facilities) are legally required to take reasonable measures short of undue hardship to accommodate the characteristics protected by statute.

For example, if an employee suffers from a physical disability that limits her from performing some or all of her duties, the employer must determine if it can accommodate her short of undue hardship by modifying her duties or providing the support that will enable her to continue working. Similarly, if a student at a college were unable to attend a scheduled exam because of her religious observances, the college would be required to assess whether it could accommodate the student by, for example, modifying the exam schedule.

In some jurisdictions, "undue hardship" is defined by statute. In Nunavut, for example, the term is defined as follows:

"undue hardship" means excessive hardship as determined by evaluating the adverse consequences of a provision in this Act that requires a duty to accommodate, by reference to such factors as

(a) health and safety;

(b) disruption to the public;

(c) effect on contractual obligations;

(d) cost; and

(e) business efficiency.[73]

The *Human Rights Act* in the Yukon Territory includes a similar definition.

---

[73] *Human Rights Act*, S.Nu. 2003, c. 12, s 1.

In other jurisdictions, such as British Columbia, Alberta, and Newfoundland and Labrador, the term "undue hardship" is not even mentioned. In general, however, similar principles are applied across Canada to determine whether the point of undue hardship has been reached. The following factors may be relevant to this assessment:[74]

- the nature of the employer's workforce, service, or facilities;
- the employer's or service/facility provider's size and financial resources;
- the extent of any disruption to the workplace, collective agreement, or learning or teaching environment;
- the effect of the accommodation on the rights or morale of other employees or students;
- the cost to the employer of the proposed accommodation, including direct monetary costs, as well as any impact on efficiency or productivity;
- the impact on the safety of the individual, other employees or students, or the general public; and
- the employer's or service provider's statutory obligations (e.g., under occupational health and safety legislation).

Accommodation is a collaborative process.[75] An institution with a duty to accommodate must actively seek the information it needs and consider and explore possible accommodation alternatives. When a collective agreement is in force, the task of determining how to accommodate individual differences also requires the participation and cooperation of the union. Finally, the person requiring accommodation must also cooperate in the attempt to find a suitable accommodation. Generally, the person requiring accommodation has obligations in the process that, if not met, may relieve the employer or service/facility provider from its duty to accommodate. This may arise when, for example, the person seeking accommodation for a disability refuses or fails to provide medical information. An institution's duty to accommodate can also be discharged when the person who seeks accommodation refuses to accept a reasonable accommodation.

Importantly, the employer or service/facility provider must meet the procedural requirements of the duty to accommodate by taking adequate steps to explore what accommodation is needed and to assess

---

[74] See, for example, factors discussed in *Central Alberta Dairy Pool v Alberta (Human Rights Commission)*, [1990] 2 SCR 489 at 439; *Central Okanagan School District No. 23 v Renaud*, [1992] 2 SCR 970 [*Renaud*]; and *Howard v University of British Columbia* (1993), 18 CHRR D/353 (BCCHR).

[75] See for example, ibid., *Renaud*.

accommodation options.[76] It is not sufficient to merely assume or speculate that no accommodation is possible, regardless of how accurate that assumption or speculation is likely to be.

Affirmative Action Programs / Special Interest Organizations

Human rights legislation in all jurisdictions except Alberta allows, by way of exemption, for discrimination in employment or the provision of services if the differential treatment forms part of a special program designed to eliminate or reduce disadvantages faced by individuals because of certain protected grounds. These types of programs are commonly known as "affirmative action" programs and involve preferential treatment on the basis of a protected ground to attempt to remedy past discrimination and promote equality. Employers with affirmative action programs should ensure that the restrictions of the program are rationally connected to the program's objectives.

Many jurisdictions have similar exemptions that allow special interest organizations, educational institutions, clubs, or organizations serving the interests of a protected group to draw a distinction based on a protected ground if it can be shown that such distinctions are made to further protect the legitimate interests of that group. For example, a student club or organization formed to represent and promote the interests of LGBT*TQIA+ students may legitimately restrict membership to persons belonging to the LGBT*TQIA+ community. In jurisdictions where the human rights legislation does not expressly exempt special interest groups from the prohibition against discrimination (i.e., Alberta, Saskatchewan, Manitoba, and New Brunswick), such groups may nevertheless justifiably rely upon distinctions based on protected grounds under the bona fide or reasonable justification exemption.

Since provisions exempting special programs and interest groups vary from jurisdiction to jurisdiction in terms of their application and the classes of persons covered, employers and service providers are advised to consult the human rights legislation and jurisprudence applicable in their jurisdiction to determine whether they fall within these exceptions.

POTENTIAL REMEDIES AND SCOPE OF DAMAGES

Adjudicative tribunals dealing with human rights matters have broad remedial powers designed to further the purposes of human rights legislation. The remedies for a contravention of a human rights statute

---

[76] See, for example, *Datt v McDonald's Restaurants of Canada Ltd.*, 2007 BCHRT 324.

can have significant implications for the finances and operation of a postsecondary institution.

Arbitrators in every jurisdiction have the power not only to interpret and apply human rights legislation, but also to fashion appropriate remedies. As stated in *Association of Professors of the University of Ottawa v University of Ottawa*,[77] arbitrators must have the full panoply of remedies envisaged by human rights legislation "in order to ensure the effective application of these important workplace laws."

Remedies for human rights violations vary from jurisdiction to jurisdiction and depend on the type of discrimination and activity at issue. Assessing the risk that postsecondary institutions may face for human rights violations requires a careful review of the applicable statutory provisions and case law.

In general, courts, tribunals, and arbitrators have the power to remedy a human rights violation by ordering the offending party to

1.   cease the contravention;
2.   make available to the complainant the opportunities or privileges that were denied contrary to the human rights scheme (e.g., reinstatement of an employee or admission of a student);
3.   pay damages for any financial loss suffered as a result of the contravention (e.g., lost wages or additional costs of obtaining alternate services); and
4.   take any other action the tribunal deems appropriate to rectify the violation (in Nunavut, for example, this requires the tribunal to take into consideration Inuit culture and values that underlie the Inuit way of life).

In addition, many statutes provide for damages for injury to dignity, feelings, and self-respect. This remedy may create significant financial liability for institutions, as tribunals in some jurisdictions increase the quantum of damages available under this head. The rough upper limit for damages for injury to dignity in British Columbia, for example, recently increased from $35,000 to $75,000.[78]

Finally, certain statutes provide for other specific types of remedies, such as

1.   exemplary or punitive damages (e.g., Manitoba and Yukon Territory);
2.   an apology (e.g., Nunavut); and

---

[77] [1999] OLAA No 945 at para 15.
[78] See, for example, *Kelly v University of British Columbia (No. 4)*, 2013 BCHRT 302.

3. an order to take measures short of undue hardship to make accessible services or facilities impeding physical access or lacking proper amenities for persons with disabilities (e.g., Saskatchewan).

DISCRIMINATION IN EMPLOYMENT

All jurisdictions in Canada have provisions in their human rights legislation that broadly prohibit discrimination in the context of employment. Discrimination is prohibited in any aspect of the employment relationship, such as recruitment and selection, compensation and benefits, dismissals, hours of work, overtime, training, promotions, performance management, layoffs, leaves of absence, vacations, and transfers. These restrictions apply to full-time and part-time employees, probationary employees, contractors, seasonal workers, temporary workers, and volunteers.

Employees who complain of a violation of their human rights must show a *prima facie* case of discrimination. This is not a particularly high bar. Employees need only show that they fall within a group characterized by one of the prohibited grounds and were treated adversely, and that the prohibited ground was a factor in the adverse treatment.

Concerns Most Relevant to Postsecondary Institutions

Employment and Contracts

As explained earlier in this chapter, an employer may lawfully discriminate, based on an otherwise prohibited ground, if it can prove a legitimate operational or business reason for the discrimination. However, in order to prove the legitimacy of such a reason, the employer must demonstrate that the workplace rule, policy, standard, or criterion relied upon is a "bona fide occupational requirement." Below, we address employment issues that most commonly generate human rights concerns in the postsecondary sector.

Recruitment and Selection (Hiring Decisions)

Because human rights legislation applies to employment advertising, employers should be mindful that the recruiting process can trigger human rights liability. The duty to accommodate is triggered as early as the applicant screening and interview process. For example, in one case before the BC Human Rights Tribunal, a prospective employee was held to have been discriminated against when the refusal to hire was based on his disclosure of a drug addiction: *Brady v Interior Health Authority.*[79]

---

[79] [2007] BCHRTD No 231.

The prohibition against discrimination and the duty to accommodate only applies to the protected grounds of discrimination discussed earlier in this chapter. The protected ground need only be a factor in the alleged adverse treatment, rather than the sole or primary factor, to establish a complaint of discrimination. There is no requirement to accommodate a lack of skills, experience, education, intelligence, or personal preferences unrelated to a protected ground. Discrimination on such unprotected grounds is a lawful and natural part of the recruitment and selection process. The key is to ensure that the assessment of candidates for employment is free from any inference that is based, in whole or in part, on a protected ground. Thus, in order to avoid liability under human rights legislation in the recruitment and selection process, it is important to have clear, objective criteria by which to evaluate candidates.

Tenure

Because tenure relates to employment, decisions regarding tenure attract the same protection against unlawful discrimination as decisions regarding hiring. An institution's tenure and promotion procedure should be clearly established and followed so as to avoid any claims that the process is discriminatory.

Miraglia v University of Waterloo[80] provides an example of the importance of having clearly established and documented procedures with respect to decisions about tenure. In *Miraglia*, a professor complained that the process followed in consideration of her promotion to full professor was discriminatory. It was also alleged that she received different treatment than a male faculty member and that, as a result, she received a lower salary. The tribunal reviewed the university's procedures and found that the promotion process involved a frank assessment based solely on a candidate's academic qualifications. It held that the claim was not substantiated, especially with respect to the differential treatment she alleged. The tribunal found that the complainant's academic and scholarship qualifications were not comparable to the qualifications of the other candidates competing for tenure.

Accommodation in a Unionized Workplace

If the workplace is unionized, the union bears a joint duty to cooperate in the accommodation process and propose alternative solutions where accommodation relates to one of its members. For example, a union must consider whether collective agreement requirements can be relaxed, waived or varied, without undue hardship, to accommodate an employee

---

[80] 2010 HRTO 1459.

with a disability. The union, for example, may be required to allow that employee to obtain a job vacancy over a more senior applicant. The union has a duty to genuinely cooperate with the employer and not simply to seek the optimal solution to the employee's problems.

Generally, a union may become a party to discrimination in two ways. The first occurs when the union is a party to a collective agreement or other agreement with the employer that is discriminatory. For example, in *UFCW, Local 401 v Alberta Human Rights and Citizenship Commission*,[81] the employer and union reopened the collective agreement to negotiate a reduction of the employer's labour costs. A buyout program was negotiated whereby high-seniority and high-wage employees would be replaced by new employees at lower wages. An eligibility period for the buyout was set at 52 weeks, and some employees who were absent for medical reasons were ineligible to participate. The Alberta Court of Appeal upheld the findings of the commission and lower court that this eligibility requirement was discriminatory and held the employer and the union jointly liable for the discrimination and failure to accommodate.

The other most common form of union involvement in discrimination occurs when a union, though not having had a part in the creation of the discriminatory rule or practice, nevertheless refuses to do what it reasonably should to accommodate an employee after learning of the discrimination. For example, in *UFCW, Local 401*,[82] the court held the union liable for failing to accommodate employees with disabilities after learning of the discriminatory effect. The union did nothing to address the discriminatory effect because it viewed the issue as the employer's problem, and it was not prepared to bear any cost itself or canvas the possibility that its membership bear some of the cost of the accommodation.

Standards and Criteria for Faculty and Staff

It is important to consider human rights obligations when developing job performance standards and criteria for faculty and staff. When an employer's workplace standard (e.g., a requirement that an employee filling a particular position must perform certain duties) discriminates against an employee on a prohibited ground (e.g., disability), that standard will violate human rights legislation unless the employer can establish that it is a bona fide occupational requirement, as described earlier in this chapter.

In order to establish that a job requirement is "reasonably necessary" for the fulfillment of a legitimate work-related purpose, the employer must demonstrate that it is impossible to accommodate an employee who

---

[81] 2003 ABCA 246 [*UFCW, Local 401*].
[82] Ibid.

cannot meet the standard without causing the employer undue hardship. This gives rise to the so-called duty to accommodate.

Even when workplace standards meet this requirement, they should not be rigidly adhered to when the issue of accommodation is raised. For example, in *McGill University Health Centre v Syndicat des employes de l'Hopital General de Montreal*,[83] the employee's absence exceeded the period that was provided for rehabilitation in the parties' collective agreement. The employer, assessing the employee's situation, extended the leave, but ultimately terminated her employment due to her prolonged absence. The Supreme Court of Canada found that the termination clause in the collective agreement was a significant factor to be considered in assessing the accommodation issue, but also stressed that accommodation needs to be considered on an individualized basis. The accommodation was held to be sufficient because the employer had considered the employee's individual circumstance and had not applied the policy strictly, without due consideration.

Discipline and Discharge

When making decisions about discipline or dismissal, it is important to bear in mind human rights obligations. Some disabilities, such as mental illness, do not manifest in obvious ways. Employers may have a duty to make inquiries about an employee's health, especially when the employee's unusual conduct provides reasonable cause to do so, before taking any steps that might affect the individual's employment. Employers must be vigilant and able to identify potential signs of physical or mental disability, which may be subtle, and make the necessary inquiries when there is reason to believe there may be a medical problem underlying an employee's performance or conduct issues.

For example, in *Wilson v Transparent Glazing Systems Ltd.*,[84] the BC Human Rights Tribunal considered an employer's duty to make further inquiries into an employee's health when the employer was aware that the employee had a back problem, suffered from migraines, and was prescribed medical marijuana. The employee was difficult to work with and was the subject of numerous complaints from co-workers. Compounding matters, the employee made a number of errors in his work. The employer ultimately dismissed the employee, relying on the employee's poor performance and productivity, his bad temper and his general inability to get along with his co-workers. The employee claimed that his dismissal amounted to discrimination on the basis of disability.

---

[83] 2007 SCC 4.
[84] 2008 BCHRT 50 [*Wilson*].

The employer acknowledged that it was aware, prior to its decision to dismiss the employee, that he had been prescribed marijuana to alleviate his symptoms. Evidence of the employer's knowledge existed in the form of a supervisor's memo, which indicated a suspicion that the employee's performance problems appeared to be affected by his medication. There was no evidence, however, that the employer made any effort to obtain further information about whether the employee's disability or his medication were affecting his performance, nor was there any evidence that the employer considered whether the employee's disability could be accommodated. The tribunal found that the employer discriminated against the employee because of his disability.

As demonstrated in *Wilson*, it is prudent for employers, when taking disciplinary action, to ensure they have not ignored signs that the employee may be suffering from a mental or physical disability. Keeping thorough personnel records can assist in identifying any sudden changes in an employee's behaviour that might trigger the employer's duty to inquire. Further, when records indicate that an employee is suffering from a disability, the employer must look at the employee's personal experience and capabilities, rather than making assumptions and generalizations about that employee's limitations.

Academic Freedom

"Academic Freedom" describes the right of university and college faculty to teach without infringements on classroom content and methods, subject to responsibility to students, colleagues, and the orderly administration of the institution: *Charles I. Stastny v Board of Trustees of Central Washington.*[85] The limits of academic freedom will often be laid out in employer policies and collective agreements.

In some cases, behaviour such as harassment or apparent discrimination may be saved by the protection of academic freedom. For example, in *Balcilek v Kwantlen Polytechnic University*,[86] the subject material an instructor assigned to students raised issues regarding human rights. The course, titled Psychology of Genocide, dealt with particularly sensitive issues concerning the psychology of different groups of people associated with genocide. The complainant, a student, complained that, among other things, the instructor assigned derogatory reading material. The tribunal summarily dismissed the complaint, finding that the articles were assigned in the context of a course about human psychology in the circumstances of genocide, and that in this context the material was not a discriminatory publication.

---

[85] (1982), Wash. App. LEXIS 2962.
[86] 2009 BCHRT 366.

DISCRIMINATION IN THE PROVISION OF EDUCATIONAL SERVICES

Concerns Relevant to Educational Service Providers

In general, human rights provisions prohibiting discrimination in the provision of services apply to the admission process for public postsecondary institutions and to services, accommodations, or facilities customarily available to students after admission: *University of British Columbia v Berg*.[87] In Saskatchewan, section 13 of the *Human Rights Code* states that every person enjoys the right to education in any school, college, university, or other institution or place of learning, and to vocational training or apprenticeship without discrimination on the basis of a prohibited ground other than age. Accordingly, human rights issues may arise in relation to many facets of a postsecondary institution's dealings with its students. For the purposes of this chapter, we have selected three areas of concern relevant to postsecondary institutions as service providers: (a) student admissions, (b) curriculum requirements and testing, and (c) accommodation of learning disabilities.

Student Admissions

As providers of a service to the "public," postsecondary institutions must not discriminate against students on the basis of a protected ground. This protection extends to prospective students. Therefore, when dealing with the admission of students to their programs, postsecondary institutions must not breach their human rights obligations.

When an institution's admission requirement, rule, or standard results in the adverse treatment of a candidate based on a protected ground (e.g., place of origin), this will amount to *prima facie* discrimination in the provision of services. The institution may, however, justify differential treatment on a prohibited ground if the rule or standard is based on bona fide or reasonable grounds. In these circumstance, the *Meiorin*[88] test applies such that the rule or standard will be justifiable if it

1. was adopted for a purpose or goal rationally connected to the institution's operations;
2. was adopted in good faith, in the belief that it is necessary for the fulfillment of the purpose or goal; and

---

[87] [1993] 2 SCR 353.

[88] *British Columbia (Public Service Employee Relations Commission) v BC Government Service Employees' Union*, [1999] 3 SCR 3.

3. is reasonably necessary to accomplish its purpose or goal, because the institution cannot accommodate persons with the characteristics of the applicant without incurring undue hardship.

Complaints of discrimination in the admissions process are usually brought by applicants who were denied admission on the basis of a standard that they claim is discriminatory. Below, we provide two examples of how tribunals in Canada have dealt with such cases.

In *Agduma-Silongan*,[89] the complainant, who completed her doctor of medicine in the Philippines, alleged that the University of British Columbia discriminated against her based on her place of origin when it failed to assess her foreign credentials as equivalent to domestic credentials. The tribunal recognized that while UBC differentiated between internationally and domestically credentialed students, this practice was not based on assumptions about the merits of educational systems around the world, but rather on information garnered from a large number of resources about the merits of worldwide educational systems.

The tribunal in *Agduma-Silongan* held that assessing the equivalence of an international credential was a necessary undertaking in fairly considering both domestically and internationally credentialed students for admission to UBC, and did not amount to *prima facie* discrimination. The tribunal stated as well that treating students unfairly is not necessarily discrimination, provided that such "unfairness" is not related to a protected ground.

In *Harvey v Woodford Training Centre Inc.*,[90] the complainant alleged discrimination on the basis of disability after her school revoked her enrolment in a spa course on learning that she had hepatitis C. The centre's decision was based on an enrolment standard that required students to submit a medical certificate confirming "freedom from communicable and contagious disease." The Board of Inquiry found that the training centre violated the *Human Rights Code* and awarded damages to the complainant as a result.

The board found that expelling the complainant from a program as a result of her physical disability amounted to a *prima facie* breach of her human rights. The board also found that the standard in question could not be justified under the second and third criteria of the *Meiorin* test. Although the requirement for students to be free of communicable disease was a goal rationally connected to enrolment in an esthetics course, the respondent was unable to prove that it adopted this standard in good faith. The requirement had been blindly adopted from the National Association of Career Colleges as part of a curriculum developed by a

---

[89] 2003 BCHRT 22.
[90] [2009] NLHRBID No 1.

person who was not identified as a medical doctor or other person with training or experience in the field of communicable diseases. There was no evidence to suggest that any thought was given by the respondent to the scope, necessity, or potentially discriminatory effect of this requirement.

Finally, the board found that the respondent could have taken steps to accommodate the complainant, such as prohibiting her from performing tasks that increased the risk of communicating her illness. In failing to even consider such options, however, the respondent failed to discharge its duty to accommodate.

Curriculum Requirements and Testing

Postsecondary institutions must also meet their human rights obligations in providing courses and assessing student performance, including accommodating students who are limited in their ability to fulfill certain curricular requirements due to a protected ground. The following cases provide specific examples.

In *Howard*,[91] a hearing-impaired student studying to become a teacher asked to be accommodated by being provided with the services of an interpreter. The university denied the request and argued that it could not bear the cost of an interpreter for such a practicum-heavy curriculum (approx. $40,000) because of its budgetary restrictions. As a result, the complainant's studies were put back three years. The Human Rights Council, as it was then, ruled that there was insufficient evidence to establish that accommodating the complainant by providing an interpreter, or funds for one, would constitute more than a minor interference with the operations of the university. Notably, however, the council emphasized that the university was required bear the burden of funding the accommodation of students with disabilities in circumstances such as this only when it is evident that funds are not otherwise available from another resource.

In *Harris v Camosun College*,[92] a student with an environmental sensitivity disability claimed she could not attend classes and requested that her lectures be recorded and her exams be convened outside of the classroom. Although the college accommodated her in a number of instances, it refused to accommodate her in three of her classes. When the student initially made the accommodation requests, the college complied without obtaining any medical information. The college later, though, requested medical information to determine the best accommodation for the student. The student claimed the request for medical information was discrimination. The tribunal held that the college had the right to

---

[91] (1993), 18 CHRR D/353 (BCCHR).
[92] 2000 BCHRT 51.

request appropriate medical information to analyze its responsibilities in meeting the duty to accommodate. The tribunal also accepted that certain courses reasonably required students to attend class. In this respect, the tribunal confirmed that accommodation measures that would remove the educational utility of a program meet the standard of undue hardship and are not required by law.

In *Brown v Trebas Institute Ontario Inc.*,[93] a visually impaired student claimed that the institute failed to accommodate him by not providing alternatively formatted course materials and refusing to allow a second deferral of his admission start date, which he had requested because the institute did not have the accommodations he required in place at that time. The tribunal held that the institute failed to properly accommodate the student and ordered the institute to waive its one deferral policy, make the alternative format materials available to the student, and designate a position to be responsible for handling accommodation issues in the future.

Finally, in *Hickey v Everest Colleges Canada*,[94] the respondent was found to have breached its duty to accommodate a dental assistant student who was limited in her ability to complete an 80-hour practicum due to a physical disability. The student had requested an accommodation to complete the practicum in four 4-hour shifts. The college refused the complainant's request because it understood that the Ministry of Training, Colleges and Universities required the practicum to be completed in two weeks. The tribunal held that, once advised of the request for accommodation, the respondent had a duty to explore with the complainant options that may have been available to accommodate her disability during the required practicum up to the point of undue hardship. The failure on the part of the college to take the first step to fully explore all the options amounted to a failure to accommodate. The tribunal awarded the complainant $3,000 in damages for injury to her dignity.

As these cases demonstrate, a variety of circumstances involving the provision of educational services to students can give rise to a human rights complaint. In each instance, a careful, thorough, and well-documented consideration of all the circumstances related to a request for accommodation is necessary to avoid potentially significant liabilities.

Accommodation of Learning Disabilities

Postsecondary institutions may face significant challenges in ensuring that students who suffer from learning disabilities receive the same learning opportunities as those who do not. The issue of whether an

---

[93] 2008 HRTO 10.
[94] 2009 HRTO 796.

accommodation might be necessary is just the first step, and it is often difficult in and of itself.

As in employment situations, it is not always obvious that an individual suffers from a disability and may be entitled to certain accommodations. It has been held that the duty to accommodate is not triggered when a post-secondary institution is unaware that a student has a learning disability, unless the institution ought to have known. For example, in *Hannaford v Douglas College*,[95] the tribunal found that the complainant had failed to make her head injury known to the college, and the symptoms of the student's alleged cognitive disability were not obvious or apparent. As a result, there was no duty on the college to accommodate the student.

When it is evident that a student has a learning disability that may require accommodation, however, an institution must act accordingly. As illustrated in *Fisher v York University*,[96] a prudent strategy for limiting the potential for liability in circumstances involving students with learning disabilities is to actively demonstrate the institution's commitment to equal access to education for all students and take measures – for example, by creating policies and programs – to address their accommodation needs.

In *Fisher*, a student alleged discrimination in the provision of services on the basis of her learning disability because, *inter alia*, the respondent refused to provide subject-matter tutoring in accordance with its policies concerning tutoring services. The tribunal rejected the complaint, finding that the university had met all of the requirements of the *Meiorin* test.

In respect of the first *Meiorin* requirement, the tribunal found that the university had adopted a policy whereby it would not fund "subject-matter tutoring" because, in the university's view, this type of tutoring was incompatible with the maintenance of academic standards. Accommodation that was intended to allow students with disabilities to demonstrate their ability to master the content and skills required to successfully pass the course without disadvantage because of their disability was permitted under the policy in a variety of other ways, including "skills tutoring" in areas such as language and essay writing to enable students to communicate their learning more effectively. The tribunal agreed with the university that such skills tutoring did not deal with the subject matter of particular courses, which students had to learn on their own. On the contrary, subject-matter tutoring could create an unfair advantage and alter the academic standards by which success in a course is determined. On this basis, the tribunal found that the university had adopted its policy for reasons rationally connected to the purpose or goal of university education.

---

[95] 2000 BCHRT 25.
[96] 2011 HRTO 1229 [*Fisher*].

The tribunal also found that the university had adopted the policy in good faith, in accordance with the second part of the *Meiorin* test. There was no evidence to support the allegation that the university adopted this policy in order to exclude or otherwise penalize students with disabilities. Rather, the tribunal found that the university devoted considerable resources to providing support and accommodation to students who had a wide variety of disabilities. It created programs and staffed them with well-trained professionals. It was evident that the university developed policies on disability and accommodation out of a strong commitment both to equal access to education for all students regardless of disability and to the creation of an equal playing field where all could learn to the best of their abilities.

The key issue in *Fisher* was the tribunal's assessment of the substantive aspect of the duty to accommodate under the third part of the *Meiorin* test – that is, whether the university made reasonable efforts to provide accommodation for the applicant's learning disability, to the point of undue hardship. The tribunal concluded that the university had complied with the recommendations that were provided in an assessment of the student by professionals at her home university. Specifically, the university provided her with extended time for exam writing, a quiet location to write the exams, exam proctors who understood the needs of students with learning disabilities, and the recording of classes to facilitate the processing of material taught.

A significant factor in the tribunal's dismissal of the complaint in *Fisher* was the abundant evidence of the university's commitment to equal access to education for all students. Such commitment and accompanying policies and programs designed to address the accommodation needs of students with disabilities will help protect institutions from liabilities related to human rights complaints.

STRATEGIES FOR DEFENDING AGAINST HUMAN RIGHTS COMPLAINTS

In most jurisdictions, human rights claims are handled by a commission that receives, investigates, and mediates complaints. Some jurisdictions, such as British Columbia, Ontario, and Nunavut, have a "direct access" model under which the human rights tribunal has the sole responsibility for receiving, processing, and adjudicating complaints under human rights legislation. Direct access models generally do not have a mechanism for investigating complaints, and the tribunals screen complaints only in a cursory manner to ensure that they raise issues that could constitute a *prima facie* violation of human rights legislation. Just as these two systems differ, strategies for defending against human rights complaints will not be the same across all jurisdictions.

General Steps

When a respondent receives a notice that a human rights complaint has been made, the first step is to review the complaint and determine if the appropriate parties have been named, and to consider the factual and legal issues raised in the complaint. In reviewing the complaint, it is important to ensure that the complaint is made within the statutory time limits, that the appropriate parties are named, and that the complaint has been made in the appropriate jurisdiction.

A respondent should also begin to gather all of the relevant documents in its possession and conduct interviews of the appropriate representatives of the respondent, as well as other potential witnesses. This exercise serves three purposes: it allows assessment of the merits of the complaint and the areas where some exposure to liability may exist; it provides the information that will be used to prepare a response to the complaint; and it lays the foundation for the preparation of supporting materials and arguments that may be used if the complaint progresses to a hearing.

Once the relevant information has been gathered, the respondent should analyze the merits of the complaint and the potential remedies that the complainant may be awarded if the complaint is successful.

Mediation Process

All jurisdictions in Canada have human rights tribunals or commissions that offer mediation or conciliation processes for parties to a human rights complaint. This process offers parties the chance to resolve their disputes with the assistance of a neutral third party. When a complaint is resolved through the mediation process, both the respondent and the complainant have a hand in negotiating the terms of the settlement. From a risk- and cost-reduction point of view, a respondent may wish to settle a complaint through mediation rather than proceeding to a hearing.

The mediation process is valuable in the resolution of human rights complaints not only because it may resolve the complaint early on in the process, but also because it often gives the respondent an opportunity to assess the strengths and weaknesses of the complainant's case.

Reasonable Settlement Offers

Offers to settle human rights complaints provide employers with several benefits: they have the potential to bring an early resolution; they allow the respondent greater control over the potential outcome of a complaint; they allow the respondent to reduce not only its own legal costs, but also the monetary awards it may be required to pay to a complainant. Finally, an offer to settle, if reasonable and rejected by the complainant, may allow the employer to have the complaint dismissed by the tribunal.

Factors that may be considered in assessing the reasonableness of a settlement offer include the evidence available to prove any financial or other losses of the complainant, the likely range of general damages the complainant might be able to expect in the circumstances, and whether the settlement offer corrects any systemic problems that were identified in the complaint.

Applications to Dismiss

In jurisdictions like British Columbia and Nunavut, which utilize the direct access model so that there is no commission investigating the merits of complaints before referring them to hearing, there are statutory provisions that permit respondents to make a preliminary application to dismiss a human rights claim. In British Columbia, for example, a complaint may be dismissed for the following reasons:

- The complaint is outside of the jurisdiction of the tribunal;
- The complaint does not disclose a contravention of the *Human Rights Code*;
- The complaint does not have a reasonable prospect of success;
- Proceeding with the complaint does not further the purposes of the *Human Rights Code*;
- The complaint was made for improper motives or made in bad faith;
- The matter has been decided in another proceeding; or
- The complaint exceeds the time limits set in the *Human Rights Code*.

This application process not only provides respondents with an opportunity to resolve a complaint by having it dismissed, but also, if it is unsuccessful, affords the respondent an opportunity to learn a great deal about the complaint, which can assist in preparation for a hearing.

Chapter 6

CANADIAN POSTSECONDARY EDUCATION ASSOCIATIONS: A VITAL PIECE OF THE POSTSECONDARY GOVERNANCE STRUCTURE

DAVID C. YOUNG AND
WENDY L. KRAGLUND-GAUTHIER

INTRODUCTION

In thinking about postsecondary educational institutions in Canada, particular consideration should be given to the governance structures, both internal and external, that provide a legal and administrative framework by which these very institutions are regulated. As Kaplin and Lee point out, this external dimension can come in the form of either public external governance exercised by a government, or private external governance through education associations.[1] In the Canadian context, there are many such education associations that impact the governance of postsecondary education.

This chapter, which does not purport to be exhaustive, will examine the multifaceted role of academic, faculty, student, and athletic associations in postsecondary education in this country. In addition to outlining the relevant agencies, attention will be devoted to examining the legal

---

[1] Kaplin and Lee, *Law of Higher Education.*

Handbook of Canadian Higher Education Law, edited by Theresa Shanahan, Michelle Nilson, and Li-Jeen Broshko.
Montreal and Kingston: McGill-Queen's University Press, Queen's Policy Studies Series.

and policy implications associated with such bodies in terms of the administration and governance of postsecondary education.

SETTING THE STAGE

As Gregor points out, postsecondary education, or higher education, is difficult to define because there are a myriad of institutional or program types that vary from province to province.[2] Further, as Jones notes, a Canadian system of higher education does not exist.[3] Despite this dilemma, for purposes of both simplicity and clarity, in this chapter postsecondary education "refers to the sum total of activities associated with institutions that focus on the provision of educational programming beyond the level of the secondary school."[4]

Data provided by the Canadian Association of University Teachers indicates that during the 2009/10 academic year, combined full-time and part-time university enrolment in this country stood at 1,203,891 students. For the same time period, 701,622 individuals were enrolled full- or part-time in college. It is interesting to note that between 1999/2000 and 2009/10, full-time university enrolment experienced a 49 percent increase.[5] Although some areas of the country are currently experiencing flat to declining numbers of students attending postsecondary education, it is clear that higher education continues to attract students in pursuit of advanced learning.

In looking at the macro-level policy dimension of postsecondary education in Canada, it is important to recognize that because of the division of powers set out in *The Constitution Act, 1867*, the federal government has little to no substantive role in coordinating policy in this area. As such, provincial and territorial governments are charged with developing and enacting policies surrounding postsecondary education. Essentially, "each province has its own regulatory framework, its own policy mechanisms and its own unique institutional structures and arrangements."[6] However, the federal government is not entirely excluded, as Ottawa's sphere of influence intersects with postsecondary education in the following areas: (a) federal-provincial transfers, (b) skills development, (c) research and development, and (d) student financial assistance.[7]

At the micro-level, internally, most universities in Canada have a similar bicameral governance structure. Regarded as largely autonomous institutions, universities normally have a corporate board of governors

---

[2] Gregor, "Introduction," 7.

[3] Jones, "Brief Introduction," 1.

[4] Jones, "Challenges of Shifting Categories," 372.

[5] Canadian Association of University Teachers, *Almanac*, 38–39.

[6] Shanahan and Jones, "Shifting Roles and Approaches," 36.

[7] Ibid., 32.

that deals with administrative and financial matters and a senate whose chief mission is setting academic priorities. The college sector is somewhat more difficult to encapsulate, as in some jurisdictions there are governing boards, while in others these institutions operate under the direct authority of the province, in the complete absence of such boards.[8]

ACADEMIC ASSOCIATIONS

In an age of increasing accountability and competition, program quality is often touted by universities and colleges as a drawing card to attract the brightest and best minds to their campuses. Unlike the United States, there exists in this country no national accreditation body to evaluate program standards. However, educational associations such as Universities Canada (formerly the Association of Universities and Colleges of Canada) do play a role in accreditation. Membership in Universities Canada, coupled with a charter granted by the provincial government, normally indicates de facto accreditation. Universities Canada, which was formed in 1911, serves as the national voice for its 97 member institutions.[9] The main role of Universities Canada is to

- serve as an advocate for higher education,
- develop public policy,
- share information on postsecondary education,
- develop seminars on leadership for university administration,
- manage scholarships and international programs, and
- publish reports and publications.[10]

In a like manner to Universities Canada, the Association of Canadian Community Colleges (ACCC) promotes quality assurance practices in colleges throughout the country. As well, it strives to promote respect, dialogue, and collaboration between colleges, countries and stakeholders.[11] Both Universities Canada and ACCC are examples of education associations that directly influence the governance of postsecondary education.

Besides the role of Universities Canada and ACCC, professional programs offered by postsecondary institutions are subject to accreditation by regulatory bodies. Teaching, nursing, and a host of other academic courses of study routinely undergo evaluations, often consisting of on-site

---

[8] Jones, "Brief Introduction," 4.

[9] Charbonneau, "Meeting of Minds."

[10] Universities Canada, "What We Do," http://www.univcan.ca/about-us/what-we-do/.

[11] Association of Canadian Community Colleges, "Operating Principles," http://www4.accc.ca/xp/index.php/en/about/strategic-plan-2013-2018/operatingprinciples.

visits. The Association of Accrediting Agencies of Canada, which serves as a representative for the accrediting agencies of many professional organizations, works to ensure high educational standards in the training and preparation programs offered by postsecondary programs.

Recently, a number of associations/organizations have begun to emerge, representing the core interests of institutions that are similarly situated. One such association is the U-15, which serves as a voice for Canada's most research-intensive universities. The following institutions are members of the U-15:

- University of Alberta
- University of British Columbia
- University of Calgary
- Dalhousie University
- Université Laval
- University of Manitoba
- McGill University
- McMaster University
- Université de Montréal
- University of Ottawa
- Queen's University
- University of Saskatchewan
- University of Toronto
- University of Waterloo
- Western University

According to Suzanne Corbeil, executive director of the U-15, the mandate of the association is to influence "policy direction on things that are of most impact to our group."[12]

Partly in reaction to the creation of the U-15, smaller comprehensive-research universities in Canada have banded together. Known as the Alliance of Canadian Comprehensive Research Universities (ACCRU), this alliance comprises approximately 20 institutions. According to Dan Weeks, vice-president research at the University of Lethbridge, ACCRU is not a lobby group; "rather, the aim of the new alliance is to discuss the challenges and issues that these smaller universities face, and to pool resources and best practices with like-minded colleagues."[13]

Much like the U-15 and ACCRU, the U4 League, composed of Acadia University, Bishop's University, Mount Allison University, and St. Francis Xavier University, is another collaborative enterprise. The goal of the U4 is

---

[12] Quoted in Berkowitz, "U-15 Begins to Formalize Its Organization," 34.
[13] Quoted in Charbonneau, "Research Vice-Presidents," 27.

to promote best practices in teaching and learning at each of the member institutions, and to foster research partnerships.

The Council of Ontario Universities is another association whose mandate is to promote the shared interests of its members. As the voice for universities in the province of Ontario, the council advocates on a range of issues that impact the 20 publicly funded universities in the province, as well as the Royal Military College of Canada.

In addition to associations such as the U-15, ACCRU, and U4, it is important to recognize the role played by governmental associations. For instance, the Council of Ministers of Education (CMEC) serves as a forum whereby information can be shared among provincial jurisdictions. More particularly, "CMEC provides leadership in education at the pan-Canadian and international levels and contributes to the exercise of the exclusive jurisdiction of provinces and territories over education."[14]

Besides CMEC, some provinces have established intermediary bodies/ agencies that advise provincial ministries of education on matters such as planning, reviews, and assessment of new programs. An example of such an arrangement is the Maritime Provinces Higher Education Commission (MPHEC).[15] The role of MPHEC is to assist institutions and governments in New Brunswick, Nova Scotia, and Prince Edward Island in establishing a high-quality postsecondary education system.

Although an arm's-length agency of the government of Ontario, the Higher Education Quality Council of Ontario (HEQCO) is also relevant. HEQCO is involved in conducting evidence-based research, at times in collaboration with Ontario colleges and universities, on three themes: (a) access to postsecondary education, (b) quality of education, and (c) accountability of institutions. Through its various publications, HEQCO occupies an important role in advising Ontario's minister of Training, Colleges and Universities.[16]

FACULTY ASSOCIATIONS

Recent labour unrest at universities in Nova Scotia, New Brunswick, and elsewhere serves as a stark reminder that relations between administration and faculty are always tenuous at best. In fact, despite resolutions to the 2014 strikes at the University of New Brunswick (UNB) and Mount Allison University, recent happenings indicate that harmony has yet to be achieved. In fact, the Faculties of Arts, Education and Engineering at UNB have passed motions of non-confidence or issued statements of

---

[14] Council of Ministers of Education, "About," http://www.cmec.ca/11/About/index.html.

[15] Shanahan and Jones, "Shifting Roles and Approaches," 38.

[16] Tamburri, "New Kid on the Block," 24.

concern regarding President Eddy Campbell. Similarly, Mount Allison's Faculty Council recently voted 60–1 on a non-confidence motion concerning President Robert Campbell and Provost Karen Grant.[17]

As postsecondary institutions face mounting challenges on multiple fronts, it seems likely that the role of faculty associations will continue to occupy a position of extreme importance. Historically, between 1920 and 1950, several institution-based faculty associations emerged. However, the recession of the 1970s was the major impetus that led to the creation of the modern faculty association as a force in university governance. Currently, most postsecondary institutions have a faculty association that represents the interests of its members in relation to the central administration. Specifically, these associations undertake activities such as (a) spearheading negotiation efforts aimed at improved salary, benefits, and working conditions; (b) assisting members with grievances; and (c) influencing university policies.[18]

The Brock University Faculty Association (BUFA), formed in 1996, is representative of the role various faculty associations undertake across the country. According to its website, BUFA offers advice to members should a dispute with the university arise, and this extends to representing the interests of members in grievance procedures. As well, BUFA works to influence salaries and benefits, pensions, and employment conditions, including promotion, tenure, sabbaticals and research grants.[19]

In addition to institution-based faculty associations, provincially based associations represent the interests of their members. For example, the Association of Nova Scotia University Teachers, composed of faculty associations from eight universities in Nova Scotia, serves as an advocate and voice for those whose interests it represents.

On the national scene, the Canadian Association of University Teachers (CAUT) is arguably the strongest presence. Formed in 1951, the initial goal of the CAUT was to transform university governance so that faculty would be the dominant force within the institutions.[20] More recently, CAUT has been actively involved on many fronts such as academic freedom, tenure and promotion, copyright, and a host of other issues that impact faculty. CAUT also plays an important role in collective bargaining. Besides offering advice and assistance to local faculty associations engaged in a strike or lockout, the CAUT Defence Fund provides members with benefits during such job action. Today, with more than

---

[17] Canadian Association of University Teachers, "Faculty at Mount Allison, UNB Lack Confidence in Administration," A1.

[18] Jones, "Structure of University Governance," 223–25.

[19] Brock University Faculty Association, "About Us," https://www.bufa.ca/show_content.php?id=23.

[20] Savage, "Higher Education Organizations," 30–31.

68,000 members based at 122 universities and colleges across Canada, CAUT is a major force on the postsecondary landscape.[21]

STUDENT ASSOCIATIONS

Since the emergence of postsecondary educational institutions in Canada, student associations have played a role. Although initially concerned with tasks such as organizing extracurricular activities, their scope has expanded considerably. Today, student associations are actively involved in representing the student body in its collective relationship with the university, and in particular, the central administration.[22]

Most universities and colleges in Canada are characterized by the presence of at least one student association, although some institutions have multiple organizations that represent specific groups or interests. These institution-based student associations may undertake a variety of activities such as operating service businesses on campus. However, student leaders indicate that the three most important roles performed by these associations are (a) influencing institutional policies, (b) monitoring institutional policies, and (c) assisting students in navigating their way through institutional red tape.[23]

Each of the aforementioned roles is vital to ensuring the best possible student experience. As such, it is not uncommon to have student representatives elected or appointed to university or college committees, including the senate and board of governors. The mission statement of the University of Winnipeg Students' Association (UWSA) is quite typical in stating that its "efforts include promoting the exchange of ideas and information among students, and within the greater University community. As well as promoting communication within the University, the UWSA advocates on behalf of students to administrative bodies."[24]

In addition to these institution-based student associations, there exists a national presence in the form of the Canadian Federation of Students (CFS). Formed in 1981, and with more than 500,000 members, CFS lobbies at the federal level for quality, accessible postsecondary education. More specifically, it has taken an active role in regard to tuition, Aboriginal education, and a host of other issues. It is worth noting that CFS also engaged in litigation to protect student interests. In 2000 CFS challenged amendments to the federal *Bankruptcy and Insolvency Act*,[25] which

---

[21] Canadian Association of University Teachers, "Faculty at Mount Allison," A1.

[22] Jones, "Structure of University Governance," 225.

[23] Ibid.

[24] University of Winnipeg Students' Association, "Canadian Federation of Students," http://the uwsa.ca/advocacy/Canadian-federation-of-students/.

[25] RS 1985, c B-3, s 1;1992, c 27, s 2.

essentially prohibited students who were unable to repay student loans from filing for personal bankruptcy.

Much like CFS, the Canadian Alliance of Student Associations (CASA), composed of 24 student associations and student unions across Canada, serves as a voice for postsecondary students. Through lobbying efforts directed at the federal government and related interprovincial organizations, CASA advocates for student interests and proposes solutions for issues impacting its constituents.

ATHLETIC ASSOCIATIONS

In Canada, Canadian Interuniversity Sport (CIS) and its regional associations (Canada West Universities Athletic Association, Ontario University Athletics, Réseau du sport étudiant du Québec, and Atlantic University Sport) as well as the Canadian Colleges Athletic Association serve as the national governing bodies of university and college sport in Canada. Although not as lucrative as television deals that some American universities have with major television networks, membership in sports associations such as the CIS affords institutions a degree of national exposure not otherwise available.

However, some lament the fact that Canadian athletic programs are not cost-effective. For example, in 2010/11 universities in this country spent over $11,000,000 on funding to varsity athletes.[26]

Another issue that should not be overlooked is the recent introduction of the US National Collegiate Athletic Association (NCAA) into Canadian postsecondary education. Although the NCAA requires member schools to be accredited through an American accreditation agency, Simon Fraser University has been granted an exemption to play in NCAA Division II.[27] It could be argued that by participating in the NCAA, student athletes at Simon Fraser will be able to compete against elite schools. Further, participating in the United States could raise Simon Fraser's overall profile, which might help in recruiting and other such initiatives.

Although athletic associations in Canada currently lack any real substantive capacity to accredit institutions, such as the power exercised by the National Collegiate Athletic Association in the United States, associations such as the CIS and NCAA will continue to play an important role in postsecondary education.

---

[26] Pettigrew, "Why Universities Should Just Say No to Expensive Varsity Athletics."

[27] Charbonneau, "SFU Becomes a Full Member of U.S. Sports Body NCAA," 7.

CONCLUSION

In thinking about postsecondary education in Canada, most of the attention inevitably focuses on the role of government. This is certainly understandable given that provincial governments, and perhaps to a lesser degree the federal government, exert a tremendous influence on the overall administration of universities and colleges. In addition to government, one also needs to consider the scope of the internal governance structure of higher education institutions. Undeniably, governing boards, senates, and senior university administrators play an important role in the overall organization of universities and colleges.

However, a third and vital piece of the Canadian postsecondary governance structure, and one that is often overlooked, is the role played by education associations. As the preceding discussion has demonstrated, there are a variety of associations that impact higher education. Be it academic, faculty, student, or athletic associations, each plays a unique role in the overall equation. While some of these associations perform roles that are largely advisory in scope, others, particularly those charged with issues such as accreditation, have considerable power. In fact, without the "stamp of approval" from a recognized accreditation agency, some professional programs would be unable to offer their degree program.

In sum, the governance of postsecondary education in Canada is a complex web of intricate parts. "There are, of course, complaints that there is no end to the making of higher education organizations, and that the number and variety of them prevent the Canadian academic community from being heard as one voice."[28] Still, ideally, each of the constituent groups works in harmony to ensure the smooth operation of the university or college. At the end of the day, all parties must remember that they are working toward the same ideal: the best possible student experience. By keeping this in mind, the parties can put differences aside and find the will to make things work. Such collaboration might seem like a lofty ideal, but the students of today and tomorrow deserve nothing less.

---

[28] Savage, "Higher Education Organizations," 34.

PART III
Faculty and Students

Chapter 7

STUDENTS

DAVID HANNAH AND DAVID STACK

HISTORICAL BACKGROUND

Modern higher education has its roots in the ancient universities of Europe and inherited many of its customs and traditions from those universities. Among these was the idea of the university as a community apart from society, and separate from the laws that bound it. Murray Ross described the medieval university as

> largely an autonomous corporation whose members were free from most, if not all, of the usual civil regulations and laws. The university thus became an almost independent community responsible for disciplining its members for their conduct both inside and outside the institution. There emerged therefore in the minds of the civic and academic authorities alike a concept of the university as a separate entity in the larger community, responsible for the conduct of its own members.[1]

Parts of this chapter have appeared previously in the following works by D.A. Hannah: "Student-Institution Legal Relationships in Colleges and Universities in the Common Provinces of Canada: An Analysis of the Case Law from 1982 to 1994" (PhD diss., Bowling Green State University, Ohio, 1996); "Postsecondary Students and the Courts in Canada: Cases and Commentary from the Common Law Provinces" (Asheville, NC: College Administration Publications, 1998); "Law Is a Many-Splendoured Thing: A Brief History and Overview of Student-Institution Legal Relationships in Canada," *Communique ICJ* 6, no. 3 (2006): 26–32.

[1] Ross, *The University*, 69.

Handbook of Canadian Higher Education Law, edited by Theresa Shanahan, Michelle Nilson, and Li-Jeen Broshko. Montreal and Kingston: McGill-Queen's University Press, Queen's Policy Studies Series.

As universities grew over the ages, they developed an independence from the law that was shared by almost no other institution. As W.A. Kaplin noted, "The law accorded postsecondary institutions extensive autonomy in their daily operations. The academic environment was thought to be delicate and complex. Outsiders such as lawyers or judges would, almost by definition, be ignorant of the special arrangements and sensitivities underpinning this environment."[2] Similarly, Terrence Leas observed that faculty and administrators were responsible for a special mission – that of discovering, preserving, and transmitting knowledge: "This combination of exclusive expertise and special mission introduced the idea that outside monitoring of academe was unnecessary, even dangerous, to society's interests."[3]

The autonomy of the university meant that students' relationship to the university in many ways superseded their relationship to society at large. In the ancient universities, "public misconduct of students ... was not tried in civil courts but was deferred to university authorities for consideration and/or discipline.... This idea – that students were less subject to civil law than non-students and responsible only to university authority –... was decisive in defining the student's role in the university.[4]

For centuries the university's right to deal with its students as it thought best was unquestioned. The university's attitude towards its students was generally authoritarian and paternalistic. "The emerging concept of the university's relation to the student was *in loco parentis*, which meant that the student was in effect a ward of the university, which was responsible for guiding and nurturing his or her development."[5] The only rights of students were those bestowed on them by their masters. In short, higher education was seen by most as

> a unique enterprise that could regulate itself through reliance on tradition and consensual agreement. It operated best by operating autonomously, and it thrived on the privacy afforded by autonomy. Academia, in short, was like a Victorian gentlemen's club whose sacred precincts were not to be profaned by the involvement of outside agents in its internal governance.[6]

Colleges and universities in both Canada and the United States shared these attitudes and operated for much of their history with little awareness of, or concern for, the law and how it affected them.[7] Academia tended

[2] Kaplin, "Law on the Campus 1960–1985," 272.
[3] Leas, "The 'Doctrine' of Academic Abstention," 136–37.
[4] Ross, *The University*, 69.
[5] Ibid., 86–87.
[6] Kaplin and Lee, *Law of Higher Education*, 16.
[7] Reidhaar, "Assault on the Citadel," 343, 346. The author described the American university in 1960 as "a citadel where administrators governed students

to think of itself as "removed from and perhaps above the world of law and lawyers."[8] Furthermore, both government and the judiciary seemed to have supported this attitude by showing a remarkable deference to colleges and universities in virtually all aspects of their operations.[9]

In the period since the end of the Second World War, higher education in North America has undergone a radical transformation. One of the consequences of this transformation is that the relationship between higher education and the law has changed dramatically, particularly as it affects students and the student-institution relationship. Commentators have identified a number of factors that contributed to this transition.[10] Certainly, the tremendous increase in college and university enrolments, combined with a much more inclusive and diverse student body, created pressures to democratize higher education. As students increasingly became aware of the extent to which higher education was supported by their tax dollars, and as tuition rates increased over the years, they began to regard themselves (for better or for worse) as "consumers or purchasers of a packaged good with the right to demand good service and a good product."[11]

This "new emphasis on students as consumers of education with attendant rights, to whom institutions owe corresponding responsibilities ... further eroded the traditional concept of education as a privilege."[12] Higher education became a service industry, subject to the same consumerist expectations, and the same legal challenges, as these industries.[13] Increased calls for accountability and institutional efficiency, combined with a general increase in litigiousness in the United States, and to a lesser extent in Canada, resulted in colleges and universities becoming subject to increased scrutiny from both inside and outside the academy.[14]

---

virtually unfettered by legal constraints."

[8] Kaplin and Lee, *Law of Higher Education*, 16. See also Bridge, "Keeping Peace in the Universities"; Whyte, "Dispute Adjudication in the University."

[9] Leas, "The 'Doctrine' of Academic Abstention,"136–37. He discusses the doctrine of "academic abstention" whereby the courts traditionally hesitated to substitute their judgment for that of the academicians.

[10] A discussion of all the factors is beyond the scope of this chapter. See, for instance, Bowden, "Evolution of Responsibility"; Likins, "Six Factors"; and Ross, *The University*, 2.

[11] Ross, *The University*, 261.

[12] Kaplin, "Law on the Campus 1960–1985," 277.

[13] Janisch, "Educational Malpractice."

[14] See Mullens, "When Students Sue," 23–26. She suggests that a "culture of entitlement" among today's students and the perception that universities are "soft targets" with deep pockets have also contributed to increased litigation.

The establishment of the *Canadian Charter of Rights and Freedoms*[15] has likely had a psychological effect on Canadians as well, in that it has raised awareness of individual rights and increased expectations for the protection of those rights.[16] As Dickinson pointed out, "even if, as a matter of law, the *Charter* does not apply to universities, its mystique has crept into the academic community and likely raised its members' rights-consciousness even more."[17] The new attitude towards individual rights that has been engendered by the *Charter* may well be contributing to a new and more demanding student body than Canadian universities have historically had to deal with.

THE STUDENT-INSTITUTION LEGAL RELATIONSHIP

The legal relationship between students and postsecondary institutions is complex and multifaceted. No single area of law fully defines or governs the relationship between colleges and universities and their students. Rather, this relationship is shaped by several important types of *public law* (i.e., those areas of law affecting the public interest and involving the relationships between public bodies and individual persons), and *private law* (i.e., those areas of law affecting private interests and involving the relationships between legal "persons").

The following areas of public law have the greatest impact on colleges and universities:

- *statutory law* – the complex network of (mostly provincial) statutes establishing and regulating academic institutions;
- *administrative law* – law that governs decision-making bodies that operate under the authority of statutes, including postsecondary decision-making bodies; and (increasingly)
- *constitutional law*, which defines Canadians' fundamental rights and freedoms in relation to the state.

Colleges and universities are also subject to aspects of *private law*. For example, Canadian courts have consistently held that certain contractual relationships exist between a college or university and its students, and thus these institutions are bound by the principles and requirements of

---

[15] *Canadian Charter of Rights and Freedoms,* Part I of the *Constitution Act, 1982,* being Schedule B to the *Canada Act 1982* (UK), 1982, c 11.

[16] Crocker, "Legal Relationship between Universities/Colleges and Students"; Devine, "Fair Procedures"; Dickinson, "Academic Autonomy"; MacKay, "Canadian Charter of Rights and Freedoms"; MacKay, *Education Law in Canada*; Thistle, "Major Legal Issues Facing Canadian Universities in the 90's."

[17] Dickinson, "Academic Autonomy," 559.

contract law. In addition, postsecondary institutions are engaged in many activities that could involve them in *tort law* duties toward students.

It is important to note here that some Canadian universities have a provision in their incorporating statute for a position or office known as the "visitor," which, when present, significantly affects the legal framework within which student-institution conflicts and issues are dealt with.[18] The jurisdiction and authority of the visitor vary from one institution to the next. However, in general terms, where the position exists, the visitor has extensive and exclusive jurisdiction over the "domestic" or internal affairs of the institution.[19]

In general, decisions of a visitor on any matter within visitorial jurisdiction are final and not appealable to the common-law courts, at least on substantive grounds.[20] However, a visitor's actions are subject to review by the courts with regard to the manner of investigation and decision-making. "That is to say the visitor is subject to the general rules of natural justice with regard to notice requirements, knowledge of the allegations, opportunities to prepare a defense and the overall fairness of the hearing process."[21]

The Student-Institution Relationship as Contractual and Private

One of the primary legal theories that partially defines the student-institutional relationship is contract theory.[22] While there is at least one very early case that is based in contract theory,[23] it was not until the 1970s that

---

[18] For an interesting discussion of the ancient roots of the visitor jurisdiction, see Irvine, "The Queen's Bench Act, 1998," 102-5. The "visiting" jurisdiction was originally a common-law mechanism for the Crown to maintain supervision of charitable institutions.

[19] The ancient office of Visitor was apparently maintained in the university context as a means of respecting university autonomy and independence: Ouellette, "Le Contrôle Judiciaire sur l'Université," 631–32, 639; Irvine, "The Queen's Bench Act, 1998," 104. Visitorial jurisdiction normally ousts the authority of the courts over domestic matters, although in some jurisdictions the courts are asked to exercise the jurisdiction of the visitor: see, for example, *Mohamed v University of Saskatchewan*, 2006 SKQB 23, 276 Sask R 87[*Mohamed*].

[20] Khan, "British Universities: Visitor's Jurisdiction."

[21] Veitch, "Case Comment." See also Bridge, "Keeping Peace in the Universities"; Petraglia, "The University Visitor"; Smith, "Exclusive Jurisdiction of the University Visitor."

[22] For a more detailed discussion of the student-institution contractual relationship, see Yang, "University v. Student."

[23] *Powlett and Powlett v University of Alberta et al*, [1934] 2 WWR 209, 1934 CarswellAlta 25 (WL Can)(Alta SC (AD)); aff'g [1933] 3 WWR 322, 1933 CarswellAlta 39 (WL Can)(Alta SC).

contract-based cases began appearing with some regularity.[24] In *Sutcliffe v Governors of Acadia University*, the Appeal Division of the Nova Scotia Supreme Court stated that "there was clearly a contract here between the appellant and the university and it is this contract which governed the relationship between the parties."[25] This principle has been consistently upheld in judicial decisions over the past 40 years.[26]

Several judicial decisions have suggested that the primary contract is an implied contract to educate. The institution contractually agrees to provide students with the appropriate instruction, educational services, and other resources necessary to complete the educational credential that they are seeking, and to grant them that credential upon successful completion of the required courses and other learning activities. The students' contractual obligation is to pay the required fees, successfully complete the appropriate courses, maintain the required academic standards, and abide by the institution's policies, rules, regulations, and bylaws.

In addition to the primary contract to educate, there may be secondary or corollary contracts between the student and the institution. In one case a corollary contract requiring a university to provide students with assistantships was found to exist based on wording contained in the institutional calendar.[27] In another, a letter signed by a student relating to sharing of information about his master's thesis was seen by the courts as a contractual document.[28] Other examples of corollary contracts might be residence or housing contracts, contracts regarding co-op placements, traffic and parking, the proper use of library or computer facilities and services, and so on.[29]

---

[24] See, for example, *Re Polten and Governing Council of University of Toronto* (1975), 8 OR (2d) 749, 59 DLR (3d) 197 (Ont H Ct J) [*Re Polten*]; Chewter, "Justice in the University," 126.

[25] *Sutcliffe v Governors of Acadia University* (1978), 95 DLR (3d) 95 (NSSC); aff'g (1978), 85 DLR (3d) 115 (NS Co Ct) at 100 [*Sutcliffe*].

[26] See, for example, *Anderson v University of Alberta*, [1996] AJ No 1337(QL)(Alta QB)[*Anderson*]; *Attaran v University of British Columbia*, [1998] BCJ No 115(QL) (BCSC)[*Attaran*]; *Ciano v York University*, [2000] OJ No 681(QL), 2000 CarswellOnt 633 (WL Can)(Sup Ct J), Winkler J; additional reasons, [2000] OTC 37, [2000] OJ No 183 (QL)(Sup Ct J), Winkler J; aff'd on other grounds, [2000] OJ No 3482 (QL), 2000 CarswellOnt 3248 (WL Can)(Ont CA), Feldman JA, Goudge JA, Laskin JA; *Hazanavicius v McGill University*, 2008 QCCS 1617, 2008 CarswellQue 3458 (WL Can), Delorme JCS [*Hazanavicius*]; *Rittenhouse-Carlson v Portage College*, 2009 ABQB 342, [2009] 11 WWR 277, Gill J [*Rittenhouse-Carlson*].

[27] *Wong v Lakehead University*, [1991] OJ No 1901 (QL)(Ont Ct J)[*Wong*].

[28] *Ogden v Simon Fraser University*, 1998 CarswellBC 3260 (WL Can), [1998] BCJ No 2288 (QL)(BC Prov Ct).

[29] See, for instance, *University of British Columbia v Magolan*, 2008 BCPC 299, 2008 CarswellBC 2267(WL Can)(BC Prov Ct), Armstrong J.

While some terms of the student-institution contract are implied, other terms of the contractual relationship are explicit, and are contained in an institution's various official publications. An institution's academic calendar is perhaps its most important publication with respect to defining the terms of the student-institution contractual relationship. The calendar typically contains the most comprehensive and "official" description of an institution's admission and degree requirements, courses, academic regulations, and grading policies. Numerous judicial decisions since the 1970s have upheld this principle, and have made it clear that the calendar should be treated as a contractual document.[30] Other institutional documents have also been identified as part of the institution-student contract.[31]

The Student-Institution Legal Relationship as Public

While the courts have relied on the contractual model in their attempts to explain and categorize the unique student-institution relationship, the contractual model does not completely define this complex relationship. Institutions are governed, to varying degrees, by public statutes that constitute colleges and universities and that regulate the educational context in various ways.

---

[30] *Sutcliffe, supra* note 25; *Simpson v University of Guelph,* 1982 CarswellOnt 2792(Ont H Ct J); *McBeth v Dalhousie College and University,* 26 DLR (4d) 321, [1986] NSJ No 159(QL)(NSSC(AD)) [*McBeth*]; *MacDonald* v *Acadia University,* [1987] NSJ No 203 (QL)(NSSC(AD)) ; *Hague v University of British Columbia* (1988), 21 BCLR (2d) 245, 47 DLR (4d) 150 (BCSC); *Brodie et al v Governors of Dalhousie College and University* (8 March 1989), Halifax Claims 16743, 16744, 16745 (NS Sm Claims Ct); *Matthews* v *Memorial University of Newfoundland* (1991), 15 CHRR D/399, 1991 CarswellNfld 359 (WL Can)(Nfld Bd of Inquiry); *Wong, supra* note 27; *Bell v St Thomas University* (1992), 97 DLR (4d) 370, 130 NBR (2d) 31(NBQB)[*Bell*]; *Wong* v *University of Toronto* (1989), 79 DLR (4d) 652, 45 Admin LR 113(Ont Dist Ct), aff'd (1992), 4 Admin LR (2d) 95 (Ont CA); *Blaber v University of Victoria* (1995), 123 DLR (4d) 255 (BCSC); *Anderson, supra* note 26; *Attaran, supra* note 26; *MacDonald v University of British Columbia,* 2003 BCSC 1103, 18 BCLR (4d) 184; *Hickey-Button v Loyalist College of Applied Arts & Technology,* [2006] OJ No 2393 (QL)(CA); *Olar v Laurentian University*49 CCLT (3d) 257, [2007] OJ No 2211(QL)(Ont Sup Ct J), Gates J [*Olar*]. But see *Turner v York University,* 2012 ONSC 4272, 298 OAC 174.

[31] *Olar, supra* note 30: promotional documents; *Sutcliffe, supra* note 25and *Crerar v Grande Prairie Regional College,* [2004] AJ No 905 (QL)(Prov Ct), rev'd [2004] AJ No 905 (QL)(QB): registration forms; *Rittenhouse-Carlson, supra* note 26: institutional policies and procedures; *Sutcliffe, supra* note 25: residence handbooks; *Morgan v Acadia University,* 69 NSR (2d) 109, [1985] NSJ No 74 (QL)(NSSC(TD)) [*Morgan*]; *Goldberg v UBC,* 2001 BCPC 0035: student handbooks; *York University v Strazds,* 1985 CarswellOnt 3299 (WL Can) (Prov Ct (Sm Cl Div))[*York University*]: vehicle registration forms and apartment leases.

For instance, while the payment of fees has been portrayed as part of the basis for the private contractual basis between the institution and the student, the courts have characterized the setting of fees by universities as a public duty restricted by statute and reviewable by the courts.[32] If legislation provides the board of governors with the duty to set fees, the board cannot abdicate this function.[33] If the university enacts fees or fines that are ultra vires, then the court can order restitution to those who have paid the amounts.[34]

The academic appeals and discipline processes of universities are not generally considered any longer to be purely internal domestic matters, but, rather, are subject to public law duties and administrative law principles.[35] Finally, as explained below, a trend is developing that purports to categorize the student-institution relationship as a relationship between the student and the state.

In many ways, the student-institution relationship is a *sui generis*, or a one of a kind legal relationship. It is regulated by a complex blend of public law and private law, and the application of these laws is tempered by academic discretion and, at least in the case of universities, institutional independence.

STUDENT RIGHTS AND RELATED ISSUES

Fundamental Rights and Freedoms

For much of the last century, the fundamental rights and freedoms of higher education students were determined by the internal rules, policies, and decisions within the student's institution. Indeed, the concept of freedom tended to refer to the fact that the student was under the tutelage of a community of scholars that enjoyed academic freedom from state interference. A number of English decisions[36] suggested that

---

[32] See *Webb v Simon Fraser University* (1978), 83 DLR (3d) 244 (BCSC); *Students' Union, University of Alberta v University of Alberta* (1990), 67 DLR (4d) 593 ("instructional fees").

[33] However, the board does not abdicate this duty by considering the recommendations of university counsel or government's reaction: *Webb v Simon Fraser University*, 85 DLR (3d) 494, 1978CarswellBC597 (WL Can).

[34] See *Barbour v University of British Columbia*, 310 DLR (4d) 130, [2009] 10 WWR 323; rev'd [2010] 316 DLR (4d) 354. The university charged fees, charges, and fines related to parking that were ultra vires. The government eventually passed legislation with retroactive effect to prevent the university from paying a significant liability.

[35] *King v University of Saskatchewan*, [1969] SCR 678, 68 WWR 745 [*King*].

[36] *R v Dunsheath, Ex parte Meredith*, [1950] 2 All ER 741 (KB) and *Thorne v University of London*, [1966] 2 All ER 338 (CA), cited with approval in *Houston v*

academic actions such as the holding of examinations and the conferring of degrees were domestic questions within the exclusive jurisdiction of the institution such that the High Court had no jurisdiction to intervene. While the Canadian common law has never adopted such a bright-line position, for most of the twentieth century Canadian case law afforded unparalleled autonomy to universities. The twenty-first century to date has witnessed case law and legislation that has steadily chipped away at this autonomy.

In *Harelkin v University of Regina*, the Supreme Court described the freedom of the university as follows:

> The Act incorporates a university and does not alter the traditional nature of such an institution as a community of scholars and students enjoying substantial internal autonomy. While a university incorporated by statute and subsidized by public funds may in a sense be regarded as a public service entrusted with the responsibility of ensuring the higher education of a large number of citizens, … its immediate and direct responsibility extends primarily to its present members and, in practice, its governing bodies function as domestic tribunals when they act in a quasi-judicial capacity. The Act countenances the domestic autonomy of the university by making provision for the solution of conflicts within the university.[37]

In *Kane v University of British Columbia*, the Supreme Court of Canada directed the courts to afford a "large measure of autonomy" to decisions of the university board of governors.[38]

In many of these mid-twentieth-century cases, the procedural right to natural justice appeared to be the only fundamental external legal constraint on the academic processes of universities. Thus, so long as the institution applied fair process when addressing a student matter, the student had little likelihood of success in applying to the courts. Indeed, in *Harelkin* it was even decided that a student was denied access to the courts until all the university's internal avenues of redress had been fully pursued by the student.

This historic autonomy even largely withstood (at least for a time) the most significant possible challenge – the advent of the *Charter*. The *Charter* was established to ensure that government respects certain fundamental rights and freedoms of Canadians such as freedom of expression and assembly and the right to equality. While the *Charter* does not generally

---

University of Saskatchewan (Joint Senate-Council Board of Student Appeals), 117 Sask R 291, [1994] 4 WWR 387 (QB). See also *King v University of Saskatchewan* (1968), 67 WWR 126, 1 DLR (3d) 721.

[37] *Harelkin v University of Regina*, [1979] 2 SCR 561 at para 78 [*Harelkin*].

[38] *Kane v University of British Columbia*, [1980] 1 SCR 1105, [1980] 3 WWR 125 [*Kane*].

impose legal restraints on private organizations, many expected that it would apply to public universities.

In a challenge to universities' mandatory retirement policies, the majority of the Supreme Court of Canada in *McKinney v University of Guelph* ruled that the *Charter* does not generally apply to universities, stating:

> The government thus has no legal power to control the universities even if it wished to do so. Though the universities, like other private organizations, are subject to government regulations and in large measure depend on government funds, they manage their own affairs and allocate these funds, as well as those from tuition, endowment funds and other sources.

What Beetz J. said of the University of Regina in *Harelkin v University of Regina*, supra, in the passage at pp. 594–95, quoted above, applies equally here.... In short, I fully share the following conclusion of the Court of Appeal (1987), 63 OR (2d) 1, at pp. 24–25:

> The legal autonomy of the universities is fully buttressed by their traditional position in society. Any attempt by government to influence university decisions... would be strenuously resisted by the universities on the basis ... of academic freedom.... There may be situations in respect of specific activities where it can fairly be said that the decision is that of the government....[39]

The same independence from government cannot be attributed to all postsecondary institutions, as was noted in *Douglas/Kwantlen Faculty Assn v Douglas College*.[40] In that case, the majority of the Supreme Court of Canada found that the college was a Crown agency established by the government to implement government policy. The actions of the college were, therefore, those of the government for the purposes of the *Charter*. The facts established that the government appointed and removed the board at pleasure, and that the government also may at all times by law direct its operation. The majority expressly noted that the college was quite unlike the universities, which managed their own affairs.

The *McKinney* decision has never sat well with many in academia and the legal profession. The decision has received much critical analysis.[41]

---

[39] *McKinney v University of Guelph* (1986), 57 OR (2d) 1, 32 DLR (4d) 65, (H Ct J), aff'd (1987), 63 OR (2d) 1, 46 DLR (4d) 193, aff'd [1990] 3 SCR 229 at 52, 53.

[40] *Douglas/Kwantlen Faculty Assn v Douglas College*, [1990] 3 SCR 570, 52 BCLR (2d) 68.

[41] Mix-Ross, "Exploring the Charter's Horizons"; Henderson, "Searching for 'Government Action'"; C. Jones, "Immunizing Universities."

Yet *McKinney* has, by and large, survived for over 20 years,[42] and appellate courts have continued to apply it.

In *Maughan v University of British Columbia*, the plaintiff claimed against the University of British Columbia and members of its staff for negligence and breaches of her civil rights in relation to a negative course assessment.[43] She alleged she had been discriminated against on the basis of her Christian religion. The British Columbia Court of Appeal rejected the claim, ruling that the *Charter* has no application as the university was not a government actor and therefore not subject to the *Charter*.

In *Lobo v Carleton University*, the plaintiffs, students of the defendant university, asserted that the defendants violated their *Charter* rights by failing to allocate space for a venue requested by the plaintiffs in order to express their social, moral, religious, or political views.[44] The Ontario Superior Court described *McKinney* as the "leading authority." The *Charter* claim was struck as it was found that when the university books space for non-academic use, it is not implementing a specific government policy or program. The Ontario Court of Appeal agreed.

The Ontario Superior Court in *AlGhaithy v University of Ottawa* also rejected the argument by a medical resident that his *Charter* right to freedom of expression had been violated when he was required to discontinue his residency.[45] The student was removed from the college due to concerns about his unprofessional and disruptive behaviour. The Court rejected his *Charter* challenge, noting:

> At issue ... is the University's decision to dismiss a student from an academic program because of unprofessional and disruptive conduct. The legislation governing the University provides that "the management, discipline and control of the University shall be free from restrictions and control of any outside body: ... Moreover, courts have long respected the autonomy of universities in academic matters...
>
> The University was not implementing a government program or policy nor exercising a power delegated by ... the College of Physicians and Surgeons of Ontario when it disciplined the applicant. Instead, the Appeals Committee was making a decision about an internal matter, the dismissal of a student for a violation of standards of academic conduct. Therefore, the Charter of Rights does not apply in the circumstances."[46]

---

[42] The decision in *McKinney* has been clarified somewhat by *Eldridge v British Columbia (AG)*, [1997] 3 SCR 624, 1997 CanLII 327, where the Supreme Court developed the test for determining if the *Charter* should apply to a private entity.

[43] *Maughan v University of British Columbia*, 2009 BCCA 447 [*Maughan*].

[44] *Lobo v Carleton University*, 2012 ONSC 254, aff'd 2012 ONCA 498.

[45] *AlGhaithy v University of Ottawa*, 2012 ONSC 142 [*AlGhaithy*].

[46] Ibid., para 76 and 79.

These decisions from Ontario and British Columbia stand in stark contrast to the Alberta Court of Appeal judgment in *Pridgen v University of Calgary*.[47] *Pridgen* involved students who were disciplined by the university for making negative comments about a professor on a social media site. The Alberta Court of Appeal ruled that universities must comply with the *Charter* when disciplining students pursuant to authority granted by legislation. The court relied heavily on the fact that non-academic discipline is expressly authorized by legislation and is not simply a private contractual dispute mechanism. Moreover, the court held that regulation of student speech in the context of non-academic misconduct is not merely an internal matter, but analogous to the regulation of expression by professional regulatory bodies, a context where the *Charter* has been applied in the past. The court further rejected the argument that the application of the *Charter* in these circumstances undermines the university's academic freedom or institutional autonomy. The following comment of the court, however, illustrates that the judges might not have ascribed much social utility to the traditional autonomy of universities: "One can no longer maintain a pastoral view of university campuses as a community of scholars removed from the rest of society."[48] The court provided no historical or factual basis to explain why universities should no longer be viewed as a community of scholars.

There are a number of difficulties with the *Pridgen* approach. From the perspective of precedent, it simply does not square with *McKinney* or the recent case law from other provinces. The judgment also purports to abandon the historic community of scholars model that treated universities as independent of government. Instead, the *Pridgen* approach appears to frame the university-student relationship as an adversarial relationship between the state and the student. University processes relating to students, however, continue to be operated by academics and administrators who remain independent of government. Thus, it is arguable that this attempted reframing of the university-student relationship is not adequate to capture its complex nature.

Pridgen will likely significantly increase the time and legal costs expended by universities on student litigation. In a *Charter* context, a student need only prove that his or her expression, for instance, has been limited in order to shift the burden to the university to prove that the expression could be justifiably limited under section 1 of the *Charter*. A university would arguably need to engage in a constitutional analysis every time a student is subject to discipline for speech or expressions that violate university policy. Indeed, the Alberta Court of Appeal in *Pridgen* suggested that the University of Calgary board of governors erred by

[47] *Pridgen v University of Calgary*, 2012 ABCA 139, 524 AR 251 [*Pridgen*].
[48] Ibid., 122.

not undertaking any *Charter* analysis.[49] Furthermore, if the decision in *Pridgen* was motivated by a judicial perception that universities can no longer be left to their own devices, stretching the scope of the *Charter* is likely unnecessary. As discussed below, the courts have in recent years exercised far more scrutiny over colleges and universities without resort to the *Charter*.

The Supreme Court of Canada will likely be called upon in coming years to consider this conflicting case law and decide whether the university-student relationship should be reframed as a relationship between the state and the student or whether it should remain a *sui generis* relationship within an independent and autonomous community of scholars.

Human Rights

Human rights legislation across Canada applies to higher education organizations, and it tends to prohibit discrimination based on prohibited grounds such as religion, creed, disability, family status, sex, and age. This legislation prohibits discrimination in all elements of the educational environment – even those elements that may appear neutral but that adversely affect a student on the basis of a prohibited ground.[50] Any academic requirement, qualification, policy, practice, service, or mode of teaching that adversely affects a student on the basis of a prohibited ground is likely to be considered *prima facie* discrimination.

Once *prima facie* discrimination is established, the onus then shifts to the institution to prove that the adverse treatment is reasonable and justifiable.[51] *Prima facie* discrimination will be considered reasonable and justified where (a) the educational element is rationally connected to the provision of the program, (b) the postsecondary institution has an honest and good faith belief that the educational element is necessary, and (c) the educational element is reasonably necessary to carry out the objectives of the institution.

In order for a higher education institution to justify an adverse treatment of a student on the basis of prohibited ground, the institution will have to establish that the student cannot be accommodated without undue hardship. The following factors are typically the most salient in

---

[49] Ibid., 127.

[50] An attempt to limit the application of human rights legislation in the university setting was rejected in *University of British Columbia v Berg*, [1993] 2 SCR 353, 79 BCLR (2d) 273.

[51] The general human rights law approach to assessing whether an adverse effect is reasonable and justifiable is set out in *Ontario Human Rights Commission v Etobicoke*, [1982] 1 SCR 202, 132 DLR (3d) 14; *British Columbia (Public Service Employee Relations Commission) v British Columbia Government Service Employees' Union*, [1999] 3 SCR 3, 66 BCLR (3d) 253.

assessing whether or not an accommodation would cause undue hardship to the institution: (a) financial cost, (b) interference with the rights of others, (c) health and safety, and (d) essential academic requirements or standards.

In the context of public postsecondary institutions, financial cost will rarely be a factor that justifies a refusal to accommodate.[52] It will, however, be undue hardship for the postsecondary institution to lower the academic bar in order to accommodate a student. While human rights law may expect the institution to modify the manner of teaching or evaluation,[53] the institution is not expected to lower academic standards or requirements. The student is still expected to meet the minimum academic standard.

For instance, in *Harris v Camosun College* the complainant, a student in the criminology program of the college, alleged that the college did not accommodate her multiple sensitivities to environmental elements such as paints.[54] The British Columbia Human Rights Tribunal found that it was reasonable and justifiable for the college to require that the complainant attend a course in person, because interaction with students was one of the essential elements of the course. The tribunal concluded that the complainant could not satisfy the goals and objectives of the program by having someone take notes in class for her, and that no other accommodation could be made without undermining one of the essential academic elements of the class.

Generally speaking, the postsecondary institution's duty to accommodate arises when the student identifies the need for the accommodation. While the institution has the responsibility to provide the accommodation, the duty to accommodate is a shared duty, meaning that the student must take reasonable steps to cooperate and facilitate the accommodation.[55] This duty entails accepting a reasonable accommodation even if the accommodation is not perfect or is not the accommodation preferred by the student.[56]

---

[52] For instance, see *Howard v University of British Columbia* (1993), 18 CHRR D/353 (BCCHR) – the tribunal found no evidence that expense of an interpreter for a deaf student would be anything other than a minor interference with the operations of the university.

[53] A typical accommodation in the academic environment could include more time to write exams: *Justice Institute of British Columbia v British Columbia* (1999), 17 Admin LR (3d) 267 (BCSC).

[54] *Harris v Camosun College* (2000), 39 CHRR D/36.

[55] *Williams v University of British Columbia*, 2007 BCSC 996, 2007 CarswellBC 1587 (WL Can).

[56] *Wang v Humber Institute of Technology and Advanced Learning*, 2011 HRTO 29 (CanLII)[*Wang*].

In the context of disabilities, there are rare cases where the nature of the disability (e.g., mental illness) may prevent the student from realizing the need for accommodation. Some human rights cases suggest that where the institution has reasonable notice that the individual is likely suffering from such a disability, the institution should take steps to attempt to accommodate the student.[57] Other cases in the higher education environment, however, have questioned whether a duty to accommodate arises in such a context, particularly if the student spurns attempts by the institution to reach out to the student.[58]

In disability cases, the institution is generally entitled to sufficient medical information to substantiate the need for accommodation and to determine the abilities and limitations of the student in order to structure the accommodation. The medical information received by the institution is confidential, and should be disclosed only to those in the institution who need the information to provide the accommodation.[59] If the student refuses to provide sufficient medical information, the institution will likely be relieved of any duty to accommodate.[60]

In the context of academic grade appeals or other academic appeals, if a student suggests that his or her poor performance was due to a disability, the academic committee likely cannot simply consider the academic performance of the student.[61] Rather, the committee may be required to apply human rights laws and assess the extent to which the disability impacted the academic performance. If academic performance was affected by the disability, the committee will need to consider whether appropriate accommodations were provided to the student.[62]

Religious accommodation is an emerging area of human rights law in the higher education context. Greater diversity in the student population has forced institutions to consider the degree to which diverse traditions,

---

[57] *Zaryski v Loftsgard* (1995), 22 CHRR D/256, 1995 CarswellSask 946 (WL Can) (Sask Bd Inq); *Re Okanagan College and Okanagan College Faculty Assn(Fu)* (2007), 171 LAC (4d) 310 (BC Arb Bdl).

[58] *Wang, supra* note 56.

[59] *Sotiropoulos v York University*, 2009 HRTO 2278 (CanLII).

[60] See e.g., *Dean v University of Victoria and another*, 2012 BCHRT 71; *Sotiropoulos v York University*, 2009 HRTO 2278. See *Tang v McMaster University*, 2014 HRTO 92 for a case where the medical information was provided, but it did not support the form of accommodation demanded by the student.

[61] The consideration of disability and human rights issues in academic appeals can become complicated in situations where a third party is involved, such as in work placement situations: *Machado v Vancouver College of Counsellor Training*, [2007] BCHRTD No 430 (QL).

[62] *Singh v University of British Columbia*, 2010 BCCA 485; *E v An Institution*, [2010] BCHRTD No 212 (QL); *Schnurr v Douglas College*, [2007] BCHRTD No 40; *Carson v University of Saskatchewan*, 2000 SKQB 322; but see *Mohamed, supra* note 19.

beliefs, and holidays can and should be accommodated. The case law indicates that this can be a divisive issue in higher education.[63]

Human rights issues have also arisen in the context of athletics.[64] In one case, a complaint was made that a university discriminated against women in the provision of public services, facilities, and education by providing less support, funding, and scholarships for a women's program relative to the men's program.[65]

Given the complexities of human rights law, many postsecondary institutions have adopted accommodation policies. These policies often involve specialized departments charged with receiving and reviewing confidential student medical information, and providing special expertise in structuring accommodations in the educational environment. These policies have an important institutional risk-management function, since there can be significant costs to the institution if accommodation cases are not administered properly.[66]

In addition to provincial human rights laws, international human rights conventions and covenants address higher education.[67] Even in situations where Canada has not formally ratified an international convention, it may still have persuasive impact in Canadian human rights cases.[68] More recently, the United Nations Declaration on the Rights of Indigenous Peoples has provided for significant human rights norms relating to education:

Article 14

1. Indigenous peoples have the right to establish and control their educational systems ... in a manner appropriate to their cultural methods of teaching and learning.

...

---

[63] See for example, *Noble v York University*, 2010 HRTO 878; *Gray v University of British Columbia-Okanagan Students' Union*, 2007 BCHRT 424.

[64] See, for instance, *University of New Brunswick v New Brunswick (Human Rights Commission)*, 2013 NBQB 148.

[65] *University of Saskatchewan v Women 2000*, 2005 SKQB 342, 267 Sask R 33.

[66] Particularly in the context of professional colleges where a failure to accommodate can result in a delayed career, see *Kelly v University of British Columbia*, 2013 BCHRT 302. Accommodation cases also can breed a multiplicity of proceedings: see *Baharloo v University of British Columbia*, 2014 BCSC 762.

[67] See Russo, "Reflections on Education," 87.

[68] *R v Keegstra*, [1990] 3 SCR 697, 77 Alta LR (2d) 193. See also La Forest, "Domestic Application on International Law in Charter Cases."

Article 15

1. Indigenous peoples have the right to the dignity and diversity of their cultures, traditions, histories and aspirations which shall be appropriately reflected in education.

...

Article 21

1. Indigenous peoples have the right, without discrimination, to the improvement of their economic and social conditions, including, inter alia, in the areas of education, employment, vocational training and retraining.

While the Canadian government initially resisted the UN Declaration, in November 2010 the Government of Canada issued a statement of support for the Declaration.[69] It is therefore likely that the Declaration will play a role in the development of educational policy in Canada and in future court cases involving Aboriginal rights and the education system.

Harassment

It has been suggested that the postsecondary institutional environment can be a breeding ground for harassment.[70] Canadian postsecondary institutions tend to address this potential hazard through policies that recognize the right of students to learn in a harassment-free environment.[71]

Harassment can include sexual harassment (which is prohibited by human rights legislation) or a pattern of other negative behaviours such as unwelcome jokes, slurs, gestures and solicitations to exclusion, physical abuse, and physical assault.[72] Harassment now often takes the form of "cyber" harassment (e.g., the use of social media, messaging, email) to

---

[69] Indian and Northern Affairs Canada, "Canada's Statement of Support."

[70] Dickerson, "Cyberbullies on Campus." See the Harassment Task Force of the Ontario Council of Regents in its *Report on Harassment and Discrimination in Ontario Colleges of Applied Arts and Technology* (May 1992), which described instances of harassment and discrimination that have been experienced at Ontario colleges.

[71] Major, "American Campus Speech Codes." The author references the argument that universities must provide an environment that is free of harassment and intimidation for all students so that they may devote their energies to their studies instead of responding to a hostile and threatening environment.

[72] Harassment can also occur in subtle, less overt ways, particularly in an imbalanced relationship like professor and student: *Dutton v British Columbia (Human Rights Tribunal)*, 2001 BCSC 1256.

carry out the harassing behaviour.[73] This form of harassment can be especially pernicious given that it allows for distance harassment and persistent maltreatment.

University and college harassment prevention policies often entail an investigative phase (which can involve the appointment of an external investigator) followed by a decision-making phase. In appropriate circumstances, the investigation can include consideration of both on-campus and off-campus maltreatment.[74] Serious or repeated harassment can be grounds for suspension or expulsion.[75]

The ability of educators to address harassment can be complicated to the extent that the *Charter* right to freedom of expression applies to postsecondary institutions.[76] In the United States, some universities have resorted to "speech codes" in an attempt to balance the First Amendment right to freedom of speech with the right to be free of harassment. The adoption of such speech codes in Canada has been suggested as a means to address the expanding application of the *Charter*.[77]

Privacy and Access to Information

In the 1990s, a number of provincial governments instituted freedom of information and protection of privacy statutes that apply to universities and colleges.[78] This legislation has two main purposes: (a) to provide the public with the right of access to records of public body to ensure openness and accountability, and (b) to protect the personal information of citizens (such as students) from unauthorized collection, use, or disclosure by public bodies.

In terms of the access to information, the Court of Appeal for Saskatchewan has suggested that the philosophy behind such legislation is that of full disclosure unless information is exempted under clearly delineated statutory language.[79] There tend to be many exemptions in these statutes.

---

[73] See Dickerson, "Cyberbullies on Campus"; Broster and Brien, "Cyber-Bullying of Educators by Students."

[74] *B and W et al*, 52 OR (2d) 738, 23 DLR (4d) 248 [*B and W*].

[75] Ibid.

[76] See Brosterand Brien, "Cyber-Bullying of Educators by Students"; *R v Whatcott*, 2012 ABQB 231; *R v Whatcott*, 2002 SKQB 399.

[77] See Major, "American Campus Speech Codes."

[78] See *Freedom of Information and Protection of Privacy Act*, RSO 1990, c F.31; *Freedom of Information and Protection of Privacy Act*, RSBC 1996, c 165; *The Local Freedom of Information and Protection of Privacy Act*, SS 1990-91, c L-27.1.

[79] *General Motors Acceptance Corp. of Canada v Saskatchewan Government Insurance*, 116 Sask R 36, [1994] 2 WWR 320 (CA).

The privacy provisions of these statutes are designed to protect privacy rights in the personal information held by public institutions and to provide individuals with a right of access to that information. The courts and privacy commissioners have referred to the privacy protections in public authority privacy statutes as "quasi-constitutional."[80]

Given the sometimes countervailing rights of access and privacy, a balancing analysis can be necessary to ensure that both the privacy and the openness objectives are met. Thus, the Alberta privacy commissioner ordered the University of Alberta to disclose to a student letters of reference submitted by third parties about the student.[81]

The application of federal privacy legislation to universities and colleges is a somewhat complicated question. Generally, the *Personal Information Protection and Electronic Documents Act* does not apply to the core activities of universities because universities are not engaged in trade and commerce.[82] A university, however, may become subject to *PIPEDA*, according to the Office of the Privacy Commissioner of Canada, when it engages in a non-core commercial activity, unless substantially similar provincial legislation applies.[83]

Intellectual Property

Students of universities and colleges will generally obtain intellectual property in the works, designs, creations, and inventions they create during their studies, barring special circumstances or special arrangements with the institution. Institutions and professors maybe liable for significant damages if a student's intellectual property rights are not respected.[84] In the complex student-institution relationship, however, intellectual property issues can be complicated.[85]

---

[80] See, for example, *Cash Converters Canada Inc v Oshawa (City)*, 2007 ONCA 502; *Lavigne v Canada (Office of the Commissioner of Official Languages)*, 2002 SCC 53, [2002] 2 SCR 773; Order F07-18; *University of British Columbia (Re)*, [2007] BCIPCD No 30 (QL).

[81] Order 2000-029; *University of Alberta (Re)*, [2001] AIPCD No 18 (QL).

[82] *Personal Information Protection and Electronic Documents Act*, SC 2000, c 5 [*PIPEDA*].

[83] See Fact Sheets, http://www.priv.gc.ca/resource/fs-fi/02_05_d_25_e.asp, where the federal commissioner suggests that *PIPEDA* would probably apply if a university sold or bartered an alumni list or personal information collected by a university in the course of operating a parking garage.

[84] *Boudreau v Lin*, 150 DLR (4d) 324, [1997] OJ No 3397(QL) (Ont Ct J Gen Div) [*Boudreau*]; *Dolmage v Erskine*, 23 CPR (4d) 495, [2003] OJ No 161 (QL) (Ont Sup Ct J) at para 176 [*Dolmage*].

[85] For a thorough discussion of these issues, see Monotti and Ricketson, *Universities and Intellectual Property*.

In some postgraduate scenarios, a student is both a student and an employee of the institution. Different intellectual property rules can apply to intellectual property developed during the course of employment.

Furthermore, the same research project could create multiple kinds of intellectual property. The project could result in a process that is capable of patent protection. The research data might be subject to copyright legislation and confidentiality law or provisions in contracts relating to the project.

Matters can also be complicated by the nature of the research project. Since research is often done in teams, it is quite possible that many students, faculty, and non-academic lab staff will have an interest in the intellectual property, which may result in an overlap of student and employment considerations.[86] If a research sponsor is involved, the sponsorship agreement may address intellectual property and research data issues. Some sponsors may claim licensing rights or a share of royalties.[87]

The unique aspects of the student-institution relationship may also have an important role in defining intellectual property rights in the academic setting. For instance, one court has ruled that the nature of the academic supervisor-postgraduate relationship gives rise to a fiduciary duty on academic supervisors in relation to the dissertation ideas and projects of postgraduate students.[88] It has also been suggested that academic conventions may result in an expansion of the rights that intellectual property laws would otherwise offer. For instance, it has been suggested in one case that an academic convention respecting the acknowledgement of student contribution to a faculty member's paper may result in greater intellectual property rights than would otherwise be provided by the law.[89] The compensation awarded to students may also be impacted by the unique circumstances of students. For example, where a faculty member fails to attribute an academic paper to the student who wrote it, damages may include an amount to reflect the lost opportunity for the student to include the reference in his or her resume.[90]

Intellectual property issues can be confused with scholarly integrity considerations. While there can be, for instance, overlap between copyright infringement and plagiarism, the concepts and standards are quite distinct. Furthermore, where a complaint of scholarly misconduct is investigated and dismissed by the institution, the complainant student will

---

[86] For example, see *A.U.P.E. v University of Calgary*, [2008] Alta LRBR 129 at paras 82, 83, and 214.

[87] Ibid., para 195.

[88] *Plews v Pausch*, 2006 ABQB 607 at para 86.

[89] Ibid, para 90.

[90] *Boudreau, supra* note 84; *Dolmage, supra* note 84 at para 176.

not likely be barred from subsequently proceeding with an intellectual property lawsuit based on the same circumstances.[91]

Universities and colleges may seek to include intellectual property provisions in institutional admissions documents or policies in attempt to clarify property rights in the event of a dispute.[92] With respect to Australia, United Kingdom, and the United States, Monotti and Ricketson identified three discernible models followed by higher education institutions: universities (a) make no express claim to intellectual property subject to individual agreements; (b) claim ownership of intellectual property created by the student in specific categories of circumstances; or (c) claim ownership of all intellectual property created during studies or while using university resources.[93]

While it would likely be difficult to find a Canadian university applying the third model, institutions in Canada have taken varying approaches relating to the commercial potential of intellectual property created from the use of university resources.[94] In some situations, institutional policy may require students and faculty to sign agreements assigning intellectual property rights to the university and setting out royalty-sharing arrangements. Other institutions take the opposite approach, vesting ownership of intellectual property in the creators rather than the institution.

Residence

Student residences are a unique form of housing. In some jurisdictions, campus residences are exempted in whole or part from residential tenancies legislation in light of this unique and temporary tenancy. Significant issues can arise if urban zoning requirements are not adequately observed in relation to off-campus residences.[95] The courts have recognized university-operated residences as part and parcel of the educational mission of the institution. As such, campus residences have been granted the same tax-exempt status enjoyed by the institution's educational buildings.[96] Privacy laws governing colleges and universities will also generally apply to institution-operated residences. A search of a student

---

[91] *Rothery v Grinnell* (2000), 262 AR 182 (QB).

[92] Monotti and Ricketson, *Universities and Intellectual Property*, 110–12.

[93] Ibid., 315–20.

[94] For a contrast see the institutional approaches discussed in *A.U.P.E, supra* note 86 at paras 82 and 214, and *University of British Columbia Faculty Assn v University of British Columbia* (2004), 125 LAC (4d) 1 at paras 16–18.

[95] *The Neighbourhoods of Winfields Limited Partnership v Death*, 2009 ONCA 277; Potts, "Universities and Housing."

[96] *Acadia University v Wolfville (Town)* (1971), 2 NSR (2d) 630, 29 DLR (3d) 441 (CA); *University of Waterloo v Ontario (Minister of Finance)*, [2002] 166 OAC 262 (CA).

residence by campus officials resulted in *Charter* issues in subsequent criminal proceedings.[97]

STUDENT DISCIPLINE (ACADEMIC AND NON-ACADEMIC)

Student Discipline and Judicial Deference

The courts have consistently maintained that colleges and universities are free to develop their own academic standards, requirements, and curricula and to confer degrees without interference from the courts.[98] Similarly, the courts have recognized these institutions' authority to take necessary remedial actions when their academic requirements and standards have not been met,[99] provided that they follow their established processes[100] and the fundamental elements of procedural fairness. Similarly, it has been suggested that the standards for the assessment of a student's work are so firmly vested with the university that "the courts have no power to intervene merely because it is thought that the standards are too high, or that the student's work was inaccurately assessed, in the absence of a

---

[97] Rigakos and Greener, "Bubbles of Governance"; *R v Fegan* (1993), 80 CCC (3d) 356 at 365.

[98] *Houston v University of Saskatchewan* (Joint Senate-Council Board of Student Appeals), 1994 CanLII 4898 (SKQB) [*Houston*].

[99] The principle of judicial deference to postsecondary institutions' academic decisions is well established in Canadian jurisprudence, and has been reaffirmed in numerous cases since the 1970s: *Harelkin v University of Regina*, [1979] 2 SCR 561, [1979] 3 WWR 676 [*Harelkin*], aff'g [1979] 3 WWR 673 (Sask CA), rev'g [1977] 3 WWR 754, 74 DLR (3d) 537 (Sask QB); *Morgan, supra* note 31; *Bancroft v University of Toronto* (1986), 53 OR (2d) 460, 24 DLR (4d) 620 (H Ct J); *Lavoie v University of Ottawa*(1986), 55 OR (2d) 28, 27 DLR (4d) 763 (H Ct J); *Aylward v McMaster University* (1991), 79 DLR (4d) 119 (Ont Ct J (Gen Div)); *Archer v Université de Moncton* (1992), 129 NBR (2d) 289 (QB); *Wong, supra* note 27; *Dawson v The University of Ottawa* (1994), 72 OAC 232 (Ont Div Ct); *Baxter v Memorial University of Newfoundland*, 166 Nfld & PEIR 183, [1998] NJ No 222 (QL) (SC(TD)) [*Baxter*]; *O'Reilly v Memorial University of Newfoundland*, 166 Nfld & PEIR 327, 1998 CarswellNfld 200 (WL Can) (SC(TD)); *Hayat v University of Toronto*, 181 DLR (4d) 496, [1999] OJ No 4238 (QL) (ONCA); *Carson v University of Saskatchewan*, 2000 SKQB 322, 196 Sask R [*Carson*]; *Dhillon v University of Alberta (General Facilities Council Academic Appeals Committee)*, 2000 ABQB 77, 81 Alta LR (3d) 65; *Mohl v University of British Columbia*, 2000 BCSC 1849, [2000] BCJ No 2572 (QL) [*Mohl*]; *Rittenhouse-Carlson, supra* note 26; *Pacheco v Dalhousie University*, 2005 NSSC 222, 238 NSR (2d) 1 [*Pacheco*]; *Bikey v University of Saskatchewan*, 2009 SKQB 340; *Hazanavicius, supra* note 26; *Mulligan v Laurentian University*, 2008 ONCA 523 [*Mulligan*]; *Deng v University of Toronto*, 2011 ONSC 835 [*Deng*].

[100] This can be done through the use of informal procedures where formal procedures do not exist; see *Koh-Adelman v University of Saskatchewan*, 2000 SKQB 303, 197 Sask R 103.

denial of natural justice."[101] When, however, the college or university is carrying out a statutory duty, the courts will employ administrative law principles in reviewing the exercise of such statutory duties, as has been routinely done in the context of student discipline.[102]

The reason for deference in academic matters was outlined in *Blasser v Royal Institute for the Advancement of Learning et al*.[103] In this case the court stated that

> in any university ... there are certain internal matters and disputes that are best decided within the academic community rather than by the courts. This is so, not only because the courts are not as well equipped as the university to decide matters such as academic qualifications, grades, and conferring of degrees and so on, but also because these matters ought to be able to be decided more conveniently, more quickly and at least as accurately by those who are specialized in educational questions of that kind. In addition, of course, there is every good reason not to risk compromising the essential independence of the universities by undue interference in their academic affairs.[104]

The courts have traditionally deferred to colleges and universities even in the area of process. The application of administrative law principles in the context of student discipline tends to involve the requirement of fair process before unbiased decision makers.[105] In *Harelkin v University of Regina*, the Supreme Court of Canada characterized the internal university processes as a domestic code that is intended to be applied by laymen rather than by lawyers.[106] While institutions are expected to follow the principles of procedural fairness set out in administrative law,[107] the Supreme Court has called it a duty of the courts to attribute a large measure of autonomy to university tribunals in respect to process.[108]

---

[101] *Yen v Alberta (Advanced Education)*, 2010 ABQB 380 at 44; *Re Polten, supra* note 24 at 206 [*Yen*].

[102] *King, supra* note 35. This approach has also been followed in regard to private schools: Brown, "Are Private Schools Really Private?"

[103] *Blasser v Royal Institute for the Advancement of Learning et al* (1985), 24 DLR (4d) 507 (Qc CA).

[104] Ibid., 515.

[105] Hamilton, "Lessons Still to Be Learned."

[106] *Harelkin, supra* note 99.

[107] *Baker v Canada (Ministry of Citizenship and Immigration)*, [1999] 2 SCR 817 [*Baker*]; Hamilton, "Lessons Still to Be Learned."

[108] In *Kane, supra* note 38, the Court stated that university tribunals need not assume the trappings of a court. It is sufficient that that they follow a judicial spirit. It has been suggested in some cases, that "manifest unfairness" or flagrant abuse of natural justice must be established before the courts should intervene. See *Yen, supra* note 101 at 42.

Some courts have suggested that no deference should be afforded to process decisions made by colleges and universities where the discipline could involve serious consequences for the student and where no academic judgment is employed.[109] On the other hand, other recent cases have afforded the highest level of judicial deference to cases of non-academic discipline.[110]

Under modern administrative law principles, judicial review is not necessarily limited to review of process. In some recent judgments, the courts have reviewed the substance of a student disciplinary decision, albeit with considerable deference.[111] The recent case law has generally indicated that the courts will not overturn a discipline decision unless the decision was unreasonable. The reasonableness standard also applies when the severity of the penalty is in question.[112] In reviewing the "reasonableness" of a disciplinary decision, the court does not consider whether the decision is right or wrong. Rather, a reasonable decision is one that demonstrates justification, transparency, and intelligibility within the decision-making process, and that falls within a range of possible, acceptable outcomes that are defensible in respect of the facts and law.[113]

Interestingly, even the substance of *academic* decisions has been the subject of a reasonableness review in recent decisions.[114] These judgments stand in contrast to cases that indicate academic judgment should never be the subject of judicial review.[115] That said, in extraordinary cases where there have been serious breaches of fairness, delays in an institution's internal decision-making processes, or concerns that internal decision-making bodies may be biased, the courts have occasionally taken a more interventionist approach and imposed substantive decisions upon universities.[116] Furthermore, the courts will address the substance of the

---

[109] *Zeliony v Red River College*, 2007 MBQB 308 [*Zeliony*].

[110] *Pacheco, supra* note 99.

[111] *SDL v University of Alberta*, 2012 ABQB 244, 531 AR 218; *Alsaigh v University of Ottawa*, 2012 ONSC 2313 [*Alsaigh*]; *Singh v University of British Columbia*, 2010 BCCA 485 [*Singh*].

[112] See *Lalani v University of Toronto*, 2014 ONSC 644 at para 4 where the court describes the issue of the proper sanction as going to the core of the academic function and internal governance.

[113] *Pridgen, supra* note 47; *Alsaigh, supra* note 111. See *Dunsmuir v New Brunswick*, [2008] 1 SCR 190 for a detailed description of the "reasonableness standard."

[114] *Alsaigh, supra* note 111; *Singh, supra* note 111.

[115] *Houston, supra* note 98; *Yen, supra* note 101.

[116] *Al-Bakkal v De Vries*, 2003 MBQB 198, 176 Man R (2d) 127; *Healey v Memorial University of Newfoundland* (1993), 106 Nfld & PEIR 304, 14 Admin LR (2d) 259 (Nfld SC(TD)); *Handa v University of Ottawa*, [2008] OJ No 2589 (QL) (Ont Sup Ct J); *Mikkelsen v University of Saskatchewan*, 2000 SKQB 45, 191 Sask R 53 [*Mikkelsen*].

disciplinary decision when a disciplinary committee purports to decide offences outside its jurisdiction.[117]

Issues of deference and jurisdiction can also arise in postgraduate discipline situations where the program involves both an academic and an employment role for the student. In *University of Saskatchewan v Professional Association of Interns and Residents of Saskatchewan*, the Saskatchewan Court of Appeal ruled that a trade union representing residents could not grieve questions related to the discipline of residents and academic appeals, and that the trade union's role was limited to addressing non-academic terms and conditions of employment, such as rates of pay and hours of work.[118]

The courts have also identified the discipline of students for non-academic misconduct as a right that universities must have in order to fulfill the institutional duty to protect members of the university community.[119] The discipline process can extend to off-campus conduct if that conduct can reasonably be seen as having an adverse effect on the ability of others to use and enjoy the university's learning and working environment.[120]

Student discipline issues can become complicated when the student's misconduct is related to a mental illness. Generally speaking, the courts have recognized that institutions must have the right to address misconduct in order to protect the campus community.[121] However, the disciplinary process needs to take into account the illness, and perhaps be accompanied by efforts to encourage the student to seek help.[122]

Procedural Fairness

One of the key provisions of administrative law is that the decisions of college and university decision-making bodies can be reviewed by the courts if they exceed their jurisdiction,[123] for example by violating the

---

[117] For instance, where the committee purports to decide if the student violated laws external to the university, such as criminal or quasi-criminal statutory offences: *Morgan, supra* note 31.

[118] *University of Saskatchewan v Professional Association of Interns and Residents of Saskatchewan*, 2002 SKCA 75, 219 Sask R 244.

[119] *Frederick Zhang v University of Western Ontario*, 2010 ONSC 6489 [*Zhang*]; *Pacheco, supra* note 99; *Kobilke v Phillips*, 2004 CanLII 7914 (Ont Sup Ct J) [*Kobilke*].

[120] See for instance, *Zhang, supra* note 119.

[121] *Pacheco, supra* note 99; *Kobilke, supra* note 119.

[122] *Pacheco, supra* note 99; *Carson, supra* note 99. But see *Mohamed, supra* note 19 where the court provided reasons why a discipline committee addressing academic dishonesty should not be required to assess psychological reasons for the behaviour.

[123] Including, in some cases, private college decision-making bodies; see *C(D) (Litigation Guardian of) v Ridley College*, 138 DLR (4d) 176, 1996 CarswellOnt 2932 (WL Can) (Ont Ct J (Gen Div)).

principles of *procedural fairness*. The process by which these decisions can be reviewed by the courts is referred to as *judicial review*. While it is well established that the courts have, and will exercise the right to review college and university administrative decisions affecting students, they generally will not do so unless and until students have exhausted all of the internal decision-making options available to them.[124]

Procedural fairness comprises two fundamental components. The first is *Audi Alteram Partem* (let the other side be heard), which "incorporates the notion of notice of any proceedings, notice of the case to be met and an opportunity to be heard and to respond."[125] The second component is *Nemo Judex in Causa Sua* (no one can be a judge in his own cause), which simply states that a decision-maker must be free from interest or bias in the decision to be made.

The Right to be Heard and to Respond

The first key element of procedural fairness is that a person who is the subject of a decision-making process has a right to be heard and to respond to the matter before the decision-making body. In practice, the "right to be heard" requires that an institutional decision-making body ensures that certain procedural protections are provided to the student whose case is being considered, as described below.

Notice. A student must be provided with adequate notice that a matter affecting his or her rights or interests will be considered by a decision-making body. Notice should be provided to the student in writing, and should generally

- specify the issue or allegation that is being considered,
- provide basic information regarding the case against the student,
- include a copy of any institutional policies or regulations that are relevant to the case, and
- indicate the possible consequences or sanctions that could result from the case.

Most importantly, sufficient notice must be provided to enable the student to prepare an adequate response. The notice should clearly identify the date, time, and location of any hearing that may be taking place, specify what additional actions, if any, the student is required to take, indicate the consequences if no response is received or if the student fails to show up for a hearing, and provide the name and contact information of the

---

[124] See for instance, *Harelkin, supra* note 99; *Rittenhouse-Carlson, supra* note 26.
[125] Devine, "Fair Procedures," 4.

person(s) to contact should the student have any questions or require additional information. Reasonable efforts should be made to ensure the notice is received by the student.[126]

Discipline policies tend to include time limits within which the notice of proceedings must be brought. Delay can undermine disciplinary proceedings.[127]

Knowledge of the Case to Be Met. In order to adequately respond, a student has the right to know the issues or "charges" that the decision-making body will be considering and the specific details of the case against him or her. The student should be provided copies of *any and all* relevant evidence that will be considered by the decision-making body in making its decision (including any written complaints, memos, letters, reports, and witness statements).

Right to Respond. Perhaps the most important right a student has is the right to respond to the case against him or her through some form of hearing. Depending on the seriousness of the matter being considered and the consequences of the decision to the student, the hearing may take a number of different forms ranging from providing written submissions to a decision-maker, to being present and making submissions while a decision-maker is deliberating,[128] to participating in round table discussions with a decision-maker and other parties, to having a full oral hearing. Oral hearings are not required in all administrative decision-making processes, particularly in cases where the issues being decided upon and their consequences are relatively minor.[129] However, oral hearings are generally recommended in cases where the matters being considered and their potential consequences are more serious, where issues are more disciplinary (as opposed to academic) in nature, where "special circumstances" arise that might warrant an oral hearing, and especially where issues of fact or credibility are in question.[130]

---

[126] Such as sending the notice via registered mail to the student's address in official records or sending a copy to the student's official email address, depending on the institution's email policy.

[127] However, even where an institution has tolerated the problems for some time, the institution may still be in a position to bring disciplinary proceedings if appropriate notice is given: *Al-Nowais v McGill University (Faculty of Medicine)*, 2013 QCCS 4559.

[128] See, for example, *Driver v Sault College of Applied Arts & Technology* (2008), 165 ACWS (3d) 91, 2008 CarswellOnt 1374 (WL Can) (Ont Sup Ct J (Div Ct)).

[129] *Re Polten, supra* note 24; *Baxter, supra* note 99; *Baker, supra* note 107; *Mikkelsen, supra* note 116.

[130] *Carson, supra* note 99; Jones and de Villars, *Principles of Administrative Law*, 5th ed.; *Khan v University of Ottawa* (1997), 34 OR (3d) 535, 148 DLR (4d) 577;

Normally, non-academic misconduct proceedings are initiated by a complaint or charge against a student who has allegedly violated the institution's student code of conduct, followed by some form of hearing (oral or otherwise) before a decision-maker (a person or body). A decision regarding guilt or innocence is made, and if guilt is found, an appropriate sanction is imposed. In emergency situations, it is possible and advisable for an institution to act without providing a hearing, especially if there is a risk to the safety or well-being of the subject student, other students, members of the university community, or the public – provided that an opportunity for a hearing is provided within a reasonable time afterwards.[131] Readers are encouraged to check their institution's founding statute and non-academic misconduct policy, and consult with their legal counsel, to confirm how to respond to emergency situations.

Right to Present Witnesses and Evidence. When an oral hearing is held, a student has a right to present evidence and call witnesses. Because a college or university hearing is not a court of law, the formal rules of evidence that apply within the courtroom setting do not apply. These bodies are therefore free to consider any evidence relevant to the case and to determine how much weight to attach to that evidence. They can even hear and consider hearsay evidence if, in their judgment, it is relevant to the issues at hand.[132]

Right to Cross-Examine. While the courts have occasionally upheld institutional decisions where the right to cross-examine was denied, most authorities suggest that if an oral hearing is provided, cross-examination should be permitted.[133] This is especially true if the evidence is controversial, if the credibility of witnesses is an issue, or if the potential consequences of the case are serious.[134]

Ghafourian v The Governing Council of the University of Toronto, 2010 HRTO 675.

[131] For example, an institution may restrict or suspend a student with the understanding that an appropriate hearing will follow such action in a timely manner.

[132] Overreliance on hearsay or weak evidence, however, can affect the reasonableness of the decision.

[133] *Ching v University of Windsor* (1984), 3 OAC 228 (Div Ct); *B and W, supra* note 74; *York University General Accountant v Bloxam* (1984), 15 Admin LR 51, 1984 CarswellOnt 779 (WL Can) (Ont Sm Cl Ct); *Re McInnes and Simon Fraser University* (1983), 52 BCLR 26, 3 DLR (4d) 708 (CA); *AlGhaithy, supra* note 45.

[134] See, for example, *Hajee v York University* (1985), 11 OAC 72, [1985] OJ No 1308 (QL) (Ont Div Ct). See also Jones and de Villars, *Principles of Administrative Law*, 5th ed., 304: "In a disciplinary hearing, where someone's reputation and livelihood is at stake, or where issues of credibility arise, the right to cross-examination will usually be present."

If the student does not request to cross-examine a witness, the student may not have a right to complain after the fact.[135]

Members of the decision-making body are often permitted to ask questions of any of the parties or of any witnesses they call in support of their case.[136]

Right to Counsel. There is no absolute right to counsel in academic or non-academic decision-making processes, especially when a decision-making body is dealing with simple or minor matters whose potential consequences are modest in nature.[137] It is advisable in more serious cases that a student accused of academic or non-academic misconduct be provided with the right to be represented by counsel.[138] Where counsel is permitted, it need not always be legal counsel; many institutions have provisions for students to be supported and/or represented by an "advocate," who could be another student, a member of the institution's student affairs staff, or even a parent.

If one party is granted the right to counsel, the other party should be offered the same right. This right may be waived, provided the parties are made fully aware "of the seriousness of the proceeding and its potential outcome."[139]

Onus and Standard of Proof. Members of administrative decision-making bodies must understand that the onus of proof is always on those who have filed a complaint, made an allegation of misconduct, or laid a charge against a student, and *not* on the student defendant (i.e., an accused student must be considered "innocent until proven guilty"). The standard of proof that must normally be met in academic and non-academic administrative hearings is the "balance of probabilities" standard, *not* the criminal standard of "beyond a reasonable doubt."[140] Generally speaking, the "balance of probabilities" standard is met if it has been proven that the alleged facts probably occurred. That said, what constitutes "the balance of probabilities" depends to some extent on the circumstances of each

---

[135] *Deng, supra* note 99.

[136] Care needs to be taken when the tribunal members ask questions to avoid creating an appearance of bias.

[137] Jones and de Villars, *Principles of Administrative Law*, 5th ed.

[138] See Blake, *Administrative Law in Canada*, 48. In some cases, "adequate presentation may require the expertise of a lawyer, particularly if the issues are complex," if the allegations or consequences are very serious, or at the final level of appeal in a multilevel decision-making process.

[139] Ibid., 50.

[140] Unless the "beyond a reasonable doubt" standard is stipulated in institutional policy; see *Khan v University of Toronto*, 130 DLR (4d) 570, 87 OAC 204 (Ont Ct J(Gen Div)).

case, and includes such things as "the nature of the facts to be proved, the seriousness of the allegations, and the gravity of the consequences that will flow from a particular finding."[141]

Who Hears, Decides. It is important that an institution's academic and non-academic misconduct policies and procedures clearly specify who is responsible for making decisions regarding allegations of misconduct (i.e., an identified person or position, a hearing board) and the process by which they do so. In cases where such decisions are made by a panel or hearing board, policies should indicate who the "voting" members are and what the quorum is for such panels or boards. So long as quorum is maintained, the hearing process can continue, but if quorum is lost, the hearing must be adjourned and reconvened at a time when quorum can again be met. It is also critical that the membership in a panel or hearing board remains consistent throughout the entire hearing, especially when the hearing spans multiple sessions, and that *only* those members who have attended for the entire duration of a hearing participate in the hearing board's decision. Finally, it is essential that no *ex parte* discussions, private interviews, or extraneous evidence that was not presented at the hearing, and that the accused student did not have an opportunity to respond to, are considered by the panel or board in making its decision.[142]

Level of Procedural Protections Required. There is no universal or standard set of hearing processes that must be followed in all cases. Rather, the requirements of procedural fairness are quite flexible, and the type and level of procedural protections that should be provided will vary depending on the circumstances of each case. Formal, trial-like, adversarial procedures are not required in most cases.[143] Generally speaking, the more "judicial" the decision and the more serious the alleged violation and the potential consequences of a decision, the greater the procedural protections required.[144] Similarly, the higher and more "final" the level of the decision-making body, or in cases where no meaningful right of appeal is available, the better argument there will be for greater procedural protections. Finally, at least one case suggests that the level of procedural

---

[141] Blake, *Administrative Law in Canada,* 69. In Ontario, some courts have suggested that if the discipline has consequences for the student's professional career (e.g., in a residency or practicum), the standard of "clear, convincing and cogent evidence" must be met; *Deng, supra* note 99.

[142]*Kane, supra* note 38; *Mohl, supra* note 99.

[143] See comments by Dickinson, "A Criminal Trial by Any Other Name," 149–54 on *Khan,* where he points out that institutions with highly legalistic adjudicatory processes may be held to higher procedural standards by the courts.

[144]See, for example, *Zeliony, supra* note 109.

fairness required in private educational institutions may be less than that required in public institutions.[145]

If a student is not satisfied with the level of process offered, the student is well-advised to make this objection known at the time. If a timely objection to the process is not made, the student may lose the ability to the challenge the process later in court.[146]

Right to an Unbiased Decision Maker

Reasonable Apprehension of Bias. The second key element of procedural fairness is that the decision maker must be free of the reasonable apprehension of bias. Put simply, the principle requires that any person involved in making a judgment or decision affecting the rights of another person be free from any personal involvement or interest in the matters to be decided that would give rise to a perception in the mind of a reasonable person that the decision maker would not likely decide the matter fairly. Any form of pecuniary interest in the outcome of a student academic or non-academic administrative process would almost certainly disqualify someone from participating in a decision on the matter. Similarly, "a close personal relationship with someone who has a direct interest in the outcome of [a] decision … will give rise to a reasonable apprehension of bias," and such relationship will disqualify a decision maker from taking part in the decision.[147] Thus, it is important that decision makers not participate in cases involving relatives, friends, close colleagues, or associates.[148] Finally, decision makers must "not hold strong, predetermined views regardless of the merits of a case" or prejudge a case before hearing it.[149] The key point here is that a decision maker must be "perceived to be able to address his or her mind openly to the questions at hand" and open to persuasion based on the facts of the case.[150]

It should be pointed out that under Canadian administrative law, it is not necessary to prove *actual* bias to establish that the rules of natural justice have been breached. Rather, the appearance or "reasonable apprehension" of bias is considered sufficient cause to void a tribunal's decision and make it subject to judicial review.[151] The test for bias requires that

---

[145] *Lisyikh v Canadian Law Enforcement Training College*, [2007] OJ No 3621 (QL) (Ont SCJ) at 40.

[146] *Lana v University of Alberta*, 2013 ABCA 327, 91 Alta LR (5d) 250.

[147] Jones and de Villars, *Principles of Administrative Law*, 5th ed., 408.

[148] Blake, *Administrative Law in Canada*, 69.

[149] Ibid., 110.

[150] Jones and de Villars, *Principles of Administrative Law*, 2nd ed., 47.

[151] Jones and de Villars, *Principles of Administrative Law*, 5th ed., 398–99.

the apprehension of bias must be a reasonable one, held by reasonable and right minded persons, applying themselves to the question and obtaining thereon the required information.... That test is "what would an informed person, viewing the matter realistically and practically – and having thought the matter through – conclude. Would he think that it is more likely than not that [the decision maker], whether consciously or unconsciously, would not decide fairly."[152]

In other words, justice should not only be done, but also be seen to have been done. The existence, or even the appearance (i.e., reasonable apprehension), of bias on the part of a decision maker will almost certainly result in justice being seen *not* to be done, which constitutes a violation of the fundamental principles of procedural fairness.

It is within a tribunal's discretion to rule on any allegations of bias when they arise, and the burden of proof is upon the student alleging bias to prove that the decision maker will likely not decide the matter fairly.[153] If the student raises no concerns about the potential bias of members of a decision-making body, the student may be considered to have waived any objections to those members' participation in the hearing, particularly if the student is asked at the start of the hearing if he or she has any objections.[154] Conversely, if concerns of bias are raised and a decision-making body finds that a member is biased, that member should be removed from or replaced on the body. If the whole panel is biased, it should be replaced by another panel. However, if the decision-making body deals with the allegations seriously and in good faith and finds no bias, it is free to continue with its proceedings.

Overlapping Membership. In some cases, bias may also be held to exist where there is overlapping membership on various levels of multitiered decision-making processes, or where there is a reasonable possibility that an appeal body is unlikely to overturn the decision of a lower-level body, even if there is no duplication of membership among the two bodies. In particular, bias may be seen to exist in instances where individuals participate in an appeal of a decision that they were involved in making initially. As Dickinson and Lewis point out, this rule has significant implications for decision-making in colleges and universities, where overlapping membership on various decision-making bodies is common. Generally speaking, colleges and universities should try wherever possible to avoid

---

[152] *Committee for Justice and Liberty v Canada (National Energy Board)*, [1978] 1 SCR 369 at 394–95, 68 DLR (3d) 716; and see Blake, *Administrative Law in Canada*, 101.

[153] *Dickson v Canadore College*, 287 DLR (4d) 570, [2007] OJ No 4125 (QL) (Ont Sup Ct J (Div Ct)) [*Dickson*]; and Blake, *Administrative Law in Canada*, 114.

[154] *Dickson, supra* note 153.

having individuals involved in various levels of multitiered decision-making processes. That said, the courts have historically recognized the unique nature and structure of decision-making in academic institutions, and have generally been willing to defer to those institutions, at least so far as prior involvement in a case or cross-membership on institutional decision-making bodies is concerned.[155]

Other Considerations regarding College and University Disciplinary Processes

There are several additional points that should be kept in mind regarding academic and non-academic disciplinary processes in postsecondary institutions. One is whether a college or university has the authority to deal with misconduct that is subject to ongoing criminal proceedings. It is true that postsecondary institutions have no authority to enforce the provisions of the Criminal Code or to initiate discipline simply on the basis of an alleged Criminal Code violation.[156] The institution, however, does have the jurisdiction to enforce its own internal non-academic standard of conduct, as outlined in its code of student conduct or other, similar policy.[157] Institutions that do not have a well-defined code of conduct or similar policy will have a more difficult time dealing with students' non-academic offences than those that do.[158]

There is no rule that discipline proceedings must be held in public.[159] The question may depend somewhat on the provincial public authority privacy legislation. It is important that the actual deliberations and decision-making of the tribunal or hearing board members be held "in camera" to ensure that members are able to discuss all aspects of the case fully and openly. Notes should be taken of both the hearing and the decision-makers' deliberations. The notes and the substance of the deliberations must be treated as confidential by the participants.

Once the tribunal or hearing board has reached its decision, it is very important that the decision *and the supporting reasons for that decision* be documented and communicated to the parties in the case. The Supreme Court of Canada has ruled that there is a common-law duty to provide reasons for a decision when the issue is one of significant importance to

---

[155] *King, supra* note 35; Lewis, "The Legal Nature of a University"; Dickinson, "A Criminal Trial by Any Other Name"; *Dickson, supra* note 153.

[156] *Mpega v University of Moncton*, 2001 NBCA 78, 240 NBR (2d) 349.

[157] *SDL v University of Alberta*, 2012 ABQB 244.

[158] The *Charter* and issues regarding the applicability (or non-applicability) of protections in the evidence legislation from self-incrimination may also arise in the context of university discipline cases.

[159] Jones and de Villars, *Principles of Administrative Law*, 5th ed., 312.

the individual.[160] There is no set format that the description of reasons must follow provided that the tribunal or hearing board explains to the parties why it reached the conclusion(s) and made the decision(s) that it did. According to Blake:

> Reasons should state the findings of fact that support the conclusions and identify the evidence on which they are based. The rejection of important items of evidence and findings of credibility should be explained. If an application is dismissed by reason of insufficient evidence, the material deficiencies in the evidence should be identified…. If several incidents of misconduct were alleged in the notice of hearing the reasons for decision should identify which incidents are proven and the reasons for the disciplinary order.[161]

While tribunal decisions may be provided to the parties orally, it is generally advised that they be given in writing, particularly in cases where the nature of the issue and the consequences of the proceeding are more serious. Finally, when communicating the decision to the parties, the tribunal or hearing board should inform them as to whether the decision is appealable and the process for initiating the appeal.

Institutional Liability

Colleges and universities are exposed to various kinds of institutional liability given their multifarious activities and roles. There are many cases where postsecondary institutions have been sued in contract and/or tort.

The Supreme Court of Canada has recognized that the contractual relationship between fee-paying students and colleges and universities gives rise to a tort law duty of care imposed on institutions to take reasonable steps to protect students from harm.[162] In *Young v Bella*, the Supreme Court of Canada dealt with a student who had been wrongly identified by faculty as a child abuser.[163] The Court held that the university owed both contractual duties *and* a tort law duty of care to students as fee-paying members of the university community. The Court noted that the tort duty is reflective of the special relationship and power imbalance between a university and a student, with the university exercising power over the careers and future lives of fee-paying students.

---

[160] *Baker, supra* note 107. In the postsecondary context, see *Dunne v Memorial University of Newfoundland*, 2012 NLTD(G) 41, 321 Nfld & PEIR 342; *Lerew v The St. Lawrence College of Applied Arts and Technology*, 196 OAC 363, [2005]OJ No 1436 (QL) (Sup Ct J(Div Ct)); *Zeliony, supra* note 109.

[161] Blake, *Principles of Administrative Law*, 90.

[162] *Young v Bella*, 2006 SCC 3, [2006] 1 SCR 108.

[163] Ibid.

Students have successfully litigated a number of cases where universities failed to fulfill their contractual responsibilities. In *Wong v Lakehead University*, Lakehead University was required to comply with clear language in its calendar indicating that "each graduate student receives a Graduate Assistantship worth $5000 per year," despite the fact that this statement was intended to apply only to students in degree programs, not those in graduate diploma programs, and that in 20 years not a single assistantship had ever been awarded to a diploma student.[164] *McBeth v Dalhousie College and University* involved a first-year law student who was unable to write a Christmas examination because of a medical disability.[165] The normal procedure under such circumstances was for the student to write a special examination or complete an assignment in lieu of the examination. A jury found that "the contract was breached when the University failed to provide a Christmas Exam to the Plaintiff within the contract year," as was the standard practice in such cases.[166] In one case, a court ordered the University of British Columbia to return a tuition deposit, even though the institution had clearly indicated that the deposit was non-refundable, on the grounds that the student had legitimate health concerns, the university sustained no damages when the student failed to attend, and the deposit was therefore penal in nature.[167]

Colleges and universities have also been held accountable to students in tort law for negligent misrepresentations in promotional or other similar material.[168] In addition, universities have been found liable for breach of contract or negligent misrepresentation in cases when they have failed to offer courses or programs as advertised. In *Chicoine v Ryerson Polytechnical Institute*, a student convinced the Ontario Provincial Court that a case involving a course he claimed had not been taught as offered and advertised should proceed to trial.[169] In *Bell v St. Thomas University*, the court held that a student had a contractual right to retake a course without conditions because a statement in the calendar permitted course repetitions without special permission.[170] When a program placed certain conditions upon the student's repeating the course, the university was found to have breached the contract. In a 2000 Ontario Supreme Court case, a student successfully sued Lakehead University for negligent

---

[164] *Wong, supra* note 27.

[165] *McBeth, supra* note 30.

[166] Ibid., 324.

[167] *Waichenberg v University of British Columbia*, 2006 CarswellOnt 4526 (WL Can), [2006] OJ No 3066 (QL) (Ont Sup Ct J).

[168] *Olar v Laurentian University*, 2007 CanLII 20787 (Ont Sup Ct J), aff'd 2008 ONCA 699, 2008 CarswellOnt 10147(WL Can).

[169] *Chicoine v Ryerson Polytechnical Institute* (1985), 15 Admin LR 261, 1985 CarswellOnt 901 (WL Can) (Ont Prov Ct (Civ Div Sm Cl Ct)).

[170] *Supra* note 30.

misrepresentation when it cancelled a program to which he had been admitted without informing him when it first became aware that the program would not be offered.[171] Perhaps the most egregious case of this type was *Olar v Laurentian University*, which involved a student who had completed two years of study at Laurentian's School of Engineering on the understanding that he would receive full credit for his courses at a number of other Ontario engineering schools, as was clearly stated in the university's calendar, student guide, promotional materials, and website.[172] While he was accepted into engineering at another university, he did not receive full credit for his courses and was required to take an extra year to complete his program. Because Olar had relied on Laurentian's misrepresentations regarding the transferability of its engineering courses, he was awarded damages in excess of $120,000. *Hickey-Button v Loyalist College of Applied Arts & Technology* is similar in many respects. In this case, a group of students entered the nursing program at Loyalist College with the understanding, based on Loyalist's promotional materials and other representations, that they could transfer to Queen's University after two years to complete their nursing degree.[173] When negotiations between Loyalist and Queen's broke down, this option was not available, and the affected students successfully petitioned the court to be certified as a class in a class-action suit for breach of contract or negligent misrepresentation.[174] *Crerar v Grande Prairie Regional College* addressed the question of whether institutions could be held liable for the provision of erroneous oral advice.[175] In this case, the Alberta Court of Queen's Bench found that students have an obligation to verify the accuracy of oral advice given to them, rather than relying exclusively on such advice.

The duty of care also likely includes a duty to protect those in the campus community from students. In one case, the court suggested that the institution may have breached its duty to the general student body to provide a "safe, constructive and orderly learning environment" by allowing a potentially dangerous student to return to campus without

---

[171] *Ibrahim v Lakehead University*, 2000 CarswellOnt 167 (WL Can)(Sup Ct J).

[172] *Supra* note 30.

[173] *Supra* note 30.

[174] See *Matoni v C.B.S. Interactive Multimedia Inc.*, 2008 CarswellOnt 7185 (WL Can) (Sup Ct J); *McKay v CDI Career Development Institutes Ltd.* (1999), 64 BCLR (3d) 386 (SC); *Nadella v Kingston Education Group, Inc.*, 2009 BCSC 1143; *Trend College (Kelowna) Ltd. v British Columbia (Private Post-Secondary Education Commission)*, 2001 BCSC 905, [2001] BCJ No 1280 (QL) for cases involving allegations of misrepresentation by private colleges.

[175] *Supra* note 30.

psychiatric clearance.[176] Some jurisdictions limit the liability of universities for the acts of students.[177]

A duty to warn is likely also a part of the duty of care, including a duty to warn against the threat of violence. While Canadian case law on university's duty to warn is not developed, American tort law suggests where a university or college has knowledge of an individual's violent intentions, a duty to warn those at risk may be imposed on the institution.[178] Given the history of violent incidents on campuses in North America, institutional policies and protocols are essential for evaluating, addressing, and communicating risks.[179]

Several cases address occupiers' liability in the university environment, and the duty of institutions to take such care as is reasonable to see that persons are reasonably safe while on the premises.[180]

Research is another area that has the potential for liability, but there is little Canadian authority for guidance. In *Law and Ethics in Biomedical Research: Regulation, Conflict of Interest, and Liability*, Mary M. Thomson argued that the present state of law is lagging behind science. It has been suggested that conflicts of interest in research have not yet been sufficiently addressed in the postsecondary environment and could be a basis for liability in the event of injuries arising out of the research.[181]

"Educational malpractice" is a developing liability phenomenon arising out of Ontario case law, and it is challenging the notion that the courts lack the jurisdiction to second-guess academic judgment. While there is no tort of educational malpractice, the courts are increasingly hearing tort and contract claims that relate to the manner in which institutions educate students. The Ontario Court of Appeal in *Gauthier v Saint-Germain*[182] ruled that the superior courts have inherent jurisdiction to hear contract and tort claims against universities *even if the dispute is academic in nature*. It was acknowledged in *Gauthier*, though, that when students enroll at a university, they agree to be subject to the institution's discretion in resolving academic matters, including student evaluations and the organization and implementation of university programs. As a result, in order to succeed in a contract or tort case, a student will usually

---

[176] *Kobilke, supra* note 119.

[177] See section 81 of *The University of Saskatchewan Act, 1995*, SS 1995, c U-6.1. The scope of this immunity has received little judicial interpretation.

[178] Pochini, "Managing Risk," 160–61.

[179] Ibid.

[180] See, for instance, *Dandell v Thompson Rivers University*, 2013 BCCA 490; *Grochowich v Okanagan University College*, 2004 BCCA 325; *Dixon v Cabot College of Applied Arts, Technology and Continuing Education* (1999), 177 Nfld& PEIR 162 (SC(TD)).

[181] Robinson, "University of Pin-Stripes," 414.

[182] *Gauthier v Saint-Germain*, 2010 ONCA 309, 325 DLR (4d) 558.

have to do more than simply argue that an academic result is incorrect or a professor is incompetent.[183]

The *Gauthier* approach has been followed in a number of cases.[184] However, there remain cases in other jurisdictions where the courts refuse to hear civil claims based on academic decisions.[185] Madam Justice Strekaf stated in *Cruickshank*:

> A matter is fundamentally academic if it focuses on the academic requirements, rules and regulations that the University applies to students. The issues in this case meet this criteria as they relate to the interpretation of an academic offence, the application of the discipline process and the penalties imposed for academic misconduct. Such matters do not fall within the jurisdiction of this Court, except when they are reviewable on an application for judicial review. A civil suit for damages is not an available remedy.[186]

The Manitoba Court of Appeal also dismissed a lawsuit over admissions. In *Walia v University of Manitoba*,[187] the court described admissions as an academic matter that should be dealt with in the world of academia and not in civil courts. A similar conclusion was reached by the Ontario Superior Court in *Ramlall v Ontario Family Medicine Programs*[188] in a claim involving refused entry into a residency program. The Ontario Court of Appeal has also resisted reviewing the admission decision, noting:

> In this regard, it has long been accepted that courts should be reluctant to interfere in the core academic functions of universities (citations omitted)... Here, the decision whether to admit the appellants to the Department of Biology M.Sc. Program was a decision going to the core of a university's

---

[183] The Court of Appeal also noted that if a student is seeking to change an academic decision (instead of suing for compensation), then judicial review should be used and the courts will be reluctant to interfere with the internal affairs of universities.

[184] *Jaffer v York University*, 2010 ONCA 654 – claims in contract and tort for university's alleged failure to accommodate his disabilities; *Amdiss v University of Ottawa*, 2010 ONSC 4738 – contract claim for refusing to admit a student. See also *Vatamanu v Baird*, [2009] OJ No 5481 (QL) (Ont Sup Ct J) in which a graduate student made a claim against her supervisor for "negligence, harassment, verbal assault, intentional interference in contractual relations, intentional infliction of economic harm, and intentional infliction of emotional harm and nervous shock." In *Miller v Thompson Rivers University*, 2013 BCSC 2138, the court refused to strike a claim that alleged breach of contract for failing to accommodate a disability.

[185] See *Yen, supra* note 101; *Cruickshank v University of Lethbridge*, 2010 ABQB 186 [*Cruickshank*].

[186] *Cruickshank, supra* note 186.

[187] *Walia v University of Manitoba*, 2013 MBCA 61.

[188] *Ramlall v Ontario Family Medicine Programs*, 2012 ONSC 7260.

functions. As the Divisional Court observed: "The decision to admit or not is discretionary; one made daily in an academic environment." We are satisfied that the decision was made reasonably.[189]

There have also been cases where the courts have dismissed civil claims on the basis that the claim appears to be a disguised or an indirect attack on an academic decision that had been already reviewed by an internal appeal process. The Ontario Court of Appeal characterized this as an abuse of process in *Aba-Alkhail v University of Ottawa*.[190]

The *Gauthier* line of cases may not have fully developed an answer to the fundamental concern that "educational malpractice" claims trespass on areas of academic judgment and scholarly expertise. As such, there is likely to continue to be challenges to actions that attack academic decisions, and the judicial approach to these actions is likely to continue to develop.[191]

It is worth noting that postsecondary institutions are not powerless to address many of the issues that devolve into lawsuits. Institutions should consider making full use of the contractual nature of the student-institution relationship by developing admissions documents, policies, regulations, and so on to effectively regulate student academic and non-academic behaviour and to provide reasonable clarity regarding the scope and limitations of the institution's services and responsibilities.[192] The case law suggests that students implicitly accept the internal policies, bylaws, and regulations of colleges and universities when they apply for admission.[193] It is nevertheless advisable that students be informed about the policies, regulations, and requirements at the point of admission or registration and be asked to formally indicate (e.g., by their signature, or by clicking "Accept" on an appropriately worded computer form) that they agree to be bound to and to adhere to them.

---

[189] *Mulligan, supra* note 99 at paras 20, 21.

[190] *Aba-Alkhail v University of Ottawa*, 2013 ONCA 633, 363 DLR (4d) 470. See also *Mortazavi v University of Toronto*, 2013 ONCA 655; *Fufa v University of Alberta*, 2012 ABQB 594, 543 AR 119.

[191] American cases have suggested that the courts can reliably assess whether grading is "arbitrary or capricious" because no academic expertise is needed to look for arbitrariness or capriciousness. See Amy Lai, "Grades Matter," 21.

[192] See *Turner v York University*, 2012 ONSC 4272.

[193] See *Wong v University of Toronto* (1989), 79 DLR (4d) 652 (Ont Dis Ct); *Rittenhouse-Carlson, supra* note 26.

Considerations and Advice for College and University Administrators

It is clear from reviewing recent trends in the law that today's students are more rights conscious than they were a generation ago, and more willing to challenge decisions both within their institutions and through litigation, especially when the stakes are high. For this reason, it is important that administrators have a solid understanding of both their rights and their legal obligations toward their students, and ensure that institutional practices and decision-making processes are established on strong legal grounds.

Canadian courts generally have not expressed a desire to get involved or intervene in universities' core business, and thus have historically shown considerable judicial deference to postsecondary institutions, especially with respect to fundamental academic matters such as admission and curriculum requirements, academic standards, and issues relating to academic judgment. That said, while the courts do not consider themselves experts in these core academic matters, they do consider themselves experts in matters of fundamental fairness, especially with respect to the *processes* that institutions use to make decisions, resolve disputes, and deal with academic and non-academic disciplinary matters that arise from time to time within the academy. The courts have clearly demonstrated that when necessary, they are prepared to intervene in the affairs of colleges and universities to ensure that they meet their constitutional, statutory, and contractual obligations; fulfill their duty of care toward their students (or are held to account when they do not); and deal fairly with alleged violations of academic and non-academic standards of conduct by students. Rarely (though increasingly), the courts have even stepped in and imposed substantive academic decisions on institutions.

With these points in mind, the authors would like to offer the following suggestions to college and university administrators with respect to how best to deal with the kinds of legal issues that might arise in connection with their students:

1. Remember that the student-institution legal relationship is complex and multifaceted, comprising elements of constitutional, statutory, administrative, contract, and tort law. Understand the ways in which this complex web of legal principles and requirements affects how you should deal with students and student situations on your campus.
2. Understand the statutes that apply to your institution and that affect your interactions with and obligations to your students. In particular, familiarize yourself with the provisions of your incorporating statute ("University Act," etc.), provincial human rights law, and freedom of information and protection of privacy legislation.

3. Accommodate students with disabilities, and help others within your institution, especially faculty members, understand the institution's duty to accommodate students to the point of undue hardship.

4. Ensure that your institution has appropriate, up-to-date policies and procedures in place for dealing with academic and non-academic misconduct, that these policies have been formally approved by the appropriate decision-making bodies, and that decisions are made according to the standards and procedures described in these policies.[194] Make sure that information about these policies is made widely available and promoted to your students.

5. If you do not currently have some kind of formal student code of conduct, develop one!

6. Remember that while colleges and universities generally have a fairly good track record when students have challenged their decisions through judicial review,[195] when they do lose these cases, it is usually because they have failed to follow their own approved institutional policies and procedures, or they have violated the principles of procedural fairness (or both).

7. For this reason, *follow your policies and procedures* as written, even if you believe they are flawed. Periodically review and revise any policies that you believe are in need of improvement, to incorporate new learnings you have gained from working with them and to reflect changes in the law.

8. For the same reason, treat students fairly when dealing with allegations of academic or non-academic discipline. Follow the principles of procedural fairness, understanding that the requirements of procedural fairness are flexible and need to be adapted to the particular circumstances. Provide more procedural protections to students when the nature of the offence and the potential consequences are serious, and at the final level of institutional decision-making. When in doubt, provide more procedural protections rather than fewer.

9. Wherever possible, try to avoid cross-membership on various levels of academic and non-academic decision-making bodies (to avoid perception of bias).

10. Understand the contractual nature of the student-institution relationship, and keep in mind that many of your institution's publications – especially your college or university calendar (or equivalent

---

[194] See *Gleason v Lethbridge Community College* (1995), 36 Alta LR (3d) 103 (QB) and *Shank v University of Toronto*, 57 OR (3d) 559, [2002] OJ No 50 (QL)(Sup Ct J (Div Ct)) for examples of cases overturned by the courts because they violated these principles.

[195] Hannah, "Student-Institution Legal Relationships."

website), promotional materials, student and residence handbooks, and other similar documents – are likely to be viewed as contractual documents by the courts.

11. Understand the "special relationship" you have and the duty of care your institution owes to your students. Ensure that you fulfill your duty of care by keeping your campus safe, providing proper instruction and supervision, and educating faculty and staff regarding their legal duties with respect to preventing harm to those who are using institutional facilities or participating in activities that are sponsored by the institution. These duties are particularly important for those who are involved in instructing, supervising, or organizing educational, recreational, or social activities that are potentially dangerous, including field trips (canoeing, rafting, skiing, camping, hiking, rock climbing, etc.), recreational and sports activities (hockey, football, basketball, etc.), and other physically demanding activities.

12. Develop alcohol policies that will help you better manage the use of alcohol on your campus. Offer information and educational programs to raise students' awareness of the problems associated with alcohol abuse, and encourage the responsible use of alcohol. Ensure that those who are responsible for organizing, supervising, and serving at alcohol-related events are thoroughly familiar with their duties toward their patrons, including the duties not to serve the intoxicated, not to serve to the point of intoxication, and to take appropriate action so that the intoxicated will not harm themselves or others. Security staff, residence assistants, and others who are likely to come into contact with intoxicated students should also receive training on appropriate methods for dealing with the intoxicated, and policies should be in place to guide these people as to the actions they should take when they encounter intoxicated students.

Chapter 8

FACULTY EMPLOYMENT AT CANADIAN POSTSECONDARY INSTITUTIONS

PATRICK GILLIGAN-HACKETT AND PAMELA MURRAY

INTRODUCTION

The law of contract provides the foundation for the employment relationship between faculty members and their employers. However, with the increase in unionization of faculty members at Canadian universities, labour law has also assumed a central role in faculty employment relationships. This chapter reviews applicable principles of the foregoing areas of law, as well as aspects of employment, statutory, and administrative law that govern the employment of faculty members in Canada.[1]

The particular focus of this chapter is on the employment contract itself. The chapter reviews the means by which the employment contract is created and its terms and conditions are established; important features of the academic setting that affect the employment contract; the general legal framework within which decisions about employment are made; discipline; and the jurisdiction over disputes arising from employment decisions, including disciplinary decisions.

---

[1] Human rights law, while increasingly significant in Canadian employment relationships including those of faculty members, is beyond the scope of this chapter. See, generally, chapter 5. Similarly, the application of the *Charter of Rights and Freedoms*, Part I of the *Constitution Act, 1982*, being Schedule B to the *Canada Act 1982* (UK), 1982, c 11 to universities and colleges is beyond the scope of this chapter, although the issue of the application of the *Charter* to universities has recently been the subject of renewed debate.

Handbook of Canadian Higher Education Law, edited by Theresa Shanahan, Michelle Nilson, and Li-Jeen Broshko. Montreal and Kingston: McGill-Queen's University Press, Queen's Policy Studies Series.

THE EMPLOYMENT CONTRACT

Formation

At a postsecondary institution where faculty members are unionized or belong to a non-unionized employee association, the collective or framework/faculty agreement may create requirements for posting of faculty positions and assignments.[2] A postsecondary institution's failure to comply with the requirements of the relevant agreement may interfere with the formation of a contract between the institution and the faculty member.

That said, while practices vary, a faculty employment relationship will typically begin with the execution of a written contract: for example, a written offer of employment – usually describing key terms and conditions of employment – which will be countersigned by the new faculty member to confirm his or her acceptance of the offer. Generally, a contract of employment will not be formed until such formal steps are taken, although an oral contract of employment is possible if the parties' actions satisfy the requirements for the formation of a contract.

In general, a postsecondary institution will not generally have any obligations to an applicant for a faculty position.[3] For example, in *Roback v University of British Columbia*, 2007 BCSC 334, the defendant did not select the plaintiff, who had simply responded to an advertisement for a faculty position. The plaintiff claimed, among other things, that a contract had been created by his application for the position. The plaintiff said that the defendant had breached that contract by hiring a candidate who allegedly failed to meet the selection criteria for the position – criteria that the plaintiff argued were set out expressly or impliedly in the advertisement. The court rejected the plaintiff's position. Among other things, the court found that the defendant had not demonstrated an intention to create a contractual relationship simply by advertising the faculty position and, further, that the advertisement did not contain either selection criteria or terms and conditions of sufficient clarity to give rise to a contractual obligation between the defendant and the plaintiff. The court also rejected

---

[2] See, for example, *Laurentian University v Laurentian University Faculty Assn. (Sessional Appointments Grievance)*, [2013] OLAA No 416 (Sheehan); *Windsor University Faculty Assn. v University of Windsor (Beaudrie Grievance)*, [2013] OLAA No 398 (Watters); *Algonquin College (College Employer Council for the Colleges of Applied Arts and Technology) v Ontario Public Service Employees Union (Full-time Appointments Grievance)*, [2012] OLAA No 5 (Knopf); and *Brock University v Canadian Union of Public Employees, Local 4207*, [2012] OLAA No 2 (Swan).

[3] Except in the event that some provision in an applicable collective or faculty/ framework agreement or written policy of an individual postsecondary institution leads to a different result: for a further discussion of such documents, see below.

the plaintiff's argument that the defendant had a freestanding duty of fairness when hiring for an advertised position.

Terms and Conditions of Employment

The Contract at Unionized Postsecondary Institutions

A critical question to answer when determining the terms and conditions of a faculty member's employment is whether the faculty members at a given postsecondary institution are unionized.

Until comparatively recently, faculty employment relationships did not involve representation by a bargaining agent certified under a labour relations statute. By one account, in 1971, there was only one certified bargaining unit for university faculty members in Canada.[4] By 2004, almost 80 percent of Canada's university faculty associations had been certified as bargaining agents under the applicable labour relations statutes.[5] Today, few universities remain at which faculty members are not represented by a certified bargaining agent. Those universities are primarily in Alberta[6] and, until recently, in British Columbia.[7] Faculty members at a few universities in other provinces are not unionized.[8] Union representation of academic staff at colleges and institutes is also widespread.

Under the Canadian labour relations model, once a union is certified, the employer "loses the option of negotiating different conditions of employment with individual employees."[9] Therefore, once faculty members are unionized, the terms and conditions of their employment are established by the collective agreement negotiated between the postsecondary institution and the bargaining agent.[10] However, there are some collective agreements which by their express terms allow an employer to negotiate aspects of the employment relationship directly with faculty members.[11]

---

[4] Adell, "Faculty Collective Bargaining," 46.

[5] Dobbie and Robinson, "Reorganizing Higher Education"; Robinson, *Status of Higher Education Teaching Personnel*, 31–32.

[6] See *Post-secondary Learning Act,* SA 2003, c P-19.5, ss 84–92.

[7] In 2014, faculty members at the University of Victoria, the University of Northern British Columbia, and Simon Fraser University voted to unionize.

[8] Robinson, *Status of Higher Education Teaching Personnel*, 30.

[9] *Noël v Société d'énergie de la Baie James*, 2001 SCC 39 at paras. 41–42 and 45; see also *Bisaillon v Concordia University*, 2006 SCC 19 at para. 24.

[10] See, for example, *York University v York University Faculty Assn. (FES Workload Grievance)*, [2013] OLAA No 389 (Kaplan) (faculty workload and entitlement to course release).

[11] See *York University Faculty Assn. v York University (Policy Grievance)* (2013), 231 LAC (4th) 288 (Larry).

Even at a postsecondary institution where faculty members are represented by a union, some faculty members will fall outside the scope of or otherwise be excluded from the bargaining unit, for example because they are not employees under the applicable labour relations statute but rather are "managers."[12] To determine the members of a given faculty bargaining unit, it is necessary to review the union's certification, the recognition and other related clauses in the relevant collective agreement, the applicable labour relations statute (see Table 8.1), and possibly the statute establishing the postsecondary institution at issue. Further, faculty bargaining units may include classes of employee such as librarians, who would not in any strict sense be considered faculty members.

TABLE 8.1
Labour Relations Legislation

Province/Territory	Legislation
Alberta	*Labour Relations Code,* RSA 2000, c L-1
British Columbia	*Labour Relations Code,* RSBC 1996, c 244
Manitoba	*Labour Relations Act,* CCSM c L10
New Brunswick	*Industrial Relations Act,* RSNB 1973, c 1-4
Newfoundland and Labrador	*Labour Relations Act,* RSNL 1990, c L-1
Northwest Territories	Generally, *Canada Labour Code,* RSC 1985, c L-2[a]
Nova Scotia	*Trade Union Act,* RSNS 1989, c 475
Nunavut	Generally, *Canada Labour Code,* RSC 1985, c L-2[b]
Ontario	*Labour Relations Act,* SO 1995, c 1
Prince Edward Island	*Labour Act,* RSPEI 1988, c L-1
Quebec	*Labour Code,* CQLR c C-27
Saskatchewan	*The Saskatchewan Employment Act,* SS 2013, c S15-1
Yukon	Generally, *Canada Labour Code,* RSC 1985, c L-2

Note: The labour relations statutes that govern faculty employment fall within provincial jurisdiction.
[a] See *Canada (Labour Relations Board) v Yellowknife (City),* [1977] 2 SCR 729.
[b] See *Nunavut Teachers' Assn. v Nunavut,* 2010 NUCJ 13.

The Contract at Non-Unionized Postsecondary Institutions

At non-unionized postsecondary institutions, or at a unionized postsecondary institution if a faculty member falls outside the scope of a bargaining unit, a faculty member's terms and conditions of employment

---

[12] See, for example, *Ryerson University v Ryerson Faculty Assn. (Norrie Grievance),* [2012] OLAA No 608 (Luborsky).

will generally be established by an individual employment contract. Ultimately, such individual employment contracts are governed by the common law.

As a practical matter, many faculty members who are not unionized are represented by employee associations. Postsecondary institutions with such associations typically enter into a contract with the association that recognizes the association as the representative of faculty members. Such contracts do not appear to constitute a voluntary recognition of the faculty association under the applicable labour relations statute.[13] The associations negotiate a framework or faculty agreement – which may incorporate certain institutional policies – with the postsecondary institution. The agreement is renegotiated from time to time, contains detailed terms and conditions of employment, and effectively subsumes the employment contracts of the association's members.

While such agreements often resemble collective agreements, the relationship between the institution, the association, and the association's members is not governed by the applicable labour relations statute but remains, at its core, a matter governed by the common law of contract and any applicable legislation.

Written Policies

A postsecondary institution's written policies often constitute a significant additional source of the legal framework governing faculty employment. Some collective and framework/faculty agreements clearly incorporate such written policies. They refer expressly to the relevant policies and confirm that they form part of the agreement with the consequence that they form contractual terms and conditions of employment.[14] In other situations, for example where the collective or framework/faculty agreement is silent, the incorporation of such policies into the employment contract will be less obvious. In this event, the issue of incorporation is likely to require careful consideration. Even in the absence of incorporation, such policies may, if they meet the required legal standard, govern aspects of the employment relationship as an exercise of management rights.

Legislation

Legislation that applies to a postsecondary institution may also have an important bearing on an institution's employment relationship with its

---

[13] *University of Victoria v University of Victoria Faculty Assn.*, BCLRB No B190/99.

[14] See, for example, *Vanek v University of Alberta*, [1974] 3 WWR 167 (Alta SC), aff'd 57 DLR (3d) 595 (Alta CA) ("*Vanek*").

faculty members. An important example of such legislation is the statute establishing the postsecondary institution.

Such legislation may impose obligations on the postsecondary institution that relate to decisions about its faculty employees. For example, in *Faculty Assn. of the University of Windsor v University of Windsor* (1998), 59 OTC 216 (Ct J (Gen Div)), the court observed that the legislation incorporating the university provided "a package of powers and requirements generally related to the subject of the appointment of various individuals including Deans." And in *Lakeland College Faculty Assn. v Lakeland College*, 1998 ABCA 221, the Alberta Court of Appeal, on judicial review, set aside a decision of the college's board of governors to redesignate a librarian who had been a member of the faculty association from an academic to non-academic position. The court found the college's board had committed a jurisdictional error when it failed to meet the standard of consultation set out in section 10(2) of that province's *Colleges Act*.

At the same time, governance provisions in the legislation that establishes a postsecondary institution may immunize a policy that affects faculty employment from arbitral review. In *Faculty Assn. of the University of British Columbia v University of British Columbia*, 2010 BCCA 189, leave to appeal refused [2010] SCCA No 232, the British Columbia Court of Appeal held that as a result of the independent nature of the university's senate under the province's *University Act*, a senate policy on student evaluation of teaching was not subject to the provisions of the collective agreement between the faculty association and the postsecondary institution and was not, therefore, subject to arbitral review.[15]

Further, the legislation establishing a postsecondary institution may affect the available remedies when an adjudicator overturns a post-secondary institution's decision about faculty employment. In *University of British Columbia v University of British Columbia Faculty Assn.*, 2007 BCCA 201, leave to appeal refused [2010] SCCA No 232, the British Columbia Court of Appeal found that as a result of the provisions of the province's *University Act*, an arbitrator had no power to substitute a recommendation that the faculty member be promoted for the university president's decision to the contrary. The court held that the appropriate remedy for defects in a tenure decision was to remit the matter to the president for reconsideration.

---

[15] See also, generally, *Kulchyski v Trent University* (2001), 204 DLR (4th) 364 (Ont CA); but see *Lakehead University (Board of Governors) v Lakehead University Faculty Assn. (Shutdown Grievance)*, [2010] OLAA No 612 (Devlin) ("*Lakehead University*").

THE ACADEMIC CONTEXT OF FACULTY EMPLOYMENT

Tenure

Tenure at universities does not have a long history in Canada. It has only been widespread since the 1950s.[16] However, it has come to be recognized as a matter of central importance to the academic mission of universities. In this regard, tenure has been described as a term of employment for university faculty members: "The right to be considered for tenure is one of the terms of employment of members of the teaching staff of the University. It is a contractual right."[17]

In *McKinney v University of Guelph*, the Supreme Court of Canada observed that tenure "provides the necessary academic freedom to allow free and fearless search for knowledge and the propagation of ideas." The Court also quoted with approval the following comments of the Ontario Court of Appeal:

> The policy of tenure in university faculties is fundamental to the preservation of academic freedom. It involves a vigorous assessment by one's peers of academic performance after a probationary period of up to five years. Once tenure is granted, it provides a truly free and innovative learning and research environment. Faculty members can take unpopular positions without fear of loss of employment. It provides stability of employment, because once an academic is found worthy of tenure by his or her peers, he or she can be assured of keeping that position until death, or the normal age of retirement, unless there is termination for cause following a properly conducted hearing before one's peers.[18]

However, tenure is not universal among academic staff. There has been an increasing trend toward temporary and part-time faculty employment.[19] As observed in *Athabasca University Governing Council, and Canadian Union of Public Employees Local 3911 with Respect to a Grievance Concerning the Employee Status of Academic Coaches and Graduate Sessional Instructors*:

> At the heart of any University is its academic staff. They have, and seek to sustain, the protections of promotion and tenure systems, which serve

---

[16] Dobbie and Robinson, "Reorganizing Higher Education," 118.

[17] *Paine v University of Toronto* (1981), 34 OR (2d) 770 (CA), leave to appeal refused (1982), 35 OR (2d) 528n (SCC) ("*Paine*") at para. 11.

[18] [1990] 3 SCR 229 at para. 62 ("*McKinney*"). See also *University of British Columbia v Faculty Assn. of the University of British Columbia (Tenure Policy Grievance)*, [2007] BCCAAA No 175 (Taylor, QC) at para. 10, citing *St. Michael's College v Richardson*, 1994, unreported.

[19] Robinson, *Status of Higher Education Teaching Personnel*, 29.

to protect academic freedom as well as career advancement. Customarily, academics have invested many otherwise employable years in obtaining their academic qualifications. The promotion and tenure system customarily provides compensation for those years of investment, with salaries and rank increasing over time, followed by a pension.

Any sense of an increase in the use of contingent part-time staff in an academic role often raises concerns that it will diminish academic freedom, academic tenure, and the availability of sufficiently compensated academic positions in the future. These fears to some extent supplement, and to some extent lie behind, the parallel concerns expressed about the insecurity, lack of benefits and low pay for contract academic workers.

However, the time has long past [sic] when the core full-time academic staff of a University were able to perform all a University's teaching functions. Sessional instructors have long been used for highly specialized subjects, but are increasingly used for core subjects. Part-time teaching opportunities have often been used to train and subsidize graduate students, and to take advantage of available non-tenured academics.[20]

Temporary and part-time faculty employment normally involves terms and conditions that are significantly different from those of tenured and tenure-track faculty.[21] Temporary faculty members such as sessional instructors and limited term instructors may also be represented by a different union than tenure-track and tenured faculty members; may not be represented by a certified bargaining agent or employee association at all; and indeed, in certain circumstances, could even be found to be independent contractors rather than employees.[22]

Academic Freedom

Academic freedom has been described as the "essence of a university."[23] The Supreme Court of Canada has also described it as "essential to our

---

[20] (2012), 224 LAC (4th) 1 (Sims, QC) at paras. 177–78, judicial review dismissed 2014 ABQB 292.

[21] See, for example, *University of Guelph v Canadian Union of Public Employees, Local 3913 (Bell Grievance)*, [2005] OLAA No 440 (Rose) (nature of sessional employment; academic freedom for sessional instructors); *York University v York University Faculty Assn. (Contract Grievance)*, [2002] OLAA No 945 (Goodfellow) (difference between faculty members appointed on special renewable contracts and tenure track faculty); *Carr v Atlantic Business College Ltd.*, 2007 NBQB 77.

[22] See *Athabasca University, supra* note 20.

[23] *Connell v University of British Columbia* (1988), 21 BCLR (2d) 145 (CA) at 152, rev'd on other grounds *Harrison v British Columbia*, [1990] 3 SCR 451.

continuance as a lively democracy."[24] Academic freedom is protected for faculty members at universities and, generally, at colleges and institutions. Yet, it has been observed that while academic freedom is an important right, it is not one with a precise definition.[25]

In 2011, the Association of Universities and Colleges of Canada (now Universities Canada) adopted a new Statement on Academic Freedom, which defines academic freedom as follows:

> Academic freedom is the freedom to teach and conduct research in an academic environment. Academic freedom is fundamental to the mandate of universities to pursue truth, educate students and disseminate knowledge and understanding.
>
> In teaching, academic freedom is fundamental to the protection of the rights of the teacher to teach and of the student to learn. In research and scholarship, it is critical to advancing knowledge. Academic freedom includes the right to freely communicate knowledge and the results of research and scholarship.
>
> Unlike the broader concept of freedom of speech, academic freedom must be based on institutional integrity, rigorous standards for enquiry and institutional autonomy, which allows universities to set their research and educational priorities.[26]

The Canadian Association of University Teachers (CAUT) also has a Policy Statement on Academic Freedom, the most recent version of which was adopted in November 2011. The statement includes the following definition:

> Academic freedom includes the right, without restriction by prescribed doctrine, to freedom of teaching and discussion; freedom in carrying out research and disseminating and publishing the results thereof; freedom in

---

[24] *McKinney, supra* note 18 at para. 69. However, although academic freedom had been recognized as being of fundamental importance in Canada – unlike at public postsecondary institutions in the United States – it is not constitutionally protected. There is nevertheless an identifiable relationship between the rights protected by the concept of academic freedom and those protected by section 2(b) of the Canadian Charter of Rights and Freedoms, which provides: "Everyone has the following fundamental freedoms … freedom of thought, belief, opinion and expression."

[25] *University of Calgary Faculty Assn. v University of Calgary*, [1999] AGAA No 104 (Sims, Chair) ("*University of Calgary*"); see also *University of Manitoba Faculty Association v University of Manitoba*, [1991] MGAD No 19 (Schulman).

[26] Association of Universities and Colleges of Canada, "New Statement on Academic Freedom."

producing and performing creative works; freedom to engage in service to the institution and the community; freedom to express freely one's opinion about the institution, its administration, or the system in which one works; freedom from institutional censorship; freedom to acquire, preserve, and provide access to documentary material in all formats; and freedom to participate in professional and representative academic bodies. Academic freedom always entails freedom from institutional censorship.[27]

Determining the scope of a faculty member's academic freedom at a given postsecondary institution requires a review of any applicable provisions in the collective or framework/faculty agreement and in written policies.

Generally, courts and arbitrators defer to the academic community when determining the scope of academic freedom. As one court has held, "No one is better qualified to determine what constitutes academic freedom, and any infringement thereof, than members of the University who are concerned with the same principles."[28] For this reason, in adjudicative disputes, expert evidence and policy statements such as those set out above may assist in defining the scope of academic freedom.[29]

Academic freedom generally extends to research; teaching, including both the right to choose methods of evaluation[30] and the ability and responsibility to assign grades;[31] public statements by faculty members;[32] and university governance.[33] There has been some debate about whether

---

[27] Canadian Association of University Teachers, "Academic Freedom." For additional policy statements on particular aspects of academic freedom, see http://www.caut.ca/about-us/caut-policy. See *College Institute Educators' Assn. v British Columbia*, 2002 BCSC 1480 for a discussion of CAUT's history and expertise.

[28] *Strofolino v Helmstadter* (2001), 55 OR (3d) 138 (Sup Ct J) at para. 48.

[29] See, for example, *University of Calgary, supra* note 25; *York University v York University Faculty Assn. (Noble Grievance)* (2007), 167 LAC (4th) 39 (Goodfellow) ("*York University*").

[30] *University of Calgary, supra* note 25 (whether essays should be required in art history classes).

[31] *Memorial University of Newfoundland v Memorial University of Newfoundland Faculty Assn. (Snook Grievance)*, [2007] NLLAA No 3 (Knopf, Chair) at para. 90 ("*Memorial University*"). However, see *University of Ottawa v Association of Professors of the University of Ottawa (Rancourt Grievance)*, unreported January 27, 2014 (Foisy, QC) ("*University of Ottawa*").

[32] *York University, supra* note 29 (discussion of balancing required of universities in fashioning public responses to controversial statements by faculty members); *University of Manitoba Faculty Association v University of Manitoba*, [1991] MGAD No 19 (Schulman).

[33] *University of Calgary, supra* note 25 (whether essays should be required in art history classes).

it applies to service obligations of faculty members.[34] However, it is unlikely to extend to such matters as how a university provides email access to its faculty.[35]

Even in relation to those academic pursuits that are generally recognized as being protected by academic freedom, academic freedom is not unlimited.[36] Further, academic freedom must be balanced with the rights of both other members of the academic community, such as students, and the institution itself.[37]

Collegial Governance

An important aspect of decision-making at postsecondary institutions, including decision-making about faculty employment, arises from the collegial nature of their governance structure. That structure is normally recognized in the processes set out in the collective[38] or framework/faculty agreement and may also be reflected in the legislation establishing a given postsecondary institution.[39]

Postsecondary institutions have been contrasted to the traditional industrial workplace model, where employees have less control over and input into the employment environment. It has been observed that at Canadian postsecondary institutions the line distinguishing faculty members from management is quite difficult to draw, with the result that faculty members normally have input into matters that would otherwise be left to the discretion of management.[40] The collegial nature of decision-

---

[34] See http://www.caut.ca/docs/default-document-library/caut_to_aucc_academic_freedom.pdf?sfvrsn=0.

[35] *Lakehead University Board of Governors v Lakehead University Faculty Assn. (Right to Privacy Grievance)* (2009), 184 LAC (4th) 338 (Carrier) (university had not violated faculty members' academic freedom by replacing its internal email system with one provided by Google).

[36] See *University of Ottawa v Assn. of Professors of the University of Ottawa (Rancourt Grievance)*, [2008] OLAA No 356 (Picher): "To the extent that such statements are not unlawful, or materially false and misleading, they should generally have the protection of academic freedom." See also, for example, *Memorial University, supra* note 32 at para. 83: "The academic rights of an individual faculty member are 'not absolute and inviolable.'" See also Schrank, "Academic Freedom and University Speech Codes."

[37] *York University, supra* note 29.

[38] See, for example, *Nicola Valley Institute of Technology v Nicola Valley Institute of Technology Employees Assn.*, [2006] BCCAAA No 22 (Ready).

[39] See *Lakehead University, supra* note 15.

[40] *Okanagan College Board v Okanagan College Faculty Assn.*, [1982] BCCAAA No 250 (Bluman) at paras. 40–42, citing *Faculty Assn. of Vancouver City College (Langara)* and *Vancouver City College*, BCLRB No 60/74.

making at postsecondary institutions has been identified as a component of academic freedom.[41]

DECISIONS ABOUT FACULTY EMPLOYMENT

Faculty Employment Decisions, Generally

While the discussion below considers the legal framework that applies generally to decisions made during the course of a faculty member's employment, specific additional requirements and processes will often attach to a particular type of decision. For example, the employment relationship for tenure-track faculty typically progresses through a number of stages: an initial term appointment without tenure; renewal for a second term appointment with the right to be considered for tenure; and if the applicable requirements have been met, the grant in due course of tenure and, frequently, promotion. Particular considerations may apply to decisions regarding tenure and promotion.

The Principles of Natural Justice

The principles of natural justice, which apply to universities and colleges making faculty employment decisions, are part of the common law. They provide for and require fairness in administrative decision-making. Every public authority making an administrative decision that is not of a legislative nature and that affects the rights, privileges, or interests of an individual is subject to a duty of procedural fairness.[42] The extent of the duty of procedural fairness varies with the factual context in which the decision is being made.[43]

In *Kane v University of British Columbia*, [1980] 1 SCR 1105 ("*Kane*"),[44] the Supreme Court of Canada confirmed that the following principles apply to decisions about faculty employment:

- The duty of the courts is to attribute a large measure of autonomy of decision to a tribunal, such as a university's board of governors, sitting in appeal pursuant to legislative mandate;

---

[41] See *University of Calgary, supra* note 25; Canadian Association of University Teachers, "Academic Freedom."

[42] See *Dunsmuir v New Brunswick*, 2008 SCC 9 at para. 87, citing *Cardinal v Director of Kent Institution*, [1985] 2 SCR 643.

[43] Ibid., para. 79; see also *Baker v Canada (Minister of Citizenship and Immigration)*, [1999] 2 SCR 817.

[44] See also *Wade v Strangway* (1996), 132 DLR (4th) 406 (BCCA) and *University of British Columbia v Faculty Assn. of the University of British Columbia (Lund Grievance)*, [2012] BCCAAA No 26 (Hall).

- As a constituent of the autonomy it enjoys, the tribunal must observe natural justice. To abrogate the rules of natural justice, express language or necessary implication must be found in the relevant statutory instrument;
- A "high standard of justice" is required when the right to continue in one's profession or employment is at stake;
- The tribunal must listen fairly to both sides. The parties to the controversy must have a fair opportunity for correcting or contradicting any relevant statement prejudicial to their views;
- Unless empowered expressly or by necessary implication to act *ex parte*, an appellate authority must not hold private interviews with witnesses or hear evidence in the absence of a party whose conduct is impugned and under scrutiny; and
- A court will not inquire whether the evidence did work to the prejudice of one of the parties. It is sufficient if it might have done so.

The above statement of the requirements of natural justice is not exhaustive. Aspects of natural justice and procedural fairness also include the right to notice of the case; a reasonable opportunity to respond to it;[45] disclosure of relevant records; in some circumstances, the right both to counsel and to cross-examine adverse witnesses; and the decision-maker's duty to be free from bias[46] and to provide reasons.[47]

---

[45] *Giroux v Ontario* (1984), 46 OR (2d) 276 (CA) (once the ad hoc committee appointed to advise the president realized that the issue might be decided against the faculty member, faculty member should have been advised and given an opportunity to make oral or written submissions); *Ruiperez v Board of Governors of Lakehead University* (1983), 41 OR (2d) 552 (CA) (a faculty member seeking tenure was entitled to be given the essence or substance of the detrimental information against him and an opportunity to respond to that information); *Wilfrid Laurier University Faculty Assn. v Wilfrid Laurier University (Harvey Grievance)* (1997), 49 CLAS 337 (Adell) (receipt of an email by the university president from the associate dean was a denial of procedural fairness because the faculty member was not given the right to respond).

[46] *Paine, supra* note 17 (members of a tenure committee acting on their own knowledge of the tenure candidate and references provided to them were not biased unless holding preconceived opinions as to candidate's suitability for tenure); *University of Waterloo v Faculty Assn. of University of Waterloo (Pan Grievance)* (2007), 168 LAC (4th) 1 (Shime) (no bias arising from three members of the department's tenure and promotion committee who also served on the merit advisory committee); *Hurd v Hewitt* (1994), 20 OR (3d) 639 (CA) (bias arising from some members of the search committee meeting at the dean's house and conspiring to pool votes to defeat the sessional applicant's application for a tenure-stream professorial position); *Said v University of Ottawa*, 2011 ONSC 6179 (bias arising from continued involvement of the dean who had recommended the applicant's dismissal in promotion application process).

[47] See, for example, *Dalhousie University v Dalhousie Faculty Assn.*, 2002 NSCA 1.

It has been held that the "high standard of justice" required by the principles of natural justice may be met where there is a collective agreement and the postsecondary institution complies with the wording of the collective agreement. In *Trent University Faculty Association v Trent University (Yee Grievance)* (2009), 188 LAC (4th) 254 (Cummings), the tenure committee of the faculty member's department recommended that she be granted tenure. However, the committee on academic personnel, the dean of the relevant faculty, and the university's president were not satisfied that she had met the applicable standard.

Under the applicable collective agreement a candidate had to show, in the judgment of those assessing the candidate's performance, high quality in both teaching and research. The committee, the dean, and the president were not satisfied that the faculty member had met the required standard in her research. The arbitrator held at para. 81:

> I believe that the parties negotiated their detailed provisions with the goal of providing a complete code. So long as they comply with those provisions, it is not appropriate for an arbitrator to create a new process or impose a different procedural standard. But because I also believe that the parties' detailed provisions arise out of and are responsive to the concerns that arbitrators have raised in the case law, even if I were to apply an over-arching high standard of justice, I would find that the standard had been met.

> As a result of the collegial governance which characterizes postsecondary institutions, the processes leading to most faculty employment decisions, including disciplinary decisions, involve multiple levels of consideration. For this reason, the administrative law rule that a fair process during a subsequent consideration of a decision can correct a procedural defect at an earlier consideration is of particular importance.[48]

Records of the Terms and Conditions of Employment

As is noticed above, postsecondary institutions normally record the terms and conditions of employment for faculty members in written documents such as a collective or framework/faculty agreement and university policies. Such documents typically contain extensive provisions governing decisions about such matters as appointments, contract renewals, promotions, and grants of tenure. If a decision is made without following the substantive and procedural requirements contained in an applicable agreement or policy, that decision is likely to be set aside if it is challenged.

---

[48] But see *Paine, supra* note 17.

In *University of Western Ontario v University of Western Ontario Faculty Assn. (Rao Grievance)*, [2010] OLAA No 14 (Brent), a decision denying a faculty member tenure was set aside because under the collective agreement, the university's provost was charged with the responsibility for approving or denying the recommendation for tenure and promotion. However, the provost relied on a file review conducted by the vice provost and on the vice provost's synopsis of the file. The synopsis usually included a recommendation. The arbitrator found that the vice provost's synopsis was not a proper consideration under the collective agreement. This was especially true because the vice provost prepared the synopsis in advance of the provost's review of the file and the synopsis included both references to things not in the file and a recommendation based at least in part on factors not referred to in the collective agreement.

And in *Dalhousie Faculty Assn. v Dalhousie University*, 2002 NSCA 1, the union argued that the university's president had, among other things, breached the terms of the collective agreement and the tenure and promotion guidelines of the relevant faculty, which had been incorporated into the collective agreement, by applying the wrong standards for tenure. An arbitrator appointed to hear the dispute found that the president's decision was unreasonable because it imposed a standard of teaching excellence while the promotion and tenure guidelines only required very good to excellent teaching. The Court of Appeal reinstated the arbitrator's decision.

DISCIPLINE

As a practical matter, the imposition of disciplinary measures on faculty members, and in particular tenured faculty members, is comparatively rare. However, because faculty members occupy positions of trust and are largely unsupervised in the execution of their duties, departures from the expected standard of conduct are treated more seriously than for employees who are closely supervised.[49]

Like other employment-related decisions about faculty members, decisions about discipline are subject to the requirements of natural justice. Aside from questions about procedural fairness, two questions will normally arise in a dispute about the discipline of a faculty member:

- whether the faculty member has engaged in conduct that justifies either the imposition of discipline or termination from employment; and

---

[49] *University of Windsor v Faculty Assn. of the University of Windsor (Taboun) (Re)* (2002), 112 LAC (4th) 1 (Adell, Chair) ("*University of Windsor*") at paras. 73–77, aff'd 2014 ONSC 1142; *Kwantlen College v Douglas and Kwantlen College Faculty Assn. (Pawson Grievance)*, [1984] BCCAAA No 302 (MacDonald) ("*Kwantlen College*") at paras. 32–33.

- whether the behaviour in question warranted the particular disciplinary action taken by the employer, including whether the discipline imposed itself violates the collective agreement.[50]

When deciding whether the behaviour in question warrants the discipline imposed by the employer, an arbitrator will consider whether there are factors in the particular case that would mitigate the disciplinary penalty.[51] Further, general labour law principles requiring an employer to use progressive discipline, except when responding to the most serious employment offences, have been accepted as applicable to misconduct by a faculty member.[52]

In discipline cases, the postsecondary institution has the onus of satisfying the applicable statutory or contractual standard – typically but not always just and reasonable cause – for the discipline imposed.[53] Examples are provided below of grounds for discipline. However, it is important to note that these examples do not reflect all of the potential grounds for discipline.

Discipline Short of Termination

While discipline short of termination is uncommon in faculty employment, it is not unknown. Conduct that might give rise to disciplinary measures short of termination normally arises from less serious misconduct.

In *University of Ottawa v Assn. of Professors of the University of Ottawa (Rancourt Grievance)*, [2008] OLAA No 356 (Picher), the postsecondary institution reprimanded a tenured full professor for having independently published, on the internet, information about one of his courses that he knew was incorrect. He wrongly described the course as "new," "bilingual," and "graduate." Despite recognizing the inherently broad scope of academic freedom, the arbitrator concluded that the postsecondary institution did have just cause to issue a written reprimand for the description of the course as "bilingual" and "graduate." The professor knew or reasonably should have known that describing the course

---

[50] See Brown and Beatty, *Canadian Labour Arbitration*, 7:0000 and *Re William Scott & Co.*, BCLRB Decision No 46/76; see also, for example, *Lethbridge College v Lethbridge College Faculty Assn. (Bird Grievance)* (2007), 166 LAC (4th) 289 (Ponack, Chair), aff'd 2008 ABQB 316 ("*Lethbridge College*").

[51] See, for example, *Lethbridge College, supra* note 50 (mitigating factors in faculty sexual relationships with students) and *Malaspina University-College v College Institute of Educators' Assn. (Chen Grievance)*, [1999] BCCAAA No 419 (Blasina).

[52] See, for example, *University of Manitoba v University of Manitoba Faculty Assn. (Re)*, [1993] MGAD No 116 (Bowman).

[53] See, for example, *University of Windsor, supra* note 49.

in the quoted terms was incorrect and that such misdescriptions were of substantial and legitimate concern to the university. However, the grievance as it related to the publicity for the course was allowed in part because the arbitrator held that academic freedom protected the activity of publicizing the course.

In *Vancouver Community College v Vancouver Community College Faculty Assn. (Grimman Grievance)* (1994), 46 LAC (4th) 72 (Thompson), the college imposed a five-day suspension on an instructor in its auto technician program for having allegedly breached its harassment policy by using abusive language, initiating unwelcome physical contact, and intimidating students during an on-campus incident. The college and the faculty association agreed there were grounds for some form of discipline, but the faculty association argued that the five-day suspension was excessive. The arbitrator upheld the discipline and observed that faculty members are required to treat their students with respect and to observe standards of conduct similar to employees who have authority over clients. The arbitrator found that the grievor's violation of those standards had not been trivial and was to some degree premeditated.

Termination

The standard for terminating a faculty member's employment is, at a minimum, just cause.[54] However, this standard may well be the subject of elaboration or refinement in the wording of the terms and conditions of employment applicable to faculty members at a given postsecondary institution.

The types of misconduct that will be sufficient to sustain the termination of a tenured faculty member are varied. They include both single serious acts and repeated lesser acts of misconduct. In *McKinney*, the Supreme Court of Canada identified "gross misconduct, incompetence, or persistent failure to discharge academic responsibilities"[55] as grounds for the termination of faculty employment.

Misconduct

The termination of a faculty member has been upheld for such employment offences as

- knowingly and repeatedly giving false information to a granting agency that was funding the doctoral research of one of the faculty

---

[54] *McKinney, supra* note 18 at para. 62; see also, for example, *University of Windsor, supra* note 49.

[55] *McKinney, supra* note 18 at para. 62.

member's students, thereby taking an active part in what the applicable collective agreement referred to as a material misuse of research funds;[56]

- "failing to disclose … related activities … committing extensive time to outside enterprises and … obtaining, and refusing to provide information with respect to, medical leave";[57]
- "insubordination, professional irresponsibility and teaching irresponsibility";[58]
- "irreparable damage to the employment relationship and gross misconduct, including repeated refusal or failure to follow directives and decisions from College management";[59]
- embarking on a campaign to smear the reputation of peers in the faculty member's department, senior officers of the university, and the university itself;[60] and
- insubordination against the background of a breach of the duty to objectively evaluate students.[61]

Incompetence

As the Supreme Court of Canada observed in *McKinney*, there is "the possibility of dismissal for cause but the level of interference with or evaluation of faculty members' performance is quite low."[62]

Incompetence may be either culpable or non-culpable.[63] The general labour law principles that govern the decision to dismiss an employee for incompetence have been accepted as equally applicable in faculty employment.[64] The postsecondary institution must

- define the level of job performance required,
- communicate that standard of performance to the employee,

---

[56] *University of Windsor, supra* note 49.

[57] *Richardson v University of St. Michael's College* (1995), 87 OAC 302 (CJ (Gen Div).

[58] *Bareau v University of Alberta* (1995), 35 Alta LR (3d) 403 (QB), aff'd 1999 ABCA 202, leave to appeal refused (2000), 252 NR 400 (SCC).

[59] *Langara College v Langara Faculty Assn. (Mirza Grievance)*, [2000] BCCAAA No 27 (Hall).

[60] *Assoc. des professeurs de l'Université Concordia c Université Concordia (grief de Petkov)*, 2014 LNSARTQ 42.

[61] *University of Ottawa, supra* note 31.

[62] *McKinney, supra* note 18 at para. 62.

[63] *Re Keyano College v Keyano College Faculty Association* (1993), 34 LAC (4th) 182 (Beattie, Chair).

[64] See, for example, *Assiniboine Community College v Manitoba Government and General Employees' Union*, [2006] MGAD No 53 (Werier).

- provide reasonable supervision and instruction and allow the employee a reasonable period of time to reach the standard,
- establish an inability on the part of the employee to reach the requisite standard to an extent rendering the individual incapable of performing the job,
- establish that reasonable efforts were taken to find alternative employment within the competence of the employee, and
- provide reasonable warnings to the employee to convey that a failure to meet the standard could result in dismissal.[65]

JURISDICTION OVER DISPUTES REGARDING FACULTY EMPLOYMENT

Despite the traditional view of a university as a self-governing community of scholars and the recognition of collegial governance as a critical feature of Canadian postsecondary institutions, various external bodies have the jurisdiction to review decisions about a faculty member's employment.

As noted above, postsecondary institutions normally have extensive internal review and appeal processes in which faculty members and, as applicable, their union, have the power to dispute a university decision. In addition, the following external bodies may play an important role.

Arbitrators

Normally, collective and framework/faculty agreements provide for the right to have disputes about a postsecondary institution's decisions about faculty employment decided by an independent adjudicator such as an arbitrator. This mechanism provides a means by which employment disputes will be resolved without resort to the courts. For this reason, many legal decisions about faculty employment will initially be made by arbitrators rather than the courts.

At Unionized Postsecondary Institutions

In *Re University of Ottawa v Association of Professors of the University of Ottawa*, the arbitration board observed that

the advent of collective bargaining in the university sector engenders a qualitative change in the relationships of the professoriate to the university.... In the scheme of the collective agreement which is before us, the university

---

[65] *Re Edith Cavell Private Hospital v Hospital Employees' Union, Local 180* (1982), 6 LAC (3d) 229 (Hope, Chair).

is the employer. The employer has agreed that in certain personnel areas, such as the promotion and tenure of academic faculty, it would be bound by the decisions of the Joint Committee of the Senate and Board of Governors. These decisions cannot be arbitrary or capricious, they must conform to the provisions of the collective agreement. They are ultimately subject to review in accordance with procedures set out in the collective agreement.[66]

In *Weber v Ontario Hydro*, [1995] 2 SCR 929, the Supreme Court of Canada held that labour arbitrators have exclusive jurisdiction over disputes arising from the interpretation, application, administration, or violation of a collective agreement. The question then becomes whether the dispute arises expressly out of the collective agreement.[67]

At Non-Unionized Postsecondary Institutions

Even where a faculty member is not unionized, but is instead a member of a non-union employee association, where the agreement between the postsecondary institution and the employee association provides a means for resolving disputes without resort to the courts, courts may not have jurisdiction over a wrongful dismissal action.[68]

The Courts

There do remain situations in which the courts will have original jurisdiction over disputes regarding faculty employment. For example, in *Jalan v Institute of Indigenous Government*, 2005 BCSC 590, the court allowed a wrongful dismissal action where the plaintiff was excluded from the

---

[66] (1978), 20 LAC (2d) 132 (Frankel, Chair) at para. 22.

[67] See, for example, *Pratt v University of Lethbridge*, 2001 ABCA 134, leave to appeal refused, [2001] SCCA No 388 (the essence of dispute was a decision to deny tenure and the process employed to reach that decision; the dispute fell within the exclusive jurisdiction of the grievance and appeal procedures in the faculty handbook); *James v Northern Lakes College*, 2012 ABQB 6 (dispute fell within the exclusive jurisdiction of the labour arbitrator, even where the plaintiff instructor was a probationary employee not entitled to access to the grievance procedure under the collective agreement); *Wiebe v Saskatchewan Institute of Applied Science & Technology*, 2007 SKQB 60 (dispute regarding intellectual property rights over lecture materials fell within the scope of the collective agreement of arbitrator's jurisdiction); *Blass v University of Regina*, 2012 SKQB 247, 400 Sask R 169 (allegations including wrongful dismissal, harassment, theft of equipment, alleged breach of labour relations legislation, safety legislation, and human rights legislation all fell within the exclusive jurisdiction of a labour arbitrator). But see *Wanke v University of Calgary*, 2011 ABCA 235.

[68] See *Ferrari v University of British Columbia*, 2014 BCCA 18.

relevant faculty bargaining unit, and the dispute therefore did not fall within the jurisdiction of a labour arbitrator.

Except in very narrow circumstances, unionized faculty members cannot pursue a legal action on their own account in any dispute about their employment. Instead, the employer and the union are the parties to the dispute.[69]

In *Yee v Trent University*, 2010 ONSC 3307, the Ontario Superior Court of Justice (Divisional Court) discussed exceptions to this principle. In *Yee*, a faculty member's union grieved a tenure denial. The arbitrator dismissed the grievance. The faculty member then applied personally for judicial review of the arbitrator's award. The court concluded that the faculty member had no standing to bring the application. The facts did not fall within any of the three "exceptional situations" in which a union member may have personal standing to litigate a decision about his or her employment: the collective agreement confers a right on the individual to pursue a matter to arbitration, the union takes a position adverse in interest to the employee, or the union's representation of the employee has been so deficient that the employee should be given a personal right to litigate the matter.

In addition to the limited instances where the courts may have jurisdiction over wrongful dismissal actions, except in British Columbia, the review of a decision of a labour arbitrator is to the courts.[70]

However, even when courts do have jurisdiction to review decisions regarding faculty employment, they have traditionally been reluctant to interfere with internal university decisions, as they recognize that universities are independent communities of scholars. As such, universities are generally recognized as enjoying substantial internal autonomy.[71] As

---

[69] See, for example, *Technical University of Nova Scotia v Collins* (1990), 97 NSR (2d) 76 (SCTD).

[70] See Palmer and Snyder, *Collective Agreement Arbitration in Canada*, 225–26. In British Columbia, generally the BC Labour Relations Board has jurisdiction pursuant to section 99 of the *Labour Relations Code*, RSBC 1996, c 244 to review awards of labour arbitrators, except if "the basis of the decision or award is a matter of general law not included in section 99(1)," in which case a party affected by the award may apply to the BC Court of Appeal for review of the arbitral award (see section 100). For a discussion of the BC Court of Appeal's jurisdiction to review arbitral awards, see *Okanagan College Faculty Assn. v Okanagan College*, 2013 BCCA 561.

[71] For a general discussion, see *Harelkin v University of Regina*, [1979] 2 SCR 561. See also, for example, *Syndicat des professeurs et professeures de l'Université Laval c Université Laval*, [1998] JQ No 450 (CA) at para. 21, where the Quebec Court of Appeal, on judicial review of an arbitral award relating to a faculty member's employment, stated: "Where the grievance related, essentially, to an evaluation of a professor's teaching skills and research, in my view, a superior court should be particularly deferential to the expertise of a specialized arbitration tribunal in the assessment of the decision of the University authorities."

Ontario's Court of Appeal has observed, "With respect to the employment of professors, they are masters in their own houses."[72]

The Visitor

The visitor has recently been described as an "ancient and somewhat obscure office."[73] It is a historical office in jurisdictions in which the English common law has been received. At some postsecondary institutions, the visitor continues to have a power to review internal university decisions, including decisions regarding faculty employment.

In *Mohamed v University of Saskatchewan*, the court described the powers of the visitor as follows:

> The visitor at common law has very broad powers available to intervene in matters of domestic jurisdiction, and how those powers are exercised by the visitor in any one matter may vary depending on the nature of the wrong alleged, and the quality and expertise of the internal processes the institution has put in place to address such matters. In the end result, the visitor has the discretion to determine what type of review will be conducted by him or her, and to decide whether it will include a review on the merits, or whether it will consist of a supervisory type of review only.[74]

Whether a given university remains under the jurisdiction of a visitor and, if so, the identity of the visitor depend on applicable statutory provisions and case law. For example, the *University of Saskatchewan Act, 1995*, SS 1995, c U-6.1 states that "the Lieutenant Governor is the visitor of the university and may exercise the rights and shall perform the duties of the visitor." Further, section 9(5) of *The Queen's Bench Act, 1998*, SS 1998, c Q-1.01, states: "On the direction of the Lieutenant Governor in a particular case, the court may exercise the jurisdiction and powers of the Lieutenant Governor as a visitor."[75]

Labour Relations Boards

At institutions where faculty members are unionized, as is noticed above, most initial decisions in disputes about faculty employment are made by labour arbitrators. However, a labour relations board may have jurisdiction to review a decision of a labour arbitrator or to hear complaints about

---

[72] *McKinney v University of Guelph*, [1987] 63 OR (2d) 1 (CA) at para. 47, aff'd *McKinney, supra* note 18.

[73] *Pearlman v University of Saskatchewan*, 2006 SKCA 105 at para. 1.

[74] 2006 SKQB 23, 276 Sask R 87 at para. 37.

[75] For further examples regarding the University of Alberta, see *Vanek, supra* note 14; regarding McGill University, see *Hafeez c Université McGill*, [1996] JQ No 884.

whether a faculty member's union has met its duty to fairly represent a member.

Review of Labour Arbitrators' Awards

In British Columbia, the BC Labour Relations Board has the jurisdiction to review awards of labour arbitrators.[76]

The Union's Duty of Fair Representation

In Canada, generally, the duty of fair representation is a statutory duty arising under the relevant labour relations statute.[77] It protects members of certified bargaining units by placing obligations on unions to fairly represent members in connection with certain actions, for example the conduct of grievances. The nature and scope of the duty will require a review of the applicable labour relations statute.

CONCLUSIONS

With the advent of widespread unionization among Canadian faculty members, there has been a significant evolution of the legal framework for faculty employment in Canada. As is apparent from the legal decisions surveyed above, this evolution has to some degree led to a reduction in the autonomy of postsecondary institutions in relation to matters of faculty employment. However, the unique features of faculty employment including tenure, academic freedom, and the collegial decision-making structure continue to play an important role throughout the faculty employment relationship.

---

[76] *Keyano, supra* note 63.

[77] *Gendron v Supply and Services Union of the Public Service Alliance of Canada, Local 50057*, [1990] 1 SCR 1298. See Table 8.1 for a list of the applicable labour relations statutes in the provinces and territories.

PART IV
Postsecondary Institutions and the Community

Chapter 9

COMPLEX VENTURES: UNIVERSITY RESEARCH, INTELLECTUAL PROPERTY, AND ACADEMIC FREEDOM

BRENT DAVIS

INTRODUCTION

Universities, largely through the efforts of their faculty, are significant producers of intellectual property. Lecture notes, syllabi, and classroom texts are commonly prepared by academic staff and are copyrightable works. Researchers create know-how and patentable works in their projects funded by government or industrial partners. Prior to the 1990s, universities received little external pressure to take closer notice of intellectual property as a significant asset capable of generating revenue. But as scrutiny of government funding of universities in Canada increased, so did the interest displayed by both universities and government in the potential value of university-created intellectual property.

In 1999, the Government of Canada received from an expert panel the report on the commercialization of university research, *Public Investment in University Research: Reaping the Benefits*. The report advised that although Canadian universities were well positioned to fuel Canada's economic growth and social well-being, they were not achieving their full potential in generating innovations from research. The consultants concluded that Canadian taxpayers had a right to expect a greater return on their

Handbook of Canadian Higher Education Law, edited by Theresa Shanahan, Michelle Nilson, and Li-Jeen Broshko. Montreal and Kingston: McGill-Queen's University Press, Queen's Policy Studies Series.

investment in universities.[1] The federal government was not alone in examining the outputs of universities. The McGuinty government in the Province of Ontario created the Ministry of Research and Innovation which, in November 2006, published its Strategic Plan requiring publicly sponsored research organizations to manage intellectual property in ways that supported Ontario's long-term innovation goals. According to the Strategic Plan, this was to be accomplished by, among other things, making intellectual property more readily available to the commercial sector.[2] Perhaps understandably, the Canadian Association of University Teachers disagreed with the direction charted by the Ontario government:

> We are deeply troubled by the call for commercialization to become a key mission of the university – alongside teaching, research and community service. Our public educational system is vital to understanding the character and purpose of Canadian social, economic and political life. To accomplish that goal, our public educational institutions must be free of encumbrances resulting from compulsory ties to the corporate and commercial world – or to any other special interest.[3]

The tension between the institutional objective of achieving a return on its intellectual property inventory and faculty's desire to preserve "academic freedom" is still profoundly felt on Canadian campuses today.

This chapter will examine the elements of intellectual property ownership in Canadian universities. In doing so, the general legal principles of intellectual property ownership in Canada will be discussed, specifically with respect to copyrightable and patentable materials created by faculty. Next, the chapter will illustrate how these legal principles co-exist, sometimes uneasily, with notions of academic customs and academic freedom that have been long-standing mainstays of academic life. Finally, the chapter will examine the intellectual property policies of research-intensive Canadian universities to determine the institutional means by which the universities seek to regulate the tension between institutional commercialization objectives and academic customs.

LEGAL PRINCIPLES OF INTELLECTUAL PROPERTY OWNERSHIP

The default ownership of patents and copyright in Canada is established by legislation, which some universities seek to either modify or embrace

---

[1] Canadian Advisory Council on Science and Technology, "Public Investment in University Research," 34.

[2] Ministry of Research and Innovation, *Strategic Plan*, 11–12.

[3] Canadian Association of University Teachers, "Minister Rapped for Reaping the Benefits."

within their intellectual property policies. Complicating the application of the law is the additional considerations required in circumstances where, as is the case in universities, inventions are created during an employment relationship. The ownership of copyrightable material created in an employment relationship in Canada is directly addressed by the *Copyright Act* while the *Patent Act* is silent on the issue. The general principle of ownership of inventions created by employees in Canada was established in *Bloxam v Elsee*[4] where it was held that if a servant, while in the employ of his master, makes an invention, that invention belongs to the servant, not to the master; however, if the master employs a skillful person for the express purpose of inventing, the inventions made by the employee will belong to the master so as to enable the master to obtain a patent for them.

The vast majority of faculty in Canadian universities are, in the legal sense, employees. Their relationship to the university satisfies the legal tests[5] used to determine employment relationships, and the large number of faculty who are members of academic unions[6] would not be eligible for membership if they were something other than employees of the university. The same conclusion can be drawn for faculty in the United States. Therefore, the statutory and common law applicable to the ownership of intellectual property created by employees should be applicable to faculty. The following discussion illustrates that, for a variety of reasons, this may not be the case.

Patents

As part of a university's research outputs, some faculty will invariably create intellectual property capable of being patented. The *Patent Act*[7] provides that an inventor of an invention may, if the conditions of the *Patent Act* are met, obtain a patent. An "invention" is defined as "any new or useful art, process, machine, manufacture or composition of matter, or any new and useful improvement in any art, process, machine, manufacture or composition of matter."[8] The grant of a patent gives to the owner the exclusive right of making, constructing, and using an invention

---

[4] (1825) 1 Car & P 558.

[5] See for example *Montreal (City) v Montreal Locomotive Works Ltd* (1946), [1947] 1 DLR 161 (Canada PC) at 169: "It has been suggested that a fourfold test would in some cases be more appropriate, a complex involving (1) control; (2) ownership of the tools; (3) chance of profit; (4) risk of loss. "

[6] One article reported that 79 percent of faculty at Canadian universities had unionized by 2004. Hackett and Pullman, "Faculty Unionization: What Difference Does It Make?"

[7] RSC 1985, c P-4.

[8] Ibid., s 2.

and offering it to others to be used. In essence, the effect of a patent is to exclude all persons except the inventor and his licensees or assignees from the exploitation of an invention for a prescribed period of years.

In the case of an invention created by an employee, the *Patent Act* is silent, and guidance must be obtained from the common law. When a person is hired to develop inventions, there is more recent authority providing that the new material, method, or process discovered belongs to the employer, unless this expectation is modified by agreement between the parties.[9] However, the mere fact of an employment relationship does not preclude an employee from patenting and retaining ownership of an invention provided it does not directly arise out of work assigned to the employee.[10] The distinction is a fine one and the ultimate result rests on the particular facts at hand. But the applicable legal principle has remained unchanged since *Bloxam*: an employee must be employed to invent in order for the employer to own the invention.

Discerning the true state of ownership of inventions created by university-employed faculty can be problematic. There is considerable debate as to whether faculty, who pursue research from which inventions can be reasonably expected to result, are employed to invent. If faculty are employed to invent, Canadian law directs that, unless a contrary agreement exists, the university is the proper owner of the invention. However, if faculty are employed to merely conduct research, without a positive duty to invent, the law directs that the faculty inventor is the owner of the resulting inventions.

Although no Canadian case has considered whether university faculty are employed to invent, decisions of Scottish and Australian courts are instructive. In *Greater Glasgow Health Board's Application*,[11] Dr. Montgomery was employed primarily as a clinician in the Department of Ophthalmology; and any teaching or research activities were permissible and expected, but secondary. Nevertheless, Dr. Montgomery invented an optic spacing device for use with an indirect ophthalmoscope in his off hours at home and outside the duties of his employment. The court concluded that he, and not his employer, was the owner of the invention. The court rejected the employer's argument that because of the employment relationship, any invention created by an employee that could be used for the purpose of their employment must necessarily belong to the employer. To adopt such a conclusion, the court reasoned, would result in a significant shift in the current practice and expectation

---

[9] *Devoe-Holbein Inc v Yam* (1984), 2 CIPR 229 (Que SC).

[10] *Techform Products Ltd v Wolda*, [2000] 5 CPR (4th) 25 at para 12 (SC) rev'd on other grounds [2001] 15 CPR (4th) 44 (CA), leave to SCC denied [2001] SCCA No 603; *C. I. Covington Fund Inc v White*, [2000] 10 CPR (4th) 49 (SC).

[11] [1996] RPC 207, PatC.

of clinical faculty by, for example, requiring them to obtain permission of the university prior to publishing details of their invention. Currently, they are not required to do so, and the court in *Greater Glasgow* saw no reason why faculty should be obligated to do so in the future.

Similarly, the court in *University of Western Australia v Gray*[12] noted with approval the special case presented by universities and their long-held custom to allow faculty freedom to pursue their individual courses of research. This unique relationship between universities and their faculty meant that although a faculty member has a duty to conduct research that may lead to an invention, faculty have no specific duty to invent. Absent a specific duty to invent, a university has no common-law right to the ownership of faculty-generated inventions. In order to establish such a right, a university must explicitly provide for it in an employment or collective agreement.

The courts in both *Greater Glasgow* and *Gray* distinguished between a faculty member's duty to conduct research and the more onerous duty to invent. A duty to invent necessarily implies the obligation to preserve the secrecy of research results until the employer makes decisions regarding a patent strategy.[13] The imposition of an obligation of secrecy in an academic setting by a university owner is likely to lead to an accusation that the university is seeking to undermine academic freedom by dictating or limiting what academics may publish. On the strength of the *Greater Glasgow* and *Gray* decisions, among other authority,[14] it would appear that university faculty are not employed to invent.[15] Therefore, the common law indicates that they are owners of their inventions created during the course of their work at the university. Understandably, universities have taken steps to enable them to share in the potential revenues of inventions created using their, sometimes considerable, research support. The only avenue available to universities to modify the common law with respect to ownership of faculty-generated inventions is through employment agreements that incorporate the university's intellectual property policies or collective agreements.

---

[12] [2008] FCA 498.

[13] Monotti, "The Legal Issues: Patenting and Technology Transfer."

[14] Van Slyke and Friedman, "Employers Rights," 141. "The key factor in determining whether an employee was hired to invent is the specificity of the task assigned to the employee. Where ... the employee is hired to 'do research' for the employer, title will ... remain with the employee/inventor." See also *Yeshiva University v Greenberg*, 681 NYS 2d 71 (App Div 1998).

[15] One case that holds a contrary view is *Speck v North Carolina Dairy Foundation*, 391 SE 2d 139 (NC 1984) in which the court held that Dr. Speck had been employed by North Carolina State University to invent. The decision has been criticized and may best be left to stand on its particular facts instead of applying to faculty generally (see Chew, "Faculty-Generated Inventions," 301–2).

Copyright

The vast majority of copyrightable works created by faculty will be literary works, and for such works the *Copyright Act* establishes the presumption that the author of a work shall be the first owner of the copyright.[16] The owner of the copyright in a literary work has the sole right to produce, reproduce, perform, publish, translate, convert, record, and communicate the work in any form and to authorize such acts.[17] One exception to the presumption noted above are works made under a contract of service. In circumstances where the author of the work was employed by some other person under a contract of service and the work at issue was made during the course of employment, the *Copyright Act* stipulates that the employer shall be the first owner of the copyright in the absence of an agreement to the contrary.[18] The authorship of the work is maintained by the employee. In contrast, the United States *Copyright Act* provides that works produced within the scope of an employee's employment are "works made for hire" and the employer is deemed to be both author and first owner of the copyright. Thus, in the United States, the employee forfeits all author rights, including the moral right to be associated with the work, effectively erasing the true author from the creative process. Nevertheless, copyright law in Canada and the United States are in agreement that employers are the first owners of copyright created by their employees.

As a result of faculty's employee status, Canadian and American law suggests that the university is the owner of copyrightable works created by their faculty. But this conclusion has not been universally accepted by academics, judges, and commentators who cite considerable and long-standing legal authority and academic tradition to the contrary. The underpinnings of the academic tradition of faculty owning their copyrightable works can be traced to the United Kingdom. As early as 1825, in *Abernethy v Hutchinson*, British courts held that professors have a common-law copyright in their lectures, which arose in the "precedent" of William Blackstone's copyright in his Vinerian Lectures: "Now, if a professor be appointed, he is appointed for the purpose of giving information to all the students who attend him, and it is his duty to do that; but I have never yet heard that anybody could publish his lectures."[19]

The notion of the employment relationship as the determining factor of copyright ownership failed to gain credence until the 1950s. In *Stephenson Jordan & Harrison Ltd v MacDonald & Evans*,[20] Justice Denning concluded

---

[16] *Copyright Act*, RS, c C-30, s 13(1).

[17] Ibid., s 3.

[18] Ibid., s 13(3).

[19] *Abernethy v Hutchinson*, (1825) 3 LJ (Ch) 209.

[20] (1951) 69 RPC 10 (CA).

that a duty to provide lectures for one's employers does not necessarily include a duty to record the lectures in writing and, should the employee do so, such written work would be outside of the employment contract and therefore ineligible for ownership by the employer.[21] *Noah v Shuba*[22] raised the issue of the employer's past practice in determining ownership of copyright in written works. The court concluded that the ongoing practice of the employer at issue not to claim ownership of copyright in works written by its employees and submitted for publication to journals was clear and, in the absence of a contravening agreement with the employee, should be upheld.[23] Although these cases did not deal directly with a faculty-university employment relationship, they demonstrate that the principle that a lecturer retains ownership of lecture notes and publishable materials is consistent and well established in the common law.

The academic custom established by the *Abernethy* line of cases outlined above was codified in the United States *Copyright Act* of 1909, which created a "teacher exception" to the principle of a "work made for hire." The exception allowed academic staff to retain copyright in their research outputs in circumstances where the law would consider their employers, in this case the university, as the first owner of the copyright. The existence of the teacher exception is controversial in the United States because the 1976 codification of the *Copyright Act* makes no reference to a teacher exception. The courts were left to determine whether the omission of the teacher exception was an oversight and that Congress intended it to continue or whether its omission was an active decision taken to alter the law. Decisions in *Weinstein v University of Illinois*[24] and *Hays v Sony Corp of America*[25] upheld the teacher exception despite there being no statutory basis. The court in *Hays* based its conclusion upholding the teacher exception on the havoc that would ensue in universities if it ceased to exist.[26] This reasoning mirrors that in *Greater Glasgow Health Board's Application*. As a result of these cases, many universities, including those in Canada, still honour the tradition of permitting faculty members to own works that might otherwise reasonably be characterized as within the scope of their employment and therefore owned by their university.[27] Further, the expectation among faculty at most universities is that the academic tradition will be upheld.

---

[21] Ibid., 18.

[22] [1990] c D-14.

[23] Ibid., 27.

[24] 811 F (2d) 1091 (7th Cir 1987).

[25] 847 F (2d) 412 (7th Cir 1988).

[26] Ibid., 416.

[27] Such works are usually limited to "traditional academic materials" such as articles, lecture notes, laboratory manuals, books, and works of visual art.

ACADEMIC FREEDOM

The reason that the letter of the law is not necessarily followed in the academy can be attributed to the unique historical rights and traditions inherent to a community of scholars. These rights and traditions have come to be termed academic freedom. The concept of academic freedom defies easy definition and, as a result, is subject to abuse when invoked improperly or applied to inappropriate situations. Academic freedom, as it is generally recognized today, had its origins in Germany in the nineteenth century with the linkage of university autonomy, research, and academic freedom. Both *Lernfreiheit*, the freedom to learn granted to the student, and *Lehrfreiheit*, the professional freedom to research and present findings, were recognized.[28] The modern Canadian concept of academic freedom combines the German concepts of freedom to learn and to conduct and disseminate research with the British notion of freedom to express political and social views in opposition to administrators, employers, and the government.[29] This understanding is reflected in the Canadian Association of University Teachers' Policy Statement on Academic Freedom,[30] which outlines six principles including searching for and disseminating knowledge, truth, and understanding; the freedom to teach, discuss, research, and publish; engage in service to the university and community; express opinions about the institution; acquire documentary material; and participate in professional bodies.

Although there is no legislative basis in Canada for either academic freedom or the academic tradition of faculty owning their intellectual property created during the course of their employment at the university, it is a fundamental expectation of many faculty. The majority of commentators, themselves academics, conclude that university ownership of inventions and copyrightable works is anathema to academic freedom. The concerns include suppression by the university of unpopular ideas;[31] restrictions on the faculty's right to choose, free from institutional pressure, the direction of their research program;[32] and the loss of publishing freedom by faculty.[33] As suggested by Rhoades, the root issue is that of control:

> As intellectual property becomes increasingly privatized, who controls its use? For many faculty members, what is at issue is not the money, but quality

---

[28] Birtwistle, "Academic Freedom and Complacency," 205.

[29] Horn, *Academic Freedom in Canada*, 7–9.

[30] See Canadian Association of University Teachers, "Academic Freedom."

[31] Kulkarni, "All Professors Create Equally," 246.

[32] Chew, "Faculty-Generated Inventions," 306.

[33] Monotti, "The Legal Issues," 7–8.

control and professional autonomy. With the advance of corporatization, academic managers have increasing say over initiatives in research and instructional programs, evaluating them, along with academic work in general, in terms of their potential commercial value. Formerly, such decisions were firmly within the domain of faculty members and based more exclusively on academic criteria.[34]

For those concerned about threats to academic freedom, according university administrators power over research outputs, whether or not they choose to exercise it, weakens the very foundation of academic freedom.

Other commentators believe that today's university has been commercialized and, set against this backdrop, traditional academic norms and the principles and purposes of academic freedom appear anachronistic. In the age of the entrepreneurial academic, traditions of academic freedom may no longer serve the goal of maintaining the integrity and objectivity of scholars. Further, should the public awaken to the reality of the new commercialized university, it may be less willing to accord scholars the same level of academic freedom as in the past.[35]

These diverging viewpoints are not easily reconciled. The interest taken by universities in owning inventions and copyright is strictly monetary while the interests of academics extend beyond monetary considerations to the very control of their intellectual output.[36] In the day-to-day practices of university technology transfer offices, there may be circumstances in which it is better for the university to own the intellectual property provided that it only retains those aspects of ownership in which it truly has interest, that is, income generation.

It is clear that some combination of academic freedom and academic traditions have had some success in eroding the legal principle that employers are to be accorded ownership of inventions and copyrightable works created during the course of faculty employment. There have been several mechanisms used to achieve these ends. The court in *Greater Glasgow Health Board's Application* sought to draw a distinction between persons hired to research and those hired to invent. The courts in *Weinstein* and *Hays* cited academic tradition as upholding a statutory provision that had been omitted from the applicable *Copyright Act*.

Regardless of the mechanism, the borderless nature of academe resulted in the easy import of such traditions to Canadian universities from the United States and elsewhere. The divergence between the legal authorities and academic practice left universities no choice but to codify their

---

[34] Rhoades, "Whose Property Is It?" 42.
[35] Leskovac, "Academic Freedom," 412.
[36] Lape, "Ownership of Copyrightable Works of University Professors," 268–69.

expectations regarding ownership of inventions and copyrightable works in their intellectual property policies.

UNIVERSITY INTELLECTUAL PROPERTY POLICIES

All of the major Canadian research universities have created intellectual property policies and embedded them either in their collective agreements with faculty or by specific reference in faculty employment contracts.[37] As previously suggested, the purpose of university intellectual property policies is to provide clarity to an area of law that may not be consistent with the presumptive application of statutory or common law. Although the terms of intellectual property policies vary, they each typically address four main points:

- disclosure of intellectual property invented by faculty to the university;
- the ownership of patents, copyright, and "academic materials" as between the faculty creator and the university;
- the control of the commercialization process; and
- the sharing of resulting revenues.

The university intellectual property policies examined below include those of McMaster, Queen's, Dalhousie, Alberta, UBC, Western, McGill, Calgary, Toronto, Waterloo, and Ottawa.

Disclosure of Intellectual Property to the University

University Policy

In order for the university to become involved in the commercialization process, the university must first be made aware of potentially commercializable inventions by the faculty creators through the invention disclosure process in the intellectual property policy. Canadian universities have employed a variety of different strategies with respect to disclosure. Dalhousie and Ottawa have opted for no disclosure, while the intellectual property policies of McMaster, Western, and Toronto all make disclosure of new intellectual property to the university industry liaison office mandatory. The remaining universities impose the disclosure obligation only where faculty intend to commercialize the intellectual property. By

---

[37] In the case of employment contracts, the intellectual property policy is typically referenced, although not included as an enclosure, in the letter offer of employment to the proposed new faculty member, which must be signed and returned to the university.

way of illustration, section 4.19 of Calgary's intellectual property policy states that the creator of intellectual property

> will disclose to the University any proposed paid assignment, sale, license, or exploitation for profit of any Intellectual Property that is covered by the revenue sharing guidelines. The Creator and University will discuss and determine ownership and revenue sharing according to this policy.

These approaches to disclosure illustrate a shifting burden to determine the worthiness of intellectual property for commercialization. For universities that only require disclosure immediately prior to commercialization, the burden to establish the intellectual property as commercializable rests with the faculty creator. For universities that require immediate disclosure, the burden is shared between the faculty creator and the industry liaison office, which often undertakes marketing efforts on behalf of the faculty creator.

Legal Implications

The failure by a faculty creator to properly disclose intellectual property to the university is actionable by the university as a breach of contract or collective agreement, as applicable. In *Fenn v Yale University*,[38] Dr. Fenn invented a method to determine the molecular weight of particles through the use of multiplied charged ions. Dr. Fenn did not immediately file a disclosure with the university and, when he ultimately did so, only included the barest details of the invention. When he was asked directly whether the invention had commercial applications, he replied that it did not. Based on this advice, Yale did not file a patent application. However, Dr. Fenn, contrary to his advice to Yale, did believe it had valuable commercial applications and filed a patent application in his own name. When Yale discovered the patent application, it requested that it be assigned to the university in accordance with the applicable patent policy. Dr. Fenn refused, and Yale commenced an action for breach of contract, fraud, and an assignment of the patent. Both the trial and appellate courts concluded that Dr. Fenn breached his contract with Yale by violating the patent policy and also committed fraud. Dr. Fenn's actions were so egregious that the court not only granted Yale an assignment of the patent, but also an entitlement to the profits received by Dr. Fenn as well as a significant damage award.

A Canadian court has not had the opportunity to consider a situation similar to that described in the Fenn case. Nevertheless, if a faculty creator at one of the universities with an intellectual property policy that

---

[38] 283 F Supp (2d) 615 (2003 D Conn).

requires disclosure – either upon invention or prior to commercialization – engaged in behaviour similar to that of Dr. Fenn, in all likelihood a Canadian court would provide a similar result.

Ownership

University Policy

The intellectual property statutes and cases discussed earlier outline the default ownership of intellectual property created by employees and how the ownership regime may be modified in the university setting by academic customs. Ownership rules regarding intellectual property generated at universities by faculty creators are modified by the institution's intellectual property policies. There is considerable nuance in the ownership provisions of the intellectual property policies examined. McMaster is the only university among those examined where the university is the first "nominal owner" of patents and copyright in non-academic materials irrespective of the normal parameters such as research funding source, creation during the course of employment, or use of university facilities. At Dalhousie and UBC, the university is the owner of intellectual property[39] created using university funds or facilities. At Western and Calgary, the university owns intellectual property if a third-party contract requires it to do so. At Ottawa, the university owns the intellectual property if either of the previous two scenarios exist. Faculty and the university are joint owners of intellectual property created at McGill when university resources, such as laboratory space and administrative services, are used. Intellectual property is also jointly owned between faculty and Toronto unless the university specifically directs its creation. At Waterloo, faculty is the owner of intellectual property unless its creation falls specifically within a task assigned by the university. Queen's has provided for a non-exclusive license for research purposes from its faculty owners. Similarly, faculty owners at Alberta are compelled to provide the university with a right to use their intellectual property for education purposes.

The situation with respect to academic materials is considerably more consistent.[40] Predominantly, faculty are the owners of academic materials with the university occasionally reserving a right to use such materials

---

[39] As used in this section, intellectual property includes both patents and copyrights to materials that are not created in the course of faculty's "academic duties," such as typical teaching responsibilities and publishing scholarly journals.

[40] The term *academic materials* is defined by section 4.3(a) of McMaster University's Joint Intellectual Property policy as "lecture notes, laboratory manuals, articles, books, artifacts, works of visual art, maps, charts, plans, photographs, engravings, sculptures and music, no matter in which format any of the foregoing materials may have been recorded or embodied."

for a certain time period[41] or for internal academic purposes.[42] The only circumstances in which a university reserved ownership of academic materials was where a third party contract was involved[43] or where the material was prepared for the purposes of "course management."[44] Allowing faculty creators to consistently own academic materials not only concurs with the tenets of academic freedom and tradition but has the added benefit of allowing faculty to freely move between universities without being required to reformulate their academic materials at their new employer.

As illustrated by the significant variety in ownership regimes, there are no standard ownership provisions in Canadian university intellectual property policies. The wide variety of ownership provisions suggests that faculty may be treated differently depending on their place of employment, and as a result, a migration might be expected away from universities with institution-owned policies toward those with faculty-owned policies. However, LaRoche et al. conclude that there is no evidence that such a migration takes place for the reason that the right to be identified as the owner of intellectual property is largely irrelevant; the most valuable rights are the control of commercialization and entitlement to share revenues, which for the most part are shared.[45]

Legal Implications

Canadian courts have not yet had the opportunity to assess the enforceability of university intellectual property contracts with respect to their provisions on ownership of faculty-generated intellectual property. In an earlier era when intellectual property policies were not included in collective agreements or specifically incorporated into faculty employment contracts, their enforceability may have been in doubt. But more recently, American courts have commented on the enforceability of intellectual property policies that are referenced in faculty employment agreements.

The faculty member in *Singer v Regents of the University of California*[46] signed a written employment agreement that required him to sign the university's Patent Agreement, which referred to the university's relevant Patent Policy. The Patent Policy contained the ownership provisions and obligation for faculty to assign their inventions to the university. The court concluded that for intellectual property policies to be incorporated by reference in other agreements, such as employment agreements, the

---

[41] At Dalhousie, one to five years after employment ceases.
[42] See Waterloo's Intellectual Property Policy.
[43] See Calgary's Intellectual Property Policy.
[44] See Waterloo's Intellectual Property Policy.
[45] LaRoche et al., "Appropriating Innovation," 8–9.
[46] 1996 WL 775106 (Cal App Super, 1996).

reference to the incorporated document must be clear and unequivo-cal. Otherwise, the ownership and assignment provisions would be unenforceable.

In *Scallen v Regents of University of New Mexico*,[47] Professors Scallen and Knight engaged in cancer research that led to inventions subsequently assigned to the university in accordance with the relevant patent policy, which was incorporated into their written employment contracts. These inventions subsequently were patented by the university. As part of the patent process, the university was required to file continuations that re-quired further assignments from Scallen and Knight, which were refused because they disagreed with the university's patent prosecutions. Both the trial and appellate court confirmed that the broad language contained in the patent policy[48] was more than sufficient to obligate Scallen and Knight to assign the inventions and related continuations to the university.

From time to time a university may be required to amend its intellectual property policy, which may raise an issue where terms of the new policy are less favourable to faculty than terms of the former policy. Authorities from the United States provide conflicting answers. In *Shaw v Regents of the University of California*,[49] the university was prevented from enforcing the terms of its new policy against a faculty member who had accepted the terms of the former policy in his employment agreement. In that case, the faculty member remained entitled to receive the 50 percent of royal-ties established in the former policy. In *Fenn v Yale University*, mentioned previously, the court concluded that because the patent policy specifically allowed the university to revoke or amend the policy, the faculty member was required to abide by any new policy.

Commercialization

University Policy

Although intellectual property may be created at universities, they are not well-suited to transforming intellectual property into marketable products by themselves. The commercialization of intellectual property generated at universities involves a complicated assessment of commercial potential. The assessment includes ascertaining the nature and status of

---

[47] 321 F 3d 1111 (Fed Cir).

[48] According to the Patent Policy, any inventions or discoveries made by staff members (a) in the course of their research funded by the university, (b) that are a direct result of their duties with the university, or (c) that are made in whole or part using university facilities shall be disclosed and belong to the university. For such inventions, every involved staff member is obliged to cooperate fully including signing of patent applications and associated documents.

[49] 58 Cal. App. 4th 44 (Cal. Ct. App. 1997).

the development of the intellectual property; the relevant market environment and identification of potential investors, partners, and customers; and the costs of commercialization. The control of the commercialization process is a key intellectual property right that university intellectual property policies address. The majority of the intellectual property policies examined grant to faculty the right to control the commercialization process.[50] Included in the right is the ability to decide whether the intellectual property will be commercialized and, if so, whether the faculty member would like to proceed with the commercialization alone or with the assistance of the university. At McMaster, the faculty creator is given the power to decide whether an invention is to be commercialized as well as the ability to choose whether the university or the faculty creator will lead the commercialization effort.[51] If the faculty creator decides that the university is to lead commercialization, and the university is interested in proceeding, the university then decides the method of commercialization while the faculty creator gains a right of consultation and is relieved of any obligation to pay for costs related to commercialization. If the university declines to proceed, the faculty creator is permitted to request an assignment of the intellectual property.[52] McMaster's policy reflects an approach to the commercialization of faculty-generated intellectual property that acknowledges the university's investment in its creation together with the fact that the university, rather than the faculty member, is better disposed to fund a patent application and the initial search for a commercial partner.

At both Alberta and McGill, faculty and the university must agree on the commercialization process before proceeding. In most cases, the commercialization process commences with seeking proprietary rights to the intellectual property. Given the expense associated with patent protection, the university is typically in a better position to file a patent.[53] While most intellectual property policies grant faculty the right to control the commercialization process, if faculty desire the university to

---

[50] Among the universities that provide faculty the right to control the commercialization process are Queen's, Dalhousie, UBC, Western, Calgary, Toronto, and Waterloo. In McMaster's case, this is despite the fact that McMaster is the first nominal owner of the intellectual property. McMaster's intellectual property policy allows the faculty member to request an assignment of the intellectual property in exchange for McMaster's right to receive 25 percent of future revenues. This illustrates the earlier point that the most valuable intellectual property right is not ownership but rather the rights to control commercialization and share in revenues.

[51] See McMaster, Joint Intellectual Property Policy, ss 6.1 and 10.2.

[52] See McMaster, Joint Intellectual Property Policy, ss 10.2, 10.3, 11.1, and 13.1–3.

[53] To the author's knowledge, there is not a single Tri-Council grant that allows a principle investigator to include patent expenses as a budget line item.

seek patent protection, intellectual property policies often require faculty to assign ownership of the invention to the university. The university then assumes financial responsibility for the commercialization of the intellectual property. Faculty are also usually given the right to seek an assignment back from the university if the university is unsuccessful in its commercialization efforts.

Legal Implications

Although the terms of the intellectual property policies clearly articulate the different responsibilities of faculty and the university in the commercialization effort, commercialization in practice occurs more as a collaboration between faculty and the university's industry liaison office.[54] A recent Canadian decision illustrates the result of a breakdown in the spirit of a university-faculty commercialization collaboration. In *Université de Sherbrooke v Beaudoin*,[55] the inventors commenced action against the university for failing to consult them regarding certain aspects of the commercialization process. The inventors had created a patented process for extracting krill oil. The university and Groupe Conseil Harland Inc. ("Harland") entered into an agreement to further develop the invention. The university and the inventors also entered into an agreement relating to the management of the intellectual property and commercialization process (the "Management Agreement"). Harland agreed to license the invention from the university and incorporated a subsidiary company – Neptune Technologies and Bioresources Inc. ("Neptune") – specifically for the task. The university agreed to transfer its agreements with Harland to Neptune as well as to modify the existing formula for determining the price by a predetermined amount. The inventors commenced an action against the university for damages on the basis that they had not been consulted on the transfer of the agreements from Harland to Neptune or the modification to the fixed price formula. The inventors had been advised that the university was proceeding in this manner and had registered their opposition.

The court interpreted the Management Agreement as requiring the university to consult the inventors on the commercialization of the invention but not to obtain their consent to any proposed action. The court also concluded that, although the university had taken a conservative approach to commercialization, it had complied with its duty to maximize the value of the invention by taking realistic steps with an invention that still had not

---

[54] Alberta's intellectual property policy goes so far as to state that, whoever proceeds with commercialization, a fiduciary duty is owed by that person/entity to the other.

[55] 2010 QCCA 28.

demonstrated its commercial potential. The university was successful in enforcing its interpretation of the applicable intellectual property policy, as extended and enhanced by the Management Agreement.

Revenue Sharing

University Policy

The majority of university intellectual property policies contain provisions that outline how commercialization revenues are to be shared between the university and faculty inventors. Where the invention is owned or commercialized by the university, the sharing calculations are generally 50-50. The intellectual property policies of McMaster, Queen's, Dalhousie, and UBC all contain some element of 50-50 sharing between the university and faculty inventor. To reimburse the university for its initial investment in the commercialization process, both Alberta (one-third) and Toronto (up to 20 percent as a "management fee") specifically reserve to the university a percentage of revenues. At Alberta, the remaining two-thirds is split evenly between the university and faculty inventor. At Toronto, the remaining revenues are split 25 percent to the university and 75 percent to the faculty inventor. McGill varies its sharing calculations based on the amount of revenues earned if commercialized by the inventor: if less than $100,000 the inventor retains 80 percent and the university is entitled to 20 percent; if $100,000 or more, the inventor retains 30 percent and the university is entitled to 70 percent. Calgary and Waterloo adopt a more relaxed approach by requiring a revenue-sharing calculation to be worked out at the time revenues are expected to be received.

Legal Implications

Several problems with the revenue-sharing provisions of university intellectual property policies have been catalogued. The revenue-sharing formulas can lack specificity and detail causing confusion regarding their application. Not all intellectual property policies impose reporting obligations on faculty or provide faculty with audit rights. As a result, revenue sharing may be taking place without a full accounting of revenue, and the process may lack transparency. An unexpected problem with the revenue-sharing process was illustrated in *Corporation de l'Ecole Polytechnique de Montreal c Fardad*[56] in which the Quebec Court of Appeal ruled in favour of the faculty inventor and against the university. Fardad, who was employed by McGill, performed some of the work that led to

---

[56] 2010 QCCA 992.

the invention at l'Ecole Polytechnique de Montreal (EPM) as part of a collaborative project between the two universities. The invention had one inventor from EPM and two from McGill. It was agreed that the commercialization would be undertaken by McGill, which received an assignment of the invention and provided an undertaking to share any revenues with EPM. The inventors would share in the revenues according to the terms of the relevant university intellectual property policy. Several years elapsed before Fardad discovered that a company had been formed to commercialize the invention and that both McGill and EPM (through its commercialization entity, Polyvalor) received shares in the new company in exchange for a grant of license rights in the invention. The shares were subsequently sold by both McGill and Polyvalor, thereby earning revenues to be shared with the inventors. Fardad received his allotted revenue share from McGill and then approached EPM for a share in accordance with EPM's intellectual property policy. EPM denied Fardad's claim on the basis that he was not an employee of EPM at the time the invention was devised. EPM's intellectual property policy was examined by the court, which noted that the policy was intended to apply not just where an employee is an inventor but also where EPM's resources or services are used. Moreover, the court decided that EPM's creation of a commercialization arrangement with Polyvalor could not be used to detrimentally affect Fardad's share of the revenues. The court therefore held that Fardad's share of commercialization proceeds should be determined based on revenues received not just from EPM but also from Polyvalor. On appeal, Fardad was denied a share of revenues stemming from Polyvalor on the basis that Polyvalor and EPM are separate entities.[57]

CONCLUSIONS

In Canadian academia, any assumption that the ownership of intellectual property follows the strict dictates of the law would be incorrect. It is clear in law that copyright and patents are owned by their creators unless an employment relationship exists. Where an employee creates copyright in the course of employment or is specifically employed to create patentable inventions, the law indicates that the employer owns such intellectual property. However, courts have tended to view academia as something other than a traditional employment relationship in the context of intellectual property. Courts outside of Canada have held that faculty are not specifically employed to invent and, therefore, remain the owners of their patentable inventions. Conversely, because of the close connection copyrightable materials have to faculty members' day-to-day employment

[57] *Corporation of the Polytechnic School of Montreal c Fardad*, 2010 QCCA 992 (CanLII).

duties, the law suggests that universities, as the employers, would be the owners. For various reasons entrenched in the history of academia, the expectations of faculty and the practice of universities do not follow the prescriptions of the law. Patentable inventions, because of their potential value and the infrastructure support provided by the university, are often characterized by shared ownership and revenue splitting between the university and faculty. Most copyrightable materials, particularly publications used to assess progress through the academic ranks, are considered to be owned by faculty creators. This is principally due to long-standing academic custom. In order to circumvent the stipulations of statutes and precedent, universities have established intellectual property policies that codify the accepted academic expectations and practices. Such policies generally apportion ownership, control, and revenue between the university and faculty creators. Notwithstanding the power imbalance between a university and individual faculty, courts, including those in Canada, have generally given considerable deference to intellectual property policies.

Chapter 10

BEYOND RESEARCH: COLLABORATIVE RESEARCH, SPIN-OFF COMPANIES, AND OTHER COMMERCIAL ACTIVITY

Jeffrey J. Lowe and Christopher M. Lennon

As the Latin *universitas magistrorum et scholarium* suggests, the core mission of a university has long been grounded in research and learning. Yet universities, colleges, and other postsecondary institutions are increasingly called on, by government, industry, and society alike, to play a more prominent role in facilitating the transfer of knowledge and discovery from concept to application. One need only look at the growth of technology transfer offices at postsecondary institutions across Canada over the past few decades to see the increasing role that such institutions have in driving innovation – no longer only through knowledge creation but also through knowledge transmission and mobilization.

When The University of British Columbia created its University Industry Liaison Office in 1984, it was the first Canadian office of its kind. According to Statistics Canada,[1] by 2008 88 percent of Canadian universities were actively managing intellectual property (IP) through technology transfer offices. Since 2008, many of these offices have broadened the scope of their mandate to include technology incubators, accelerators, and other entrepreneurship support services for faculty, staff, students, and alumni.

---

[1] Statistics Canada, *2008 Survey of IP Commercialization*, 10.

Handbook of Canadian Higher Education Law, edited by Theresa Shanahan, Michelle Nilson, and Li-Jeen Broshko. Montreal and Kingston: McGill-Queen's University Press, Queen's Policy Studies Series.

The development and commercialization of IP by educational institutions complement the institution's core mission, yet that mission invariably remains quite distinct from the goals of industry. Indeed, in many respects the policies, procedures, and practices – and even the values of these postsecondary institutions – are incongruent with business practices prevalent in the for-profit sector. Compounding these competing objectives is the emerging realization that the exploitation of IP is a challenging endeavour often requiring significant investment and boasting few financial successes. Consequently, the issues, considerations, and nature of advice sought from legal counsel when postsecondary institutions engage with industry are unique and require a balancing of institutional and commercial interests.

Historically, the primary function of most industry liaison offices was the protection of institution-owned intellectual property. Over time, in order to compete for research dollars and better exploit their technology, institutions have taken on a more aggressive marketing and sales role. As the process of technology transfer within the postsecondary environment matured, institutions became more creative in structuring transactions that engage industry partners, while simultaneously furthering the institution's mandate. A corresponding need developed for legal advice that was sensitive to the institutional parameters yet accommodated the objectives of industry. In an attempt to canvass some of the avenues commonly utilized, and to introduce a selection of the issues that may arise in each case, this chapter is divided into six sections. The first section, Partnering with Industry, will explore a sample of the unique issues and practical concerns that arise when postsecondary institutions attempt to contract with business entities. The next section, IP Policy, will introduce the importance of a well-conceived IP policy and some of the considerations that should be addressed in relation to the institution's interaction with industry. The third section, Sponsored and Collaborative Research, will canvass in more detail some of the specific challenges that arise in the context of research endeavours sponsored or supported in some fashion by industry partners. The fourth section, Licensing in the University Context, will look at situations in which an institution partners with industry by licensing some form of IP to the industry partner to exploit and commercialize. Next, in Spin-off Ventures, the instance in which the institution or one or more of its inventors take an equity ownership interest in a new venture will be considered. Finally, Knowledge Mobilization will look at some alternative ways and recent initiatives being utilized to support the development and dissemination of technology without great concern for financial returns.

The purpose of this chapter is not to be comprehensive or to provide definitive answers on any of the issues discussed, but rather to offer some preliminary observations and high-level comments gleaned from our experiences that may be helpful to postsecondary institutions or their advisors as they work through various relationships with industry partners.

PARTNERING WITH INDUSTRY

Despite the fact that many postsecondary institutions, and in particular the research-focused institutions, are drivers of innovation and play an important role in the development of the Canadian economy, postsecondary institutions, or at least the public ones, have a very different mandate than industry. Through their technology transfer offices and other relationships with industry, they do at times operate in the for-profit sphere and contract with for-profit businesses. At the same time, the operational mandates, core values, and even motivations of postsecondary institutions on specific projects of collaboration are typically quite distinct from those of business. Where businesses are generally interested in generating profits and maximizing shareholder value, postsecondary institutions are predominately interested in facilitating discovery, diffusing knowledge, and minimizing risk. To the extent that postsecondary institutions operate in the for-profit sphere at all, they generally do so to augment or further their core values – not at the expense of them.

Accordingly, a number of unique issues and practical concerns can arise as institutions attempt to balance, within the parameters of any proposed commercial transaction, the demands of industry and the values and culture of the institution. Oftentimes the industry partner struggles to appreciate the issues raised on the institutional side. Industry partners do not inherently identify with the concerns and priorities of postsecondary institutions, which at times seem contrary to routine business practice. Take for example the almost standard business practice of entering non-disclosure agreements in advance of negotiations to establish some form of business relationship or to keep the results of a joint project confidential. Businesses routinely enter these types of commitments without much difficulty. Yet for postsecondary institutions, entering the same commitments can be quite challenging on a number of fronts.

First, any time an institution committed to the promotion of discovery and the free exchange of knowledge and ideas restricts the ability of its members to share the product of their research, the institution is arguably straying from its mission and potentially constraining the academic freedom of its faculty.[2]

---

[2] Despite having been described by Ronald B. Standler, in his paper "Academic Freedom in the USA," as "an amorphous quasi-legal concept that is neither precisely defined nor convincingly justified from legal principles," academic freedom is undeniably a foundational tenet of the modern university. The Association of American Colleges and Universities has a statement on academic freedom (American Association of University Professors, "1940 Statement of

Second, and added to this general conflict of values and priorities, is a related practical concern that arises from a difference in operational conduct between academic institutions and industry. It is quite common for the terms of a non-disclosure agreement to require that the parties ensure that any personnel who might come into contact with confidential information be bound by similar written obligations of confidentiality. Viewed from the point of view of the industry partner, such an obligation is reasonable. However, applied in the context of a postsecondary institution, such a commitment may be administratively untenable to implement and thus problematic to make. Unlike a business corporation, which often has obligations of confidentiality built directly into the employment agreements of its personnel, postsecondary institutions typically encourage at least a subset of their personnel – namely faculty, graduate students, and other researchers (arguably the subset most likely to come into contact with confidential information of a research nature) – to share ideas and to publish their findings. Moreover, the categories of personnel likely to access confidential information in an academic community are much more diverse than in a commercial operation. In addition to the usual involvement of employees and perhaps consultants, a university is likely to have students, faculty members, visiting professors, and others involved. The culture and practice of postsecondary institutions is simply not one where commitments of confidentiality are easily implemented.

Third, in the event the institution determines it can reasonably enter some commitment of confidentiality in a specific situation and implement a system to meet those commitments, there is also the matter of scope, a concern uniquely relevant to the academic setting. Postsecondary institutions need to be very careful to ensure that the subject matter to which an obligation of confidentiality applies is defined both clearly and narrowly. Similarly, the commitment itself should be constrained as narrowly as possible to ensure that the obligations of confidentiality apply only to the information arising from the joint project or research, and only to the personnel involved in the specific project. On a related note, the matter of scope is relevant not only to the control of knowledge and discoveries but also to any agreement with respect to the ownership of IP arising from a joint project. The overarching concern of the institution, in both cases, is that an obligation of confidentiality or an interest in IP granted

---

Principles on Academic Freedom"), as does the Association of Universities and Colleges of Canada (Murphy, "Canada's Universities Adopt New Statement on Academic Freedom"). Peter MacKinnon, former president and professor of law at the University of Saskatchewan, has defined academic freedom as "the freedom to teach and conduct research constrained only by two things – the professional standards of the relevant discipline and the legitimate and non-discriminatory institutional requirements for organizing the academic mission." MacKinnon, "What Do We Mean When We Talk about Academic Freedom?"

in relation to a specific project involving one subset of the institution's members (e.g., the faculty members and graduate students working in a particular lab) might somehow constrain or impact research being conducted by an entirely separate unit of the institution. Such a concern is all the more problematic because large institutions, which encourage their faculty and graduate students to research and generate ideas and discoveries on an ongoing basis, cannot possibly know of all matters being researched at the institution at any one time, nor can they anticipate the range of discoveries, knowledge, and IP that might be produced from that research and thus become subject to the institution's commitments.

Consequently, postsecondary institutions struggle to balance the call of industry to maintain the confidential nature of its proprietary information with the freedom of the institution's faculty, staff, and students to research and publish their work. The juxtaposition of industry's desire to own and control the dissemination of discoveries arising from joint projects housed within the institutional setting creates an awkward tension that is by definition present when educational institutions enter the commercial arena. These issues frequently arise repeatedly throughout the life cycle of any relationship with industry partners. In short, educational institutions need to carefully consider every proposed commitment of confidentiality or grant of rights to IP in terms of who will be bound by the commitment, how any subordinate commitments will be implemented, and more generally how such commitments will impact the broader activities of the institution, particularly if potentially overlapping discoveries may arise from research conducted in distinct disciplines.

Another common area where challenges can arise in relation to an institution's dealings with industry is in the interactions of an institution's faculty with the industry partner, often without the direct involvement of the postsecondary institution. Industry partners often attempt to forge relationships with key researchers at institutions, and outside consulting work is often permitted and encouraged under institutional policies. In fact, according to the Canadian Association of University Teachers, "by definition employment in a tenured position involves responsibilities of teaching, research, professional activity, and service."[3] While this statement has not been universally adopted by all stakeholders, it is not uncommon for tenured faculty members to carry on outside professional activities and interests that could place them in actual or perceived conflicts of commitment or conflicts of interest. The researchers may find themselves in a new type of relationship with an industry partner, yet they are still bound by their fiduciary obligations to their employer. If there are any misunderstandings in the two distinct roles of institutional employee and industry consultant, the researcher may need clarification

---

[3] Canadian Association of University Teachers, "Policy Statement on Tenure."

as to their obligations to each party, as well as advice on how to avoid conflicts of interest, particularly with respect to follow-on discoveries. While a thorough discussion is outside the scope of this chapter, these issues permeate much of the interaction between institutions and industry. Accordingly, in addition to implementing broadly applicable policies, procedures, and practices, institutions must address these issues in various aspects of their interactions with industry. We return to these issues below in the sections IP Policy and Spin-off Ventures.

All of this is not to say that a postsecondary institution and an industry partner cannot find workable solutions to these and other matters where interests diverge, sufficient to allow the parties to move forward with a commercial transaction or collaboration. An educational institution must simply be aware of the requirements entailed in entering into a commercial agreement with an industry partner and balance its own requirements against these.

IP POLICY

An advisable first step to prepare a postsecondary institution for collaboration and commercial relationships with industry is the implementation of a well-considered IP policy or policies. Such a policy will be instrumental in setting out the process for commercialization as well as addressing ownership, benefits of commercialization, and related issues. Ideally, this policy or policies would be drafted to account for all means of structuring commercialization transactions with industry while also addressing some primary and almost foundational issues regarding IP created or developed at the institution. The policy must balance IP law and employment law in a way that supports the strategic direction of the institution, yet leaves the technology transfer professional with the requisite tools to commercialize or otherwise transfer technology into applications that stand to benefit society.

IP transactions can be complex commercial arrangements, particularly when outside financing is involved. This may be unknown territory for an academic researcher. Thus, the IP policy together with other supporting policies such as conflict of interest will set the ground rules for any transaction involving researchers and industry partners. An IP policy should provide a framework that establishes the rights and obligations of both the institution and the researcher in a form that is clear and unambiguous to potential industry partners and other third parties. It will provide a road map on both the process and the allocation of any benefits received from commercialization.

A well-considered IP policy can also decrease potential liabilities. Educational institutions are structured to foster learning, transfer knowledge, and facilitate research. Industry is seeking control over proprietary technology and clear definition of ownership. These differing objectives can be met only if the contributions are identified, public disclosure is managed, and third party claims are avoided.

Most often, when business corporations and postsecondary institutions consider potential liability in relation to the development and commercialization of intellectual property, they tend to focus on claims by external parties – claims of patent infringement or misappropriation of IP, for example. However, significant liabilities may also arise from within the institution itself. This is particularly so for research institutions with tenured faculty, visiting professors, and graduate students at times all contributing to research at the institution. We are aware of a number of distinct circumstances in which inventors brought such claims against an institution. Some claims arise from inventors who, for one reason or another, were not seen by the institution as an inventor.[4] In other instances, these claims have alleged that an institution mismanaged the commercialization of a particular technology.[5] In one somewhat unique case, inventors sued an institution for failing to adequately share the revenue from commercialization because the institution had mischaracterized royalty revenues as research funds.[6]

The conflict at the core of many of the IP disputes arising from within an institution often centres on the ownership of and entitlements to particular inventions. While even the best IP policy is unlikely to prevent every potential claim, having a clear and unambiguous policy in place can go a long way to decreasing an institution's exposure to such actions.

The range of IP policies utilized by Canadian universities include inventor-owned policies, institution-owned policies, and a variety of policies that allocate ownership jointly to inventors and the institution. It is outside the scope of this chapter to compare and contrast the variety of approaches taken across Canada. Still, well-crafted policies address a number of common items:

- ownership of discoveries and inventions,
- obligations and restrictions on disclosure,
- authority to make and the process to follow with respect to decisions related to any potential commercialization, and
- allocation of proceeds and expenses.

---

[4] See, for example, *Fardad v Ecole Polytechnique*, 2010 QCCA 992, [2010] QJ No 4729. In this case, an inventor who the institution believed was not covered by its IP policy contributed to technology that the institution licensed for equity but did not share with the inventor. The court disagreed and awarded a share of the equity to the inventor.

[5] See, for example, *University of Sherbrooke v Beaudoin*, 2010 QCCA 28, [2010] RJQ 89. In this instance the institution renegotiated a cap on a buy-out option of a license agreement without the agreement of the inventors.

[6] *Singer et al v Regents of University of California*, 1997 WL 34594173 (California Court of Appeal).

Ownership of Discoveries and Inventions

Unless addressed elsewhere, such as collective agreements with faculty and staff, an appropriate IP policy will address the ownership of all IP created by faculty, staff, students, or any combination of them. As best as possible, it should attempt to contemplate all foreseeable scenarios in which IP may be developed at or in any way related to the institution.

The common-law presumption in Canada is that employees are entitled to ownership of their inventions.[7] This presumption can be displaced either by an express contract to the contrary or by terms of employment that include the express purpose of inventing or innovating.[8] Unfortunately for postsecondary institutions, the *University of Western Australia v Gray* decision out of Australia, which likely also reflects the law in Canada, stands for the proposition that faculty members do not have a duty to invent.[9] The *Gray* decision involved the head of the University of Western Australia's department of surgery and the production of micro-particles used in the treatment of cancer. In arriving at its decision, the court reviewed the law in a number of common-law jurisdictions including Canada and concluded, "Dr. Gray had no duty to invent anything. He had a duty to undertake research and to stimulate research amongst staff and students at UWA. He was working for a university."[10]

In situations where staff are employed to produce specific intellectual property, institutions may be able to address ownership of IP by contract, but such situations seldom give rise to inventions that are commercialized. Moreover, universities are severely restricted from negotiating individual agreements with faculty due to collective bargaining issues. Thus, postsecondary institutions in Canada generally have two means of altering the common-law presumption of ownership by the inventor: collective agreements and institutional policy.

If the institution wishes to be the owner of the IP, the policy may provide, as a term of using the institution's resources for the research, that any invention or discovery will be assigned to the institution. In British Columbia, the *University Act* specifically contemplates that an institution can require as a term of employment or assistance that a person assign an interest in IP arising from an invention.[11]

Some postsecondary institutions in Canada elect not to alter the common-law presumption; they allow ownership of the invention to remain

---

[7] *Comstock Canada v Electec Ltd* (1991), 45 FTR 241, 38 CPR (3d) 29 (FCTD) [*Comstock*]; *Spiroll Corp v Putti* (1976), 77 DLR (3d) 761, [1976] BCJ No 788 (SC) [*Spiroll*].

[8] *Comstock, supra* note 7 at para 53.

[9] *University of Western Australia v Gray (No 20)*, [2008] FCA 498 [*Gray*] affirmed in *University of Western Australia v Gray (No 20)*, [2009] FCAFC 116.

[10] *Gray, supra* note 9 at 1360.

[11] *University Act*, RSBC 1996, c 468 s 27(2)(v).

with the inventor but mandate some form of revenue-sharing model. As mentioned above, it is outside the scope of this chapter to compare and contrast the benefits of institution-owned and inventor-owned IP policies. Let us simply conclude by stating first that it is important to differentiate between ownership and financial returns, as the two concepts are not necessarily connected; and second that the capacity and experience of most Canadian institutions to assist with patenting, licensing, and other activities associated with the commercial exploitation of technology has been growing over the last two decades.

Obligations of Disclosure

In order for any IP policy to be effective, a protocol for disclosure of the discovery must be established. The issues in this respect are generally twofold: First, when has a discovery progressed enough to warrant disclosure to the institution, particularly given that almost all of the technology will be very early stage? Second, is disclosure required or might the decision whether to disclose be left to the inventor?

Where disclosure is mandated or chosen, the protocol must include reference to all contributing parties, and the institution must decide the methodology for confirmation of this information in the situations of multiple inventors. The IP policy must also acknowledge and accommodate the objective of exchanging information, whether through publication, presentations, or otherwise. This objective must be balanced against the need to preserve the ability to patent an invention. The policy may address the time frames necessary to file a patent application before the researcher makes public disclosure of the invention. The policy may not necessarily require disclosure of all inventions to the institution; nevertheless, the consequences of any decision to publish discoveries or to disclose an invention to the institution prior to public disclosure, and the requirements of any such disclosure, need to be clear and unambiguous.

Authority to Make Decisions

All IP policies should set out the rights and obligations of both the researchers and the institution. If the institution will be managing the process to commercially exploit the technology, it will require an assignment of any right the inventor may have, whether through common law or under the policy.

One very difficult area, however, is the autonomy of the institution to make decisions. For example, does the institution have a contractual obligation or perhaps even fiduciary obligation to consult with the researchers during the process of exploiting the technology? A researcher may not agree with the financial terms or the party receiving the rights to the technology. This situation is compounded by the fact that most industry partners want, as a condition of the transaction, the continued support of the key researcher.

Thus an IP policy must establish the level of consultation required and the authority of either party to make decisions. The increasing prevalence of creative commons licensing and the increasing realization that revenue generation should not be the primary objective when licensing inventions have only added to the importance of clearly allocating the power to make decisions.

Revenue Sharing

The policy will, of course, deal with the sharing of the benefits from the commercialization of the technology. Depending on the policy structure, this may mean allocating a share of revenue to the institution or to the inventors. While straightforward in concept, revenue sharing raises many related concerns that must be addressed. For example, if the policy mandates that revenues will be split, it must similarly contain a robust means of determining the revenue to be apportioned. Typically, IP policies contemplating revenue sharing will establish some concept of net revenue, which usually recovers direct costs such as patent filing costs, research and development expenses, legal fees, and other potential administrative fees.

The allocation of benefits among multiple researchers should be addressed. Consideration must be given to how co-inventors will be identified and how relative contributions will be determined. Likewise, the manner in which equity from commercialization received as consideration is allocated among researchers and institutions will have to be addressed in the policy. Consideration will also need to be given to the timing of any equity transfer as part of a revenue-sharing scheme as there are likely tax consequences to any such transfer and potentially a lack of funds to bear an immediate tax burden.

Finally, an IP policy should clearly stipulate any situations in which a party can or must waive their entitlement to a share of revenue, and the process for doing so. One likely scenario in which an inventor may be required to waive his or her entitlement to revenue would be a situation where an inventor takes an equity position in a spin-off corporation.

Miscellaneous Other Issues

In conjunction with tackling the four concepts itemized above, decisions will need to be made with respect to the scope of the IP to be caught by the policy. For example, will the policy address the ownership of all IP coming out of the institution or just some subset loosely characterized as inventions? A policy that captures copyright in scholarly works may be troublesome for academics. On the other hand, copyright subsists in many traditional inventions (e.g., software) and thus cannot simply be carved out of the policy. In addition, institutions may see a need to treat certain curriculum materials (e.g., jointly developed problem sets or materials created through significant investment by the institution) differently from traditional textbooks and lecture notes. It would also be advisable for institutions to take steps to preserve their ownership of works for hire in any IP policy. This area is complex and may require a distinct approach to preserve an institution's ownership in works for hire.

To close the loop, it is also important to be able to demonstrate that the policy is binding on all inventors. Thus the policy must somehow be incorporated as a condition of secondment, enrolment, or employment. Often this is done by incorporating all institution policies into the employment or student relationship via an employment or student handbook. As this issue is not unique to IP policies, we have not canvassed it in any more detail.

Due to the number of stakeholders, IP policies can be quite difficult to draft and garner consensus. In addition, existing policies are often very difficult to amend, and the legal consequences of such amendments on existing employees must be reviewed carefully. As a result, it is sometimes beneficial to confine the policy to the general and permit the institution's executive to prescribe procedures for the implementation of the policy in much the same way regulations are prescribed under a statute. Finally, having the policy is only part of the battle; it is also critical that the policy be applied appropriately. While a discussion about the means of implementation is outside the scope of this chapter, the first step to successful implementation is clear and unambiguous drafting.

SPONSORED AND COLLABORATIVE RESEARCH

Sponsored research agreements can create both inbound and outbound issues. While outside funding of research is always welcome, the research is of course done within the parameters of existing IP and employment policies of the institution. The party sponsoring the research may have objectives that are difficult to attain within the existing institutional environment. These objectives need to be identified and analyzed at the outset of the negotiation.

The conditions of the sponsored research may also require certain protocols to be put in place both at the commencement of and during the research project. These protocols may include getting acknowledgements from the researchers with respect to confidentiality, ownership of the IP, and other related matters. It is imperative that the lead researchers be vigilant in obtaining similar covenants from all parties involved as the research progresses. The leader of the research project should also be cautioned about using other technology or materials without seeking the appropriate clearances or fully considering the implications of such actions. For example, open source software, although free to use, is generally made available pursuant to certain license terms. At least, the terms may restrict the ability to sublicense the open source technology in new inventions; at most, they could infect the entire invention. Likewise, it is important to ensure there are no other research funds being used that might have competing or conflicting obligations.

Collaborative research agreements may require the policies and procedures of two institutions to interface. The typical interinstitutional agreement will preserve the policies of each institution; however, there are situations when the policies clearly conflict.

As mentioned, outbound issues may also be created through sponsored research and collaborative research agreements. Put simply, the financial pedigree of research is often overlooked in the face of a commercial deal. This is particularly true of aging technology. The institution must make sure the technology does not have a historic set of obligations that would either prevent or at least impact the deal being negotiated. By way of an example, a Canadian institution had a visiting scholar collaborating on a research project. His salary was being paid by the United States Air Force where he held the rank of major. The project carried on long after he left the institution. By reason of his salary being paid by the United States government, the *Bayh-Dole Act* mandated that the US government receive a non-exclusive license to the technology.[12] This would have been problematic for this potential licensee; however, a waiver was obtained from the US government in this case. As part of all outbound transactions, the provenance of the technology must be reviewed carefully.

LICENSING IN THE UNIVERSITY CONTEXT

Licensing is a common means of commercializing technology developed within the university context. The challenges most often flow from the fact that institutions are typically licensing early stage technology. No one really knows if the technology will develop further, can be scaled, can be productized, or will ultimately fill a commercial need. This means that it is difficult to negotiate business terms with complete confidence or accuracy. That having been said, we would suggest that there are some well grooved paths that have stood the test of time for many institutions.

There are three key areas to identify when developing a licensing strategy for a particular technology:

- financial terms,
- mandatory terms, and
- desirable terms that may or may not survive in the negotiations.

---

[12] *Bayh-Dole Act*, PL 96-517, s 6(a), Dec 12, 1980, 94 Stat. 3018 also known as the *University and Small Business Patent Procedures Act* of 1980.

The financial terms of the license must relate to the investment to date by the institution, the stage of development of the technology, the cost to move the technology forward, and lastly, the likely size of the market and potential financial upside for the licensee. This last factor can be an exercise in manipulating variables with widely varying results. In most industry segments, there are, however, fairly established ranges of royalty rates.

The institution should consider up-front licensing fees as a method of recouping investment to date. The royalty rates may also be complemented by milestone payments. In addition, the license can be used to diminish the financial burden on the institution by causing the licensee to pay patent costs, legal costs, and other out-of-pocket expenses. Often, the license is accompanied by a sponsored research agreement, with the licensee agreeing to take over all research costs.

Each institution will develop a number of terms that they view as mandatory for all license agreements. These may relate to minimizing risk, or sometimes to historical experiences in prior licenses. The financial terms will be mandatory inclusions, including royalties, up-front licensing fees, milestone payments, recovery of patent costs, and perhaps equity participation in the license. In addition to these financial terms, an institution may consider termination clauses, insurance, confidentiality, and indemnity clauses as mandatory clauses.

Any negotiation will also see give and take on those provisions less important to the parties. Matters such as ownership of improvements, field of use, use of the technology by affiliated companies, security for financial obligations, the right to sublicense, and management of the patent portfolio may be the subject of negotiation. It is unlikely that an institution will achieve every desired term in the negotiation. By deciding which terms are mandatory and which are merely desirable, the institution will be more likely to negotiate successfully.

In drafting a license, it is worth noting a few key considerations. Particular attention must be paid to the definition section of the document, as the complexity of license agreements have increased. The need for interlocking and cross-referenced definitions makes this particularly challenging and important. The representations and warranties within the license are a mechanism for allocating risk between the parties. An institution must control its representations and warranties and likely will have to undertake some due diligence to ensure that what is being represented is not exposing the institution to any future liability.

The confidentiality provisions must relate to the nature of the intellectual property. Researchers may want to carry on with research and publications. This work could be problematic if the institution is granting an exclusive license of know-how. The right to preview all publications may be required. It may also be very important to set out performance milestones for the licensee to meet, failing which the license can be terminated. Lastly, an institution should always consider the most appropriate way to resolve disputes. Arbitration allows a rapid timeline and use of an expert as an arbitrator, yet can sometimes lack the discovery process and enforcement remedies offered by the court system. Further, due to freedom of information legislation, public institutions need to assume that arbitration proceedings will not remain entirely confidential.

SPIN-OFF VENTURES

Universities often find themselves in the awkward position of trying to exploit technology before it has proven commercially viable. Very often the technology will require a significant further investment before its commercial value can be established.

Finding favourable terms, at this stage in the development of the technology, often requires some flexibility on the part of the postsecondary institution to structure the transaction in creative ways other than simply through a license that includes royalties and initial license fees. One such alternative is the participation of the postsecondary institution as a shareholder in licensee companies. Spin-off companies are usually created by a combination of the institution's researchers and financial partners seeking to develop a promising technology.

A postsecondary institution taking an equity position in a technology company provides the aura of a flexible and willing licensor or investor who is cognizant of both the risks and the benefits of expensive and time-consuming research. As an owner of the technology, the institution can either license or assign the technology to the spin-off company. Technology companies often view equity as a reasonable way to reduce royalty rates and up-front licensing fees. If the technology has not yet proven itself commercially viable, a company may be reluctant to pay significant licensing fees and commit to a royalty rate until after the completion of clinical trials, development of a prototype, or continuation of research. Taking an equity position in the spin-off company provides a mechanism to address the concerns of the licensee, while also assuring the postsecondary institution that it will participate in any successes the licensee may enjoy as a result of the technology.

There are also a number of public policy reasons why a postsecondary institution may be inclined to accept equity in a company being granted a license of intellectual property. As discussed in more detail below under the heading Knowledge Mobilization, most postsecondary institutions feel they have an obligation to ensure that their inventions reach the community. Postsecondary institutions are also under constant financial pressures. The exploitation of inventions and discoveries can attract research dollars as well as produce revenues. By taking an equity position in a licensee company rather than insisting upon royalties and up-front fees, a postsecondary institution may be able to structure a deal to exploit a discovery that would otherwise languish or have been mobilized without the possibility of financial reward. Revenues from research contracts, capital appreciation of shares, and license fees all enable postsecondary institutions to expend greater amounts of money on research, which in turn attracts talent to participate in the research. If successful, this approach can add a great deal of momentum to the postsecondary institution's research program.

On the flip side, although equity ownership provides a postsecondary institution with potential capital appreciation of the shares in licensee companies, it raises a number of issues that can be controversial within the academic environment. For example, speculative ventures can put an educational institution at risk of becoming involved in a company that needs to raise venture capital or make difficult management decisions. Taking an equity stake in a spin-off company is also a marked departure from the historic tradition of intellectual independence that postsecondary institutions, and particularly universities, have jealously guarded.

The role of the inventor in completing the transaction must also be analyzed. A postsecondary institution might find itself in an awkward position if the researcher does not agree with the structure of a transaction. As a practical matter, the researcher will usually be required to carry on with future research relating to the licensed technology, and so he or she must be comfortable with the transaction. If possible, the university should try to delineate the roles each party will take in the process of licensing the technology. As already discussed, much of this can be addressed in the institution's IP policies.

A postsecondary institution must ensure that the taking of equity will work within the parameters of its existing IP policy or policies vis-à-vis the inventors. As discussed above, many postsecondary institutions have a sharing formula whereby the inventors have an interest in revenues generated from the licensing of the technology that they develop. The institution's policies governing this relationship must be reviewed very carefully as it is quite likely that the policy was not drafted to accommodate the issuance of shares in licensee corporations as part of the institution's compensation for granting a license.

One issue that frequently arises is the mechanism (or lack of a mechanism) for the transferring of shares to the researcher pursuant to any revenue-sharing formula. For tax and other reasons, the timing of when ownership of shares vests in a researcher can be very important. A postsecondary institution may even ask a licensee company to directly issue shares to the inventor to avoid some of these complications.

Although there are no immediate tax consequences for the issuance of shares to a postsecondary institution, if a researcher is entitled to an interest in a portion of those shares, there may be certain tax ramifications for the inventor. Shares are a taxable benefit earned pursuant to the researcher's contract of employment. The institution's financial office should issue a T4 or T4A slip to the researcher representing the fair market value of those shares. A postsecondary institution and the relevant inventor may be able to argue to Revenue Canada that shares in a start-up technology company have nominal value. As a general rule, the sooner that a researcher can receive the shares the stronger the argument will be that they have a low or nominal value. The effect of this is that the adjusted cost base of those shares will be zero, and the researcher will be taxed on the full value when the shares are sold.

It should also be noted that if the value of the shares is uncertain, it may be incumbent upon the postsecondary institution to have the shares valued by a qualified, independent valuator using standard valuation techniques.

If the shares have more than a nominal value and if the licensee corporation is a Canadian Controlled Private Corporation within the meaning of the *Income Tax Act*, it may be possible to grant the researcher an option to acquire shares, rather than issuing the shares, and thus enable the researcher to avoid paying tax until the shares are sold.

In the case of a public company issuing shares to a researcher, the share option plan mentioned above will not work. In the case of a public company, the measure of the value of the employee benefit is calculated when the share option is exercised (i.e., the difference between the option price and the fair market value of the shares will be taxable) not when the shares are sold.

Another option is to ensure that the institution has the means to delay the inventor's recognition of revenue in the form of equity until such time as the shares can be sold freely. Care must be taken to not have this be characterized as a salary deferral arrangement under the *Income Tax Act*. However, if the shares do not vest immediately with the researcher, the postsecondary institution must be very careful that it does not incur any liability through the mismanagement of those shares. One possible solution may be for the institution to retain the services of a professional investment advisor who handles the management of the shares.

It is also very important that a postsecondary institution not trade in shares of licensee companies if the institution is in possession of insider information. Insider trading issues may be another reason to appoint an independent fund manager who handles the shares of the licensee companies as they would any other investments completely outside the institutional environment. The university must advise all researchers and personnel in possession of insider information of the prohibition against insider trading.

In addition to the insider trading concerns, many jurisdictions across Canada have a "closed" security system, meaning that unless there is an exemption under the applicable securities act or regulations, a company cannot distribute any of its shares unless a prospectus has been filed. There are a number of exemptions that allow a company to issue shares without the use of a prospectus. Thus a postsecondary institution receiving shares from a licensee company should ensure that there is an appropriate exemption and that it has complied with all applicable securities laws. Usually there is a requirement to file a report of an exempt distribution with the appropriate securities commission. The postsecondary institution should also be advised of its obligation to file "insider reports."

Through the issuance of shares, universities and/or researchers may become minority shareholders in privately held corporations. This raises issues about control, liquidity, and the general operation of the business. It may be appropriate to consider the use of a shareholders' agreement to govern the operations of the company.

In order to maintain some control over the licensee company, another trend seems to be to negotiate the right to nominate a director or officer of the company. However, there is an inherent conflict of interest in assuming the role of director or officer of the licensee company as once having assumed that position, the director or officer has the obligation to act in the best interest of the company. The best interest of the licensee company may or may not be parallel to the best interest of the postsecondary institution.

If the licensee company gets into financial difficulties or is on the verge of being in breach of a license agreement or research agreement, a university nominee will find themselves in an awkward position. A director can disclose this conflict in accordance with the relevant corporate legislation, but disclosure will not solve the problem. In practice, when a conflict arises, the university nominee usually resigns prior to the institution taking any action with respect to the license agreement or research agreement between the university and the company.

Directors and officers may also incur statutory liabilities (income tax, GST, and unpaid wages), and therefore university nominees should ensure that they have the permission of the postsecondary institution and perhaps an indemnity from the university for such liabilities. It is recommended that a letter from the president of the institution be directed to any employee who will be assuming the role of director or officer in a company on behalf of the university, clearly giving them the direction to do so.

Equity ownership allows a university to participate in the success of a technology at a point in its development when it may be difficult to quantify the value. Equity should not, however, become an excuse for doing business with an undercapitalized industry partner. Equity may be an appropriate means of realizing the future potential of a technology but should be approached with caution. In structuring an equity participation transaction, an educational institution should be aware of the securities issues, tax consequences, minority shareholder issues, and the potential liabilities of nominees, directors, and officers.

It is our experience that if institutions do not get more creative in the structuring of their transactions, it is likely that those industry partners and the research dollars that they can contribute will find their way to other institutions that are willing to participate in both the risk and the benefits of the development of technology. The participation as a shareholder in a licensee company is perhaps one more signal that many aspects of the traditional relationship between the university and the community that supports it have changed.

KNOWLEDGE MOBILIZATION

Although technology transfer offices were often established in an attempt to capture and create economic value from the intellectual pursuits conducted within the walls of the nation's colleges and universities, it has become clear that statistically there are few inventions that are profitably commercialized. As a consequence, many institutions have begun to look at ways to make technology available more freely for the greater good of society, rather than simply to create financial rewards. For some institutions this involves focusing more commercialization efforts and attention on technology projected to have a sufficiently high commercial value, and making other technologies perceived to be less valuable available at little or no cost. The fundamental underpinnings of the industry liaison model must be reviewed and considered within the emerging realization that technology transfer for profit is a challenging endeavour. This realization may well impact the manner in which an institution approaches collaborations, licenses, and other forms of knowledge transfer described in this chapter.

Professor Stephen Toope, former president of The University of British Columbia, referred to the university's core business as "higher education and knowledge creation." He went on to say that "patents and licensing are all very well, but it's estimated that 73 percent of new knowledge generated by university research is transmitted into the economy through its graduates."[13] Indeed, in recent years we have seen an influx of efforts by institutions to support their graduates and researchers through incubators, accelerators, and other entrepreneurial support services.

Whatever means of disseminating knowledge and discovery are utilized in the postsecondary context, interactions will occur between postsecondary institutions and industry. While there is no doubt that these interactions have enormous potential benefit for the institution, the industry partner, and society more generally, any time research institutions embark on commercial or quasi-commercial endeavours, unique and nuanced considerations will continue to arise and will need to be managed.

---

[13] Toope, speech to Life Sciences British Columbia, October 2010, http://www.lifesciencesbc.ca/.

Chapter 11

LAND DEVELOPMENT ISSUES APPLICABLE TO HIGHER EDUCATION INSTITUTIONS

McCarthy Tétrault LLP

ACQUISITION OF LAND

Legislative Framework

In the vast majority of cases, the enabling legislation for a higher education institution provides the specific authority for the institution to acquire land.[1] The means by which higher education institutions can acquire land are typically quite broad; some statutes simply grant the institution the authority to "acquire" land,[2] while others list specific means such as

This chapter was written collaboratively by the following practitioners in McCarthy Tétrault LLP, counsel for Higher Education Institutions across Canada: Alexandre Blanchard, Kristina Bocharov, Jessica Dorsey, Annie Gagnon-Larocque, Kimberly J. Howard, Sherena Hussain, Kara M. Levis, Stephen L. Livergant, Vanessa Lunday, Michael E. Mitchell, Alexander Paruk, Tara L. Piurko, Shannel Rajan, Godyne N. L. Sibay, Brenda Swick, Lisa Vogt, and Elizabeth Yip.

[1] Examples of exceptions to this general rule are *The Brandon University Act*, SM 1998, c 48, CCSM c B90 and *The University of Winnipeg Act*, SM 1998, c 50, CCSM c U70, which do not contain specific provisions enabling those universities to acquire land.

[2] *Post-secondary Learning Act*, SA 2003, c P-19.5, s 66(1).

Handbook of Canadian Higher Education Law, edited by Theresa Shanahan, Michelle Nilson, and Li-Jeen Broshko. Montreal and Kingston: McGill-Queen's University Press, Queen's Policy Studies Series.

"acquire, take, accept, and receive by grant, purchase, lease, gift, devise, bequest or otherwise howsoever."[3] A higher education institution may also have the authority to acquire land by way of expropriation.[4] Possible restrictions on these powers of expropriation are discussed in the third section of this chapter.

Universities generally do not need to obtain the approval of a provincial minister or other governmental authority to acquire land (except in the case of acquisition by expropriation, where governmental approval is often a prerequisite).[5] It is more common for colleges, university-colleges, or institutions to require approval to acquire land.[6] The process for obtaining such approval varies from jurisdiction to jurisdiction. By way of example, in British Columbia the process currently involves submitting to the Ministry of Advanced Education a request for approval to acquire that includes a legal description of the property, the cost of the acquisition, and future operating costs.[7]

The Meaning of "University Purposes"

A common restriction on the ability of Canadian universities to acquire land is that they may do so only for "the purposes of the university" (or some variation on this phrasing).[8] In addition, property tax exemptions for university lands are often provided only for land that is owned, held, used, and/or occupied (depending on the jurisdiction) for "university purposes."[9] However, most universities' enabling statutes leave "univer-

---

[3] *The University of Manitoba Act*, CCSM c U60, s 4(a).

[4] See, for example, *An Act respecting the Université du Québec*, CQLR c U-1, s 5.

[5] Ibid.

[6] See, for example, *College and Institute Act*, RSBC 1996, c 52, s 50(2); *The Regional Colleges Act*, SS 1986-87-88, c R-8.1, s 14(b); *New Brunswick Community Colleges Act*, SNB 2010, c N-4.05, s 37(1).

[7] British Columbia Ministry of Advanced Education, *Capital Asset Reference Guide*, section 14.2.1.2.

[8] See, for example, *The University of Regina Act*, RSS 1978, c U-5, s 5(1)(a). Other higher education institutions, such as colleges, may be similarly restricted in acquiring land. See, for example, *The Regional Colleges Act*, SS 1986-87-88, c R-8.1, s 14, which requires that the acquisition be for the "purposes of the college."

[9] Again, the precise wording varies considerably in each jurisdiction and even within different statutes in a jurisdiction. See, for example, *University Act*, RSBC 1996, c 468, s 54(1); *An Act to incorporate Laurentian University of Sudbury*, SO 1960, c 151, s 11. The property tax exemption in Alberta is for "property, other than a student dormitory, used in connection with *educational purposes* and held by any of the following: (i) the board of governors of a university, technical institute or public college under the *Post-secondary Learning Act* ..." [emphasis added]; *Municipal Government Act*, RSA 2000, c M-26, s 362(1).

sity purposes" undefined.[10] This may create an element of uncertainty regarding whether land can be acquired or will benefit from a property tax exemption.

University Purposes: Case Law Arising from Property Tax Disputes

It is predominantly in the context of litigation over property tax exemptions that courts have considered the meaning of "university purposes." While no comprehensive definition of "university purposes" has been formulated, several general principles have taken shape in the case law. For instance, the Supreme Court of Canada determined that the phrase "university purposes" is not synonymous with the "duties" of a university set out in its legislation, but neither does it mean simply "for the benefit of a university."[11] The meaning lies somewhere in between. "University purposes" has also been said to encompass the promotion of the objectives, and the advancement of the interests, of the university.[12]

Overall, there is a growing recognition of the varied roles and the array of services provided by modern universities beyond the formal provision of education, such as housing and food services, counselling, and athletic and recreation services; courts have been willing to take

---

[10] Even where a university's enabling statute defines the purposes of the university, "purposes of the university" may extend beyond the specifically enumerated purposes. For example, in *University of Windsor v Windsor (City) Assessment Commissioner*, 1965 CarswellOnt 131, [1965] 2 OR 455 [*University of Windsor* cited to CarswellOnt], the court was determining whether the president's residence was "actually used and occupied for the purposes of the University" such that it qualified for a property tax exemption. These deliberations included not only the university's legislated objects and purposes, namely, "(a) the advancement of learning and the dissemination of knowledge; and (b) the intellectual, spiritual, moral, social and physical development of its members and students and the betterment of society," but also "the promotion of those activities which are reasonably necessary in order that these broad objectives can be obtained." See paras 22-23. The president's residence ultimately qualified for the property tax exemption.

[11] *Victoria (City) v University of Victoria*, [1972] SCR 160 at 164 [*UVic*].

[12] *University of Windsor, supra* note 10 at paras 21, 22, 37; see also *Assessors of Areas #1 and #10 v University of Victoria*, 2010 BCSC 133 at para 154 [*Assessors*], which echoes this language; the court in that case stated that the services provided by commercial entities in the student union building, while not "indispensible or critically necessary to the attainment of the university's educational objectives, … have a substantial and reasonably connection to the furtherance and advancement of the multiple *bona fide* broad objectives of a modern Canadian university, including attracting and retaining the ever vital student body."

this into account when considering "university purposes."[13] To that end, the Ontario Court of Appeal has noted that in addition to lecture halls and labs, land and buildings used for student lounges, snack bars, and football stadiums also come within the tax exemption for lands "actually used and occupied for university purposes." Noted the court, "to hold otherwise would unduly limit the meaning of the section and would disregard the true nature and scope of activities which we have come to consider necessary to a university."[14]

University Purposes and Property Tax Exemptions: Additional Considerations

There is increasing acceptance across jurisdictions that a dual purpose (in other words, both a "university purpose" and some alternate purpose) will not disentitle university land to a property tax exemption.[15] Moreover, it is not necessarily fatal to the property tax exemption that the other purpose is of a commercial or for-profit nature.[16] Thus, in *Assessors v University of Victoria*, premises in the Student Union Building that were leased to private, for-profit commercial enterprises remained exempt from property tax. The services they provided were for university purposes, in the sense of being important and convenient to the student body and beneficial to the quality of university life.[17] Note, however, *Donaldo Pianezza Beauty Salon et al v Borough of North York et al*,[18] where property vested in York University was exempt from tax so long as it was "actually used and occupied for the purposes of the University." The land in question was vested in York University but was leased to private entrepreneurs. The court found that the property was "occupied by the occupants for

---

[13] *Assessors, supra* note 12 at paras 28, 68, and 154. See also *Acadia University v Wolfville (Town)*, 1971 CarswellNS 54 at paras 85–90.

[14] *University of Windsor, supra* note 10, para 24.

[15] See, for example, *University of Windsor, supra* note 10, where the president's residence was held to be tax exempt despite its use for both the purposes of the university and as a private residence; *Assessors, supra* note 12, in which the relevant lands were used for both university and commercial purposes and were tax exempt; and *University of Alberta v Edmonton (City)*, 2005 ABCA 147, where the food service areas were entitled to a property tax exemption despite being run by an independent contractor on a profit-sharing basis.

[16] *Assessors, supra* note 12. See also *University of Alberta, supra* note 15 at para 14, where the Alberta Court of Appeal noted that commercial and educational purposes are not mutually exclusive and that commercial services may be connected with educational purposes.

[17] *Assessors, supra* note 12 at para 154.

[18] [1978] OJ No 3315, 19 OR (2d) 343 at para 9.

profit and for the purposes of the occupants" and that the property was not entitled to the exemption.[19]

In that respect, it is worth noting the differences in the BC and Ontario property tax exemptions. In British Columbia, the requirement is that the land be "held *or* used for university purposes," while statutes in Ontario tend to import a more restrictive "use *and occupation*" standard.[20] Moreover, in British Columbia, third party holders or occupiers (such as lessees) of university land that is held or used for university purposes may still be liable to pay property tax.[21] What this illustrates is the critical importance of examining the wording of the exemption at issue and any exceptions thereto in order to determine whether land will be exempt from property taxation or who may be liable to pay any taxes levied. Each case may be distinguishable based on its particular facts and the exemption at issue.

The Meaning of Land Being "Vested" in a University

For university land to qualify for an exemption from property taxation or for protection against expropriation (or both), certain enabling statutes specify that the land must be vested in the university.[22] The term "vested" has both a technical, legal meaning and a more general meaning akin to "ownership." In real property law, the term vested is used to refer to an interest in real property that is limited to a currently existing and ascertained "person" (for present purposes, a higher education institu-

---

[19] Ibid., paras 9–10.

[20] See *University Act, supra* note 9, s 54(1); *University of Ottawa Act*, SO 1965, c 137, s 21; *Assessment Act*, RSO 1990, c A.31, s 3(1) 4.

[21] *Assessment Act*, RSBC 1996, c 20, s 27: "(1) Land, the fee simple of which is held by or on behalf of a person who is exempted from taxation under an Act, and which is held or occupied otherwise than by or on behalf of that person, is, with its improvements, to be assessed in accordance with this section. (2) The land and improvements referred to in subsection (1) must be entered in the assessment roll in the name of the holder or occupier, whose interest must be valued at the actual value of the land and improvements determined under this Part."

[22] See, for example, *University of Ottawa Act*, SO 1965, c 137, ss 21–22. Land may also have to be "vested" in other types of higher education institutions to receive property tax exemptions or protection against expropriation. See, for example, *Holland College Act*, RSPEI 1988, c H-6, s 3(7), which protects from expropriation real property vested in the college. Conversely, there are enabling statutes that provide these benefits without specifying that the land in question be vested in the higher education institution. See, for example, *Post-secondary Learning Act*, SA 2003, c P-19.5, s 120: "The power to expropriate land conferred by any statute on a municipality or any other person does not extend to the land of a public post-secondary institution […] unless the statute conferring the power is made in express terms to apply to the land of a public post-secondary institution."

tion), and that is not subject to the fulfillment of some condition.[23] While the use of vested relating to land in higher education statutes can likely encompass this meaning, a more appropriate interpretation is probably more generic. "Vest" is defined, in part, as "to confer ownership (of property) upon a person," while owner is defined as "one who has the right to possess, use and convey something; a person in whom one or more interests or vested."[24] It seems that this meaning related to ownership was intended in most higher education institutions' statutes where land must be vested in a higher education institution.

The Supreme Court of Canada has indicated that "the term 'vested' denotes title."[25] Land can be vested in an entity that holds only beneficial, and not legal, title to the land.[26] Furthermore, land that is owned by a higher education institution is vested in the institution even if it is leased to others.[27]

Property Transfer Tax

Unless an exemption exists, higher education institutions in certain jurisdictions must pay provincial property transfer or land transfer tax when they acquire land.[28] This tax is generally calculated as a percentage of the purchase price or market value of the land being acquired.[29] In British Columbia, designated universities, colleges, and other educational institutions are exempt from property transfer tax when the land being transferred to them will be used for an educational purpose.[30] Higher education institutions in other jurisdictions may not be exempt.[31] Land transfer taxes are not currently levied in Alberta, Saskatchewan, or rural Nova Scotia.

---

[23] La Forest, *Anger & Honsberger Law of Real Property*, s 9:20.10.

[24] *Black's Law Dictionary*, 9th ed., s.vv. "vest" and "owner."

[25] *City of Vancouver v Canadian Pacific Railway Co.* (1894), 23 SCR 1 at 22.

[26] *Whistler Village Land Co. v North Shore-Squamish Valley Area Assessor* (1981), 15 MPLR 192, 121 DLR (3d) 284 (BCSC).

[27] *Simon Fraser University v Burnaby (District)* (1968), 67 DLR (2d) 638 at para 32 (BCSC), aff'd 1 DLR (3d) 427 (BCCA).

[28] See, for example, *The Tax Administration and Miscellaneous Taxes Act*, RSM 1987, c R150, CCSM c T2, s 112(1).

[29] See, for example, *An Act respecting Duties on Transfers of Immovables*, CQLR c D-15.1, s 2.

[30] *Property Transfer Tax Act*, RSBC 1996, c 378, s 14(4). See also *Income Tax Act*, RSC 1985, c 1 (5th Supp), s 118.6(1).

[31] For example, section 1.1 of the *Land Transfer Tax Act*, RSO 1990, c L.6 provides that "no person otherwise subject to tax under this Act is exempt therefrom by reason of an exemption granted to the person, or to or in respect of the personal or real property of the person, by or under any other Act, unless the other Act expressly mentions this Act."

Application of the Ultra Vires Principle

Canadian higher education institutions are corporations created by legislation or by charter.[32] Their capacity to act and to undertake obligations, therefore, is circumscribed to the extent of the powers and obligations granted to them by their incorporating statutes or set out in their charter documents. Any act or obligation that a higher education institution undertakes that is not contemplated in its incorporating statute or charter documents is void by reason of being ultra vires (beyond its power), even if it is in the interests of the higher education institution. A recent BC case illustrates the significance of this concept. In *Barbour v The University of British Columbia*, the University of British Columbia was ordered to repay millions of dollars in fines it had collected pursuant to parking regulations that were ultra vires the public law powers delegated to the board of governors in the *University Act* (British Columbia) to enact (though the decision was reversed on appeal as a result of retroactive amendments to the *University Act* that made the regulations intra vires).[33]

The powers granted to higher education institutions can be defined either more or less broadly, depending on the statute or charter documents at issue. For example, currently in British Columbia, universities governed by the *University Act* (British Columbia)[34] have "the power and capacity of a natural person of full capacity."[35] Conversely, the University of Winnipeg has "the capacity, rights and powers of a natural person *for carrying out its purposes and objects.*"[36] Governing statutes also tend to *specify* certain permitted powers and obligations, or prohibited actions.[37] Certain of these may be directly relevant to the acquisition (or disposition) of land. For example, the BC *University Act* authorizes universities (with

---

[32] See, for example, *Memorial University Act*, RSNL 1990, c M-7, s 3(1); Victoria R Proclamation, 1841 para 1, reprinted in *Consolidated Royal Charter of Queen's University* (Kingston: Queen's University).

[33] 2009 BCSC 425, rev'd 2010 BCCA 63, [2010] BCJ No 219, leave to appeal to SCC ref'd June 24, 2010, [2010] SCCA No 135.

[34] University of British Columbia, Simon Fraser University, University of Victoria, University of Northern British Columbia, and the special purpose, teaching universities designated by BC Reg 355/2008: Capilano University, Emily Carr University of Art and Design, Kwantlen Polytechnic University, Vancouver Island University, and University of the Fraser Valley.

[35] *University Act, supra* note 9, s 46.1.

[36] *The University of Winnipeg Act*, SM 1998, c 50, CCSM c U70, s 4 (emphasis added).

[37] This may be done, for example, by specifying certain powers of the higher education institution, such as degree-granting functions, or by specifying certain powers held by its board of governors. See, for example, *University of Ottawa Act*, SO 1965, c 137, ss 7 and 11.

ministerial approval) to borrow money to purchase land,[38] while Prince Edward Island's Holland College is prohibited from incurring liabilities for the purchase of land (except with the approval of the Lieutenant Governor in Council or unless the college's annual income can cover the expenditure).[39]

Because of the often fine distinctions in the powers granted to higher education institutions and the great variety in the powers granted to and proscribed for them, those working with and for higher education institutions should be familiar with an institution's governing legislation and should be alert to the possibility that a contemplated acquisition, disposition, or other action relating to land may be ultra vires the institution.

DISPOSITION OF LAND

Introduction

Higher education institutions in Canada have varying abilities to dispose of real property. Some provinces have broadly applicable statutes that dictate the conditions under which higher education institutions may transfer and lease property (e.g., British Columbia, Alberta), while in other provinces institution-specific statutes set the parameters (e.g., Ontario, Quebec). Even within the provinces with statutes of broad application, there can be subtle but significant differences between the powers of universities and the powers of colleges and institutions.

This section sets out the legislative framework for property disposition by higher education institutions in the ten Canadian provinces. It identifies which rules are applicable to which higher education institutions, and the issues that these institutions must be aware of when contemplating or pursuing disposition of property. The British Columbia section is in slightly more depth as the Ministry of Advanced Education issued an updated "Capital Asset Reference Guide" in 2014. However, the lessons that can be culled from British Columbia are applicable to other jurisdictions in which approval of a governmental authority is a prerequisite to property disposition (e.g., Alberta, New Brunswick). While ministerial requirements vary from jurisdiction to jurisdiction, the "Capital Asset Reference Guide" provides insight into the types of issues to which ministries are attuned. Within each provincial section, the applicability (or inapplicability, as the case may be) of the rule against perpetuities is also discussed.

---

[38] *University Act, supra* note 9, ss 27 and 58.
[39] *Holland College Act,* RSPEI 1988, c H-6, ss 11(a) and (b).

British Columbia

Universities

In British Columbia, disposition of land by universities is governed by the *University Act*.[40] Section 50(2) of the Act mandates that universities seeking to dispose of land must obtain the approval of the minister.[41] Section 50(2) also states that disposal of land is subject to "the terms of any grant, conveyance, gift or devise of land," meaning that the terms attached to the university's acquisition and/or ownership of the land may impact the ability to dispose of the land.

"Dispose" has a broader meaning than just "sell." Section 50(2) of the *University Act* explicitly includes "mortgage, sell, transfer, lease for not more than 99 years, or otherwise dispose of its land." Moreover, section 29 of the *Interpretation Act*[42] states that "'dispose' means to transfer by any method and includes assign, give, sell, grant, charge, convey, bequeath, devise, lease, divest, release and agree to do any of those things." If a university is seeking to do any of the aforementioned actions with its property, it must obtain approval of the minister.

As noted above, section 50(2)(a) includes disposal by "lease for not more than 99 years." However, section 50(2)(b) allows universities to lease land to an "affiliated college" for any length of time (subject, as always, to ministerial approval and any applicable terms of ownership).

The Ministry of Advanced Education issued a *Capital Asset Reference Guide* in 2014, which outlines the approval processes for higher education institutions to acquire and/or dispose of property.[43]

---

[40] RSBC 1996, c 468. Section 3 specifies the institutions that are "universities" for the purposes of the Act: Simon Fraser University, University of British Columbia, University of Northern British Columbia, and University of Victoria. Section 3(2) states that institutions designated by the Lieutenant Governor in Council ("LGC" under item 1) as "special purpose, teaching universities" pursuant to section 71(3)(a) also constitute "universities" within the Act. By virtue of BC Reg 355/2008, Capilano University, Emily Carr University of Art and Design, Kwantlen Polytechnic University, Vancouver Island University, and University of the Fraser Valley are "special purpose, teaching universities." Section 4(1) of the *Thompson Rivers University Act*, SBC 2005, c 17 makes the majority of the *University Act* applicable to Thompson Rivers University (including section 50(2) on disposition of land, discussed below). Section 16 of the *Royal Roads University Act*, RSBC 1996, c 409 does the same for Royal Roads University.

[41] The "minister" refers to the Minister of Advanced Education; the *University Act* is under his or her purview.

[42] RSBC 1996, c 238.

[43] BC Ministry of Advanced Education, *Capital Asset Reference Guide*. The guide states that disposal requests are to be submitted by the university to the Ministry of Advanced Education. Disposal requests should be accompanied by a copy of

Colleges and Institutes

The disposal of land by a college or institute in British Columbia is governed by the *College and Institute Act*.[44]

Colleges and institutes are those corporations designated as such by the Lieutenant Governor in Council pursuant to his/her power under section 5(1) of the *College and Institute Act*. As of 2014, there are eleven colleges and three institutes in British Columbia.[45]

In order for a college or institute to dispose of property, section 50(2) of the *College and Institute Act* states that "consent of the minister *and the Minister of Finance*" is required (emphasis added). As with the *University Act*, "the minister" refers to the Minister of Advanced Education. "Dispose" has the same broad meaning from section 29 of the *Interpretation Act* set out above. The BC *Reference Guide* outlines the approval process for colleges and institutes, just as it does for universities. Except for the certificate of title, which is not required, colleges and institutes are required to submit the same documentation.[46]

Issues to Consider in the Sale or Lease of Land

Proposed dispositions should be discussed with the regulatory authority before investing significant time or money. As ministerial approval is a prerequisite to any disposition of land, communication with the regulatory authorities is always paramount. The *Capital Asset Reference Guide* expressly states that higher education institutions wishing to dispose of land should discuss the proposal with the ministry before investing time or money, lest assets be wasted.[47]

If disposition by a college or institute is approved by the applicable ministers, section 50(4) of the *College and Institute Act* further provides

---

the estimated value of the property as determined by one or more independent appraisals; a board resolution approving the request, including a statement that disposal of the property will not affect the future delivery of educational programs by that institution; a copy of the survey plan with the property outlined in red; a copy of the Certificate of Title verifying any specific public purpose limitations on the land established by a Crown land grant; and the legal description of the property, among other things; see s 14.1.2.3. The same documentation is required regardless of the type of disposition sought by the university, including leases.

[44] RSBC 1996, c 52.

[45] The colleges are Camosun College, College of New Caledonia, College of the Rockies, Douglas College, Langara College, North Island College, Northern Lights College, Northwest Community College, Okanagan College, Selkirk College, and Vancouver Community College. The institutes are BC Institute of Technology (BCIT), Justice Institute of BC, and Nicola Valley Institute of Technology.

[46] BC Ministry of Advanced Education, *Capital Asset Reference Guide*, s 14.2.4.2.

[47] Ibid., s 14.1.2.1.

that "if an institution disposes of land or buildings, it must not spend the proceeds of the disposition without the consent of the minister."

The *University Act* does not contain a similar provision and, consequently, universities have greater freedom with respect to proceeds of disposition.

The Ministry of Advanced Education has stated that any provincial debt extant on a property at the time of disposition must be paid with the net proceeds from the disposition.[48] For instance, if a university receives $1 million in net proceeds from the sale of a piece of land, but there is a $100,000 debt registered by the province against the property, the debt will have to be paid out of the $1 million.

The Application of the Rule against Perpetuities

The common law "rule against perpetuities" is the rule in property law "prohibiting a grant of an estate unless the interest must vest, if at all, no later than 21 years ... after the death of some person alive when the interest was created."[49] In other words, the effective date for a grant of an estate must reference a living person, and the estate must vest (i.e., take effect) within 21 years of that living person's death. The rule is designed to prevent creation of inalienable property. As Geoffrey Cheshire wrote, "The view of the law is that no disposition should be allowed which tends to withdraw land from commerce, and in pursuance of this policy... rules have emerged which have successfully prevented the particular evil of 'perpetuities' ... The modern rule against perpetuities invalidates an interest that may vest at too remote a date in the future."[50]

At common law, it is not the result that matters but the potential. If a grant *could*, at its inception, violate the rule against perpetuities, then it *has* violated the rule against perpetuities. In 1966, the Supreme Court of Canada illustrated this aspect of the rule: "The rule against perpetuities is concerned with the certainty of vesting, not the likelihood of vesting. It is elementary that in Canada there is no wait and see rule: the interest must be good in its creation."[51]

The *University Act* and the *College and Institute Act* state, at sections 52 and 27 respectively, that "the rule against perpetuities and other rules restricting the holding of land do not apply to property of [postsecondary institutions]."

---

[48] Ibid., s 14.1.2.2.
[49] *Black's Law Dictionary*, 9th ed., s.v. "rule against perpetuities."
[50] Cheshire, *Modern Law of Real Property*, 234 and 235.
[51] *Politzer v Metropolitan Homes Ltd*, [1976] 1 SCR 363 at 372.

Alberta

Legislative Framework for the Disposition of Land

In Alberta, disposition of land by any higher education institution is governed by the *Post-secondary Learning Act*, SA 2003, c P-19.5. To comply with section 67 of the *Post-secondary Learning Act*, a higher education institution (including universities and public colleges) must obtain approval of the Lieutenant Governor in Council (LGC) prior to disposing of land. Prior approval is unnecessary, however, if the land was donated to the higher education institution.

The *Post-secondary Learning Act* allows the Lieutenant Governor to make any order respecting the disposition of property that the LGC considers necessary. This applies to universities, public colleges, and technical institutes by virtue of sections 4(5) and 41(5).[52]

The Application of the Rule against Perpetuities

The *Post-secondary Learning Act* does not explicitly exempt higher education institutions from the rule against perpetuities. Alberta's *Perpetuities Act*, RSA 2000, c P-5, section 2 states, "Except as provided by this Act, the rule of law known as the rule against perpetuities continues to have full effect." Sections 3 and 4 of the *Perpetuities Act* create a "presumption of validity" (if a grant *could* vest within the perpetuity period, it is valid until and unless it does not vest within the perpetuity period); section 5 states that the perpetuity period is a life in being plus a finite period of

---

[52] The relevant statutory provisions of the *Post-secondary Learning Act* read as follows:

67(1) In this section,

(a) "donated land" means land that has been donated or devised to a public post-secondary institution or its board, other than land donated by a municipality, the Government of Alberta or the Government of Canada;

(b) "support services" has the meaning given to it in the regulations.

(1.1) A board shall not, without the prior approval of the Lieutenant Governor in Council,

(a) sell or exchange any interest in land, other than donated land, that is held by and being used for the purposes of the board, or

(b) lease for a term that exceeds 5 years any land held by the board unless the lease is to a person that will use the land for the purpose of providing support services to the students, faculty or staff of the public post-secondary institution.

(2) Notwithstanding subsection (1.1), a board may dispose of minerals held by it in any manner it considers proper.

(3) A sale, exchange or lease referred to in subsection (1.1) is subject to any trust in accordance with which a board holds the land or the interest in land.

time. If a grant does not reference a life in being, the perpetuity period is 21 years.

Like the *Post-secondary Learning Act*, the *Perpetuities Act* does not explicitly exempt higher education institutions. Therefore the common-law rule against perpetuities continues to apply against higher education institutions in Alberta, except to the extent that the *Perpetuities Act* has modified the rule.

Saskatchewan

Legislative Framework for the Disposition of Land

The two universities in Saskatchewan (i.e., University of Regina and University of Saskatchewan) are each governed by a particularized statute: *The University of Regina Act*, RSS 1978, c U-5 and *The University of Saskatchewan Act*, SS 1995, c U-6.1, respectively. The Acts grant the universities broad power to dispose of property as each sees fit,[53] save for a few circumscriptions: in order to lease property for more than 21 years, the universities must have ministerial consent;[54] even with consent, the universities may not lease land for more than 99 years;[55] and if property was gifted or devised to the universities, or is held in trust by the universities, the universities are generally unable to dispose of it in a manner that contravenes the terms of the gift, devise, or trust.[56]

Colleges in Saskatchewan are governed by *The Regional Colleges Act*, SS 1986-87-88, c R-8.1. Section 14(e) gives the board of governors of a college the power to sell, lease, or otherwise dispose of real property that is not required for the purposes of the college, subject to approval of the Minister of Advanced Education.

The Application of the Rule against Perpetuities

The *Trustee Act* abolishes the rule against perpetuities in Saskatchewan,[57] but allows a judge to invoke the rule if "in the opinion of the court hearing the matter, it is just and equitable that the rules against perpetuities should continue to apply."[58]

---

[53] *The University of Saskatchewan Act, 1995*, SS 1995, c U-6.1, s 7(1)(c); *The University of Regina Act*, RSS 1978, c U-5, s 5(1)(b).

[54] *The University of Saskatchewan Act*, ibid., s 7(d); *The University of Regina Act*, ibid.

[55] Ibid.

[56] *The University of Saskatchewan Act*, ibid., s 7(2) and (3); *The University of Regina Act*, ibid., s 5(2) and (3).

[57] *Trustee Act*, SS 2009, c T-23.01, s 58.

[58] Ibid., s 60(2)(b).

The University of Saskatchewan Act and *The University of Regina Act* do not contain provisions on the rule against perpetuities.

Manitoba

Legislative Framework for the Disposition of Land

As in Saskatchewan, universities in Manitoba are each governed by their own statute: *The Brandon University Act*, SM 1998, c 48, CCSM c B90; *The University of Manitoba Act*, RSM 1987, c U60, CCSM c U60; and *The University of Winnipeg Act*, SM 1998, c 50, CCSM c U70.

The University of Manitoba Act, section 4(b) grants the University of Manitoba a broad power to dispose of real property.[59] *The Brandon University Act* and *The University of Winnipeg Act* do not contain express provisions on the disposition of land. However, section 12(2)(i) of *The Brandon University Act* and section 12(2)(h) of *The University of Winnipeg Act* grant Brandon University and the University of Winnipeg, respectively, plenary power to enter into agreements to further the universities' purposes.

Moreover, section 13(a) of *The University of Winnipeg Act* prohibits bylaws or resolutions that authorize "the sale or disposition of all or part of the property bounded by Portage Avenue, Ellice Avenue, Balmoral Street and Spence Street in the City of Winnipeg ... unless it is approved by the general council." This contingency on the disposition of a certain area implies that other property may be disposed of without meeting the same criterion.

Section 18(1)(b) of Manitoba's *Colleges Act*[60] states that the board of governors of a college may, subject to ministerial approval, "sell, lease or otherwise dispose of any of its property that it considers to be no longer necessary for its purposes." This implies that colleges may not sell property necessary for its purposes, even with ministerial approval.

---

[59] This section of the Act provides:

"4. In addition to the powers, rights, and privileges, conferred upon and vested in corporations by *The Interpretation Act*, the university may ...

(b) sell, exchange, lease, mortgage, hypothecate, pledge, or otherwise deal with or dispose of, all or any of its real or personal property and any right, title, or interest, it may have in, to, or out of it, and make and execute all instruments and documents and do all acts, matters, or things, requisite or necessary to carry the same into effect."

[60] SM 1991-92, c 26, CCSM c C150.1.

The Application of the Rule against Perpetuities

Section 3 of Manitoba's *Perpetuities and Accumulations Act*, RSM 1987, c P33, CCSM c P33 states that the rule against perpetuities is no longer the law of Manitoba. Consequently, the rule against perpetuities is inapplicable to higher education institutions in Manitoba.

Ontario

Legislative Framework for the Disposition of Land

Universities in Ontario are, for the most part, each governed by their own statute.

Queen's University at Kingston Act, SC 1912 c 138, as amended by SC 2011 c 27 is an oft-revised statute dating back to the late nineteenth century. There is no statutory limitation on Queen's University's power to dispose of property in the original Act nor any of its amendments.

The York University Act, SO 1965 c 143, section 16 grants York University a broad power to dispose of property. The section provides that the university has the power to "sell, grant, convey, mortgage, lease or otherwise dispose of the same or any part thereof from time to time and as occasion may require, and to acquire other estate or property in addition thereto or in place thereof without licence in mortmain and without limitation as to the period of holding."

University of Toronto Act, SO 1971 c 56, as amended SO 1978 c 88, section 2(14)(l) grants the Governing Council of the University of Toronto the power to "acquire, hold without limitation as to the period of holding, sell, lease or otherwise deal with real property." Section 14 provides that any property granted, devised, or bequeathed to the university, or to be held in trust for the benefit of the university is vested in the Governing Council of the University of Toronto (subject to other trusts affecting the property).

A number of Ontario universities, though they are governed by particularized statutes, have substantively identical property disposition powers, as follows:

> [i]n addition to the powers, right and privileges mentioned in section 26 of the *Interpretation Act*, … the power to purchase or otherwise acquire, take or receive by gift, bequest or devise and to hold and enjoy any estate or property whatsoever, whether real or personal, and to sell, grant, convey, mortgage, lease or otherwise dispose of the same or any part thereof from time to time and as occasion may require, and to acquire other estate or property in addition

thereto or in place thereof without licence in mortmain and without limitation as to the period of holding.[61]

As with universities, no one piece of legislation defines the powers of property disposition for all colleges in Ontario. The *Ministry of Training, Colleges and Universities Act*, RSO 1990, c M-19, the *Ontario Colleges of Applied Arts and Technology Act, 2002*, SO 2002, c 8, Sch F, and the *Ontario College of Trades and Apprenticeship Act, 2009*, SO 2009, c 22 do not specify if or how colleges may dispose of land.

Section 11 of the *Ontario College of Art and Design Act, 2002*, SO 2002, c 8, Sch E grants the Ontario College of Art and Design the power to "purchase or otherwise acquire, take by gift, devise or bequest and hold such property as the board considers necessary for the objects of the University, and may mortgage, sell or otherwise dispose of the same as the board, in its absolute discretion, considers appropriate."[62]

The Application of the Rule against Perpetuities

Section 2 of Ontario's *Perpetuities Act*, RSO 1990, c P 9 states, "Except as provided by this Act, the rule of law known as the rule against perpetuities continues to have full effect." Like Alberta's Act of the same name, Ontario's *Perpetuities Act* creates a presumption of validity: all grants that could vest within the perpetuity period are valid unless and until they do not vest within the perpetuity period.[63] The Act does not expressly exempt universities, but has a number of qualifications and exemptions for property held in trust.

The Acts pertaining to individual institutions in Ontario, discussed above, do not contain provisions on the rule against perpetuities either. However, the Governing Council of the University of Toronto is expressly

---

[61] See University of Windsor (via *An Act to incorporate the University of Windsor*, SO 1962 as amended in 1968, s 9); Lakehead University (via *An Act respecting Lakehead University*, SO 1965, c 54, s 19); Laurentian University (via *An Act to Incorporate Laurentian University of Sudbury*, SO 1960, c 151, s 4(f)); University of Western Ontario (via *University of Western Ontario Act*, SO 1988, c-Pr 26, s 6(2)); University of Ottawa (via *An Act respecting Université d'Ottawa*, SO 1965, c 137, s 20); Ryerson University (via *Ryerson University Act*, 1977, SC 1977, c 47).

The wording is rearranged in the latter two Acts, but the same powers are granted; and section 15 of *Ryerson University Act*, 1977 does not explicitly mention the *Interpretation Act*.

[62] Note that this institution is referred to as a "university" within its enabling statute in spite of its moniker.

[63] *Perpetuities Act*, RSO 1990, c P 9, ss 3 and 4.

given the power to hold property "without limitation as to the period of holding."[64]

Quebec

Legislative Framework for the Disposition of Land

There is no one Act in Quebec that governs disposition of land by universities. Each university is subject to the provisions of its own statute. By way of example, section 2 of McGill University's enabling statute – *An Act respecting the Royal Institution for the Advancement of Learning*, SQ 1861, c 17 – states that the trustees of the university may "purchase, take, hold and possess, without license in mortmain or *letters d'amotissement*, all real or immoveable property … paid, given, granted, purchased, appropriated, devised or bequeathed in any manner whatsoever, for and in favour of the said School and Institutions of Royal foundation, to and for the purposes of education and the advancement of learning." Section 3 provides that "the said Trustee may demise, let and lease any immoveable property so given, granted, purchased, appropriated, devised or bequeathed, for any term of years not exceeding twenty-one years, or grant emphyteutic leases or any such immoveable property for any term of years not exceeding ninety-nine nor less than nine years."[65]

The board of governors of Concordia University (formerly known as Sir George Williams University) has the power "to sell, transfer, make over and assign or otherwise alienate, dispose of and deal with property of all kinds, moveable and immoveable, real and personal, tangible and intangible."[66] Further, the "Statutes of Bishop's University," (June 8, 2012) do not state what powers the university or its board of governors has with respect to disposition of property. The absence of statutory restrictions suggests the corporation has plenary power to deal with its property.

Colleges in Quebec are governed by the *General and Vocational Colleges Act*, CQLR c C-29. Section 6(h) states that "a college is a legal person; it may, in particular … acquire, possess, lease, hold, administer and alienate

---

[64] *University of Toronto Act*, SO 1971, c 56, as amended SO 1978, c 88, s 2(14)(l).

[65] Section 11 goes on to state: "The said Corporation of the *Royal Institution for the Advancement of Learning* [now known as McGill] may alienate and dispose in perpetuity of all such portions of all lands or real estate by them held in trust for McGill College, or for any department or branch thereof … as they deem expedient for the ends of such trust … subject to all terms and conditions, whether in reference to time and mode of redemption of any such rent or otherwise, and with such formalities only of procedure, as they may deem advisable."

[66] *Concordia University Act*, SQ 1948, c 91, s 7.

property by all legal methods and under any title." Section 6 specifies that the powers granted by subparagraphs (b), (c), and (d) may not be exercised without consent of the Minister of Education, Recreation and Sports; as 6(h) is not specified, colleges may alienate property without ministerial consent.

The Application of the Rule against Perpetuities

There is no real equivalent in the civil law jurisdiction of Quebec to the rule against perpetuities; the trust rules are the most analogous. There exist other rules in the Civil Code of Quebec that limit the duration of certain property and quasi-property rights, and such rules should be considered and reviewed by a civil law lawyer.

Newfoundland and Labrador

Legislative Framework for the Disposition of Land

By virtue of section 4(1) of *Memorial University Act*, RSNL 1990, c M-7, all disposition of land by Memorial University is subject to the approval of the Lieutenant Governor in Council (LGC) and to the terms of any grant, conveyance, gift, or trust applicable to the land. Memorial University may not lease out its land for longer than 99 years, even with approval of the LGC.

Newfoundland and Labrador's *College Act, 1996*, SNL 1996, c C-22.1 does not specify the powers of a college or its board of governors to dispose of property.

The Application of the Rule against Perpetuities

An Act Respecting Memorial University of Newfoundland does not exempt the university from the rule against perpetuities. Moreover, the rule is not expressly continued or abolished in other Newfoundland and Labrador legislation.

Nova Scotia

Legislative Framework for the Disposition of Land

There is no broadly applicable Act pertaining to the power of higher education institutions to dispose of property in Nova Scotia.

By way of example for institution-specific legislation, *Cape Breton University Act*, RSNS 1989, c 484, section 3(3)(a) grants the board of governors of Cape Breton University the broad power to "hold, sell, lease, mortgage, pledge, charge or hypothecate" real and personal property. It does not specify any restrictions on those powers.

Colleges in Nova Scotia are governed by the *Community Colleges Act*, SNS 1995-96, c 4. Section 65(1)(a) of Nova Scotia's *Community Colleges Act* grants the Minister of Education and Culture the power to "purchase or otherwise acquire, hold, improve and maintain any real and personal property and lease, sell or convey the same for such consideration and on such conditions as the Minister deems proper."

Section 66(1)(b) grants a similar power to the board of governors, but stipulates that the land must no longer be necessary for the purposes of the college: "The Board may ... sell, lease or otherwise dispose of any of its property that it considers to be no longer necessary for the purpose of the College."

The Application of the Rule against Perpetuities

Neither *Cape Breton University Act* nor the *Community Colleges Act* provides express exemptions from the rule against perpetuities. The rule is not abolished or altered in the statutes of Nova Scotia. A few statutes, such as the *Trustee Act*,[67] provide express exemptions from the rule. This suggests that, to the extent the rule against perpetuities continues to be part of the common law of Canada, it is applicable to higher education institutions in Nova Scotia.

Prince Edward Island

Legislative Framework for the Disposition of Land

University Act, RSPEI 1988, c U-4, section 4(h) gives the governing body of the University of Prince Edward Island the authority to "sell, convey, lease or otherwise dispose of ... property." There are no ostensible restrictions on its ability to do so.

Holland College Act, RSPEI 1988, c H-6, section 3(3) grants Holland College the power, subject to approval of the LGC, to "mortgage, sell, transfer, lease or otherwise dispose of any of its real property." In order to give effect to section 3(3), section 3(4) grants the college the power to "make and execute all necessary instruments and documents as required."

---

[67] RSNS 1989, c 479, s 66(1).

The Application of the Rule against Perpetuities

The *University Act* does not expressly exempt the University of PEI from the rule against perpetuities. Section 1 of PEI's *Perpetuities Act*, RSPEI 1988, c P-3 codifies the rule against perpetuities and develops its own perpetuity period disparate from that at common law. However, it does not exempt universities from its application.[68]

New Brunswick

Legislative Framework for the Disposition of Land

The *University of New Brunswick Act*, SNB 1984, c 40 gives the University of New Brunswick the power to dispose of property, subject to approval of the Lieutenant Governor in Council. Without approval of the LGC, the university may only grant rights of way and easements over its property or lease property for fewer than 21 years.[69]

Section 37(2) of the *New Brunswick Community Colleges Act*, SNB 2010, c N-4.05 gives colleges the power, subject to approval of the Minister of Post-Secondary Education, Training and Labour to "lease, sell or otherwise dispose of real property."

The Application of the Rule against Perpetuities

New Brunswick has no statutory codification or abolition of the rule against perpetuities. The *University of New Brunswick Act* does not expressly exempt the university from the rule against perpetuities. Therefore, to the extent the rule against perpetuities continues to be the common law of Canada, it is applicable to the University of New Brunswick.

---

[68] Section 1 of the *Perpetuities Act* states:
Notwithstanding any other law or statute in force in this province, the period during which the existence of a future estate or interest in any hereditament, right, profit, easement or other property, real or personal, may be suspended, and during which the rents, revenues, fruits, profits or income of any real or personal property may be allowed to accumulate, either in whole or in part, may extend to, but must not exceed the life of a person or of the survivor of several persons born or conceived but not born at the time of the creation of the future estate or interest and ascertained for that purpose by the instrument creating the same, and sixty years to be computed from the dropping of such life or lives and ascertained for that purpose by such instrument.
[69] See sections 7, 13, and 14.

STRUCTURE ISSUES AFFECTING DEVELOPMENT

Introduction

Structuring considerations in relation to land development projects undertaken by higher education institutions shape some of the fundamental administrative frameworks of such development. A higher education institution's development projects may be carried out by the institution itself, or through one or more development arrangements or subsidiary entities. The following section explores some of the considerations when choosing the structure of a development project, the pros and cons of such structures, and some structuring pitfalls higher education institutions should take into account. Specifically, this section will review choices available for a development entity (corporation, trust, partnership, joint venture, direct development), tax and non-tax considerations affecting such choices, impact on charitable status, limitation of liability, and governance and control of the development entity.

Structuring Considerations – Legislative and Regulatory Framework

Higher education institutions operate within a unique legislative and regulatory framework, which can impact the choice of business vehicle that is appropriate to undertake a development project. The primary legislative and regulatory constraints affecting the choice of business vehicle are the higher education institution's status as a charitable organization[70] and the provincial regulation of universities and other higher education institutions.

Status as a Charitable Organization

Most higher education institutions with the size and scope to take on a development project will be registered charitable organizations for the purpose of the advancement of education. This charitable registration status affords the higher education institution certain privileges (tax exempt status,[71] ability to issue charitable tax receipts for donations[72]) but also carries with it certain obligations. These obligations include conducting the higher education institution's affairs in such a way as to maintain its charitable status.

---

[70] As defined in subsection 149.1(1) of the *Income Tax Act*, RSC 1985, c 1 (5th Supp), as amended [*ITA*].

[71] *ITA, supra* note 70, s 149(1)(f).

[72] *Income Tax Regulations*, CRC c 945, ss 3500 and 3501(1).

Definition of Charitable Organization

The term "charitable organization" is defined in the *Income Tax Act* as generally an organization that devotes all of its resources to charitable activities carried on by the organization itself; is not operated for personal benefit of any director, trustee, or like official; is not controlled by any major donor or contributor; and whose officials deal with each other at arm's length.[73] This definition focuses on the activities carried on by a charitable organization.

The definition of "registered charity" in the *Income Tax Act* incorporates the definition of "charitable organization" within it.[74] A registered charity is

> a charitable organization, private foundation or public foundation, within the meanings assigned by subsection 149.1(1), that is resident in Canada and was either created or established in Canada, [...] that has applied to the Minister in prescribed form for registration and that is at that time registered as a charitable organization, private foundation or public foundation.

As such, if a registered charity ceases to have the characteristics of its defined category (charitable organization, public foundation, or private foundation as the case may be), it will no longer fall within the definition of "registered charity."

The Minister of National Revenue has the power to revoke the registration of a charitable organization where, among other things, it "carries on a business that is not a related business of that charity" or where a registered charity ceases to comply with the requirements of the *Income Tax Act* for its registration as a registered charity.[75] If the Minister of National Revenue were to exercise the power of revocation of registered charity status, significant adverse consequences for a higher education institution would result.[76] In light of the prohibition of a charitable organization carrying on a business that is not a related business, and the consequences of carrying on such a business or other non-permitted activities,[77] it is recommended that a higher education institution use a

---

[73] ITA, *supra* note 70, s 149.1(1) "charitable organization."

[74] *ITA, supra* note 70, s 248(1) "registered charity."

[75] *ITA, supra* note 70, ss 149.1(2)-(4.1).

[76] See *ITA, supra* note 70, ss 188(1), (1.1), 188.1(1)(b) and (2)(b), and 188.2(1) and (2).

[77] The sanctions that the Minister of National Revenue may impose on a registered charity when that charity is not complying with its registration obligations under the *Income Tax Act* include revocation of a charity's registration status, payment of a revocation tax, suspension of receipting privileges, loss of tax-exempt

development subsidiary, and ensure the separation between the higher education institution and the development subsidiary when undertaking any development projects that are not directly related to the advancement of education.

In order to remain a registered charity, a higher education institution must continue to comply with the definition of "charitable organization" or risk losing its registered status. One significant element of the definition of "charitable organization" is that the organization devote all of its resources to charitable activities carried on by the organization.

Devotion of all resources to charitable activities means the higher education institution should dedicate the different resources at its disposal, such as the property, facilities, personnel, or financial resources, to activities related to its charitable purpose, generally the advancement of education. Any resources of the higher education institution that are integral to a proposed development project should be carefully considered and a strategy put in place to allow the project to proceed without violating the higher education institution's obligations as a charitable organization.[78]

Related Business

Charitable organizations that are registered charities are prohibited from carrying on a business other than a "related business" of that charitable organization.[79] In general, a related business is a business linked to and subordinate to the charitable purposes of a charitable organization;[80] in the case of a higher education institution, a related business should be

---

status, and certain penalty taxes for carrying on a business that is not a related business of the "registered charity."

The *Income Tax Act* sets out certain penalties for charities that are found to be carrying on businesses that are not related businesses of the charity. Under subsection 188.1(1) of the *Income Tax Act,* such a charity is liable for a penalty equal to 5 percent of its gross revenue for a taxation year from any business that it carries on that is not a related business of the charity. If a second occurrence of carrying on an unrelated business is found within five years of the first finding, the penalty will be equal to 100 percent of the gross revenue for the taxation year from the unrelated business. The penalty as applied to gross revenue does not take into account any expenses incurred to operate the business; therefore the second penalty level of 100 percent of gross revenue would mean a loss for the charity equal to the amounts expended in operation of the business.

[78] *ITA, supra* note 70, s 149.1(1) "charitable organization," para (a).

[79] *ITA, supra* note 70, s 149.1(2)(a).

[80] Registered Charities Policy Statement CPS-019, "What Is a Related Business?," March 31, 2003, para 17.

linked to the advancement of education.[81] Most development projects will not be sufficiently related to the advancement of education to qualify as a related business of a higher education institution. The primary method available to prevent a higher education institution from being found to be carrying on an unrelated business when undertaking a development project is to isolate such a project in a separate legal entity that will carry out the project itself.

Choice of Business Organization

A number of options for business organizations are available to a higher education institution to undertake a development project without carrying out the project itself. Corporations, trusts, partnerships, and joint ventures are each explained further below. As depicted in Figure 11.1, a combination of the various business organizations may be used in conjunction to achieve the desired degree of separation.

Corporation

A business corporation is the most straightforward business vehicle to use to undertake activities separated from the activities of a higher education institution. A corporation is a distinct legal entity with separate legal personality from its shareholders. A higher education institution may be a passive investor in a corporation and continue to devote all of its resources to charitable activities carried on by the higher education institution. It is important that any business corporation set up to undertake development activities be independent from the higher education institution. If the higher education institution were to dictate the terms of the corporation's projects or otherwise carry out the development projects alongside the corporation, the corporation could be found to be an agent or a partner of the higher education institution, which would jeopardize the higher education institution's status as a charitable organization.

Trust

A business trust is another way in which a higher education institution may benefit from a development project without carrying out the project itself. As a potential beneficiary of a business trust that carries out

---

[81] A business run solely by volunteers also qualifies as a related business pursuant to the extended definition of "related business" contained in s 149.1(1); however, due to the complexity and risk involved in commercial real estate development projects, a volunteer-run business seems unlikely.

FIGURE 11.1
Business Structure Options

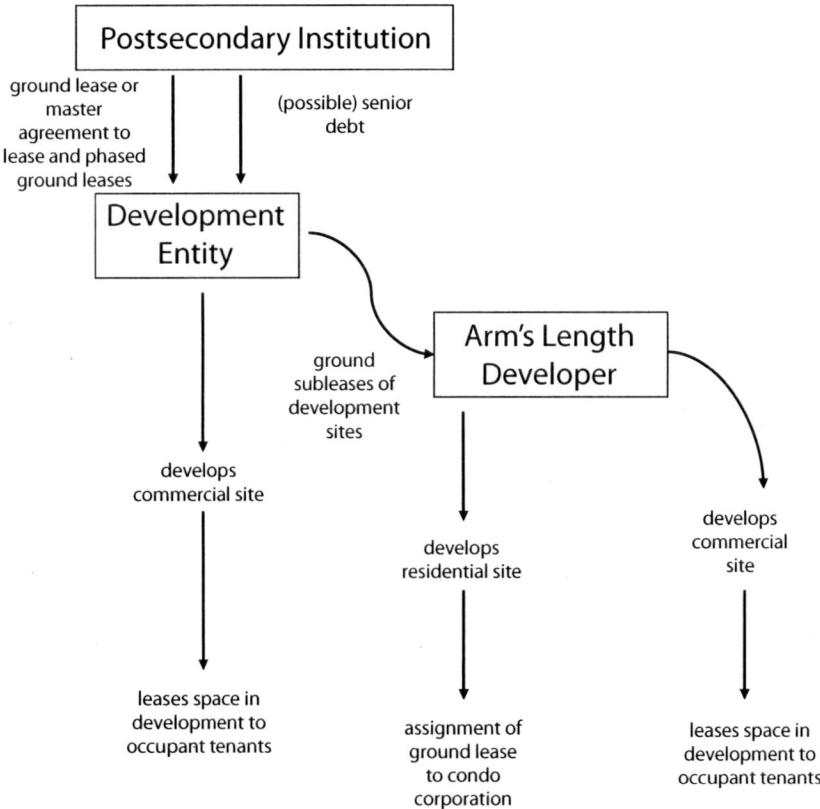

the development project, the higher education institution obtains the income from the proposed development project without carrying out the development activities itself. As long as the higher education institution does not interfere in the administration of the trust's affairs, and other clear separations between the higher education institution and the trust are put in place, a higher education institution should not be considered to be carrying out the development activities on its own behalf.

Partnership

A higher education institution may consider carrying out a development project through the use of a general or limited partnership with another entity, related or unrelated to the higher education institution. The use of a partnership is not recommended, however, because the very nature of a partnership is that of two or more parties coming together to carry on business in common with a view to a profit.[82] Even in a limited partnership (where the limited partner does not take an active part in the management of the business and enjoys some measure of limited liability), the business of the partnership is attributed to all of the partners, including the limited partners.[83] Therefore, operation of a development project through a partnership does not provide the required separation between a higher education institution and a proposed development project to ensure that the higher education institution is not carrying on a business that is not a related business. Due to these factors, the other aspects of the use of a partnership for such a development project will not be explored further below.

Note that higher education institutions are increasingly involved in public-private partnerships (PPP; see the subsection "Intergovernmental Cooperation" below). However, the term "partnerships" in PPPs is a term of common usage and not a reference to a legal partnership structure.

Joint Venture

A joint venture is somewhat similar to a partnership in which each joint venturer brings particular resources to the venture, be they physical assets, know-how, or business connections, and the joint venturers cooperate to undertake a particular business activity. Like a partnership, each joint venturer is carrying on certain activities that could be considered business activities. Even if a higher education institution that is involved in a joint venture does not take an active part in the joint venture but instead contributes the use of assets, this contribution could be construed as a failure by the higher education institution to use all its resources to carry on activities that further the advancement of education. In such circumstances, similar to the comments above relating to partnerships, it is not advisable for a higher education institution to undertake its development projects using a joint venture structure.

---

[82] This common-law principle has been codified in various provincial statutes on the matter. See *Partnership Act*, RSS 1978, c P-3, RSA 2000, c P-3, RSPEI 1988, c P-1, RSNS 1989, c 334, RSNL 1990, c P-3, RSBC 1996, c 348, RSNWT (Nu) 1988, c P-1, RSNWT 1998, c P-1, RSNB 1973, c P-4, RSO 1990, c P.5 and RMS 1987, c P30, CCSM c P30.

[83] *Robinson (Trustee of) v The Queen*, [1998] 2 FC 569 (FCA).

Tax Considerations

When Using a Business Corporation

Corporations that are resident in Canada pay income tax on income that the corporation earns in the year.[84] The most common source of income for a corporation is income from a business. Income from a business is calculated by determining the net profit of the business for the year.[85] Reasonable expenses incurred to earn the revenue of a business may be deducted from that revenue to arrive at the net profit of the business. The income earned by a corporation is taxed at corporate income tax rates (which are generally lower than personal income tax rates);[86] however, any taxable income of the corporation will be subject to some tax at the corporate level.

Since a corporation's income is its profit from business activity, the corporation may minimize its income through certain expenses that are payable by it to a higher education institution. For example, payments of interest on a loan made from a higher education institution to the corporation would be deductible in computing the corporation's income,[87] so long as such interest payments were reasonable in the circumstances (e.g., the rate of interest approximates a fair market value or arm's-length terms for such loan).[88] The corporation will be entitled to deduct other reasonable expenses from its income such as salaries, expenses for third party services, office rental, or other location expenses and utilities.

Taxable income of a corporation also may be reduced by making a gift to a charitable organization (for example, a higher education institution). Under the *Income Tax Act*, a corporation may donate, and receive a deduction from its taxable income for, up to 75 percent of its income for the year.[89] A yearly donation by the corporation undertaking the proposed development project of 75 percent of its taxable income to a higher education institution would reduce the tax paid on the corporation's income to 25 percent of what would otherwise be paid if no such donation were made.

---

[84] *ITA, supra* note 70, s 2; *ITA* Part I, Division E, subdivision b. Corporations incorporated in Canada after 1965 are deemed to be resident in Canada pursuant to the *ITA*, s 250(4).

[85] *ITA, supra* note 70, s 9.

[86] *ITA, supra* note 70, ss 123(1) and 124(1).

[87] *ITA, supra* note 70, s 20(1)(c).

[88] *ITA, supra* note 70, s 67.

[89] *ITA, supra* note 70, s 110.1(1).

When Using a Business Trust

In contrast to a corporation, a trust generally is taxed as a flow-through entity, and the entity itself pays no tax. This means that any income earned by the trust that is either actually paid, or made payable to, its beneficiaries in the year will not be taxable in the hands of the trust pursuant to the provisions of the *Income Tax Act*.[90] For the trust to obtain such a deduction, the amount payable to the beneficiaries from the trust is included in the beneficiaries' respective incomes.[91] As a beneficiary of a trust, a higher education institution would nevertheless be required to include such amounts in its income, yet a higher education institution would not be taxed on its income if the higher education institution is a tax-exempt charitable organization.

Unlike the charitable donation limit of 75 percent of a corporation's income, the trust achieves 100 percent flow through of taxable income to a higher education institution. A trust would have one or two beneficiaries to which to distribute its income. The constating documents of the trust should have provisions that require the trust to distribute all of its taxable income to its beneficiaries before the end of each year. Should, for any reason, the trust not make all of its income payable to its beneficiaries in the year, then the trust would be subject to tax at the highest marginal personal tax rate on any income not paid or made payable to its beneficiaries in the year.[92] This rate is generally higher than the corporate tax rate that would be applicable if the same taxable income were earned in a corporation. As long as the trust makes all amounts payable to beneficiaries before the end of the year, however, it should not incur this higher tax rate.

Limited Liability Considerations

Corporation

In respect of the governance of a proposed development project, a higher education institution should be concerned about any potential legal liability for any acts of the corporation organized to implement the development project. Through the use of a corporation, it is virtually guaranteed that a higher education institution will not be subject to liability for the acts of the corporation. However, if the corporation were found to be acting as an agent of a higher education institution, then the higher education institution would be responsible for any acts of its agent undertaken on the higher education institution's behalf.

---

[90] *ITA, supra* note 70, s 104(6).
[91] *ITA, supra* note 70, ss 104(13) and 105(1).
[92] *ITA, supra* note 70, s 122(1).

Business Trust

There may be some concern that, as a beneficiary of a commercial trust, a higher education institution may not be protected from liability for the acts of the trust in undertaking its development activities. Although the limited liability nature of a trust in relation to its beneficiaries is not as established as the relationship between a corporation and its shareholders, a higher education institution should not be found responsible for any of the actions of the trust that the trust undertakes on its own behalf. Because of the lack of separate statutory legal personality of a trust, the threshold for a trust to be found an agent of a beneficiary is somewhat lower. As such, a higher education institution should not interfere with or control the decisions of the trustees who oversee the trust. Should a higher education institution exercise such control, it is possible that the trust will be held to be an agent or a partner of the higher education institution.

Selected Governance Issues

Agency

It is important that the development entity of a higher education institution be more than just a bare trust. As an example, a higher education institution could structure its development entity as a trust, with the higher education institution as the sole beneficiary of the trust, and a new corporation that is wholly owned by the higher education institution acting as trustee. There must be clear separation, however, between the trustee corporation and the beneficiary higher education institution. When a trust is subject to the direction and control of its beneficiaries, it may be considered to be acting as agent for the beneficiaries, and almost certainly jeopardizes the beneficiaries' limited liability status with respect to the actions of the trustee in carrying on the business of the trust.

The Canada Revenue Agency stated in a 1996 technical interpretation that one must be careful to ensure that a business trust includes a fiduciary, and not an agency, relationship between the trustee and the beneficiaries. Particularly, "if the beneficiaries, as a group, have the ability to direct or control the manner in which the 'trustee' carries on the business, then the arrangement may constitute a partnership with the 'trustee' acting as the agent of the partnership."[93]

When the beneficiaries have effective control over the day-to-day business affairs of a trust, the trust is characterized as a "bare trust." Such a bare trust was found in the Ontario Supreme Court, Court of Appeal decision of *Trident Holdings Limited v Danand Investments Limited*[94] and

---

[93] Canada Revenue Agency, "Unincorporated Business Trust Organization."
[94] (1988), 64 OR (2d) 65, 25 OAC 378.

the beneficiaries of the trust were held personally liable on contracts made by the trustee in the name of the trust. The use of a trustee was a convenient way to hold title to certain property, but because the trustee had virtually no independent powers, discretions, or responsibilities, it was not the trustee that was liable but the beneficiaries who controlled the trust. Where the trust cannot act independently but only on the instructions of the beneficiaries, an agency relationship will predominate over the trust relationship. While the property could still be held in trust, the beneficiaries would not have the limited liability benefit of the trust relationship. On the facts of the *Trident* case, the characterization of the trust as a bare trust was very obvious; nevertheless, any interference by the higher education institution with or fettering of the discretion of the trust in carrying out its development business could lead to a finding of an agency relationship.

The terms of the trust constituting the development entity should provide broad discretionary powers to the trustees as to how to operate the business. If the higher education institution is carrying on business, it is liable for any acts undertaken in the course of that business. The higher education institution will be carrying on business if it actually does so itself or if it does so through its agents. The development entity will be a bare trustee if it cannot act without the approvals and instructions of the higher education institution or the people who control the higher education institution. To ensure independence, there are four operational areas in which this separation should be maintained:

Control of the Development Entity's Business. The board of the development entity must operate independently of the higher education institution, and the higher education institution should not direct or control how the board of the development entity carries on the business of the entity.

Financial Firewall. There must be a financial firewall between the higher education institution and the development entity, so that the higher education institution's assets are not used to benefit the development entity. The development entity should obtain financing from sources other than the higher education institution. Security should be granted by the development entity. To ensure independence, the higher education institution should not guarantee the financing of the development entity. The higher education institution's assets should not be exposed to financing liabilities incurred by the development entity. If it is financially advantageous for the higher education institution to carry out certain functions for the development entity, or vice versa, these transactions should be documented and the business terms should be commercially reasonable. There should be documentary evidence of the development entity and the higher education institution's full compliance.

Development of Lands. Control of the higher education institution lands should be transferred to the development entity. Control can be transferred to the development entity by various means, including without limitation, transferring the legal title, or granting a long-term lease.[95] There should be no direct higher education institution involvement in the various commercial activities and conduct of the development entity. The higher education institution may wish to approve specific land uses and broad architectural guidelines; however, aside from this indirect oversight on land use, there should be no direct involvement by the higher education institution in the various commercial activities and conduct of the development entity.

Management. Management and control of the development entity must not only be independent from, but it must be seen to act independently of, the higher education institution. The development entity should be the public face of the development, and the development entity's senior officers such as the president and chief executive officer should have extensive real estate development experience. This does not preclude the higher education institution, as the shareholder of the development entity or the development entity's trustee, from having the power to elect directors. Some of the key indicia of a separation of management and control include the development entity maintaining separate and distinct office space, employees, logos, websites, and as discussed above, finances.

Governmental Approvals

Formation of the Development Entity. The creation of the development entity and financial transactions completed by the higher education institution and the development entity may be subject to provincial regulation by virtue of the relevant provincial statues governing higher education institutions as well as the relevant financial administration Acts. For example, in Alberta, pursuant to the *Post-secondary Learning Act*[96] and the *Financial Administration Act*,[97] two approvals are required for a higher education institution to either incorporate or acquire a subsidiary corporation.[98]

---

[95] If a long-term lease is used, the rights of the higher education institution as head landlord should be restricted to matters normally vested in a landlord.

[96] SA 2003, c P-19.5 [*PSLA*].

[97] RSA 2000, c F-12 [*FAA*].

[98] First, pursuant to section 77 of the *PSLA, supra* note 97, the higher education institution requires approval from the Minister of Innovation and Advanced Education. The board of governors of a higher education institution must obtain ministerial approval for the incorporation or the acquisition of a subsidiary corpo-

Financial Approvals. The development entity should have powers equal to any private entity to deal with financial matters, as they are set out in the entity's constating documents or trust indenture. However, as a subsidiary of the higher education institution, the development entity may have additional obligations under the relevant provincial financial administration legislation when undertaking financial transactions, including without limitation:

- A provincial minister may prescribe the amount and manner in which money can be raised and the rate of interest that may be paid if the development entity has the power to borrow money by overdraft or line of credit.
- A provincial minister may be the sole agent for the negotiation and determination of the terms and conditions of a loan entered into through the issuance of securities.
- If the development entity wishes to borrow money by issuing securities, then ministerial approval may be required before that can take place.[99]
- The development entity may be required to furnish financial statements to the provincial minister under the financial administration Acts.

Approvals in Respect of the Transfer of Lands by the Higher Education Institution. As discussed above, control of the development lands should be transferred to the development entity. The transfer of the subject lands, whether by long-term lease or by a transfer of the fee simple interest may also be subject to government approval. For example, in British Columbia, a higher education institution may only mortgage, sell, transfer, or lease any of its lands for not more than 99 years with the approval of the minister.[100]

---

ration either directly or indirectly through the acquisition of a majority of shares in the corporation. By implication, therefore, if the board of governors were only to acquire a minority of shares in the corporation, approval by the minister would not be required. Second, the higher education institution must obtain approval from the Lieutenant Governor-in-Council pursuant to section 80 of the *FAA*, ibid.

[99] For example, approval is required pursuant to s 81(1) of the *FAA*, *supra* note 98.

[100] *University Act*, RSBC 1996, c 468, s 50. Approvals are also required in numerous other provinces; see also *PSLA*, *supra* note 97, s 67; *The Colleges Act*, SM 1991-92, c 26, CCSM c C150.1, s 18; *The Regional Colleges Act*, SS 1986-87-88, c R-8.1, s 14(e); *The University of Regina Act*, RSS 1978, c U-5, s 5(b); *The University of Saskatchewan Act, 1995*, SS 1995, c U-6.1, ss 7(1)(c)-(d); *New Brunswick Community Colleges Act*, SNB 2010, c N-4.05, s 37.

PROPERTY DEVELOPMENT ISSUES

Introduction

Canadian higher education institutions are instrumental in shaping community landscapes through the planning and implementation of forward-thinking development projects. Institutions such as the University of Northern British Columbia,[101] York University,[102] Simon Fraser University,[103] and Sheridan College[104] have engaged in development that has revitalized the physical, social, and economic environment of their local municipalities. As an engine for change and growth, the development process is a fundamental part of the long-term strategic plan of higher education institutions and the surrounding communities.

Property development is a process involving the application of regulations, principles, and policies to direct the physical change and effects of such development on the social, economic, and natural environment of an area.[105] All Canadian provinces regulate property development to some degree, and the regulatory process varies from jurisdiction to jurisdiction. Often development involves the resolution of numerous provincial, municipal, and sometimes federal issues, which contributes to the complexity of the development process. The purpose of this section is to provide an overview of the planning and development issues that in-house counsel, development managers, senior officers, and administrative personnel at higher education institutions should consider when engaging in development projects.

---

[101] The University of Northern British Columbia has been instrumental in shaping the redevelopment of Prince George through the establishment of its Greenfield campus. See Hoekstra, "A Behind the Scenes Look."

[102] The development of a private residential community on York University's Keele campus has been a key factor in the introduction of a new subway to York University. See York University Development Corporation, "Success Stories."

[103] The SFU Community Trust was the recipient in 2011 of an Award for Planning Excellence from the Canadian Institute of Planning for its development of UniverCity on Burnaby Mountain. See http://www.univercity.ca.

[104] Sheridan College's new Mississauga campus is anticipated to transform the Mississauga City Centre. See Chin, "Sheridan College Brings Council Up to Speed."

[105] *Planning Act*, RSO 1990, c P-13, s 16(1). See also MacFee Rogers, *Canadian Law of Planning and Zoning*.

Sources of Development Law

The regulation of property development generally occurs at the municipal level[106] subject to various degrees of provincial oversight.[107] Official plans, zoning bylaws, development permits, subdivision bylaws, and servicing bylaws are the primary means by which municipalities control land use and development. There are also private forms of land use control that can affect development projects, such as restrictive covenants and easements contained within various types of contractual agreements.

In Canadian provinces, planning statutes outline statements about the object and purpose of planning.[108] These statutes express provincial policies to enable municipalities to devise and implement a plan for an area through official plans, bylaws, approval requirements, and permits. Tiered municipalities may also introduce additional approval and public consultation requirements. Each development policy, regulation, and municipal tool seeks to address one of numerous issues affecting property development, ranging from service charges and municipal taxation to land use restrictions.

The public and social dimension of Canadian higher education institutions introduces an additional layer of complexity into the development process. Such institutions are governed by private or public statutes, or in some cases royal charters.[109] These statutes may exempt an institution from specific regulations or impose additional obligations as it relates to property development. As well, provinces and municipalities may introduce exceptions to planning regulations for institutions within specific development statutes, municipal codes, or bylaws. The next section provides an overview of several development issues that may affect higher education institutions.

Selected Development Issues

The following is a brief discussion of several development issues that higher education institutions should consider when engaging in develop-

---

[106] *Re Bruce and Toronto*, [1971] 3 OR 62 at 67, 19 DLR (3d) 386 (CA).

[107] See *Building Act*, CQLR c E-1.1.

[108] See, for example, *Local Government Act*, RSBC 1996, c 323; *Municipal Government Act*, RSA 2000, c M-26; *The Municipalities Act*, SS 2005, c M-36.1; *The Municipal Act*, SM 1996, c 58, CCSM c M225; *Planning Act*, RSO 1990, c P-13; *Municipal Code of Quebec*, CQLR c C-27.1; *Municipalities Act, 1999*, SNL 1999, c M-24; *Municipal Government Act*, SNS 1998, c 18; *Municipalities Act*, RSNB 1973, c M-22; *Municipalities Act*, RSPEI 1988, c M-13.

[109] Victoria R, Proclamation, 1841, as reprinted in *Consolidated Royal Charter of Queen's University* (Kingston: Queen's University).

ment. To navigate the legal issues involved, institutions are encouraged to consult experienced legal counsel in these various areas.

Land Expropriation

An institution may be able to expropriate land for the purpose of institutional development if the right to do so is specified in its incorporating or governing statute.[110] Often expropriation powers are to be exercised in accordance with the applicable provincial *Expropriation Act*.[111] In some situations the incorporating or governing statute may deem an institution to be an agent of the Crown such that the expropriation of land for institutional purposes will be subject to the rules affecting the Crown.[112] Prior government authorization may be necessary to effect an expropriation.[113] In Alberta, for example, the *Post-secondary Learning Act* allows the minister to expropriate land for the purpose of a postsecondary institution if the board of an institution has so requested and the Lieutenant Governor in Council considers it appropriate.[114] In the event of expropriation, the board must pay the minister the costs of the expropriation and the compensation payable to the land owner.[115]

---

[110] Examples of statutes enabling universities to expropriate land for university purposes include the following: *University Act*, RSBC 1996, c 468, s 51(1); *Post-secondary Learning Act*, SA 2003, c 19.5; *The University of Saskatchewan Act, 1995*, SS 1995, c 15, s 83(1); *The University of Regina Act*, RSS 1978, c U-5, s 8(1); *Ryerson University Act, 1977*, SO 1977, c 47, s 16(1); *An Act to Incorporate Laurentian University of Sudbury*, SO 1960, c 151, s 4(1)(g); *An Act to Grant Certain Powers to the Royal Institution for the Advancement of Learning*, SQ 1962, c 101; *Concordia University Act*, SQ 1948, c 91, s 2(e); *University Act*, RSPEI 1988, c U-4, s 5(3). This list is provided for illustration purposes only.

Higher education institutional land may also be protected from expropriation. By way of illustration, in British Columbia, land that is vested in a university or college is not liable to be entered, used, or taken by any municipal or other corporation or any person with the right to expropriate land for any purpose. See *College and Institute Act*, RSBC 1996, c 52, s 28 and *University Act*, RSBC 1996, c 468, s 53(1).

[111] See, for example, *Ryerson University Act, 1977*, ibid., s 16(1).

[112] See, for example, *Holland College Act*, RSPEI 1988, c H-6; *College and Institute Act*, RSBC 1996, c 52, s 65(1); *College Act, 1996*, SNL 1996, c C-22.1 s 4(1).

[113] See, for example, *College and Institute Act*, RSBC 1996, c 52, s 65(1). However, approval may be denied if property is being used for religious or educational purposes. See *General and Vocational Colleges Act*, CQLR c C-29, s 7.

[114] *Post-secondary Learning Act*, SA 2003, c P-19.5, s 66(2).

[115] Ibid., s 66(3).

Development Charges

Development charges are fees that are levied against land, often through municipal bylaws, to recover the capital costs associated with the increased service needs arising from new development.[116] Development undertaken by institutions may be exempt from development charges in certain circumstances. Land, building, and structures owned or used by higher education institutions in the City of Toronto, for example, are not required to pay development charges.[117]

To identify a higher education institution's exempted status, several sources of development law should be considered. If the incorporating or governing statute of an institution does not contain an exemption, institutions should look to provincial charging statutes, such as the *Ontario Development Charges Act, 1997*[118] or municipal bylaws and municipal codes to identify whether a specific exemption exists. The imposition of development levies as a condition of the approval of a development plan is discretionary in certain provinces.[119] In these circumstances, institutions may not be subject to fees depending on the development proposed. Furthermore, the incorporating or governing statute of an institution may deem the institution an agent of the Crown such that a development charge may not apply as long as the Crown is exempt from payment.[120]

Municipal Property Taxation

The value added to land in relation to a development project will increase an institution's municipal property tax liability unless an exemption exists. Often the real property of an institution is exempt from provincial, municipal, or other local taxation while the property is used for educational purposes.[121] Institutions may also receive exemptions in the form

---

[116] See, for example, *Ontario Development Charges Act, 1997,* SO 1997, c 27, s 2(1).

[117] *City of Toronto Municipal Code,* 2010, c 415, s 415-6B.

[118] *Supra* note 117.

[119] See *An Act respecting Land Use Planning and Development,* CQLR c A-19.1, s 145.14; *Municipal Government Act,* SNS 1998, c 18, s 274.

[120] See *New Brunswick Community Colleges Act,* SNB 2010, c N-4.05, s 8; *College and Institute Act,* RSBC 1996, c 52, s 50(1).

[121] Examples of incorporating or governing statutes exempting higher education institutions from municipal property taxation include the *University Act,* RSBC 1996, c 468, s 54(1); *Municipal Government Act,* RSA 2000, c M-26, s 362(1)(d); *The Regional Colleges Act,* SS 1986-87-88, c R-8.1, s 25; *The Municipal Act,* SM 1996, c 58, CCSM c M225, s 334; *University of Toronto Act,* SO 1971, c 56, as amended SO 1978, c 88, s 17(1); *Memorial University Act,* RSNL 1990, c M-7, s 43; and *College Act, 1996,* SNL 1996, c C-22.1, s 6. This list is provided for illustration purposes only.

of a grants-in-lieu of taxes from its local municipality.[122] However, certain non-educational uses may trigger the assessment of taxation, such as land used for a retail mall or third party signage. In Ontario, an exemption from property tax has been held to also apply during the construction phase as long as the construction work is subject to the approval of an institution during all phases of construction.[123] A higher education institution may be exempted from taxation by way of one of several legal documents, including an institution's incorporating or governing statute, provincial property tax legislation,[124] and relevant planning statutes. For example, section 18 of the *York University Act, 1965* exempts university land from any form of taxation as long as it is used or occupied for purposes of the university.[125]

Application of Land Use and Zoning Bylaws

Development projects must conform to land use bylaws regulating construction standards, lot locations, and building forms.[126] In addition, projects must respect zoning bylaws that divide a municipality into zones restricting the uses of land within such zones, subject to successful zoning amendments.[127] Only in limited circumstances are institutions exempt from the application of municipal bylaws. Memorial University in Newfoundland, for example, may avoid full compliance with municipal development procedures if it obtains approval of the Lieutenant-Governor in Council to pursue a particular development.[128] To determine whether institutions are waived from compliance, the incorporating or governing statute of an institution must be examined, in addition to provincial planning statutes, official plans, municipal codes, and relevant bylaws.

---

[122] *The Municipal Act*, SM 1996, c 58, CCSM c M225, s 334 as it applies to universities.

[123] *Ryerson University v Municipal Property Assessment Corp.*, 2005 MPLR (4th) 4 (Ont SCJ).

[124] See, for example, *Assessment Act*, RSO 1990, c A.31, s 3(1)(4); *An Act respecting Municipal Taxation*, CQLR c F-2.1, Chapter XVIII "Fiscal Provisions," Division I "Taxable Immovables," § 2; *Assessment Act*, RSNS 1989, c 23, s 5(1); *Real Property Tax Act*, RSPEI 1988, c R-5, s 3(1)(f).

[125] SO 1965, c 143.

[126] Land use bylaws are defined in *Innisfil (Township) v Shakell* (1982), 19 MPLR 117, 137 DLR (3d) 117 (Ont CA).

[127] Ibid. at 124 for definition of zoning bylaws.

[128] *Memorial University Act*, RSNL 1990, c M-7, s 4(2).

Parkland Dedication Requirements

Municipalities may establish regulations to require all development projects to dedicate a portion of land under development for use as a public park, or oblige the developer to pay the municipality an amount in lieu of such dedication. An exemption to this requirement can be determined with reference to municipal sources of development law, such as official plans, municipal codes, and relevant bylaws.[129]

Development Application Fees

Depending on the municipality, an institution may not be required to pay development application fees. This entitlement can be determined with reference to municipal sources of development law, such as official plans, municipal codes, and relevant bylaws among other sources. Where application fees are discretionary for certain entities, institutions may not be subject to fees depending on the proposed development project. Furthermore, the incorporating or governing statute of an institution may deem the institution to be an agent of the Crown such that development fees may not apply to the extent that fees are waived for the Crown.[130]

Additional Development Considerations

Duty to Consult

When engaging in development, higher education institutions may influence the interests of First Nations groups. While federal and provincial governments are currently the only parties legally bound to engage in consultation and accommodations for First Nations groups, pronouncements by the Supreme Court of Canada permit the Crown[131] to delegate certain "procedural" elements of consultation to industry proponents such as higher education institutions. This suggests that institutions should carefully approach First Nations issues to avoid liability for negligence, breach of contract, or dishonest dealings.[132]

---

[129] In the City of Toronto, lands used for college and university purposes are exempt from the requirement to dedicate 5 percent of developable land for park uses. See City of Toronto By-law No. 1020 (2010), as amending *City of Toronto Municipal Code*, c 415, s 415-30(a).

[130] See *New Brunswick Community Colleges Act*, SNB 2010, c N-4.05, s 8; *College and Institute Act*, RSBC 1996, c 52, s 50(1).

[131] Rowinski, *Duty to Consult*.

[132] Ibid.

Environmental Assessments

Higher education institutions may be required to conduct environmental assessments in relation to development projects that can impact the environment of the property and surrounding area.[133] For example, in Ontario environmental assessments include consultations with government agencies and the public, the consideration and evaluation of alternative project forms, and the management of potential environmental effects.[134] The length and type of assessment will vary according to the type of development proposed.

Administrative Tribunals for Planning and Development Matters

In several jurisdictions, provincial statutes have established administrative tribunals to hear appeals on planning and development matters.[135] To launch an appeal, institutions should be aware of the developed policies of practice of a particular tribunal.[136] The judiciary may review tribunal decisions on questions of law or jurisdiction. Depending on the jurisdiction, the minister, municipal councils, and specialized committees may also hear appeals. In Quebec and British Columbia,[137] specific provincial tribunals have not been established to hear and resolve appeals related to development approvals.

---

[133] See, for example, *Environmental Assessment Act*, RSO 1990, c E.18; *The Environmental Assessment Act*, SS 1979-80, c E-10.1; *Environmental Assessment Act*, SBC 2002, c 43; *Canadian Environmental Assessment Act*, 2012, c 19, s 52.

[134] Ministry of the Environment, "Environmental Assessments."

[135] MacFee Rogers, *The Law of Canadian Municipal Corporations*, s 140.4(b). Specific provincial tribunals are available in Prince Edward Island, Nova Scotia, New Brunswick, Ontario, Manitoba, Saskatchewan, and Alberta. In Newfoundland and Labrador, local appeal boards are subject to provincial legislative authority.

[136] Tribunal rules include the Rules of Practice Procedures of the Ontario Municipal Board and the local rules established by the Lieutenant Governor in Council for municipal Development Appeal Boards in Saskatchewan. See *Ontario Municipal Board Act*, RSO 1990, c O.28, s 91; *Planning and Development Act, 2007*, SS 2007, c P-13.2, ss 216(6) and (7).

[137] In British Columbia there is limited appeal to the Environmental Appeal Board for environmental matters, as well as to the judiciary in accordance with administrative appeal processes created in standard development application guides. See *Environmental Management Act*, SBC 2003, c 53, s 93.

Heritage Listing and Heritage Designation

Provincial governments may enact legislation[138] or administer programs[139] to limit an institution's ability to demolish and develop privately owned properties in order to protect historically significant buildings, structures, and resources. Under the *Ontario Heritage Act*[140] for example, when property is "listed" as a heritage site, the owner must give the municipality 60 days' notice of its intention to demolish or remove a building or structure on the property. If property is "designated," the owner is required to apply to the municipality for permission to alter or demolish the property with differing rights of appeal depending on the type of application.[141]

Examples of Other Provincial Statutes and Provincial Policy Documents

There may be other provincial statutes and policy documents that will affect higher education institutional development. In Ontario and Manitoba, for example, the relevant *Endangered Species Act*[142] prohibits any person from damaging or destroying the habitat of an endangered, threatened, or extirpated species. This suggests that institutions cannot undertake development that may threaten the habitat of certain species.

Similarly, the Alberta *Land Stewardship Act* will enable the provincial government to develop regional plans that will influence the types of land uses permitted under municipal regulatory instruments.[143] Regional plans may, for example, limit certain forms of development, facilitate government expropriation of institutional land, and encourage the creation of conservation areas by directive.[144] Higher education institutions may seek compensation or appeal municipal regulations on questions of jurisdiction.[145]

---

[138] See, for example, *Historical Resources Act*, RSA 2000, c H-9, s 20.

[139] See, for example, Répertoire du patrimoine culturel du Québec, *About Répertoire du patrimoine culturel du Québec*.

[140] RSO 1990, c O.18, s 27(3).

[141] Ibid.

[142] See *Endangered Species Act, 2007*, SO 2007, c 6, s 10(1); *The Endangered Species Act*, SM 1989-90, c 39, CCSM c E111, s 10(1).

[143] *Alberta Land Stewardship Act*, SA 2009, c A-26.8, s 20(1). One regional plan – Lower Athabasca Region – has been approved; the following website provides the status of the various regional plans: https://landuse.alberta.ca/RegionalPlans/Pages/default.aspx.

[144] Ibid. at ss 9 and 49.

[145] *Supra* note 145 at Part 2, Division 2.

Intergovernmental Cooperation

Federal and provincial agencies may encourage higher education institutional development projects in a variety of ways. A key example is the increased use of public private partnerships (PPP) or alternative finance and procurement (AFP) for the delivery of infrastructure projects for broader public sector partners such as higher education institutions. In these arrangements, design, construction, financing and maintenance risks, as well as other risks are transferred to, managed by, and shared with private entities. Institutions such as York University[146] and McGill University[147] have used PPP to develop innovative campus buildings.

PROCUREMENT ISSUES

Introduction

Canadian higher education institutions are increasingly subject to a more complex and diverse set of rules regarding their purchases of goods, property, and services. This reality is part of a general trend in Canada and worldwide toward expanding open public procurement at all levels of government. This represents an enormous challenge for Canadian higher education institutions as they seek to establish and enhance their open procurement systems. It also represents a tremendous opportunity for suppliers worldwide who are anxious to participate in an increasingly open and competitive public procurement environment.

Sources of Procurement Law

Public procurement law for Canadian higher education institutions consists of legislation governed by common-law principles and the obligations contained in trade agreements.

---

[146] The Ontario Realty Corporation, Archives of Ontario, York University, and private entities were involved in the development of the Archives Building of Ontario using a PPP. See York University Development Corporation, "Success Stories."

[147] The McGill University Health Centre is anticipated to be the largest Greenfield hospital project in Canada. See McGill University Health Centre, "A Winning Partnership."

Common Law

Procurements, including those by Canadian higher education institutions, are founded on the principles set forth in the Supreme Court of Canada decision in *The Queen (Ontario) v Ron Engineering*.[148]

The Court in *Ron Engineering* introduced the concepts of "Contract A" and "Contract B." When a call for proposals is issued, this constitutes an offer, and when a bid is submitted, this constitutes an acceptance. Contract A is thereby created, such that the potential supplier is accepting the terms of the bid solicitation document, and its bid generally becomes irrevocable. Contract B is formed between the purchaser and the successful supplier once the winning contractor is selected.

In *MJB Enterprises Ltd. v Defence Construction (1951) Limited*,[149] the Supreme Court held that it is an implied term of Contract A that the bid is compliant with the requirements of the tender document. It also held that a contract does not need to be awarded to the lowest compliant bidder, and that bids cannot be selected based on undisclosed criteria. The Court also noted that the dual contract approach is not applicable to all types of bid solicitation.[150]

In *Martel Building Ltd. v Canada*,[151] the Supreme Court of Canada held that it is an implied term of Contract A that all bids must be treated fairly and equally by the purchaser. Further, while purchasers are entitled to select their preferred evaluation criteria, they must not deviate from those criteria when selecting bids.

The purchaser owes no duty to the unsuccessful bidders.[152] In other words, Contract A ends after the purchaser fairly evaluates the bids and selects the successful bidder. No duty is owed by the purchaser to unsuccessful bidders once it enters into Contract B with the successful bidder.

In regard to the duties owed to subcontractors, the Supreme Court of Canada held in *Design Services Ltd. v Canada*[153] that purchasers do not owe a duty of care to subcontractors in the tendering process, and that the burden is on the bidder and not the subcontractor to seek redress against the purchaser in the event of a dispute in the tendering process.

---

[148] [1981] 1 SCR 111.

[149] [1999] 1 SCR 619.

[150] For example, standing offers are not contracts. A contract is only formed if and when the procuring entity issues a call-up to the supplier against its standing offer.

[151] [2000] 2 SCR 860.

[152] *Double N Earthmovers Ltd. v Edmonton*, [2007] 1 SCR 116.

[153] [2008] 1 SCR 737.

Trade Treaties

Solicitation processes by higher education institutions in the common-law provinces are governed by the case law described above subject to relevant provincial and territorial legislation. For example, in most provinces, procurement policies include an electronic tendering system, no preference for local vendors, and a conflict of interest policy.[154]

Currently, Canada's internal trade treaties apply to procurements by provincial governments and higher education institutions. Canada's internal trade treaties include the Agreement on Internal Trade (AIT)[155] and the New West Partnership Trade Agreement (NWPTA).[156]

Regarding international trade treaties, the current procurement obligations and the bid dispute mechanisms in Chapter Ten of the North American Free Trade Agreement (NAFTA),[157] the WTO Agreement on Government Procurement,[158] and the permanent concessions of the Agreement between the Government of Canada and the Government

---

[154] For example in Ontario, the *Ministry of Government Services Act*, RSO 1990, c-M25 requires the provincial government to follow policies and directives established by the Management Board of Cabinet when undertaking certain procurements relating to construction, renovation, or repair of a public work.

[155] http://www.ait-aci.ca/index_en.htm. The AIT came into effect on July 1, 1995, and governs the trade of goods and services within Canada. Annex 502.4 of the Consolidation of the Agreement on Internal Trade 2012 sets out the procurement disciplines for MASH entities including higher education institutions.

[156] http://www.newwestpartnershiptrade.ca. The Canadian provinces of British Columbia, Alberta, and Saskatchewan are parties to the New West Partnership Trade Agreement. NWPTA generally requires that the three provinces and their subprovincial entities conduct their procurement processes in a non-discriminatory manner in regard to suppliers from the other two provinces for prescribed procurements above stated monetary thresholds. The procurement rules of the NWPTA have applied since July 1, 2010, to all British Columbia and Alberta government entities, including departments, ministries, agencies, boards, councils, committees, and commissions, as well as municipalities, school divisions, health regions, and publicly funded higher education institutions. The procurement rules of the NWPTA have applied to all Saskatchewan government ministries and most agencies and boards since July 1, 2010. Saskatchewan Crown corporations, the remaining agencies and boards, as well as municipalities, school divisions, health regions, and publicly funded higher education institutions have been covered by the procurement rules since July 1, 2012. The Trade, Investment and Labour Mobility Agreement (TILMA) was entered into by British Columbia and Alberta in 2006. TILMA remains in effect but due to changes being requested by Saskatchewan, Saskatchewan did not become a party to TILMA, and the three provinces entered into the NWPTA.

[157] http://www.international.gc.ca/trade-agreements-accords-commerciaux/agr-acc/nafta-alena/index.aspx?lang=eng.

[158] http://www.wto.org/english/tratop_e/gproc_e/gp_gpa_e.htm.

of the United States of America on Government Procurement[159] do not apply to the provinces,[160] although this is likely to change in the not too distant future as Canada continues to agree with its trading partners to "open up" procurement processes at the subcentral level. In particular, there is a strong likelihood that procurements by higher education institutions will be subject to the procurement obligations of the Canada-EU Comprehensive Trade Agreement (CETA), regarding which an agreement in principle was reached between Canada and the European Union in October 2013.[161] Higher education institutions will be forced to re-think and revise many of their current procurement processes to bring themselves into compliance with the procurement disciplines in these international agreements. In particular, current practices of sole sourcing and limited tendering will have to be revised to reflect the more onerous conditions and restrictions surrounding sole source awards in the international agreements.

Remedies

With the exception of procurements subject to the NWPTA and the AIT, the available remedies for disappointed bidders relating to procurements by provincial entities and higher education institutions are those available at common law, including breach of contract. The most common remedy sought against higher education institutions is an order for damages for lost profits that the bidder would have earned if it had won the contract. Procurements by higher education institutions in some provinces may be subject to judicial review by the courts.

The NWPTA has its own dispute resolution process including provision for binding monetary awards and an independent bid review authority. The AIT also has an enforcement mechanism, albeit likely less effective than that found in the NWPTA and the other international procurement agreements.[162]

---

[159] http://www.international.gc.ca/trade-agreements-accords-commerciaux/topics-domaines/gp-mp/agreement-accord.aspx?lang=eng.

[160] The permanent concessions of the Canada-US Agreement on Government Procurement do apply to higher education institutions in the provinces of Ontario and Quebec.

[161] http://www.international.gc.ca/trade-agreements-accords-commerciaux/agr-acc/eu-ue/can-eu.aspx?view=d.

[162] Section M(1) of Annex 502.4 of the Consolidation of the Agreement on Internal Trade 2012 requires the MASH entities, which include universities, to follow and document a non-judicial compliant process. If the dispute is not resolved in the non-judicial process, the supplier can file a complaint with its province, which may trigger the establishment of a review panel to hear the complaint.

CONSTRUCTION PROJECTS

Introduction

Construction activity is constantly underway at most higher education institutions, with new buildings associated with campus growth. The often more complicated remedial construction related to aging infrastructure is also ongoing. Higher education institutions have unique requirements that need to be considered in addition to the typical concerns in any commercial construction project. Failing to properly consider the special requirements of the institution at the earliest stages of planning a new construction project or the remediation of an existing facility can result in financial loss or unnecessary claims against the institution or its personnel. The purpose of this section is to identify a number of critical issues for the institution to incorporate in its construction project planning and to adequately address those issues in appropriate construction documents as a "best practice" process for the growth of the institution.

The order of the steps outlined below is suggested as the most appropriate sequence in which to address these particular issues to best protect the interests of the institution.

Engaging Construction Consultants

Soon after the executive decision has been made to proceed with a project, outside expertise is usually required in the form of architectural or engineering consulting services to develop design concepts, address the functional goals of the project, and ultimately develop plans and specifications required for contractors to evaluate for pricing and bid purposes. Typically, architects and engineers are engaged by higher education institutions pursuant to the terms of the industry standard form contracts, which were primarily created by their professional associations.[163] Consequently, the institutional "client" served by such contracts needs to carefully review the standard terms. The most significant provisions to examine include the following:

The services provider is often named as a partnership or other entity. If the services of a particular architect, engineer, or other design professional are desired or required by the institution, the requirement to have the personal services of the specifically named professional should be included in the contract.

The scope of the services to be provided by the design or engineering professional needs to be as detailed as possible in order to avoid what

---

[163] The Canadian industry standard form most often used by architects is the RAIC Document #6. The commonly used engineering services standard form agreement is the ACEC-Document 31.

could become costly "additional services" if misunderstandings occur during the course of construction. In addition to developing plans and specifications, consideration should be given to whether the following services should be included for the quoted fee, rather than dealt with later as an "extra":

- assisting the institution in obtaining particular approvals for the project or participating in any presentations to other bodies;
- participating in the creation of contract documents;
- preparing and administering the tendering process;
- acting as the "consultant" and performing the duties of the consultant pursuant to contracts with contractors engaged on the project. These duties could include acting as the "payment certifier" in respect of payment claims made by contractors under construction contracts and performing numerous other duties potentially prescribed by the construction contract terms;[164]
- performing redesign services within its fee quote if the lowest acceptable bid is outside of the postsecondary institution's budget; and
- performing mediation, arbitration, or other dispute resolution services if required and at an agreed cost.

The terms of the professional services fee should be considered. For example, is the professional services fee fixed for the duration of the project or is it subject to adjustment on some calendar basis? Is it payable monthly on a basis that properly recognizes the percentage of services remaining to be delivered?

It has become common in a number of standard form consulting services contracts for the service providers to attempt to limit their liability to the amount of their available insurance coverage. Through no fault of the institution, in the event of a service provider's error or negligence, a limitation of liability provision can result in little or no financial recourse against the service provider and therefore should be considered carefully.[165]

---

[164] Consultants under the CCDC-2-2008 standard for construction contract take on many administrative functions during construction, and they are the first arbiters of disputes between the Owner and the Contractor.

[165] This concern highlights the need for institutions to consider the appropriate insurance coverage for the entire project at the earliest possible stage. Prior to project contracts being tendered, institutions should consider whether professional service providers or contractors should provide better specific coverage and whether a project "wrap up" policy obtained and controlled by the institution should be obtained.

Developing Appropriate Contract Documents

The debate that is often undertaken by administrators of higher education institutions and private developers is whether standard form construction documents should be created for use on all future projects or whether the industry standard form documents will be adequate. The usual industry approach is to modify the standard form construction documents with "supplementary conditions" as discussed below. A hybrid approach is often a good compromise, recognizing that small projects under a certain financial threshold may be most efficiently dealt with using a small projects contract form developed by the institution with legal assistance.

Larger projects with greater capital requirements may benefit from the use of industry standard forms, suitably modified, for a number of reasons. The majority of commercial, industrial, and institutional projects in Canada are constructed using versions of the standard form construction contract documents created by the Canadian Construction Documents Committee (CCDC).[166] As the CCDC documents are widely known to a great number of potential contractors who might bid on any given project, using such documents should encourage the widest participation of contractors and create a desirably competitive bidding process.

By way of example, one of the most often used CCDC contract forms, the CCDC-2-2008 stipulated price contract form (CCDC-2), outlines a number of duties for the architect or engineer who will perform the role of the consultant pursuant to the CCDC-2 requirements. Most architects and engineers engaged to work on higher education construction projects in Canada are familiar with the duties of the consultant as outlined in CCDC-2, and this familiarity usually helps to ensure that significant service scope requirements for the consultant are addressed and included.

In light of the two points noted above in favour of using the nationally recognized standard documents, it follows that a decision to instead use wholly custom documents developed by a particular institution may reduce the number of bidders (partly due to unfamiliarity and partly due to a reluctance to incur additional review time and costs, including legal

---

[166] The CCDC is a national joint committee responsible for the development, production, and review of standard Canadian construction contracts, forms, and guides. It is made up of volunteers from public and private sector owners, the Canadian Bar Association, the Association of Canadian Engineering Companies, the Canadian Construction Association, Construction Specifications Canada, and the Royal Architectural Institute of Canada. It is the stated intention of the CCDC to create contract documents using a consensus-building process aimed at balancing the interests of all parties on the construction project. However, most owners require modifications pursuant to supplementary general conditions in order to properly use the standard forms for particular projects.

review costs). In addition, project consultants may be less familiar with what is expected of them under the customized documents.

Notwithstanding the intention of the CCDC to create balanced standard forms, many higher education institutions and their consultants will wish to create supplementary general conditions to amend and modify the otherwise "standard form" contract to be used for the project. This is a standard approach in the construction industry. These supplementary general conditions (SGCs) should be created and settled by the institution, its consultant, and its legal advisors before any tendering or bid process is commenced. The creation of appropriate SGCs allows higher education institutions to effectively use a standard form document but modify it to become a suitably amended "standard" document for the institution. It is an opportunity to deal with unique requirements of the institution or the project and also to address certain applicable compliance issues such as specific funding requirements.

Some of the significant issues typically addressed in the SGCs include the following:

- compliance by the contractor with site-specific requirements such as university security requirements, site safety, and coordination with the numerous other activities typically going on at other facilities near the site;
- the importance of achieving the construction schedule; the efforts to be required of the contractor to stay on schedule and responsibility for the consequences if not on schedule.
- specific identification of the documentation and the process that the contractor is required to follow to ensure timely payment during construction. Depending on the source of the funding, some institutions will have to satisfy government-imposed requirements in order to obtain funding during construction. These requirements must be matched or referenced in the SGCs.
- Higher education institutions often have virtually no budget flexibility, and the SGCs may need to highlight that the contract price is ultimately the budget cap – the absolute limit of the institution's liability to the contractor.
- Applicable local laws or policy requirements may need to be referenced. These could include builders' lien legislation procedures and workers' compensation requirements (such as designating the contractor as the "prime contractor").
- Depending on the nature of the project, higher education institutions may have special insurance requirements that require compliance by the contractor or a price adjustment if the institution itself decides to obtain coverage through a "wrap up" policy.
- Post-construction warranties required by the institution may well go beyond the limited standards of the CCDC document. For example,

specialized facilities like athletic or gymnasium space or theatre facilities will incorporate expensive and specialized equipment or materials that will need to be addressed in the SGCs.

• If there will be an optional or a mandatory mediation or arbitration process to resolve disputes that the consultant is unable to resolve in the first instance, details should be included in the SGCs.

Engaging Contractors – the Tendering Process

The construction tendering process in Canada has been treated as a special area of contract law in which fairness and protection for the integrity of the process have been guiding principles. Courts have both read implied terms into bid contracts that oblige owners to act fairly and interpreted wide discretionary clauses narrowly. Whether a process is described as a request for proposals, an invitation to bid, or a tender request, courts in Canada will frequently impose the law as it has been developed in connection with the tender process in order to ensure that all participants are treated fairly.

The case law developed in this area is extensive and cannot be covered in detail in this outline. However, when developing rules in connection with a tendering process, care should be taken in preparing instructions to participants, using clear and relevant selection criteria, and avoiding vague or inapplicable instructions. Most importantly, institutions selecting a successful contractor following a review of bid submissions must clearly follow and strictly abide by the rules that they have created within their bid instructions in order to avoid claims by unsuccessful participants.

Owners attempting to maximize their control over the selection of contractors submitting bids have typically attempted to fine-tune instructions aimed at limiting their own liability. In the case of *Tercon Contractors Ltd. v British Columbia (Ministry of Transportation and Highways)*,[167] the British Columbia Ministry of Transportation and Highways (MOTH) issued a tender call for the construction of a gravel highway. Although the bid instructions prohibited joint venture bids, MOTH accepted a proposal submitted by a joint venture consisting of two parties, one of which might have alone been a qualified bidder. MOTH directed the "acceptance" to the single member of the two-party joint venture. Tercon Contractors Ltd. was one of the unsuccessful bidders. It sued MOTH on the basis that the contract could not be awarded to a non-compliant participant. While MOTH had broken its own procurement rules, it relied on the exclusion

---

[167] 2010 SCC 4 [*Tercon Contractors*].

clause included in the MOTH procurement instructions to reject Tercon's claim for compensation:

> Except as expressly and specifically permitted in these Instructions to Proponents, no Proponent shall have any claim for any compensation of any kind whatsoever, as a result of participating in this RFP, and by submitting a proposal each Proponent shall be deemed to have agreed that it has no claim.[168]

The British Columbia Supreme Court found for Tercon. It determined that the contract had been awarded to a non-compliant bidder and exercised its discretion to restrict the enforceability of the clause. MOTH appealed the trial decision. The Court of Appeal did not consider it necessary to determine whether the successful bid was non-compliant with the procurement instructions. Instead, it focused on the exclusion clause and found "the words of the exclusion clause so clear and unambiguous that it is inescapable that the parties intended it to cover all defaults, including fundamental breaches."

Tercon appealed to the Supreme Court of Canada. The Court, by a 5–4 majority, allowed Tercon's appeal and restored the original decision in favour of Tercon. The majority concluded that the words in the exclusion clause, "participating in this RFP," must mean "participating in a contest among those eligible to participate."[169] Consequently, the majority decided that MOTH had accepted a bid from a party who should not have been eligible to participate, and a process involving ineligible bidders could not be covered by the clause. The minority agreed with the BC Court of Appeal and considered the exclusion clause to be clear, unambiguous, and applicable.

The SCC unanimously agreed that a clearly drafted Tercon clause could be enforced and that a court would need to consider three factors when a party is attempting to avoid the effect of such a clause: (a) whether the clause applies to the circumstances, as a matter of interpretation; (b) if the clause applies, whether it was unconscionable at the time it was made and therefore invalid, such as in the case of an inequality of bargaining power between the parties; and (c) whether the clause offends "an overriding public policy … that outweighs the very strong public interest in the enforcement of contracts"[170] (this third part of the analysis replaces the doctrine of fundamental breach as a policy basis for avoiding a contract provision).

The message from the Supreme Court of Canada is that clearly drafted, unambiguous exclusion clauses will be permitted in the absence of

---

[168] Variations on this clause have since become known as "Tercon clauses."
[169] *Tercon Contractors*, at para 74.
[170] *Tercon Contractors*, at paras 121–23.

egregious conduct by the party conducting the bidding process. As a result, future exclusion clauses will require more detail and clarity in order to avoid judicial interference. The *Tercon* decision also provides useful general guidance on the principles to be followed in the development of any bidding process.

In developing instructions to bidders, postsecondary institutions should be guided by the following factors:

- A distinction should be made between essential requirements to be imposed on a bidder and those that are desirable but not mandatory. Consider including only those requirements that the institution would not waive and that would be sufficient to disqualify a bidder for noncompliance. For example, requiring a bidder to attend a scheduled site visit should be identified as either mandatory or as "helpful but not strictly required."
- The contract documents – including the SGCs, carefully developed with the assistance of the consultant and legal counsel – should be identified as the form of the contract to be entered into by the successful bidder, subject only to such amendments as may be accepted by the institution in its sole discretion. The point of the timely development of the contract documents is to reduce or eliminate time-consuming and costly future document negotiations with the potentially successful bidder.
- An appropriately drafted Tercon clause should be considered to attempt to protect the institution from claims arising from unsuccessful bidders.

Managing the Project, Defaults, and Disputes

Most higher education institutions will have identified a project manager or senior administrator who will act as the main contact person of the project for consultants and contractors to deal with on project issues and communications. This contact person will play a pivotal role in protecting the interests of the institution during the normal progress of construction and in the event of a dispute. This representative should carry out or delegate a number of important functions, including the following:

- Prior to the commencement of construction, create a schedule for routine meetings that will require attendance by the consultants and representatives of the contractor to assess progress as against the contract schedule; assess any problems or issues encountered since the previous meeting; and forecast and discuss the planned construction activities in the period prior to the next meeting. Most importantly, minutes of these meetings should be recorded in writing and circulated to all key participants.

- It should be "policy" that no change to the work defined in the construction contract or any significant decision regarding the schedule or requirements of the contract should be accepted, modified, or dealt with unless clearly documented in a written change order.
- Any activity of the contractor or other activity that is not in compliance with the progress of the project as outlined in the construction contract should be acted on immediately in writing. The views of the consultant should be obtained, and if a "clarification" instruction from the consultant or a default notice to the contractor is appropriate, it should not be delayed.
- Default by a contractor may require timely notices under insurance policies and/or performance bonds or other security documents, and these issues should be acted on immediately.

This review of significant issues to be considered in respect of construction projects undertaken by higher education institutions is a brief outline. The best use of such a summary may be as a planning tool or checklist to be referenced prior to the commencement of a project. The time taken to address and document the important issues in advance will prevent unnecessary expenses and perhaps minimize the risk of certain claims later.

CONCLUSION

Chapter 12

KEY AND EMERGING ISSUES IN CANADIAN HIGHER EDUCATION LAW

MICHELLE NILSON

INTRODUCTION

While this volume provides a foundation for administrators, practitioners, and academics interested in higher education law in Canada, higher education administrators and counsel are well advised to approach their practice with the notion that "an ounce of prevention is worth a pound of cure." This text is intended to provide tools for administrators and students to have a foundational basic understanding of the issues across higher education so that they can be preventative in their approach to decision-making and policy formation. Throughout the discussions in both higher education trade journals (see *Change Magazine*) and law texts (Kaplin and Lee, for example), the primacy of prevention as the best investment of resources cannot be overemphasized. The emphasis on prevention and forethought is evident in each of the 11 previous chapters.

The purpose of this chapter is to highlight key and emerging issues raised in this volume. This chapter will also draw together ideas from across the chapters, making connections between the issues and tensions that might otherwise appear to be isolated. As the text is organized into four main sections, so is this chapter. The first section provides an overview of postsecondary education in Canada and describes the legislative framework and corresponding roles of the federal and provincial governments. The second section provides an overview of institutional governance, offering insight on governance and administration of

Handbook of Canadian Higher Education Law, edited by Theresa Shanahan, Michelle Nilson, and Li-Jeen Broshko.
Montreal and Kingston: McGill-Queen's University Press, Queen's Policy Studies Series.

institutions and their particular issues of concern, including human rights issues and jurisdictional questions in the relationships with education associations. The third section continues along the lines of institutional concerns by highlighting the legislation concerning students and faculty. Finally, the fourth section draws connections between the university and the external communities by exploring cases and legislation that pertain to intellectual property, academic research, and collaborations, and by providing frameworks for considering land development issues. Each section concludes with a summary of emerging issues related to the topics discussed. These emerging issues represent the professional observations of this volume's authors as well as issues that are currently under consideration in the courts.

LEGISLATIVE FRAMEWORK AND THE ROLE OF FEDERAL AND PROVINCIAL GOVERNMENTS

The first three chapters lay the foundation for understanding the legislative frameworks that inform postsecondary education governance, as established both federally and provincially. As noted in chapter 1, Canada is a constitutional monarchy with a parliamentary government based in the British system where higher education regulation and governance take place at the provincial level. As noted, the absence of a federal coordinating body poses challenges to efforts that might negotiate, regulate, or consolidate services across higher education in Canada.

Despite the separation of powers laid out in the legislative frameworks described in chapter 1, a system of mechanisms for funding from the federal government to provincially housed programs, referred to as "fiscal federalism" in chapter 2, provides a framework for the national research and human resource development infrastructure. In this chapter, Shanahan notes that over the past two decades, the federal government's approach to funding postsecondary education has taken shape around four pillars. First, transfer payments from federal to provincial governments changed from targeted (which included postsecondary education) to general funding. Shanahan argues that this change in transfer payments allowed provinces to distribute the money to other sectors, which resulted in increased fiscal pressure on postsecondary institutions. Second, direct funding to research through the Tri-Councils (Social Science and Humanities Research Council, Natural Science and Engineering Research Council, and Canadian Institutes of Health Research) provides support to research agendas through grants and to researchers through Canadian Research Chair positions. She argues that this funding has not only shaped the direction of research in Canadian postsecondary institutions but has also created disparities between the institutions themselves. Third, the federal government provides financial assistance directly to students through a series of need- and merit-based scholarship and loan programs. Finally, the federal government has largely shifted its funding for the delivery of workforce and skills training to the provinces and private sector over publicly funded institutions.

The primary source of legislation and regulation of higher education is located at the provincial level, as outlined in chapter 3. This chapter highlights the various types of postsecondary institutions that exist across Canada, and provides a rich discussion about governance arrangements and regulation.

Emerging Issues

The chapters identify three main issues that affect postsecondary education in Canada: lack of harmonization of provincial laws, quality assurance, and institutional accountability.

As there is no federal system of higher education in Canada to serve as an intermediary between the provinces and external pressures (e.g., interinstitutional, interprovincial, or international credential recognition, transfer, and articulation agreements), the burden of policy and legislative harmonization and interpretation resides with the provinces and institutions. Further, there is little incentive and no funding to provide a system of harmonization between the provinces, as this function resides outside of the jurisdiction of the federal government and is not a priority for any individual or group of provinces. This lack of a coordinating body at the federal level has had some significant consequences for understanding and describing the Canadian postsecondary education sector. For example, each province is an independent "system" with its respective version of a Freedom of Information and Protection of Privacy Act, and none of these Acts are yet harmonized across the provinces. Consequently, datasets regarding aspects of workforce development, university completion, tuition discounting, and several related areas have not been developed to inform national decisions or policy-making. At best, the federal government pieces together the publicly available provincial or census data.

Quality assurance and institutional accountability are two emerging issues identified by Shanahan in chapter 3. These two issues are interlinked in that the formal resolutions or policy tools that aim to ensure quality and institutional accountability are often the same – accreditation and transfer/articulation agreements. While accreditation of professional programs largely remains within the oversight of the professional associations, where accreditation of academic programs exists, it remains largely with the individual institutions. Two pressures are bringing accreditation to the forefront. As noted in chapter 3, several provinces have articulated their own provincial accreditation system for institutions in an effort to stem the proliferation of proprietary institutions. While British Columbia and Alberta lead the way in articulation and transfer agreements at the interprovincial level, these agreements are largely developed and implemented on an individual institutional level. These agreements, where in place, serve to recognize transferable credits and facilitate the ease of mobility of students between institutions and provinces and should be one of the primary tools of provinces seeking to increase capacity to meet market demands for a workforce with employable skills.

INSTITUTIONAL GOVERNANCE, HUMAN RIGHTS, AND EDUCATION ASSOCIATIONS

Canadian universities operate within a complex system of federal and provincial laws, in conjunction with a set of academic customs and institutional policies. The primary federal legislation that influences the governance of these institutions is *The Constitution Act, 1867* and the *Canadian Charter of Rights and Freedoms. The Constitution Act, 1867* grants provinces the power to make laws pertaining to education, which includes postsecondary education. While the *Charter* outlines protected individual rights and freedoms, its application to university environments depends largely on the context in which the conflict of rights occurs. Historically, because universities were not quite operationally public institutions, nor were they exactly private, they were largely exempt from *Charter* responsibilities and could autonomously make decisions. That view was reinforced in 1990, when the courts found that universities had their own governing structures and therefore were not under the legal obligation to uphold *Charter* rights as agents of the government. However, several subsequent cases[1] propose a more nuanced interpretation of the role of the *Charter* in universities. The application of *Charter* protections differs across each of the provinces, depending on the role of universities prescribed in the legislation. That said, it is generally understood that when universities are acting in a manner that is "governmental," the *Charter* likely applies.

Institutional governance within Canadian universities is largely autonomous from provincial control and follows structural academic traditions from both the United States and the United Kingdom. With only a few notable exceptions, the majority of Canadian universities have a bicameral system of governance. This system is characterized by a board of governors, which at least symbolically represents the public interests, and a senate, which represents the faculty and student interests. The next layer of university governance is the executive level, which includes the chancellor, vice-chancellor, president, and other senior officers of the institution. The interpretation and implementation of senate and board decisions largely take place at the level of faculties (also called "Schools" or "Colleges" at some universities).

---

[1] *Eldridge v British Columbia (Attorney General)* and *Pridgen v University of Calgary.*

In chapter 5, Poskitt and Wojda argue that university executive officers have an obligation to uphold human rights statutes prescribed by provinces and federal *Charter* rights. They note that "postsecondary institutions must look to human rights tribunal decisions, arbitration awards, and decisions of the courts to understand their human rights obligations."[2]

Human rights violations typically manifest as discrimination based on a protected characteristic or defined disability that requires duty to accommodate. In most provinces, discrimination is not defined in legislation and has gained its meaning through decisions coming from the courts or tribunals. Chapter 5 provides the legal framework for determining whether or not discrimination has occurred, the prohibited grounds of discrimination, possible justifications or defenses for discrimination, and remedies.

The primary concerns for postsecondary institutions in employment discrimination include employment and contracts, accommodation, standards and criteria for job performance, discipline and discharge, and academic freedom.[3] Chapter 5 identifies three primary areas of concern related to discrimination in the provision of educational services: the rules and standards for student admissions, curriculum requirements and testing, and accommodation of learning disabilities. These three areas intersect, especially where duty to accommodate is concerned.

In the final chapter of this section, Young and Kraglund-Gauthier outline the relationships between postsecondary institutions and Canadian educational associations. They note four main types of associations affiliated with postsecondary institutions in Canada: academic associations (such as Association of Universities and Colleges of Canada, now known as Universities Canada), faculty associations (such as Canadian Association of University Teachers), student associations (such as Canadian Federation of Students), and athletic associations (such as Canadian Interuniversity Sport). These associations play a key role in establishing, recognizing, and maintaining programs and institutions, both directly and indirectly, through their requirements for accreditation and membership.

There are several conflicting interests that arise when faced with satisfying multiple stakeholders such as those required in accreditation, and in particular when the stakeholders derive from multiple cultures or perspectives. These perspectives can be reflective of individuals, groups of individuals, or organizations and their expectations. For example, when Simon Fraser University sought membership in the National Collegiate Athlete Association, it was also required to obtain academic accreditation

---

[2] Poskitt and Wodja, this volume, 80.
[3] For a fuller discussion of academic freedom, see chapter 9 of this volume.

through a US-based accreditation agency, as none existed in Canada at the time of application. Further, there are requirements that programs must meet in order to obtain their own professional accreditation and recognition that span national boundaries. Without the recognition and accreditation of professional bodies, several academic programs would not be able to continue to offer prerequisite courses for licensure to their students.

Emerging Issues

A perennial issue of concern for postsecondary institutions is the tension between their organizational autonomy and concomitant role as agents of government. In an acute observation of this tension, Davis notes in chapter 4 that "universities have been described as quasi-public institutions."[4] The commitments to autonomy and government arise most distinctly in the obligation to uphold the rights and freedoms outlined in the Canadian *Charter*.

A second tension exists between institutional autonomy on the one hand and commitments to education and professional associations on the other; these commitments include accreditation standards and licensure. Canadian education associations provide institutions with vital connections to networks of students, athletes, professions, and academic agencies that offer not only (inter)national recognition but also standards of care and practice. The intersection between the institutional commitments of universities and those of professional associations is illustrated in the case of Trinity Western University's application for and subsequent accreditation of a law school. This case is the perfect storm of human rights, student rights, freedom of religion, freedom from discrimination, and accreditation and licensure for postsecondary institutions. Trinity Western University is a private, non-profit Christian university that requires that students and staff sign a "community covenant agreement." In this agreement, students and staff are asked to "voluntarily abstain from … sexual intimacy that violates the sacredness of marriage between a man and a woman."[5] One of the primary arguments being made against accreditation of the law school is the potential for discriminatory practices during admissions. On the other hand, those in support of TWU argue that to deny its application for accreditation amounts to discrimination on the basis of religious expression.

In a case currently under consideration, the Ministry of Advanced Education of British Columbia approved the application of TWU to offer law degrees. However, in order for graduates to be able to practice law,

---

[4] Davis, this volume, 61.
[5] Trinity Western University, "Community in Covenant."

TWU must also seek accreditation from the Federation of Law Societies of Canada (FLSC) and each of the provincial law societies. While several provinces have deferred their own determination to that of the FLSC, which has granted preliminary approval,[6] British Columbia, Ontario, and Nova Scotia have decided to make their own determinations. The benchers of the Law Society of British Columbia approved accreditation of TWU's law school on April 11, 2014.[7] In June 2014, the members called a special general meeting to vote on a resolution to deny accreditation of TWU's law school, which resulted in a referendum of the members of the profession on the issue;[8] however, the final decision resides with the benchers, who upon consideration of the referendum ultimately decided not to approve the law school.[9] Despite preliminary approval from the FLSC, the Law Society of Upper Canada, which governs Ontario's lawyers, has determined that it will not approve accreditation of Trinity Western's law school.[10] Finally, Nova Scotia has passed a conditional accreditation, which specifies among other conditions either that law students are exempt from signing the Community Covenant or that TWU "amends the Community Covenant in a way that it ceases to discriminate."[11] Ultimately, the preliminary approval of TWU's law program will not be lifted until its first class of students graduates and takes the bar in 2019.

As noted earlier in this chapter, the role of the *Charter* within public postsecondary institutions has been clarified in recent years. The case of TWU's law school application presents a unique opportunity for judicial review to further clarify the role of private postsecondary institutions with regard to their obligations to uphold the *Charter*. Additionally, this case serves to clarify the obligations and commitments of the Law Societies as professional associations, and their direct impact on post-secondary admissions and accreditation.

FACULTY AND STUDENTS

The relationship between universities and students has historically been characterized by the term *in loco parentis*, which means *in the place of parents*. Universities were expected to treat students in a developmental manner that was similar to that of a parent; punishment for student transgressions in the community were handled by university administrators. Throughout the development of universities in Canada, the laws that governed behaviour on campuses stood in parallel to those in society

---

[6] Federation of Law Societies of Canada, "Preliminary Approval."
[7] Law Society of British Columbia, "Bencher Meeting."
[8] Law Society of British Columbia, "Trinity Western University."
[9] Law Society of British Columbia, "Highlights."
[10] Law Society of Upper Canada, "Treasurer's Statement."
[11] Nova Scotia Barrister's Society, "Council Votes."

at large. However, since the expansion of postsecondary access in the mid-1960s, the relationship between students and universities has also changed. In chapter 7, Hannah and Stack propose several causes of these changes, including increased enrolment of diverse student populations; a change in the intergenerational agreements about the private/public mix of funding for postsecondary costs; a shift in the view of education toward its commodification; and increased awareness of rights of individuals with the establishment of the *Charter* in 1982.

There are several sources of law outlined in chapter 7 that govern the relationship between students and universities: statutory (provincial), administrative, private, contract, tort, and constitutional law. The primary document that outlines the interactions and expectations between students and universities is the university calendar, which specifies degree requirements, regulations, and grading policies. Another is the student handbook, which stipulates appropriate behaviour and expectations. Depending on the campus amenities that the student uses within the institution, there may also be parking registration forms, housing leases, and registration forms. These contracts represent an explicit relationship between the institution and students; the payment of fees can be construed as an implicit relationship or contract.

While Poskitt and Wojda note in chapter 5 the obligation of university administrators to uphold *Charter* rights, in chapter 7 Hannah and Stack argue that, based on several cases over the past 40 years, the obligations of institutions to uphold these rights has become highly contextualized. These two perspectives serve to highlight the ambiguity that surrounds the relationship between the *Charter* and Canadian postsecondary institutions. This ambiguity has a significant impact on the interpretation of and policies governing the duty to accommodate, the rights of students with disabilities, definitions of harassment, privacy and access to information, and intellectual property.

Given the highly specialized standards and requirements of colleges and universities, postsecondary institutions have historically been granted administrative autonomy over both student discipline and faculty employment decisions. Specifically, as noted by Hannah and Stack in chapter 7, "The application of administrative law principles in the context of student discipline tends to involve the requirement of fair process before unbiased decision makers."[12] This principle also holds in the case of faculty appeals. Further, the courts generally review the "reasonableness" of a disciplinary decision rather than whether the decision was right or wrong. Hannah and Stack state, "A reasonable decision is one that demonstrates justification, transparency, and intelligibility within

---

[12] Hannah and Stack, this volume, 147.

the decision-making process, and that falls within a range of possible, acceptable outcomes that are defensible in respect of the facts and law."[13]

There are several areas in both tort and contract law concerning the institutional liability to protect students. Higher education institutions owe a duty of care to take reasonable steps to protect students from harm. This duty has been clarified with regard to the curriculum, calendar, transfer and articulation agreements, and academic program offerings. The duty to warn students against the threat of violence also falls under the umbrella of duty of care. While this aspect of the duty of care is underdeveloped in Canada, general guidelines and policies have been developed in the United States to assist in evaluating, addressing, and communicating threats. A final area of institutional liability is the potential conflict of interest and harm arising out of research.

Procedural fairness (chapter 7) or natural justice (chapter 8) is a principle that prevails in the relationships between students, faculty, and post-secondary institutions when conflicts arise. This notion consists of two main components. First, there must be a hearing of both sides; in order for that to happen, there needs to be sufficient notice of the allegations, a reasonable opportunity to respond to them, and disclosure of relevant records (chapter 8). During this process, the respondent also has the right to respond, the right to cross-examine, and the right to counsel. Whether it is a complaint brought against a student by the institution or one brought by the faculty member against the institution, the burden of proof is on the complainant and should meet the standard of the "balance of probabilities" (chapter 7), in which upon weighing of the body of evidence, the probability that the event has occurred is more likely than not. The policies governing the decision body for the hearing of these cases must be outlined, transparent to all parties, and adhered to – otherwise the hearing should be adjourned. The second fundamental element of procedural fairness is the right to an unbiased decision maker. That is, the person or people making the decisions regarding the case must be free of any material or other interest in the outcome of the case. Additionally, they must be at "arm's-length" from anyone with an interest in the case. There only needs to be an appearance of bias to breach this principle of procedural fairness. Should a respondent be made aware of a potential bias, they may either request the panelist be replaced or waive their rights. Panelists should also be aware of any potential biases that may arise when their membership crosses several levels of the organization.

While the primary contractual agreement between students and colleges and universities is primarily found in the academic calendar, the primary agreement between faculty and institutions is the employment contract. Beyond that, where there is a union or faculty association, the

---

[13] Ibid., 148.

collective agreement also provides a layer of policy and procedural agreements between the institution and faculty.

Disciplinary action of tenured faculty members is rare. When disciplinary action is considered, two questions guide the determination of discipline, as outlined by Gilligan-Hackett and Murray in chapter 8. First, do the actions of the faculty member justify discipline or termination from employment? and second, is the disciplinary action within the guidelines of the collective agreement? Once it is determined that discipline is appropriate and within the collective agreement framework, it can range from reprimand to suspension for a single non-recurrent event to termination where the events are patterns or proven to be intentional and egregious. In cases where termination occurs, it is typically on the grounds of either gross misconduct or incompetence. When these decisions are contested, the appeals typically go to arbitrators rather than to the courts, and this appeal process is provided for in most collective agreements. This system provides an expedited and affordable alternative to hearing cases, especially when compared to slow and expensive courts, which are reluctant to get involved in university affairs.

Emerging Issues

With the United Nations Declaration on the Rights of Indigenous Peoples, Hannah and Stack note in chapter 7 that the concerns of First Nations students will move to the forefront. These concerns will likely manifest in three ways: development, support, and enhancement of First Nations and Indigenous universities; accommodations for Indigenous ways of knowing; and articulation of Indigenous students' (and faculty) rights.

The tensions between individual rights as they play out between the various stakeholders in the institutions have implications for several areas of postsecondary operations. As campus security issues increase in prevalence and a wider variety of incidents are made possible through technology, institutions are clarifying and developing their duty to warn students (and others) of possible threats. As institutions consider the duty to warn, they are also compelled to weigh the privacy rights of the individuals who may pose a threat on campus. Typically, where a single individual poses a potential threat to a campus, to a set of individuals (students, faculty, administration, or staff), or to a single individual, campus security services and local law enforcement officials coordinate the effort to contain and de-escalate the threat. In particular, the historical relationship between campuses and students as *in loco parentis* poses a challenging tension to universities in the current climate, where individual privacy rights are privileged. As campus violence and harassment continue to make headlines, it will be important for institutions to develop clear policies and procedures.

Competing students' rights also emerged in a current case at York University, where a male student requested accommodation to not have to work on a group project with a female student, citing expression of his culture or religion.[14] In yet another example of competing rights, the boundaries between academic and administration as they apply to academic freedom and freedom of speech are illustrated in a case where a University of Saskatchewan dean criticized budget plans and restructuring decisions made by the president of that institution and was subsequently fired for his comments.[15] The president was subsequently terminated from her position and is suing the institution for damages.[16]

Finally, further research is both emerging and needed on conflicts of interest – in particular, those that might arise in relation to university research. Similar to the campus security issues, individual privacy and public welfare are both factors in the complex calculus of policies and procedures to guide practice. Additionally, given the power that faculty members have over grading and determining student success, policies governing credit for participation in research and related conflicts of interest need to be clearly outlined in the institutional calendar, student handbook, and related materials.

POSTSECONDARY INSTITUTIONS AND THE COMMUNITY

In this section, which comprises chapters 9 to 11, the authors examine issues related to what are typically referred to as "town-and-gown" relationships. Chapter 9 highlights the relationships between university research and public good through a discussion of intellectual property and copyright law. Chapter 10 extends the discussion through an examination of collaborative research, ancillary services, spin-off companies, and related university commercial activities. The final chapter of this section explores land development issues within the context of postsecondary institutional development.

Intellectual property within the context of postsecondary institutions takes many forms including but not limited to lecture notes, syllabi, slides, classroom readers, research findings, innovations, and curriculum. The protections for these intellectual properties take two main forms – patents and copyrights. Patents provide the patent owner the "exclusive right of making, constructing, and using an invention and offering it to others

---

[14] Hopper, "York University Professor."

[15] Professor Robert Buckingham was reinstated as a tenured professor but not as dean; he has subsequently resigned his position.

[16] CBC News, "Ilene Busch-Vishnaic."

to be used" for a period of time.[17] By contrast, copyrights within the postsecondary context consist largely of literary works that are protected under the *Copyright Act of Canada*, which "establishes the presumption that the author of a work shall be the first owner of the copyright."[18] This legislation provides the owner the right to reproduce, distribute, and communicate their work, and to transfer or extend that right to others. In the case where an employee produces work as service for a contract, the work remains the property of the employer but the employee retains authorship. While the law suggests that ownership of literary works and curriculum (lecture notes) goes to universities, common law has established that these works belong to the author.

Related to the issues of intellectual property and copyright is the matter of academic freedom. Davis notes in chapter 9 that academic freedom in Canada is derived from the German concepts of *Lernfreiheit* and *Lehrfreiheit* – the freedom to learn granted to students, and the professional freedoms to research and present findings – and the "British notion of freedom to express political and social views in opposition to administrators, employers, and the government."[19] Academic freedom is directly connected to the rights of intellectual property, as the ownership rights afforded to faculty through copyright and patents affords them the ability to express those rights in an unfettered manner.

Since there is no federal or provincial legislation that governs the intellectual property generated at universities, all major Canadian research universities have created their own set of policies, which are found in collective agreements or faculty contracts. There are four main points covered in these policies, which are outlined in both chapters 9 and 10, all of which seek to clarify the boundaries of these relationships: disclosure, ownership, commercialization, and revenue sharing. These policies can be used to reinforce the rights of institutions against academic tradition.

Another area of potential intersection between universities and commercialization is that of licensing. Universities and university researchers can license or grant permission for the use of intellectual property or copyrighted materials toward the development of a product or fulfillment of a commercial need.[20] Davis suggests three main areas of licensing terms: financial, mandatory, and desirable. The financial terms outline the past, current, and anticipated future expenditures and revenues for the product(s) developed. Mandatory terms are those that are standard across all licensing agreements that the institution engages in and gen-

---

[17] Davis, this volume, 195–96.
[18] Ibid., 198.
[19] Ibid., 200.
[20] Lowe and Lennon, this volume, 213–30.

erally include the financial terms along with termination, insurance, confidentiality, and indemnity clauses.[21]

Where institutions retain a share of licensee companies through spin-off ventures, they retain some flexibility in their ownership while providing for the marketization of research developments. Spin-off companies are typically composed of the licensee, the university, and a financing organization such as a venture capital firm. These arrangements are important to manage, as the entities have differing priorities and objectives: universities rely on academic freedom, while corporations generally thrive on secrecy; universities have a mandate to serve the public good, while corporations are responsible to shareholders and investors. In chapter 10, Lowe and Lennon outline several considerations when entering into these types of relationships including researcher participation, dividend payouts, board governance, and weighing risks and benefits.

It is important to note that Lowe and Lennon suggest that the number of inventions and patents that generate revenue for universities is quite small and that the largest benefit of knowledge mobilization or commercialization is through the public good.

In the final chapter of Part IV, Gagnon-Larocque, Howard, Hussain, Levis, Livergant, Lunday, Mitchell, Paruk, Piurko, Sibay, Vogt, and Yip present an overview of land acquisition, divestment, and development issues as they apply to higher education institutions. This final area of the "town-gown" relationship can involve local or municipal legislation, provincial legislation, as well as contract and case law. Most Canadian provinces restrict universities to purchasing land that will be used for "university purposes," a definition that varies across provinces but generally refers to land that will be held and/or used by the university and its students. Where the intended or actual purpose of land acquisition and use does not appear to be directly related to university purposes, there are direct implications for tax exemption. That said, there is increasing acceptance of extended tax-exempt status even in "dual purpose" circumstances, where the land is used or leased to private for-profit companies that serve the campus community.[22] The second section of chapter 11, on the disposition of land by postsecondary institutions, reinforces and elaborates on the legislative frameworks that establish universities, which were laid out in chapter 2 of this volume. The legislative framework for property disposition for each of the ten provinces is outlined, along with special considerations and application of the rule against perpetuities.

The third section of chapter 11 explores the range of options available to higher education institutions when establishing development projects

---

[21] See chapter 10 for further details about inclusions and exclusions.

[22] McCarthy Tétrault LLP, this volume, 231–82.

for campus facilities. Specifically, the authors examine the tax and non-tax, charitable status, limitation of liability, and governance benefits and drawbacks of corporations, trusts, partnerships, joint ventures, and direct development. The particular choice that an institution makes will depend on the balance of the competing interests of that organization at the given time in question.

The fourth section of this chapter outlines potential property development issues such as land expropriation, development charges, municipal taxation, zoning, parkland dedication requirements, and application fees. In addition, the authors discuss the duty to consult and accommodate First Nations groups, environmental assessments, administrative tribunals for planning and development, and heritage status as emerging areas for universities to consider. The fifth section of this chapter outlines the common-law rulings that have had an influence on procurement practices in higher education. In particular, the authors explain the concept of "Contract A" and "Contract B,"[23] where Contract A is an implied contract; that is, when a bidder responds to the purchaser's request for proposals, the bid is in compliance with the stipulations set forth in the request and begins when the purchaser accepts a vendor's proposal. Contract B is then the resultant explicit contract between vendor and purchaser. Importantly, they state that "while purchasers are entitled to select their preferred evaluation criteria, they must not deviate from those criteria when selecting bids."[24] An area of growing attention is the impact of trade treaties, both internal (Agreement on Internal Trade) and international (Canada-EU Comprehensive Trade Agreement).

As higher education institutions have increased the numbers of students they serve, they have simultaneously had to increase the size of their campuses. At the same time, the infrastructure of many Canadian universities is suffering from deferred maintenance.[25] These demands have led to a large number of construction projects on campuses across Canada. The final section of this chapter on land development issues takes a sequential approach to highlighting the considerations when working on construction projects. Whether the project is large or small, the authors recommend hiring a construction consultant, with a clearly outlined contract and description of the scope of work that will be expected. Given the prevalence of construction services, the authors recommend relying on the standardized construction contract documents developed by the Canadian Construction Documents Committee (CCDC) or variations of these documents as a foundation for contracts and supplementary

---

[23] Ibid., 272.

[24] Ibid.

[25] Canadian Association of University Business Officers, *Deferred Maintenance at Canadian Universities*.

conditions. The authors reiterate the importance of first determining clear selection criteria for vendors and contractors, and then strictly following those selection criteria in order to avoid claims by unsuccessful bidders.

The interactions between organizations with different purposes, such as universities and external businesses or communities, present opportunities for new types of collaboration as well as possibilities for conflict. As the ways in which universities engage their communities grows increasingly complex, the recommended practices and policies remain consistently aligned with the premise of procedural fairness.

Emerging Issues

The possible conflicts between the modern commercialized university and the integrity and objectivity of scholars is of increasing concern and will likely be brought to the forefront with issues of research ethics that were raised in Part III of this volume. In particular, such conflicts may arise when students are participating in academic research as subjects while enrolled in a course where the researcher is also the instructor.

Gagnon-Larocque et al. suggest that an area of increasing attention is the rights of First Nations peoples of Canada. They note that the move toward viewing postsecondary institutions as an arm of government has implications for the duty to consult First Nations groups with regard to development of land and suggest this as a distinct area of future consideration for postsecondary institutions.[26]

Given the complexity and competing purposes of various parts of postsecondary institutions, there are several possible areas of tension that arise when postsecondary institutions engage with the external world. As this volume illustrates, while some of these tensions are unique to the context of an institution, several transcend institutional type, location, and context and can be characterized and mitigated through proactive policies and clear procedures.

---

[26] McCarthy Tétrault LLP, this volume, 231–82.

APPENDIX

PROVINCIAL REGULATION OF POSTSECONDARY EDUCATION

Alberta	
Ministry responsible for postsecondary education	Ministry of Innovation and Advanced Education
Sectors and types of institutions	PSE system includes six sectors: • comprehensive academic and research institutions • baccalaureate and applied studies institutions • polytechnical institutions • comprehensive community institutions • independent academic institutions • specialized arts and culture institutions **Public** 26 publicly funded postsecondary institutions: • 6 universities • 2 public institutes of technology • 2 public arts and culture institutions • 11 public colleges • 5 independent university-colleges that receive public funding **Private** 140 private vocational training institutions 13 other private and out-of-province institutions with approval to offer degree

These profiles rely extensively on information from the CMEC, *Postsecondary Education Systems in Canada: Provinces and Territories* (Toronto: Canadian Information Centre for International Credentials, 2013) and its website, in addition to information on government ministry websites and provincial postsecondary organization and agency websites as listed under each province.

Provincial legislation and documents organizing the system	The concept of Campus Alberta sets out principles for an integrated system of adult learning and formalizes collaboration between the 26 publicly funded postsecondary institutions.
	Government of Alberta, *Roles and Mandates Policy Framework for Alberta's Publicly Funded Advanced Education System* (2007) sets out the quality and accountability framework for the system.
	The *Post-secondary Learning Act,* SA 2003, c P-19-5 sets out the government authority for public postsecondary education in Alberta.
	The *Apprenticeship and Industry Training Act*, RSA 2000, c A-42 and its associated regulations provide the legislative authority for the apprenticeship and industry training system.
	The delivery of vocational training programs by private providers in Alberta is governed by the *Private Vocational Training Act*, RSA 2000, c P-24 and associated regulations.
Provincial legislation constituting institutions	The *Post-secondary Learning Act,* SA 2003, c P-19-5 establishes public universities, colleges, and technical institutes and recognizes their distinct mandates, which are approved by the minister. The Act establishes the governance structures and authority of universities, colleges, and institutes.
Provincial legislation providing degree-granting powers	The *Post-secondary Learning Act,* SA 2003, c P-19-5 restricts the use of the term "university" and provides universities with the power to grant degrees for programs approved by the minister.
Provincial quality assurance mechanisms	Quality assurance mechanisms include legislation; institutional mandate review and approval by the minister; program approval or licensing processes; system coordination review by the Ministry of Innovation and Advanced Education; degree program review by the Campus Alberta Quality Council consistent with the Council of Ministers of Education Canada (CMEC) document, *Ministerial Statement on Quality Assurance of Degree Education in Canada*; licensing requirements for private vocational training; credit transfer; articulation; the institutions' own external and internal reviews and governing board reports to ministry; systemwide institutional reporting on a variety of key performance indicators; incentive-based and performance-based funding envelops that reward quality based on institutional performance indicators; professional accreditation of programs leading to professional licensing; membership in ACCC for colleges and Universities Canada (formerly the AUCC) for universities; and membership in the (Canadian) Interprovincial Standards Red Seal Program, which offers quality assurance through standardized exams for provincial and territorial apprenticeship training and certification.
	The Alberta Government plans to publish a Comprehensive Credentials Framework for Alberta's postsecondary system in 2015; see Alberta Innovation and Advanced Education, "Credentials and Programs Offered in Alberta," http://eae.alberta.ca/post-secondary/credentials/definitions.aspx.

	Vocational training programs offered by private institutions must be licensed by the Private Vocational Training branch in accordance with the *Private Vocational Training Act*, RSA 2000, c P-24 and associated regulations. This legislation allows private institutions to participate in Alberta's postsecondary system and provides consumer protection to students enrolled in licensed programs. The *Alberta Public Agencies Governance Act*, SA 2009, c A-31.5, along with the Government of Alberta's *Public Agencies Governance Framework*, provides the legislative and policy framework for quality governance and accountability in Alberta's public sector agencies. The *APAGA* requires that all agencies have a publicly available mandate and roles document, a code of conduct, and a competency-based recruitment process. All agencies must be reviewed by the relevant minister at least every seven years. In postsecondary education, this Act and Framework captures all the governing boards of all publicly funded postsecondary institutions, the Campus Alberta advisory boards and councils, and the research and innovation boards. The *Roles and Mandates Policy Framework for Alberta's Publicly Funded Advanced Education System* document sets out these requirements for postsecondary education.
Provincial coordinating or advisory bodies[a]	The Campus Alberta Quality Council is an arm's-length quality assurance agency that makes recommendations to the Minister of Innovation and Advanced Education on applications from postsecondary institutions seeking to offer new degree programs in Alberta under the terms of the *Post-secondary Learning Act*, 2003, c P-19-5 and *Programs of Study Regulation* (91/2009). Other than degrees in divinity, all degree programs offered in Alberta, including degrees offered by non-resident institutions, must be approved by the minister. The council also conducts periodic evaluations of approved degree programs to ensure that quality standards continue to be met. The Alberta Council on Admissions and Transfer is an advisory agency responsible for providing advice and guidance regarding postsecondary admission and transfer to Enterprise and Advanced Education and the Alberta Transfer System member institutions. The *Online Transfer Alberta Guide* provides information on Alberta Transfer System agreements negotiated and approved by member postsecondary institutions in the province. Alberta Apprenticeship and Industry Training Board is responsible for establishing the standards and requirements for training and certification in programs under the Act. The board also makes recommendations to the minister responsible for advanced education about the needs of Alberta's labour market for skilled and trained workers.

[a]This section includes only Crown or independent organizations that directly advise government or assist government in coordinating the postsecondary system in each province. Due to space limitations, this appendix excludes the various PSE constituent organizations – such as provincial faculty associations, student federations, university presidents councils, and college associations – that also play important advocacy, leadership, or advisory roles.

Sources	Alberta Innovation and Advanced Education, "Credentials and Programs Offered in Alberta," http://eae.alberta.ca/post-secondary/credentials/definitions.aspx
	Alberta Innovation and Advanced Education, "Data Collection Applications for Post-Secondary Institutions," http://eae.alberta.ca/post-secondary/funding/supportsinstitutions/resources/data.aspx
	Alberta Innovation and Advanced Education, "Post-Secondary System," http://eae.alberta.ca/post-secondary.aspx
	Alberta Innovation and Advanced Education, "Roles and Mandates Policy Framework," http://eae.alberta.ca/post-secondary/policy/roles.aspx
	Campus Alberta Quality Council, http://www.caqc.gov.ab.ca/
	Canadian Information Centre for International Credentials, "Learn about the Education System in the Province of Alberta, Canada," http://cicic.ca/1131/Alberta/index.canada
	CMEC, *Postsecondary Education Systems in Canada*
	Government of Alberta, *A Learning Alberta: Quality in Alberta's Advanced Education System*, http://eae.alberta.ca/media/134943/quality.pdf

British Columbia	
Ministry responsible for postsecondary education	Ministry of Advanced Education
Sectors and types of institutions	The PSE system includes universities, colleges and institutes, private degree-granting institutions, private theological institutions, private career-training institutions, and apprenticeship programming.
	Public
	25 publicly funded postsecondary institutions (research-intensive universities, teaching-intensive universities, colleges, and institutes):
	• 11 public universities, including five new universities effective September 1, 2008
	• 11 public colleges serving rural and metropolitan communities in BC; may offer 4-year applied bachelor degree and master's degrees
	• 3 public institutes offering a variety of specialized programs; may offer wide variety of 4-year applied bachelor and master degrees.

	Private 17 private and out-of-province public institutions offering degree programs under the *Degree Authorization Act*, SBC 2002, c 24 340 private career colleges registered with the Private Career Training Institutions Agency 13 private theological institutions with statutory authority under Private Acts to grant theological degrees only 2 private universities operating under the authority of private Acts of the Legislature: Quest University is governed by the *Sea to Sky University Act*, SBC 2002, c 54, and Trinity Western University by *An Act respecting Trinity Western University* [Title amended, 1972-65-2, 1985-63-3], SBC 1969, c 44
Provincial legislation and documents organizing the system	The province's public postsecondary institutions are governed by the following legislation: **Universities** *University Act*, RSBC 1996, c 468 governs most of the university sector and constitutes the following universities: University of British Columbia, Simon Fraser University, University of Victoria, and University of Northern British Columbia. The Act also designates the following as special purpose, teaching universities: Capilano University, Emily Carr University of Art and Design, Kwantlen Polytechnic University, Vancouver Island University, and University of the Fraser Valley. Each university has in its own right and name the power to grant degrees established in accordance with the Act. **Private Degree-Granting Institutions and Public Out-of-Province Institutions** *Degree Authorization Act*, SBC 2002, c 24 prescribes the process whereby private or public institutions from other jurisdictions may obtain authority to offer degree programs and grant degrees in BC. The granting of degrees and use of the word "university" without authorization of the minister are restricted. **Colleges** *College and Institute Act*, RSBC 1996, c 52 constitutes and governs public colleges and institutes. The *Industry Training Authority Act*, SBC 2003, c 34 governs the industry training and apprenticeship system. The *Private Career Training Institutions Act*, SBC 2003, c 79, governs the private career colleges.
Provincial legislation constituting institutions	*University Act*, RSBC 1996, c 468 constitutes the University of British Columbia, Simon Fraser University, University of Victoria, and University of Northern British Columbia. It designates the following as special purpose, teaching universities: Capilano University, Emily Carr University of Art and Design, Kwantlen Polytechnic University, Vancouver Island University, and University of the Fraser Valley. *Royal Roads University Act*, RSBC 1996, c 409 constitutes Royal Roads University, a university specializing in applied and professional fields.

	Thompson Rivers University Act, SBC 2005, c 17 constitutes Thompson Rivers University, which offers baccalaureate and master's degree programs, adult basic education and training, and an open learning educational credit bank for students. *College and Institute Act*, RSBC 1996, c 52 constitutes and governs public colleges and institutes.
Provincial legislation providing degree-granting powers	*University Act*, RSBC 1996, c 468 *Degree Authorization Act*, SBC 2002, c 24 *Royal Roads University Act*, RSBC 1996, c 409 *Thompson Rivers University Act*, SBC 2005, c 17
Provincial quality assurance mechanisms	In addition to internal institutional quality assurance mechanisms, British Columbia has legislated external quality assurance mechanisms including the Degree Quality Assessment Board, an independent advisory board appointed by the government that oversees the quality assurance process for degree-level education in the province. All public and private postsecondary institutions offering degrees must undergo a quality assurance process for new degree programs. Public colleges and institutes are regulated under the *College and Institute Act*. Each institution has a board of governors that reports to the government and is responsible for managing the affairs of the institution. Each institution also has an education council that advises the governing board on a variety of quality assurance and accountability areas including implementation and evaluation of programs, standards of admission, curriculum content, and faculty qualifications. The Private Career Training Institutions Agency is an arm of the government and sets standards of quality for registered private career-training institutions seeking government accreditation. BC also employs legislation, affiliation, external and internal reviews of institutions (universities must have internal program review procedures based on institutional policies, and they annually report to the ministry), provincial registration of some institutions, and professional accreditation of programs leading to professional licensing as tools of quality assurance. Memberships in professional associations are another quality assurance mechanism: in ACCC for colleges and Universities Canada (formerly the AUCC) for universities, and in the (Canadian) Interprovincial Standards Red Seal Program, which offers quality assurance through standardized exams for provincial and territorial apprenticeship training and certification. Education Quality Assurance (EQA) is British Columbia's brand for quality postsecondary education. EQA is a voluntary mechanism available to all eligible postsecondary institutions in BC. The ministry is responsible for setting acceptable quality assurance standards for designation and for establishing and determining policy relating to EQA. The ministry is also responsible for determining whether an institution will be granted or maintain the EQA designation, including permission to use the EQA certification mark.

	In addition to the quality assurance framework, British Columbia has an Accountability Framework that includes reporting of key performance indicators and the preparation of institutional reports and plans. As part of this framework, government and public postsecondary institutions signed the Government's Letter of Expectations (GLE) for the 2014/15 fiscal year, reflecting agreement on respective roles and responsibilities, including strategic priorities and public policy issues. The GLE document lists the Ministry of Advanced Education's reporting requirements for BC's public postsecondary institutions. Additionally, every year the ministry provides the public postsecondary institutions with budget letters that outline the student enrolment targets and operating budget allocations to support targeted programs and priority issues for the coming fiscal year.
Provincial coordinating or advisory bodies[a]	The Degree Quality Assessment Board was established by the ministry to meet the statutory requirement under the *Degree Authorization Act* (*DAA*) for a quality assessment process. The board conducts quality assessment activities to ensure that new proposed degree programs at both private and public postsecondary institutions meet consistent quality criteria. The board makes recommendations in support of the minister's statutory powers to approve new degree programs at BC's public postsecondary institutions and those authorized under the *DAA*.
	The BC Council on Admissions & Transfer shapes the policy and processes that support articulation and student mobility in BC. Council members are appointed by the minister responsible for postsecondary institutions. Representatives are selected from universities, colleges, institutes, university and college faculty, postsecondary students, private postsecondary institutions, and the public secondary school system.
	The *Private Career Training Institutions Act,* SBC 2003, c 79 establishes the Private Career Training Institutions Agency as the regulatory agency for private career colleges. The agency is governed by a board composed of 3 minister-appointed public interest representatives and up to 7 industry-elected members. It is a Crown corporation under the Ministry of Advanced Education.
Sources	Ministry of Advanced Education, "B.C. Post-Secondary Education – Overview," http://www.aved.gov.bc.ca/publicpsed/welcome.htm
	BC Council on Admissions & Transfer, http://bccat.ca/about/council/
	Canadian Information Centre for International Credentials, "Learn about the Education System in the Province of British Columbia, Canada" http://cicic.ca/1132/British-Columbia/index.canada
	CMEC, *Postsecondary Education Systems in Canada*
	Fisher et al., "British Columbia."

Ontario	
Ministry responsible for postsecondary education	Ministry of Training, Colleges and Universities
Sectors and types of institutions	The PSE system includes public universities, private and out-of-province institutions with authority to grant degrees in Ontario, public colleges, apprenticeships programming, and private career colleges. **Public** 22 universities, degree granting 24 Colleges of Applied Arts and Technology (CAATs), not feeder institutions, no transfer function to university; some designated as Institutes of Technology and Advanced Learning (ITALs), may offer applied degrees 3 agricultural colleges affiliated with the University of Guelph Michener Institute of Applied Health Science offers diplomas in health technologies with 60 hospitals and is funded by the Ministry of Health and Long-Term Care **Private** 17 privately funded institutions with limited degree-granting authority, mostly bible colleges with religious affiliation Additional (in province and out-of-province) private institutions offer degree programs with the consent of the minister; see list at http://www.peqab.ca/completed.html. Over 500 registered private vocational career colleges offer diplomas and certificates in over 600 locations across the province, privately owned, commercial enterprises – "shadow/phantom sector"
Provincial legislation and documents organizing the system	*Ministry of Training Colleges and Universities Act*, RSO 1990, c M.19 *Ontario Colleges of Applied Arts and Technology Act*, SO 2002, c 8 *Private Career Colleges Act*, SO 2005, c 28 *Ontario College of Trades and Apprenticeship Act*, SO 2009, c 22
Provincial legislation constituting institutions	Individual institutional royal charters or Acts of the provincial or federal legislature constitute each university. *Ontario Colleges of Applied Arts and Technology Act*, SO 2002, c 8 Schedule F sets out governance of the public colleges. Apprenticeship training and trade-certification systems are governed by *Ontario College of Trades and Apprenticeship Act*, SO 2009, c 22, which established the governing body the College of Trades and sets out the legislative and regulatory framework for the skilled trades in Ontario.

Provincial legislation providing degree-granting powers	*Postsecondary Education Choice and Excellence Act, 2000*, SO c 36, sets out conditions for degree granting in the province for public and private institutions. It also gives the minister authority to grant consent to private and out-of-province public institutions and colleges of applied arts and technology to grant degrees and applied degrees, or to operate as universities in Ontario.
	Individual institutional royal charters or Acts of the provincial or federal legislature enable each university to offer degrees.
Provincial quality assurance mechanisms	Quality assurance mechanisms include legislation; institutional reporting on a variety of key performance indicators mandated by government; annual report of the institutional governing board to the ministry; affiliations/federations between institutions; transfer and articulation agreements on an institutional basis (there is no provincewide, mandated transfer process, but the systemwide online portal *ONTRANS* facilitates credit transfer); external and internal programmatic reviews; professional accreditation of programs; arm's-length to government quality assurance organizations that review and report on institutional quality assurance processes (details below for publicly funded universities and colleges processes); membership in ACCC for colleges and Universities Canada (formerly the AUCC) for universities; and membership in the (Canadian) Interprovincial Standards Red Seal Program, which offers quality assurance through standardized exams for provincial and territorial apprenticeship training and certification.
	The Ontario Qualifications Framework outlines all non-religious postsecondary certificate, diploma, and degree programs offered under the auspices of the Province of Ontario, including apprenticeship certificates, the qualifications awarded by private career colleges, the qualifications awarded by public colleges, and degrees offered by public universities and institutions authorized to award degrees by consent of the Minister of Training, Colleges and Universities of Ontario; see https://www.tcu.gov.on.ca/pepg/programs/oqf/oqf.pdf.
	The Ontario Universities Council on Quality Assurance is responsible for quality assurance in publicly assisted universities. It was established by the Ontario Council of Academic Vice-Presidents of the Council of Universities. The Council on Quality Assurance operates at arm's-length from both Ontario's publicly assisted universities and Ontario's government. The council is the provincial body responsible for assuring the quality of all programs leading to degrees and graduate diplomas, including new undergraduate and graduate programs, and for overseeing the regular audit of each university's quality assurance processes.
	The Quality Assurance Framework oversees the quality assurance of academic programs offered at publicly assisted universities in Ontario. Under the Institutional Quality Assurance Process, institutions design and implement their own processes in accordance with the protocols outlined in the framework. The Council on Quality Assurance has the final authority over appraisal and approvals of programs. See more at http://oucqa.ca/.

The Postsecondary Education Quality Assessment Board assesses applications from institutions for ministerial consent to offer degrees under the *Postsecondary Education Choice and Excellence Act*. The Postsecondary Quality Assessment Board makes recommendations to the Minister of Training, Colleges and Universities on applications to offer degree programs from new and existing private Ontario degree-granting institutions, out-of-province institutions, colleges of applied arts and technology, and all others not authorized to award degrees by an Ontario statute.

Ontario Colleges Quality Assurance Service for CAATs, created by the *Ontario Colleges of Applied Arts and Technology Act, 2002*, is an oversight body for publicly funded colleges. The OCQAS is responsible for establishing self-regulatory mechanisms for quality assurance at both the program level and the institutional level in publicly funded colleges. Although it is mandated by the government, it is independent from the government and does not report to the government. It is owned, operated, and funded by the 24 public colleges in Ontario. In the past, college institutional quality assurance processes have taken the shape of "quality audits" of colleges. However, in September 2015 the process is transitioning into an accreditation process whereby a college will have to show evidence that it clearly meets all six of the OCQAS Quality Standards in order to receive a decision of being fully accredited. See more at http://ocqas.org/?p=9334.

The Higher Education Quality Council of Ontario (HEQCO), established by the government under the *Higher Education Quality Council of Ontario Act, 2005, SO 2005, c 28, Sch G*, is an arm's-length body that conducts research on and monitors quality in the system, and advises government on best ways to measure performance. Publicly funded universities must work with HEQCO to develop and monitor performance under terms of *Multi-Year Accountability Agreements* and *Strategic Mandate Agreements*.

Key performance indicators are also part of the higher education regulatory quality and accountability framework in Ontario. Publicly funded colleges and universities in Ontario have a portion of their operating grant determined by their performance in various areas including employment rates, graduation rates, and student and employer satisfaction. Private colleges and degree-granting institutions must also publish key performance indicators in order for their students to receive government financial assistance, but no institutional funding from government is attached to private institutions.

Formerly, *Multi-Year Accountability Agreements*, institutional contracts between institutions and government, had performance funding attached. In 2013 these agreements were re-profiled as interim accountability reporting mechanisms for the new *Strategic Mandate Agreements, 2014*, which are the mechanisms by which colleges and universities articulate their unique mandate,

	strengths, and aspirations. Institutions must align their missions and activities with the government's priorities as outlined in the *Differentiation Policy Framework, 2013*. The *Strategic Mandate Agreements* operationalize the *Differentiation Policy Framework* and include reporting on institutional and systemwide metrics connected to enrolments and financial sustainability. Policy, processes, and funding are attached to the *Differentiation Policy Framework* and the *Strategic Mandate Agreements*. University and colleges are also captured under broad public sector accountability requirements in public sector legislation (i.e., *Freedom of Information and Protection of Privacy Act*, RSO 1990, c F.31 and the *Accessibility for Ontarians with Disabilities Act*, 2005, SO 2005, c 11, as well as human rights codes and employment equity legislation). *Private Career Colleges Act*, SO 2005, c 28 sets out conditions for registration of private career colleges with the government and receipt of OSAP (Ontario Student Assistance Program) funds for attending students. By law, private career colleges must be registered in Ontario and must have their programs "approved" by the superintendent of private career colleges. Approvals are around consumer protection as opposed to programmatic quality.
Provincial coordinating or advisory bodies[a]	The College Compensation and Appointment Council provides advice and strategic planning, appoints college boards, and deals with governance, collective bargaining, and human resources issues (governance of CAATS is highly centralized in ministry). The council was created by the *Ontario Colleges of Applied Arts and Technology Act*, SO 2002, c 8. The Higher Education Quality Council of Ontario conducts research on quality, participation, and access, and advises government on the best ways to measure performance. The Postsecondary Quality Assessment Board makes recommendations to the Minister of Training, Colleges and Universities on applications to offer degree programs from new and existing private Ontario degree-granting institutions, out-of-province institutions, colleges of applied arts and technology, and all others not authorized to award degrees by an Ontario statute. The Ontario Council on Articulation and Transfer facilitates and supports academic collaboration and the development of transfer pathways among Ontario's publicly funded colleges and universities to optimize postsecondary options for students and reduce duplication of prior learning. It was established in 2011 by the Ministry of Training, Colleges and Universities. Members of the council were appointed collectively by its sponsors: the Council of Ontario Universities, Colleges Ontario, and the Ontario Ministry of Training, Colleges and Universities.

Sources	Canadian Information Centre for International Credentials, "Learn about the Education System in the Province of Ontario, Canada," http://cicic.ca/1138/Ontario/index.canada
	CMEC, *Postsecondary Education Systems in Canada*
	Government of Ontario, *Ontario's Differentiation Policy Framework*, http://www.tcu.gov.on.ca/pepg/publications/PolicyFramework_PostSec.pdf
	Higher Education Quality Council of Ontario, http://www.heqco.ca/en-CA/Pages/Home.aspx
	Klassen, "Quality Assurance in Ontario's Postsecondary Education Sector"
	Milan and Hicks, "Ontario Private Career Colleges"
	Ontario Ministry of Training, Colleges and Universities, "About the Ministry," http://www.tcu.gov.on.ca/eng/about/
	Ontario Qualifications Framework, https://www.tcu.gov.on.ca/pepg/programs/oqf/oqf.pdf
	Ontario Universities Council on Quality Assurance, http://oucqa.ca/
	Postsecondary Education Quality Assessment Board, http://www.peqab.ca/
	Shanahan et al., "Ontario"
	Strategic Mandate Agreements for Ontario publicly funded universities can be found at http://www.tcu.gov.on.ca/pepg/publications/vision/universities.html
	Strategic Mandate Agreements for Ontario publicly funded colleges can be found at http://www.tcu.gov.on.ca/pepg/publications/vision/colleges.html

Manitoba	
Ministry responsible for postsecondary education	Ministry of Education and Advanced Learning
Sectors and types of institutions	The PSE system includes universities, private religious institutions, public colleges, apprenticeship programming, and private vocational institutions.
	Public postsecondary institutions, degree granting:
	• 4 universities (one French language)
	• 2 colleges
	• 1 university-college (Aboriginal focus with tri-council governance: elder, learning, and governing councils)
	1 public technical college

	Private theological degree-granting institutions: • 1 university • 1 bible college • 2 university-colleges 50 Private vocational institutions (registered with the Government of Manitoba as of Jan 2015)
Provincial legislation and documents governing and organizing the system	*The Advanced Education Administration Act*, SM 2010, c 27, sch. A, governs postsecondary education in the province and sets out the minister's powers. Each university is governed by its own statute. *The Colleges Act*, 1991 CCSM, c C150.1 establishes governance of the colleges. *The Colleges Amendment Act,* 2009 gives community colleges authority to grant applied degrees. Manitoba's registered private vocational institutions are governed by *The Private Vocational Institutions Act*, CCSM c P137 and Manitoba Regulation 237/02. *The Apprenticeship and Certification Act*, CCSM c A110 governs apprenticeship training and establishes the Apprenticeship and Certification Board and the Minister of Jobs and the Economy as the co-authorities for training and certification in trades designated for apprenticeship training in Manitoba. *The Manitoba Institute of Trades and Technology Act*, CCSM c T130 establishes the Manitoba Institute of Trades and Technology (formerly Winnipeg Technical College), a public provincial institute with a mandate to provide both secondary and postsecondary technical career education.
Provincial legislation constituting institutions	*The University of Manitoba Act*, CCSM c U60 *The University of Winnipeg Act,* SM 1998, c 50, CCSM c U70 *The Brandon University Act*, SM 1998, c 48, CCSM c B90 *The University College of the North Act*, SM 2004, c 16 *The Université de Saint-Boniface Act*, SM 2011, c 16 *The Mennonite College Federation Act*, CCSM c M105 establishes and provides degree-granting authority for the Mennonite college. *The Providence University College and Theological Seminary Incorporation Act*, RSM 1990, c 217 establishes and gives degree-granting authority to Providence University.
Provincial legislation providing degree-granting powers	Degree-granting authority is set out in individual statutes constituting universities above. *The Degree Granting Act*, CCSM c D25 restricts who may grant degrees to those institutions already having degree-granting authority in their legislation, or to those listed in *The Degree*

	Granting Act. Restricts use of term "university" and "varsity," and defines "degree." No restrictions on the use of the term "college."
	The Colleges Amendment Act, 2009, gives community colleges authority to grant applied degrees.
Provincial quality assurance mechanisms	Quality assurance mechanisms include legislation (statutes and regulations), affiliation, provincial registration, professional accreditation, internal peer-reviewed reviews and reporting of quality established by governing board of university, similar internal reviews and reporting for colleges that are Crown corporations, and formal affiliations and agreements between various institutions (Université de Saint-Boniface is affiliated with University of Manitoba). Credit transfer and articulation agreements are done on an institutional basis; no systemwide credit transfer or articulation yet, but Inter-University Services and eCampus Manitoba are two public-institution consortia that aim to provide system-level pathways for students. Quality assurance in the form of program approvals is conducted by the government through its Advanced Learning Division within the Department of Advanced Learning.
	Membership in ACCC for colleges and Universities Canada (formerly the AUCC) for universities also offers some assurance of quality. Membership in the (Canadian) Interprovincial Standards Red Seal Program offers quality assurance through standardized exams for provincial and territorial apprenticeship training and certification.
	The Private Vocational Institutions Act, CCSM c P137 sets out requirements for the operation of registered private vocational institutions in Manitoba. Private career colleges must register with the minister, and the Act sets out limited consumer protection to students enrolled. Applications for registration must be reviewed and approved by the director of the Private Vocational Institutions Unit.
	The Advanced Education Administration Act, SM 2010, c 27, sch. A establishes the minister's authority to, among other things, review and evaluate postsecondary programs.
Provincial coordinating or advisory bodies[a]	Prior to 2014, the Council on Postsecondary Education (COPSE) conducted external reviews of quality and approved university and college programming, set funding allocations to institutions, and provided advice and policy direction to the government. In 2014 COPSE was dismantled and its functions were assumed by the Minister of Education and Advanced Learning. In 2014 the Advanced Education Advisory Committee was established by an amendment of *The Advanced Education Administration Act.* The committee is an arm of the government and provides advice on long-term planning to the Minister of Education and Advanced Learning. Now the Manitoba government through its Advanced Learning Division within the department is now directly responsible for system planning, funding allocations, regulation of programs of study, and regulation of tuition and fees as well as quality assurance of colleges and universities in the province. For more information, see http://www.edu.gov.mb.ca/ald/index.html.

Sources	Advanced Learning Division, http://www.edu.gov.mb.ca/ael/
	Canadian Information Centre for International Credentials, "Learn about the Education System in the Province of Manitoba, Canada" http://cicic.ca/1133/Manitoba/index.canada
	CMEC, *Postsecondary Education Systems in Canada*
	D. Smith, "Erosion of University Autonomy in Manitoba"
	University College of the North, "Governance," https://www.ucn.ca/sites/governance/Pages/Governance.aspx

New Brunswick

Ministry responsible for postsecondary education	Department of Postsecondary Education, Training and Labour
	Note: New Brunswick is officially bilingual
Sectors and types of institutions	The PSE system has universities, community colleges, apprenticeship programs, and private training institutions.
	Public
	4 universities (with 7 campuses across the province, 1 university is French speaking, largest in North America outside of Quebec)
	2 community colleges (11 campuses)
	2 specialized colleges: New Brunswick Colleges of Craft and Design, and Maritime College of Forest Technology
	Private
	not-for-profit denominational universities/colleges
	for-profit degree-granting institutions
	private career colleges
Provincial legislation and documents organizing the system	*Higher Education Foundation Act,* RSNB 2011, c 169
	Degree Granting Act, RSNB 2011, c 140
	Private Occupational Training Act, RSNB 1973, c P-16.1 and its general regulations require private career colleges to register with the government.
	The *New Brunswick Community Colleges Act,* SNB 2010, c N-4.05 governs New Brunswick's community colleges, while the *Adult Education and Training Act,* RSNB 2011, c 101 governs other college-level education, including the New Brunswick College of Craft and Design.
	The *Apprenticeship and Occupational Certification Act,* SNB 2012, c 19 assigns responsibility for administration of apprenticeship training and certification of trades to the Minister of Post-Secondary Education, Training, and Labour.
	Maritime Provinces Higher Education Commission Act, RSNB 2011, c 187

Provincial legislation constituting institutions	*Higher Education Foundation Act,* RSNB 2011
	Publicly Chartered Universities
	Université de Moncton
	University of New Brunswick
	Mount Allison University
	St. Thomas University
	Universities Recognized under the *Degree Granting Act, 2011*
	Meritus University
	Yorkville University
	University of Fredericton
	Privately Chartered Universities
	Crandall University
	Kingswood University
	St. Stephen's University
Provincial legislation providing degree-granting powers	The *Degree Granting Act,* RSNB 2011, c 140, provides for two processes giving institutions the right to grant degrees, namely, by designation by the Lieutenant-Governor in Council or authorization by an Act of the New Brunswick Legislature.
Provincial quality assurance mechanisms	Quality assurance mechanisms include legislation (statutes and regulations), affiliation, provincial registration, professional accreditation, membership in other organizations related to quality assurance, internal self-study reviews and reporting of quality established by governing board of university, similar internal reviews and reporting for colleges that are Crown corporations, external reviews of quality by the Maritime Provinces Higher Education Commission (MPHEC) of all new programs and significant changes to programs, MPHEC's monitoring of quality assessment procedures used by institutions (within the *Degree Granting Act's* framework), formal affiliations and agreements between various institutions (but no systematic provincewide process for conducting university credit transfers to and from colleges and universities), some articulation agreements that are institution or program specific (case by case basis), membership in ACCC for colleges and and Universities Canada (formerly the AUCC) for universities, and membership in the (Canadian) Interprovincial Standards Red Seal Program, which offers quality assurance through standardized exams for provincial and territorial apprenticeship training and certification.
	The *Maritime Degree Level Qualifications Framework* sets out information on undergraduate and graduate degrees. Colleges are reviewed annually on key performance indicators including retention, graduation and employment rates, and student satisfaction.

The Maritime Provinces Higher Education Commission is a significant mechanism of quality assurance and system coordination. The MPHEC is an "agency of the Council of Maritime Premiers," including the ministers of education in New Brunswick, Nova Scotia, and Prince Edward Island. Its main functions are to monitor quality assurance, analyze data and information, facilitate cooperative action, promote regional programs, and provide specific services to one or more provinces or institutions as agreed to by the ministers. The commission focuses primarily on university education. See http://www.mphec.ca/about/mandateandact.aspx.

The *Maritime Degree Level Qualifications Framework* is used within the New Brunswick education system. It provides information on postsecondary undergraduate and graduate degree programs; see http://www.mphec.ca/resources/DegreeLevelFrameworkEn.pdf.

The *Degree Granting Act*, RSNB 2011, c 140 establishes a framework for evaluating the quality of programs leading to a degree offered by all public and private institutions, except those created by an Act of the New Brunswick Legislature prior to the Act coming into force (before March 1, 2001).

The *Private Occupational Training Act* requires private career colleges to register with government. The Act provides some financial protection for students attending private sector training organizations, and requires a contract between the training organization and the student that covers competencies expected, teacher-instructor qualifications, course content, maximum class size, and prerequisites for admission. The training organizations are monitored to ensure compliance with the Act and its regulations.

Provincial coordinating or advisory bodies[a]	The Maritime Provinces Higher Education Commission states: "There are currently seventeen post-secondary institutions within the scope of the MPHEC, fifteen of which are publicly-funded universities. Of these fifteen, three (Cape Breton University, Dalhousie and Université Sainte-Anne) also offer college-level or technology-based certificate and diploma programs in addition to degree programs. The remaining two institutions (Holland College in Prince Edward Island and the Maritime College of Forest Technology in New Brunswick) offer primarily college-level programs." See http://www.mphec.ca/about/mandateandact.aspx.
	The Apprenticeship and Occupational Certification Board and program advisory committee advise the government on apprenticeship training.
	The Atlantic Apprenticeship Council shares common concerns and opportunities for apprenticeship programs in the four Atlantic provinces (Newfoundland and Labrador, New Brunswick, Nova Scotia, and Prince Edward Island). The council's priority is to adopt common standards for training in selected trade apprenticeship programs, including standards for curriculum development.

Sources	Canadian Information Centre for International Credentials, "Learn about the Education System in the Province of New Brunswick, Canada," http://cicic.ca/1134/New-Brunswick/index.canada
	CMEC, *Postsecondary Education Systems in Canada*
	Maritime Provinces Higher Education Commission, "Maritime Degree Level Qualifications Framework," http://www.mphec.ca/resources/DegreeLevelFrameworkEn.pdf
	Maritime Provinces Higher Education Commission, "The Maritime Provinces Higher Education Commission Mandate," http://www.mphec.ca/about/mandateandact.aspx
	Post-Secondary Education, Training and Labour, *Degree Granting Act*, http://www2.gnb.ca/content/gnb/en/departments/post-secondary_education_training_and_labour/post-secondary_education/content/post-secondary_institutions/degree_granting_act.html
	Post-Secondary Education, Training and Labour, http://www2.gnb.ca/content/gnb/en/departments/post-secondary_education_training_and_labour/post-secondary_education/content/post-secondary_institutions/universities.html
	Post-Secondary Education, Training and Labour, http://www2.gnb.ca/content/gnb/en/departments/post-secondary_education_training_and_labour.html

Newfoundland and Labrador	
Ministry responsible for postsecondary education	Department of Advanced Education and Skills
Sectors and types of institutions	The PSE system has universities, public colleges, private training institutions, and apprenticeship programming.
	Public
	1 university – Memorial University has 3 campuses across the province.
	1 college – College of the North Atlantic has 17 campuses including one in Qatar.
	Private
	25 private training institutes (PTIs)
Provincial legislation and documents organizing the system	*Apprenticeship and Certification Act*, SNL 1999, c A-12.1
	College Act, 1996, SNL 1996, c C-22.1
	Degree Granting Act, RSNL 1990, c D-5
	Memorial University Act, RSNL 1990, c M-7

	Council on Higher Education Act, PSNL 2006, c C-37.001
	Private Training Institutions Act, RSNL 1990, c P-25
Provincial legislation constituting institutions	*Memorial University Act*, RSNL 1990, c M-7, establishes the university and the Marine Institute as part of the university.
	College Act, 1996, SNL 1996, c C-22.1 establishes the College of the North Atlantic.
Provincial legislation providing degree-granting powers	*Degree Granting Act*, RSNL 1990, c D-5
Provincial quality assurance mechanisms	Quality assurance mechanisms include legislation, and affiliations and federations with institutions. The Department of Advanced Education and Skills compiles an annual transfer guide that includes transfer of credit arrangements for courses and programs within the provincial postsecondary system. Additionally, Memorial University and the College of the North Atlantic have a credit transfer mechanism. Publicly funded PSE institutions provide annual external reporting by institutional boards to the minister under the *Transparency and Accountability Act, 2004*, c t-8.1. Publicly funded institutions also conduct internal reviews and undergo professional accreditation of professional programs. PSE institutions may also be members of the ACCC for colleges and Universities Canada (formerly the AUCC) for universities, and the (Canadian) Interprovincial Standards Red Seal Program, which offers quality assurance through standardized exams for provincial and territorial apprenticeship training and certification.
	Private institutions are governed by the *Private Training Institutions Act*, RSNL 1990, c P-25, which requires registration of private institutions with the government and creates the position of superintendent of private training institutions. The superintendent reviews and approves all programs of study before registration is allowed, and reviews the quality of programs, instruction, equipment, and admissions, and the qualifications of instructors.
Provincial coordinating or advisory bodies[a]	The Council on Higher Education is a mechanism of collaboration; it provides recommendations to Memorial University, the College of the North Atlantic, and the Minister of Education, and compiles transfer information. The council was reconfigured and recognized through legislation, the *Council on Higher Education Act, 2006*.
	The Provincial Apprenticeship and Certification Board is directly accountable to the minister. The board oversees and advises government on issues and policies relating to apprenticeship training and accreditation of apprenticeship programs.
	The Atlantic Apprenticeship Council shares common concerns and opportunities for apprenticeship programs in the 4 Atlantic provinces (Newfoundland and Labrador, New Brunswick, Nova Scotia, and Prince Edward Island). The council's priority is to adopt common standards for training in selected trade apprenticeship programs, including standards for curriculum development.

Sources	Canadian Information Centre for International Credentials, "Learn about the Education System in the Province of Newfoundland and Labrador, Canada," http://cicic.ca/1135/Newfoundland-and-Labrador/index.canada
	CMEC, *Postsecondary Education Systems in Canada:*
	Department of Advanced Education and Skills, http://www.aes.gov.nl.ca/services.html

Quebec	
Ministry responsible for postsecondary education	Ministère de l'Enseignement supérieur, de la recherche, de la science et de la technologie (Quebec Ministry of Higher Education, Research, Science and Technology)
Sectors and types of institutions	PSE system includes CEGEPs (collèges d'enseignement général et professionnel) and universities.
	18 universities (including the multiple campuses and institutes of the University of Quebec and of the University of Montreal)
	College-level programs are offered in
	• 48 public CEGEPs
	• 25 subsidized private colleges (i.e., accredited for government funding)
	• 26 licensed non-subsidized private colleges (2 are governed by international agreement)
	• 4 public institutions (governed by agency other than the Ministry of Higher Education, Research, Science and Technology)
Provincial legislation and documents organizing the system	No specific legislation that designs the system.
	Each university is created and internal institutional governance is set out by a specific Act of Incorporation (for example, University of Quebec) or by a charter (all Quebec universities created prior to 1968).
	Loi sur les collèges d'enseignement général et professionnel (General and Vocational Colleges Act), CQLR c C-29 governs the public college sector and college vocational education.
	An Act respecting the ministère de l'éducation, du loisir et du sport, CQLR c M-15 governs the institutions offering PSE programs not under the authority of Ministry of Higher Education, Research, Science and Technology.
	An Act respecting the conseil supérieur de l'éducation, CQLR c C-60 creates the *conseil supérieur de l'éducation* (see below).

	Loi sur l'enseignement privé (An Act respecting Private Education), CQLR c E-9.1 governs the private education sector. *An act respecting the commission d'évaluation de l'enseignement collégial*, CQLR c C-32.2 sets out quality assurance processes for college sector. *Loi sur les établissements d'enseignement universitaire (An Act respecting Educational Institutions at the University Level)*, CQLR c E-14.1 sets out the accountability framework for Quebec universities, especially for required annual reporting to government. It also establishes the framework for recognition of institutions that can offer university-level programs, lists university-level institutions, and specifies provisions for using the term "university." *Loi sur la formation et la qualification professionnelle de la main-d'oeuvre (An Act respecting Workforce Vocational Training and Qualification)*, CQLR c F-5 governs vocational and apprenticeship training and sets out apprenticeship training typically in school boards hands but governs continuity and transition between secondary- and college-level apprenticeship programming.
Provincial legislation constituting institutions	*Loi sur les établissements d'enseignement universitaire (An Act respecting Educational Institutions at the University level)*, CQLR c E-14.1 Each university is created by specific Act of Incorporation or by a charter. *An Act respecting the Université du Québec*, CQLR c U-1 establishes the University of Quebec institutions.
Provincial legislation providing degree-granting powers	*Loi sur les établissements d'enseignement universitaire (An Act respecting Educational Institutions at the University Level)*, CQLR c E-14.1
Provincial quality assurance mechanisms	Quality assurance mechanisms include legislation, regulations, orders-in-council, policies, university affiliations between some university-level institutions but not between colleges and universities, program equivalency, program harmonization, external and internal reviews of institutions, annual governing board reporting to ministry including institutional reporting on a variety of key performance indicators, professional accreditation of programs leading to professional licensing, membership in Universities Canada (formerly the AUCC) for universities and ACCC for colleges, and membership in the Fédération des CEGEPs. The Office des professions du Québec is responsible for implementing the Code des professions. Membership in the (Canadian) Interprovincial Standards Red Seal Program offers quality assurance through standardized exams for provincial and territorial apprenticeship training and certification.

Quebec also employs performance funding tied to various targets and indicators that include quality of teaching, research, competitive positioning, and sound administration and management of universities. The performance funding is secured by agreements between the government and each university. This funding is in addition to the government's allocations for institutional operating grants. For details on performance indicators and funding, see Finance Quebec, *A Fair and Balanced University Funding Plan.*

University program quality control is performed via the voluntary coordinating body Bureau de Coopération Interuniversitaire (formerly Conférence des recteurs et des principaux des universités du Québec – CREPUQ).

Institutions' quality assessment practices are reviewed by CREPUQ's Commission de la vérification de l'évaluation des programmes (Program Evaluation Review Commission), which audits institutional policies and practices within the frame of reference defined in the *Policy of Québec Universities on the Periodic Evaluation of Current Academic Programs.* New programs leading to a university degree (bachelor's, master's, or doctoral) are submitted to CREPUQ's Commission de l'évaluation des projets de programmes (New Program Evaluation Commission), which renders an opinion as to academic quality. At that point the Ministère de l'Enseignement supérieur, de la Recherche, de la Science et de la Technologie reviews the opinion. Decisions on funding enrolment in new programs are taken based on the provisions in the document entitled *Procédure liée à l'examen d'opportunité des projets de programmes conduisant à un grade présentés au ministre de l'Enseignement, de la Recherche, de la Science et de la Technologie aux fins de financement.* See details at http://cicic.ca/1173/Quality-assurance-practices-for-postsecondary-institutions-in-Quebec/index.canada; and also at http://www.crepuq.qc.ca/spip.php?rubrique60&lang=en

Quality assessment for programs offered by public CEGEPs is provided by the Commission d'évaluation de l'enseignement collégial (College Education Evaluation Commission). The *Loi sur la Commission d'évaluation de l'enseignement collegial,* CQLR c C-32.2 sets out quality control across the college system for all pre-university programs and for technical programs over and above each institution's internal policies. (Private institutions are required to be licensed by the minister and are subject to the same quality control mechanisms as the public CEGEPs.) For details, see http://www.ceec.gouv.qc.ca/en/Assurance_quality/Default.htm.

The framework for college quality assurance is set out in *Evaluating the Effectiveness of Quality Assurance Systems in Québec Colleges: Guidelines and Framework.*

Provincial coordinating or advisory bodies[a]	*An act respecting the conseil supérieur de l'éducation* established the conseil supérieur de l'éducation that collaborates with the Minister of Education, Recreation and Sports and the Minister of Higher Education, Research, Science and Technology, and advises the ministers on any matter relating to education.
	The National Assembly Culture and Education Commission is an advisory body made up of members of the National Assembly that has competence over culture, education, vocational training, higher education, and communication in the province. The commission requires universities to submit an annual report.
	Quebec also has three independent, government-funding agencies, similar to the federal government research councils, that advise the provincial government on research, innovation, and economic development in the province as well as administer research funding.
Sources	CMEC, *Postsecondary Education Systems in Canada*
	An Act respecting the Conseil Supérieur de L'éducation, http://www2. publicationsduquebec.gouv.qc.ca/dynamicSearch/telecharge. php?type=2&file=/C_60/C60_A.html
	Bureau de coopération interuniversitaire, "Current Program Evaluation Review, http://www.crepuq.qc.ca/spip. php?rubrique60&lang=en
	Canadian Information Centre for International Credentials, "Learn about the Education System in the Province of Quebec, Canada," http://cicic.ca/1140/Quebec/index.canada
	Commission d'évaluation de l'enseignement collégial, *Evaluating the Effectiveness of Quality Assurance Systems in Québec Colleges: Guidelines and Framework*, http://www.ceec.gouv. qc.ca/publications/anglais/Effectiveness_Quality_Assurance_ Orientation_Framework_2013.pdf
	Commission d'évaluation de l'enseignement collégial, "Quality Assurance," http://www.ceec.gouv.qc.ca/en/Assurance_quality/ Default.htm
	Éducation, Enseignement supérieur et Recherche, http://www. mesrs.gouv.qc.ca/personnel-duniversite/formation-universitaire/ examen-dopportunite-des-projets-de-programmes-conduisant- a-un-grade/
	Éducation, Enseignement supérieur et Recherche, "Laws and Regulations, http://www.education.gouv.qc.ca/en/references/ laws-and-regulations/
	Finance Quebec, *A Fair and Balanced University Funding Plan*
	Trottier et al., "Quebec"

Saskatchewan	
Ministry responsible for postsecondary education	Saskatchewan Ministry of Advanced Education (responsible for postsecondary and adult learning)
Sectors and types of institutions	The PSE system includes universities, colleges and institutes, apprenticeship programs, and private training institutions.
	2 publicly funded universities and their federated and affiliated colleges (University of Regina and University of Saskatchewan)
	Note: First Nations University of Canada is a federated college of the University of Regina. It was formerly known as Saskatchewan Indian Federated College.
	The Saskatchewan Polytechnic, formerly known as Saskatchewan Institute of Applied Science and Technology, is authorized under *The Degree Authorization Act,* SS 2012, c D-2.1 to offer the Bachelor in Psychiatric Nursing degree.
	7 regional colleges that broker programs with the 2 universities and Saskatchewan Polytechnic to communities throughout the province
	The Saskatchewan Indian Institute of Technologies (SIIT)
	41 private vocational schools
Provincial legislation and documents organizing the system	*The Degree Authorization Act,* SS 2012, c D-2.1
	Private Vocational Schools Regulation Act, SS 1995, c P-26.2
	The Apprenticeship and Trade Certification Act, 1999
	The Apprenticeship and Trade Certification (Designated Trades) Regulations, RRS c A-22.2 Reg 1
Provincial legislation constituting institutions	*The University of Saskatchewan Act, 1995,* SS 1995, c U-6.1
	The University of Regina Act, RSS 1978, c U-5
	The Saskatchewan Polytechnic Act, SS 2014, c S-32.21
	First Nations University of Canada Act, 2008 (passed by the Federation of Saskatchewan Indian Nations Legislative Assembly). First Nations University is under the jurisdiction of the Indian Government of Saskatchewan, the Federation of Saskatchewan Indian Nations (FSIN).
	The Saskatchewan Indian Institute of Technologies Act, SS 2000, c S-25.
	The Regional Colleges Act, SS 1986-87-88, c R-8.1.
Provincial legislation providing degree-granting powers	*The University of Saskatchewan Act,* SS 1995, c U-6.1
	The University of Regina Act, RSS 1978, c U-5
	The Degree Authorization Act, SS 2012, c D-2.1 and associated regulations enable the government to extend degree-granting authority to postsecondary education institutions other than the University of Saskatchewan and the University of Regina. The Act

	was proclaimed in 2012 based on a quality assurance process. The Universities of Saskatchewan and Regina are exempt from the quality assurance process under the Act. The Act also restricts the use of the term "university."
	First Nations University of Canada Act, 2008. The First Nations University is a full member of the Association of Universities and Colleges of Canada (AUCC).
Provincial quality assurance mechanisms	Quality assurance mechanisms include legislation; affiliations and federations with institutions; credit transfer and articulation agreements on a case by case basis by institution and programs – no systemwide transfer system for either colleges or universities; external and internal institutional reviews; annual governing board reporting to ministry; professional accreditation of professional programs; membership in the (Canadian) Interprovincial Standards Red Seal Program, which offers quality assurance through standardized exams for provincial and territorial apprenticeship training and certification; and memberships in various organizations related to quality assurance including ACCC for colleges and Universities Canada (formerly the AUCC) for universities.
	The Saskatchewan Higher Education Quality Assurance Board evaluates new degree programs proposed by both in-province institutions (other than the two Saskatchewan universities) and out-of-province institutions. It was authorized by *The Degree Authorization Act,* 2012 to oversee a quality assurance review of institutions seeking degree-granting status in Saskatchewan.
Provincial coordinating or advisory bodies[a]	The Saskatchewan Higher Education Quality Assurance Board oversees the provincial quality assurance review process and provides its recommendations to government as to whether proposed new degree programs should be authorized.
	The Saskatchewan Apprenticeship and Trade Certification Commission creates, manages, and administers all apprenticeship training and certifications but does not deliver the programs. *The Apprenticeship and Trade Certification Act 1999* authorizes the Commission to manage the Apprenticeship and Trade Certification system.
Sources	Canadian Information Centre for International Credentials, "Learn about the Education System in the Province of Saskatchewan, Canada," http://cicic.ca/1164/Quality-assurance-practices-for-postsecondary-institutions-in-Saskatchewan/index.canada
	CMEC, *Postsecondary Education Systems in Canada*
	Government of Saskatchewan, "Degree-Granting in Saskatchewan," http://www.ae.gov.sk.ca/degree-granting
	Saskatchewan Higher Education Quality Assurance, http://www.quality-assurance-sk.ca/

Nova Scotia	
Ministry responsible for postsecondary education	The Department of Labour and Advanced Education is responsible for PSE. The Department of Education and Early Childhood Development is responsible for private training institutions. The Minister of Labour and Workforce Development is responsible for the general supervision and management of apprenticeship training.
Sectors and types of institutions	The PSE system has universities and university-colleges, colleges, apprenticeship training programs, and private training institutions including: • 11 publicly supported degree-granting institutions • 1 provincewide community college (the Nova Scotia Community College) with 13 campuses
Provincial legislation and documents organizing the system	*Apprenticeship and Trades Qualifications Act*, 2003, c 1, s 1, amended 2006, c 23 and regulations *Community Colleges Act, 1995-96*, c 4, s 1, amended 2002, c 31, s 13; 2010, c 2, ss 93-95 *Degree Granting Act*, RS, c 123, s 1, amended 2006, c 26 *Degree Granting Act, Degree-Granting Institution Authorizing Regulations*, NS Reg. 388/2008 *Maritime Provinces Higher Education Commission Act, 2004*, SNS 2004, c 30 *Private Career Colleges Regulation Act, 1998*, c 23, s 1 and General Regulations *University Foundations Act, 1991*, c 8, s 1 and Regulations *Adult Learning Act*, 2010, c 31
Provincial legislation constituting institutions	Individual university Acts constitute each university or university-college. The *Community Colleges Act*, c 4 of the Acts of 1995-96 as amended by 2002, c 31, s 13; 2010, c 2, ss 93-95; 2014, c 3, ss 16-26, established the Nova Scotia Community College.
Provincial legislation providing degree-granting powers	*Degree Granting Act*, RSNS 1989, c 123, amended 2006, c 26 gives power to government to authorize degree granting. Universities and university-colleges offer degrees and are established through institutional charters/Acts.
Provincial quality assurance mechanisms	Quality assurance mechanisms consist of legislation, professional accreditation of programs leading to licensing in a trade or profession, internal self-study reviews and reporting of quality established by governing board of university, external reviews of quality by the Maritime Provinces Higher Education Commission (MPHEC) of all new programs and significant changes to programs,

MPHEC's monitoring of quality assessment procedures used by institutions, formal affiliations between various institutions (but no systematic provincewide process for conducting university credit transfers to and from colleges and universities), some articulation agreements that are program specific, membership in ACCC for colleges and Universities Canada (formerly the AUCC) for universities, and membership in the (Canadian) Interprovincial Standards Red Seal Program, which offers quality assurance through standardized exams for provincial and territorial apprenticeship training and certification.

The *Maritime Degree Level Qualifications Framework* sets out information on undergraduate and graduate degrees.

Under the *Community Colleges Act*, the minister is responsible for approving guidelines for conducting internal reviews of existing college programs. Approval of all new programs also rests with the minister. The minister may delegate this power. Colleges must submit annual reports and financial statements to the minster. The *Community Colleges Act* establishes a board of governors as the governing body of the college responsible for operations and management, programs of study, academic reporting, and cyclical operational reviews.

According to the Canadian Information Centre for International Credentials,

> The *Private Career Colleges Regulation Act* sets out requirements for the registration of private postsecondary training institutions in Nova Scotia. No private postsecondary training school may operate in the province unless it has a certificate of registration issued by the Department of Education and Early Childhood Development or exempt under the legislation. Through the regulations under the *Private Career Colleges Regulation Act*, the department has authority to prescribe the qualifications for instructors, entrance requirements for students, and impose industry standards for curriculum. The department also sets the parameters around professional development for instructors.

The Department of Education and Early Childhood Development requires detailed reporting from private career colleges and conducts annual reviews. See http://cicic.ca/1186/Quality-assurance-practices-for-postsecondary-institutions-in-Nova-Scotia/index.canada.

The Maritime Provinces Higher Education Commission (MPHEC) is a significant mechanism of quality assurance and system coordination. The MPHEC is an "agency of the Council of Maritime Premiers," including the ministers of education in New Brunswick, Nova Scotia, and Prince Edward Island. Its main functions are to monitor quality assurance, analyze data and information, facilitate cooperative action, promote regional programs, and provide specific services to one or more provinces or institutions as agreed to by the ministers. The commission focuses primarily on university education. See http://www.mphec.ca/about/mandateandact.aspx.

	The *Maritime Degree Level Qualifications Framework* is used within the Nova Scotia education system. It provides information on postsecondary undergraduate and graduate degree programs.
Provincial coordinating or advisory bodies[a]	The *Community Colleges Act* establishes college program advisory committees primarily composed of representatives from industry. The committees advise the college board of governors and make recommendations regarding new and existing programs of study.
	The Provincial Apprenticeship Board advises the minster on apprenticeship training and conducts research.
	According to the Maritime Provinces Higher Education Commission (MPHEC), "There are currently seventeen post-secondary institutions within the scope of the MPHEC, fifteen of which are publicly-funded universities. Of these fifteen, three (Cape Breton University, Dalhousie and Université Sainte-Anne) also offer college-level or technology-based certificate and diploma programs in addition to degree programs. The remaining two institutions (Holland College in Prince Edward Island and the Maritime College of Forest Technology in New Brunswick) offer primarily college-level programs." See http://www.mphec.ca/about/mandateandact.aspx.
	The Atlantic Apprenticeship Council shares common concerns and opportunities for apprenticeship programs in the four Atlantic provinces (Newfoundland and Labrador, New Brunswick, Nova Scotia, and Prince Edward Island). The council's priority is to adopt common standards for training in selected trade apprenticeship programs, including standards for curriculum development.
Sources	Canadian Information Centre for International Credentials, "Learn about the Education System in the Province of Nova Scotia, Canada," http://cicic.ca/1137/Nova-Scotia/index.canada
	CMEC, *Postsecondary Education Systems in Canada*
	Department of Labour and Advanced Education, http://novascotia.ca/lae/
	Maritime Provinces Higher Education Commission Act, http://nslegislature.ca/legc/statutes/marprhig.htm
	Maritime Provinces Higher Education Commission, http://www.mphec.ca/about/mandateandact.aspx
	Nova Scotia Legislation, http://novascotia.ca/lae/legislation/

Prince Edward Island	
Ministry responsible for postsecondary education	Department of Innovation and Advanced Learning
Sectors and types of institutions	The PSE system has universities, colleges, apprenticeship programming, and private training institutions, including: • 1 publicly funded university (University of Prince Edward Island, which includes the Atlantic Veterinary college) • 1 publicly funded community college (Holland College has 11 training centres throughout the province) • 1 publicly funded francophone community college (Collège Acadie Î.-P.-É.) • Private vocational training schools (career colleges) • 1 private degree-granting theology college (Maritime Christian College)
Provincial legislation and documents organizing the system	*University Act*, RSPEI 1974, c U-4, s 2; 1981, c 39, s 1; 1983, c 33, s 66 *Maritime Provinces Higher Education Commission Act*, 2002 c 34, RSPEI 1988, c M-2.01 [proclaimed Jan31/05] *Apprenticeship and Trades Qualifications Act*, 2012 RSPEI 1988, c A-15.2 [proclaimed Dec8/12] *Private Training Schools Act*, RSPEI 1988, c P-20.1
Provincial legislation constituting institutions	*University Act*, RSPEI 1974, c U-4, s 2; 1981, c 39, s 1; 1983, c 33, s 66 *Holland College Act*, RSPEI 1988, c H-6
Provincial legislation providing degree-granting powers	*University Act*, RSPEI 1974, c U-4, s 2; 1981, c 39, s 1; 1983, c 33, s 66, establishes the one university and prohibits other institutions from using the term "university."
Provincial quality assurance mechanisms	Quality assurance mechanisms consist of legislation, professional accreditation of programs leading to licensing in a trade or profession, internal self-study reviews and reporting of quality established by governing board of university, external reviews of quality by the Maritime Provinces Higher Education Commission (MPHEC) of all new programs and significant changes to programs, MPHEC's monitoring of quality assessment procedures used by institutions, articulation and transfer agreements and affiliations for Holland Colleges (but no systematic provincewide process for conducting university credit transfers), student and employer surveys for colleges, membership in ACCC for colleges and Universities Canada (formerly the AUCC) for universities, and membership in the (Canadian) Interprovincial Standards Red Seal

Program, which offers quality assurance through standardized exams for provincial and territorial apprenticeship training and certification. The *Maritime Degree Level Qualifications Framework* sets out information on undergraduate and graduate degrees.

The board of governors of Holland College is accountable to report annually to the minister. The board is responsible for the government, conduct, management, and control of the institution including educational policies and activities that relate to quality assurance in the following areas:

- courses of study
- standards of admission
- qualifications for diplomas
- examinations and examiners
- academic boards and committees
- recruitment of all employees including the president

Maritime Christian College offers only theology degrees. The college is governed by a board of directors and is not accountable to the Department of Innovation and Advanced Learning or other external organizations for program quality assurance.

Private vocational training schools (career colleges) are regulated under the *Private Training Schools Act*. The law requires that such schools be registered by the province. To become registered, a school must meet the requirements set out in the law regarding curriculum, learning resources, equipment, and instructors, and must also meet a number of administrative and management practices (student contract, fees, advertising, refunds, etc.). The law provides for enforcement of standards by the Department of Innovation and Advanced Learning's administrator of private training schools.

The Maritime Provinces Higher Education Commission (MPHEC) is a significant mechanism of quality assurance and system coordination. The MPHEC is an "agency of the Council of Maritime Premiers," including the ministers of education in New Brunswick, Nova Scotia, and Prince Edward Island. Its main functions are to monitor quality assurance, analyze data and information, facilitate cooperative action, promote regional programs, and provide specific services to one or more provinces or institutions as agreed to by the ministers. The commission focuses primarily on university education. See http://www.mphec.ca/about/mandateandact.aspx.

The *Maritime Degree Level Qualifications Framework* is used within the PEI education system. It provides information on postsecondary undergraduate and graduate degree programs.

Provincial coordinating or advisory bodies[a]	According to the Maritime Provinces Higher Education Commission (MPHEC), "there are currently seventeen post-secondary institutions within the scope of the MPHEC, fifteen of which are publicly-funded universities. Of these fifteen, three (Cape Breton University, Dalhousie and Université Sainte-Anne) also offer college-level or technology-based certificate and diploma programs in addition to degree programs. The remaining two institutions (Holland College in Prince Edward Island and the Maritime College of Forest Technology in New Brunswick) offer primarily college-level programs." See http://www.mphec.ca/about/mandateandact.aspx.
	The *Apprenticeship and Trades Qualifications Act* establishes the Department of Innovation and Advanced Learning as the authority responsible for apprenticeship matters. The Act requires that the government appoint a provincial apprenticeship board. The board's main function is to advise the minister of Innovation and Advanced Learning on labour market matters that relate to training and the certification of people in designated trades and occupations. In advising the minister, the board draws upon the expertise of various committees. See http://cicic.ca/1169/Quality-assurance-p.
	The Atlantic Apprenticeship Council (AAC) shares common concerns and opportunities for apprenticeship programs in the four Atlantic provinces (Newfoundland and Labrador, New Brunswick, Nova Scotia, and Prince Edward Island). AAC's priority is to adopt common standards for training in selected trade apprenticeship programs, including standards for curriculum development.
Sources	Canadian Information Centre for International Credentials, "Learn about the Education System in the Province of Prince Edward Island, Canada," http://cicic.ca/1139/Prince-Edward-Island/index.canada
	CMEC, *Postsecondary Education Systems in Canada*
	Department of Workforce and Advanced Learning, "Post Secondary and Continuing Education," http://www.gov.pe.ca/ial/index.php3?number=1027713&lang=E
	Maritime Provinces Higher Education Commission, http://www.mphec.ca/about/mandateandact.aspx

Northwest Territories	
Ministry responsible for postsecondary education	Department of Education, Culture and Employment
	The minister is responsible for establishing programs and courses and for determining college operational policies for Aurora College.
	The minister is responsible for apprenticeship training.
Sectors and types of institutions	The PSE system has colleges, apprenticeship programming, and private training institutions.
	1 publicly funded college, Aurora College, with 3 campuses and a network of 23 learning centres throughout the territory and numerous transfer agreements with PSE institutions in southern Canada, provides a wide range of postsecondary programming including university-level transfer, certificate, and diploma programs, prescribed degrees, adult education and literacy programs, skills development programs, trades training, educational assessment, and counselling.
	Some private vocational training institutions.
Provincial legislation and documents organizing the system	*Aurora College Act*, RSNWT 1988, c A-7
	Apprenticeship, Trade and Occupation Certification Act, SNWT 2010, c 13, in force since October 2012
Provincial legislation constituting institutions	*Aurora College Act*, RSNWT 1988, c A-7
Provincial legislation providing degree-granting powers	*Aurora College Act*, RSNWT 1988, c A-7
Provincial quality assurance mechanisms	A combination of legislation, professional accreditation of programs, internal and external reviews of programming, transfer agreements with southern universities, and membership in ACCC.
	The *Aurora College Act* gives the minister of education the authority to create a board of governors for the college. The board is responsible for the operations and management of the college and must report to the minister annually. Degree, diploma, and certificate programs are internally reviewed following a schedule approved by the board of governors. External review is conducted as deemed necessary by the ministry and external partners.
	Professional accreditation of programs leading to licensing in a trade or profession. NWT Education unit is a member of the (Canadian) Interprovincial Standards Red Seal Program, which offers quality assurance through standardized exams for provincial and territorial apprenticeship training and certification.

	The *Apprenticeship, Trade and Occupation Certification Act* establishes the Apprenticeship, Trade and Occupation Certification Board. The board's main function is to advise the minister of education on matters relating to training and the certification of people in designated trades and occupations. The Act also establishes the position of supervisor of Apprenticeship, Trade, and Occupation Certification with the authority over content, standards, program delivery, exams, and instructors' qualifications.
	The NWT Apprenticeship Review Board, made up of industry representatives and government, conducts accreditation reviews for all the trades training at Aurora College.
	No legislation requiring registration of private training institutions. Instead the Private Vocational Training Designation process offers consumer protection for students and identifies which programs in private vocational training institutions meet the criteria for eligibility for student financial assistance.
	As of 2013 there was no formal provincial qualifications framework in place for the NWT. However, degrees offered by Aurora College in partnership with southern universities are captured by the provincial framework where the southern university is located.
Provincial coordinating or advisory bodies[a]	The *Apprenticeship, Trade and Occupation Certification Act* establishes the Apprenticeship, Trade and Occupations Certification Board. The board's main function is to advise the minister of education on matters relating to training and the certification of people in designated trades and occupations.
Sources	Canadian Information Centre for International Credentials, "Learn about the Education System in the Northwest Territories, Canada," http://cicic.ca/1188/Postsecondary-education-in-the-Northwest-Territories/index.canada
	CMEC, *Postsecondary Education Systems in Canada*

Yukon	
Ministry responsible for postsecondary education	Department of Education (Advanced Education Branch of the Dept. of Education is responsible for postsecondary education)
Sectors and types of institutions	The PSE system has colleges, apprenticeship programming, and private vocational institutions. Yukon is working toward establishing a university. To that end the *Yukon College Act* was amended in 2009 to allow the college to offer degrees.
	Yukon College is the only public community college in the Yukon. It is multi-campus, and offers degree alone and in partnership with other southern universities (14 campuses across the Yukon).
	Some private trade schools.

Provincial legislation and documents organizing the system	*Yukon College Act*, RSY 2002, c 234; amended by SY 2009, c 12, establishes the only public community college in Yukon. *Apprentice Training Act*, RSY 2002, c 7 *Occupational Training Act*, RSY 2002, c 160 *Trades Schools Regulation Act*, RSY 2002, c 221
Provincial legislation constituting institutions	*Yukon College Act*, RSY 2002, c 234; amended by SY 2009, c 12, establishes the only public community college in Yukon.
Provincial legislation providing degree-granting powers	The *Yukon College Act*, RSY 2002, c 234; amended by SY 2009, c 12, provides authority for Yukon College to provide educational programs leading to certificates, diplomas, and degrees. Degrees are also granted in partnership with southern universities.
Provincial quality assurance mechanisms	A combination of legislation, professional accreditation of professional programs, internal and external reviews of programming, and membership in ACCC. The *Yukon College Act*, RSY 2002, c 234; amended by SY 2009, c 12, provides the authority and responsibility of the college's board of governors who report and are accountable directly to the minister of the Department of Education for the management and operations of the college. The board sets up the quality assurance processes within the college. The Academic Council of Yukon College under the *Yukon College Act* determines and regulates the college's policies with regard to the following: • admissions and registrations • terminations and withdrawals • transfer credit, advanced credit, and prior learning assessment and recognition • curriculum content for courses • student academic conduct and student appeals on academic matters • requirements for graduation • awards recognizing academic excellence Committees with college and community representation, set up by the president, conduct internal institutional reviews to approve new and significantly altered programs. The Department of Education conducts external reviews of some programs. Yukon's Advanced Education unit is a member of the (Canadian) Interprovincial Standards Red Seal Program, which offers quality assurance through standardized exams for provincial and territorial apprenticeship training and certification. Yukon College is a member of the ACCC, which promotes quality but does not audit quality assurance processes.

	Occupational Training Act, RSY 2002, c 160, establishes the government of Yukon as the authority for private occupational training. The Yukon government establishes boards or committees to advise and assist as needed on policy and procedures.
	Private trade schools must register with the government under the *Trades Schools Regulation Act,* RSY 2002, c 221.
	As of 2013 there was no formal provincial qualifications framework in place for the Yukon. However, degrees offered by Yukon College in partnership with southern universities are captured by the provincial framework where the southern university is located.
Provincial coordinating or advisory bodies[a]	*Apprentice Training Act,* RSY 2002, c 7, sets out the apprenticeship advisory board appointed by the government as the body responsible for apprenticeship training. The board advises the minister on certification and training in the trades.
	Yukon College is part of the BC Council on Admissions and Transfer (BCCAT), which creates the policy and processes that support articulation and student mobility in BC. Yukon College credits are transferrable to BC and Alberta institutions through BCCAT and through individual agreements to other institutions in Canada and the US.
Sources	Canadian Information Centre for International Credentials, "Learn about the Education System in the Yukon, Canada," http://cicic.ca/1159/Postsecondary-education-in-Yukon/index.canada
	CMEC, *Postsecondary Education Systems in Canada*
	Yukon College, "Academic Council," http://www.yukoncollege.yk.ca/about/pages/academic_council

Nunavut	
Ministry responsible for postsecondary education	Department of Education, minister of education is responsible for the postsecondary system in Nunavut.
	However, there is a separate minister, the minister of Nunavut Arctic College, who is responsible for the college, overseeing the establishment of programs and courses, and college operational policies.
	The minister of education is responsible for apprenticeship, trade and occupational training, and certification.
Sectors and types of institutions	PSE system has 1 college, and apprenticeship training programming.
	Nunavut Arctic College includes
	• 3 campuses
	• 25 community learning centres that have transfer and cooperative arrangements with southern institutions

	• Nunavut Research Institute (Iqaluit) • Nunavut Trades Training Centre (Rankin Inlet) In addition to providing university-level transfer, certificate, and diploma programs, the college provides adult education and literacy programs, skills development programs, trades training, educational assessment, and counselling. No private training institutions in Nunavut.
Provincial legislation and documents organizing the system	*The Nunavut Arctic College Act* , *Consolidation of Nunavut Arctic College Act,* RSNWT 1988, c A-7 as amended *Apprenticeship, Trade and Occupations Certification Act and Regulations,* RRNWT 1990, c A-8, as amended by R-024-98, R-039-98, R-077-98 *Consolidation of Occupational Training Agreements Act,* RSNWT 1988, c16 (Supp.) *Consolidation of Universities and Degree-Granting Institutions Act,* SNu 2008, c 15
Provincial legislation constituting institutions	*The Nunavut Arctic College Act,* RSNWT 1988, c A-7 as amended
Provincial legislation providing degree-granting powers	*Consolidation of Universities and Degree-Granting Institutions Act,* SNu 2008, c 15
Provincial quality assurance mechanisms	A combination of legislation, articulation agreements, professional accreditation of professional programs, board reporting, membership in ACCC, and internal reviews of programming including graduate and employer satisfaction surveys. Under the *Nunavut Arctic College Act,* the president of the board of governors for Nunavut Arctic College reports to the minister for approval of new programs and significant changes to existing programs. Nunavut Arctic College has articulation agreements with individual universities in a number of programs whereby the first two years of college programs can be taken and accredited by the universities. Nunavut Arctic College is a member of the (Canadian) Interprovincial Standards Red Seal Program, which offers quality assurance through standardized exams for provincial and territorial apprenticeship training and certification. Nunavut Arctic College is a member of the Association of Canadian Community Colleges (ACCC), which promotes quality but does not mandate quality assurance processes.

	As of 2013 there was no formal provincial qualifications framework in place for the Nunavut, nor is Nunavut part of a provincial transfer council. However, programs offered by Arctic College in partnership or cooperation with individual southern institutions would be captured by the provincial framework where the southern institution is located.
Provincial coordinating or advisory bodies[a]	There is no review organization outside of the Government of Nunavut to which the Nunavut Arctic College is formally accountable to ensure program quality. However, the *Apprenticeship, Trade and Occupations Certification Act* establishes a Nunavut Apprenticeship, Trade and Occupations Certification Board. The board's main function is to advise the minister of education on matters relating to training and the certification of people in designated trades and occupations.
Sources	Canadian Information Centre for International Credentials, "Learn about the Education System in Nunavut, Canada," http://cicic. ca/1183/Postsecondary-education-in-Nunavut/index.canada
	CMEC, *Postsecondary Education Systems in Canada*
	Nunavut Arctic College, http://www.arcticcollege.ca/en/ arctic-college-overview

Note: ACCC = Association of Canadian Community Colleges. AUCC = Association of Universities and Colleges of Canada. CMEC = Council of Ministers of Education, Canada.

BIBLIOGRAPHY

Works Cited

Adell, B. "Establishment of Faculty Collective Bargaining: The Developing Law." In *Universities and the Law*, edited by P. Thomas. Winnipeg: University of Manitoba Legal Research Institute, 1975.

Alberta Innovation and Advanced Education. "Credentials and Programs Offered in Alberta." http://eae.alberta.ca/post-secondary/credentials/definitions.aspx.

—. "Data Collection Applications for Post-Secondary Institutions." http://eae.alberta.ca/post-secondary/funding/supportsinstitutions/resources/data.aspx.

—. "Post-Secondary System." http://eae.alberta.ca/post-secondary.aspx.

—. "Roles and Mandates Policy Framework." http://eae.alberta.ca/post-secondary/policy/roles.aspx.

American Association of University Professors. "1940 Statement of Principles on Academic Freedom and Tenure with 1970 Interpretive Comments." October 2006. http://www.aaup.org/AAUP/pubsres/policydocs/contents/1940statement.htm.

Arthurs, H. "The Question of Legitimacy." In *Governments and Higher Education – The Legitimacy of Intervention*, edited by C. Watson, 3–16. Toronto: Higher Education Group, 1987.

Assembly of First Nations. *First Nations PSE Review*. Ottawa: Assembly of First Nations, 2000.

Association of Canadian Community Colleges. "Operating Principles." 2014. http://www.accc.ca/xp/index.php/en/about/strategic-plan-2013-2018/operatingprinciples.

Association of Universities and Colleges of Canada (AUCC). "About Quality Assurance." Accessed July 31, 2013. http://www.aucc.ca/about-us/what-we-do/.

—. "About Us." 2014. http://www.aucc.ca/about-us/what-we-do/.

—. "Back to School – Quick Facts." October 2012. http://www.aucc.ca/wp-content/uploads/2012/09/quick-facts-back-to-school-2012.pdf.

—. "Canada's Universities Adopt New Statement on Academic Freedom." Media release, October 25, 2011. http://www.aucc.ca/media-room/news-and-commentary/canadas-universities-adopt-new-statement-on-academic-freedom.

—. *Momentum: The 2008 Report on University Research and Knowledge Mobilization*. Ottawa. 2008. Ottawa: AUCC, 2008. http://www.aucc.ca/wp-content/uploads/2011/05/momentum_2008.pdf.

—. "Our Universities." 2013. http://www.aucc.ca/canadian-universities.

Axelrod, P., T. Shanahan, R. Wellen, and R. Desai Trilokekar. "The Politics of Policy-making in Postsecondary Education in Canada and the Province of Ontario, 1990–2000." In *University Governance and Reform: Policy, Fads and Experience in International Perspective*, edited by H.G. Schuetze, W. Bruneau and G. Grosjean, 77–95. London: Palgrave, Macmillan, 2012.

Axelrod, P., T. Shanahan, R. Desai Trilokekar, R. Wellen. "People, Processes and Policy-Making in Canadian Post-secondary Education." *Higher Education Policy* 24, no. 2 (Spring 2011): 43–66.

Bakvis, H. and G. Skogstad, eds. *Canadian Federalism: Performance, Effectiveness and Legitimacy*. 2nd ed. Toronto: Oxford University Press, 2008.

Bakvis, H. "The Knowledge Economy and Postsecondary Education: Federalism in Search of a Metaphor." In *Canadian Federalism: Performance, Effectiveness and Legitimacy*, 2nd ed. Edited by H. Bakvis and G. Skogstad, 205–22. Toronto: Oxford University Press, 2008.

Berkowitz, P. "University Senate – Is It Still Useful?" Accessed January 10, 2011. http://www.universityaffairs.ca/university-senate-it-it-still-useful.aspx.

Berkowitz, P. "U-15 Begins to Formalize Its Organization." *University Affairs* 53, no. 7 (2012): 33–34.

Birtwistle, T. "Academic Freedom and Complacency: The Possible Effects If 'Good Men Do Nothing.'" *Education and the Law* 16, no. 4 (2004): 203, 205.

Blake, S. *Administrative Law in Canada*. 4th ed. Markham, ON: LexisNexis/Butterworths, 2006.

Boggs, A. "Ontario's Royal Commission on the University of Toronto, 1905–06: Political and Historical Factors That Influenced the Final Report of the Flavelle Commission." Master's thesis, OISE, University of Toronto, 2007.

Bourgeois, D.J. *The Law of Charitable and Not-for-Profit Organizations*. 3rd ed. Markham, ON: Butterworths, 2002.

Bowden, R. "Evolution of Responsibility: From 'In Loco Parentis' to 'Ad Meliora Vertamur.'" *Education* 127, no. 4 (2007): 480–89.

Boychuk, G.W. "Differences of Degrees: Higher Education in the American States and Canadian Provinces." *Canadian Public Administration* 43, no. 4 (2008): 453–72.

Bradshaw, J. "Independent Panel to Be Struck to Review Concordia Governance." *Globe and Mail*, February 22, 2011, A4.

Bridge, J.W. "Keeping Peace in the Universities: The Role of the Visitor." *The Law Quarterly Review* 86 (1970): 550.

British Columbia. Ministry of Advanced Education. "B.C. Post-Secondary Education – Overview." http://www.aved.gov.bc.ca/publicpsed/welcome.htm.

—. *Capital Asset Reference Guide – Version 1.2*. March 31, 2014. Victoria: Ministry of Advanced Education. http://www.aved.gov.bc.ca/cppm/documents/carg-2014/carg.pdf.

Brock University Faculty Association. "About Us." 2014. https://www.bufa.ca/show_content.php?id=23.

Broster, R., and K. Brien. "Cyber-Bullying of Educators by Students: Evolving Legal and Policy Developments." *Education and Law Journal* 20, no. 1 (2010): 35–61.

Brown, D.J.M, and D.M. Beatty. *Canadian Labour Arbitration*. 4th ed. (looseleaf). Aurora, ON: Canada Law Book, 1996. http://www.carswell.com/product-detail/canadian-labour-arbitration-fourth-edition/.

Brown, D. "Fiscal Federalism: Searching for Balance in Fiscal Federalism." In *Canadian Federalism: Performance, Effectiveness and Legitimacy*. 2nd ed. Edited by H. Bakvis and G. Skogstad, 63–88. Toronto: Oxford University Press, 2008.

Brown, D.M. "Are Private Schools Really Private? Judicial Review of Discipline Decisions in Private Schools." *Education and Law Journal* 8 (1996–1998): 453–70.

Burke-Robertson, J. *Primer for Directors of Not-for-Profit Corporations*. Ottawa: Industry Canada, 2002.

Cameron, D. *More than an Academic Question: Universities, Government and Public Policy in Canada*. Halifax: Institute for Research on Public Policy, 1991.

Cameron, D.M. "The Federal Perspective." In *Higher Education in Canada: Different Systems Different Perspectives*, edited by G.A. Jones, 9–29. New York: Garland Publishing, 1997.

Canada Revenue Agency. "Unincorporated Business Trust Organization." Technical Interpretation No. 9616675, September 27, 1996.

—. "What Is a Related Business?" Registered Charities Policy Statement CPS-019, March 31, 2003.

Canadian Advisory Council on Science and Technology. "Public Investment in University Research: Reaping the Benefits." Report of the Expert Panel on the Commercialization of University Research, May 4, 1999. http://acst-ccst.gc.ca/canm/rpaper_html/report_4_e.html.

Canadian Association of University Business Officers. *Deferred Maintenance at Canadian Universities: An Update*. Guilford, CT: Sightlines, LLC, 2014. http://www.caubo.ca/sites/137.149.200.5.pilot/files/CAUBO_Deferred_Maintenance_2014.pdf.

Canadian Association of University Teachers. *CAUT Almanac of Post-Secondary Education in Canada*. Ottawa: Canadian Association of University Teachers, 2013.

—. "Faculty at Mount Allison, UNB Lack Confidence in Administration." *CAUT Bulletin* 61, no. 4 (2014): A1.

—. "Academic Freedom." Approved by the CAUT Council November 2011. http://www.caut.ca/about-us/caut-policy/lists/caut-policy-statements/policy-statement-on-academic-freedom.

—. "Minister Rapped for Reaping the Benefits." *CAUT Bulletin* 46, no. 5 (1999). Accessed April 28, 2015. https://www.cautbulletin.ca/en_article.asp?ArticleID=2228.

Canadian Association of University Teachers Council. "Policy Statement on Tenure." November 2005. http://archive.caut.ca/pages.asp?page=455&lang=1.

Canadian Council on Learning. *Navigating Post-Secondary Education in Canada: The Challenges of a Changing Landscape*. 2010. http://www.ccl-cca.ca/CCL/Reports/Postseoncdary Education.

Canadian Federation of Students. Home page. 2014. http://cfs-fcee.ca/.

Canadian Information Centre for International Credentials. "Learn about Provincial and Territorial Education Systems in Canada." http://cicic.ca/851/Education/index.canada.

Canadian Millennium Scholarship Foundation. "Changing Course: Improving Aboriginal Access to Post-Secondary Education in Canada." Millennium

Research Note #2, September 2005. http://www.millenniumscholarships.ca/images/Publications/mrn-changing-course-en.pdf.

CBC News. "Ilene Busch-Vishniac, Former University of Saskatchewan President, Sues over Dismissal." June 3, 2015. http://www.cbc.ca/news/canada/saskatoon/ilene-busch-vishniac-former-university-of-saskatchewan-president-sues-over-dismissal-1.3099250?cmp=rss.

Charbonneau, L. "A Meeting of Minds in Montreal." *University Affairs* 52, no. 9 (2011): 10–15.

Charbonneau, L. "Research Vice-Presidents of Smaller Canadian Universities Form New Alliance." *University Affairs* 52, no. 8 (2011): 27–29.

Charbonneau, L. "SFU Becomes a Full Member of U.S. Sports Body NCAA." *University Affairs* 53, no. 9 (2012): 7.

Cheshire, G. *Modern Law of Real Property*. 10th ed. London: Butterworths, 1967.

Chew, P.K. "Faculty-Generated Inventions: Who Owns the Golden Egg?" *Wisconsin Law Review*, no. 2 (1992): 259–314.

Chewter, C. "Justice in the University: Legal Avenues for Students." *Dalhousie Journal of Legal Studies* 3 (1994): 105–36.

Chin, J. "Sheridan College Brings Council Up to Speed." *Mississauga.com*, April 16, 2010. http://www.mississauga.com/news/article/801489--sheridan-college-brings-council-up to-speed.

Commission d'évaluation de l'enseignement collegial. *Evaluating the Effectiveness of Quality Assurance Systems in Québec Colleges: Guidelines and Framework*. Quebec City: Government of Quebec, 2013. http://www.ceec.gouv.qc.ca/publications/anglais/Effectiveness_Quality_Assurance_Orientation_Framework_2013.pdf

Commission on the Financing of Higher Education (Bladen Commission). *Financing Higher Education in Canada*. Toronto, University of Toronto Press, 1965.

Council of Ministers of Education, Canada (CMEC). "About." http://www.cmec.ca/11/About/index.html.

—. *Best Practices in Increasing Aboriginal Postsecondary Enrolment Rates*. May 2002. Report prepared by R.A. Malatest & Associates, Victoria. http://www.cmec.ca/postsec/malatest.en.pdf.

—. *Education in Canada: An Overview*. Toronto: CMEC, 2008.

—. *Ministerial Statement on Quality Assurance of Degree Education in Canada*. Toronto: CMEC, 2007.

—. *Postsecondary Education Systems in Canada: An Overview*. Toronto: Canadian Information Centre for International Credentials, 2009.

—. *Postsecondary Education Systems in Canada: Provinces and Territories*. Toronto: Canadian Information Centre for International Credentials, 2009.

—. *Postsecondary Education Systems in Canada: Provinces and Territories*. Toronto: Canadian Information Centre for International Credentials, 2013.

Council of Ontario Universities. *Quality Assurance Framework*. Toronto: Council of Ontario Universities, 2010.

Crocker, B. "The Legal Relationship between Universities/Colleges and Students." In *Universities and Colleges and the Law: Not All You Need to Know*. Ottawa: Canadian Society for the Study of Higher Education, 1987.

Dennison, J., and P. Gallagher. *Canada's Community Colleges*. Vancouver: University of British Columbia Press, 1986.

Desai Trilokekar, R., T. Shanahan, P. Axelrod, and R. Wellen. "Making Postsecondary Education Policy: Toward a Conceptual Understanding." In *Making*

Policy in Turbulent Times: Challenges and Prospects for Higher Education, edited by P. Axelrod, T. Shanahan, R. Desai Trilokekar, and R. Wellen, 33–59. Montreal: McGill-Queen's University Press, 2013.

Devine, S.M. "Fair Procedures for Students in Universities and Colleges." In *Universities and Colleges and the Law: Not All You Need to Know*. Ottawa: Canadian Society for the Study of Higher Education, 1987.

Dickerson, D. "Cyber Bullies on Campus." *University of Toledo Law Review* 37, no. 1 (2005): 51–74.

Dickinson, G.M. "A Criminal Trial by Any Other Name." *Education and Law Journal* 7 (1996): 149–54.

—. "Academic Autonomy and Legal Prescription: An Investigation of the Intrusion of Law into Decision-making within Universities." PhD diss., University of Toronto, 1988.

Dobbie, D., and I. Robinson. "Reorganizing Higher Education in the United States and Canada: The Erosion of Tenure and the Unionization of Contingent Faculty." *Labor Studies Journal* 33, no. 2 (2008): 117–40. http://www-personal.umich.edu/~eian/Reorg_Higher_Ed_LSJ.pdf.

Donald, J. (1997). "Higher Education in Quebec: 1945–1995." In *Higher Education in Canada: Different Systems, Different Perspectives*, edited by G.A. Jones, 161–88. New York and London: Garland Publishing, 1997.

Edwards, R. "Historical Background of the English Language CEGEPs of Quebec." *McGill Journal of Education* 25, no. 2 (1990): 147–74.

Farrington, D.J., and D. Palfreyman. *The Law of Higher Education*. Oxford: Oxford University Press, 2006.

Federation of Law Societies of Canada. "Federation Grants Preliminary Approval of Trinity Western University's Proposed Law Program." News release, December 16, 2013. http://flsc.ca/federation-grants-preliminary-approval-of-trinity-western-universitys-proposed-law-program-2/.

Finance Quebec. *A Fair and Balanced University Funding Plan*. Quebec City: Government of Quebec, 2011. http://www.budget.finances.gouv.qc.ca/Budget/2011-2012/en/documents/Educationen.pdf.

Fisher, D., and K. Rubenson. "The Changing Political Economy: The Public and Private Lives of Canadian Universities." In *Universities and Globalization: Critical Perspectives*, edited by J. Currie and J. Newson, 77–98. Thousand Oakes: Sage, 1998.

Fisher, D., K. Rubenson, R. Clift, M. MacIvor, J. Meredith, T. Shanahan, G. Jones, C. Trottier, and J. Bernatchez. *Canadian Federal Policy and Postsecondary Education*. Vancouver: Centre for Policy Studies in Higher Education and Training, 2005.

Fisher, D., K. Rubenson, T. Shanahan, and C. Trottier, eds. *The Development of Postsecondary Education Systems in Canada: A Comparison between British Columbia, Ontario and Quebec, 1980–2010*. Montreal: McGill-Queen's University Press, 2014.

Fisher, D., K. Rubenson, J. Lee, R. Clift, M. MacIvor, and J. Meredith. "British Columbia." In *The Development of Postsecondary Education Systems in Canada: A Comparison between British Columbia, Ontario and Quebec, 1980–2010*, edited by D. Fisher, K. Rubenson, T. Shanahan, and C. Trottier, 35–121. Montreal: McGill-Queen's University Press, 2014.

Garner, B.A., ed. *Black's Law Dictionary*. 4th ed. St. Paul, MN: West Publishing, 1996.

—, ed. *Black's Law Dictionary*. 9th ed. St. Paul, MN: West Publishing, 2009.

Government of Alberta. *A Learning Alberta: Quality in Alberta's Advanced Education System.* Edmonton: Business Policy and Analysis Branch, Alberta Advanced Education, 2005. http://eae.alberta.ca/media/134943/quality.pdf.

—. *Public Agencies Governance Framework.* Edmonton: Government of Alberta, 2008.

—. *Roles and Mandates Policy Framework for Alberta's Publicly Funded Advanced Education System.* Edmonton: Advanced Education and Technology, 2007.

Government of Canada. *Budget.* Ottawa: Department of Finance, 1998.

—. *Budget.* Ottawa: Department of Finance, 2007.

—. "Canada Excellence Research Chairs." Last modified February 20, 2014. http://www.cerc.gc.ca/home-accueil-eng.aspx at www.serc.gc.ca.

—. *Canadian Opportunities Strategy.* Ottawa: Department of Finance, 1998. Archived at http://fin.gc.ca/budget98/pamph/edupa-eng.asp.

—. "History of Health and Social Transfers." Department of Finance, Canada. Accessed July 25, 2013. http://www.fin.gc.ca/fedprov/his-eng.asp/.

—. *The Next Phase of Canada's Action Plan: A Low-Tax Plan tor Jobs and Growth.* Ottawa: Public Works and Government Services Canada, 2011. http://www.budget.gc.ca/2011/plan/Budget2011-eng.pdf.

—. "Repayment Assistance Plan." Last modified November 20, 2014. http://www.canlearn.ca.

—. *Report of the Royal Commission on National Development in the Arts, Letters and Sciences, 1949–1951* (Massey Commission). Ottawa: King's Printer, 1951. http://www.collectionscanada.gc.ca/2/5/h5-400-e.html.

—. *Royal Commission on Canada's Economic Prospects: Final Report.* Ottawa, Queen's Printer, 1958. http://www.archivescanada.ca/english/search/RouteRqst.asp?sessionKey=999999999_142&r=2&i=NA&l=0&v=0&coll=0&lvl=1&t=Royal+Commission+on+Canada%27s+Economic+Prospects.

Government of Ontario. *Ontario's Differentiation Policy Framework for Postsecondary Education.* Toronto: Government of Ontario, 2013. http://www.tcu.gov.on.ca/pepg/publications/PolicyFramework_PostSec.pdf.

—. *Private Career Colleges (PCC): Operating a Private Career College in Ontario.* Toronto: Ministry of Training, Colleges and Universities, 2014. http://www.tcu.gov.on.ca/pepg/audiences/pcc/operate.html.

—. *Royal Commission on the University of Toronto, 1905–06* (Flavelle Commission). Toronto: Government of Ontario.

Gregor, A.D. "Introduction: Higher Education in Canada." In *Higher Education in Canada,* edited by A.D. Gregor and G. Jasmin, 7–13. Ottawa: Minister of Supply and Services, 1992.

Hackett, R., and A. Pullman. "Faculty Unionization: What Difference Does It Make?" Accessed May 18, 2011. http://sfufa.ca/UnionizationMagazineArticle.pdf.

Hamilton, M. "Lessons Still to Be Learned: Fairness in Academic Discipline Proceedings." *Education Law Journal* 18, no. 3 (2009): 221–47.

Hannah, D.A. "Law Is a Many-Splendoured Thing: A Brief History and Overview of Student-Institution Legal Relationships in Canada." *Communique ICJ* 6, no 3 (2006): 26–32.

—. *Postsecondary Students and the Courts in Canada: Cases and Commentary from the Common Law Provinces.* Asheville, NC: College Administration Publications, 1998.

—. "Student-Institution Legal Relationships in Colleges and Universities in the Common Provinces of Canada: An Analysis of the Case Law from 1982 to 1994." PhD diss., Bowling Green State University, 1996.

Harassment Task Force of the Ontario Council of Regents in its *Report on Harassment and Discrimination in Ontario Colleges of Applied Arts and Technology*. May 1992. Toronto.

Harris, R.S., ed. *Changing Patterns of Higher Education in Canada*. Toronto: University of Toronto Press, 1986.

—. *A History of Higher Education in Canada 1663–1960*. Toronto: University of Toronto Press, 1976.

Henchey, N., and D.A. Burgess. *Between Past and Future: Quebec Education in Transition*. Calgary: Detselig, 1987.

Henderson, C. "Searching for 'Government Action': Post-Secondary Education as a Case Study in the Conceptual Weakness of the Charter's Government Action Doctrine." *Education and Law Journal* 15, no. 3 (2006): 233–62.

Hodges, L. "Fear Is the Key to Naming and Shaming." *The Independent*, June 11, 1998. Accessed February 27, 2011. http://www.independent.co.uk/life-style/fear-is-the-key-to-naming-and-shaming-1164120.html.

Hoekstra, G. "A Behind the Scenes Look at Development That Could Change P.G.'s Downtown Core." *The Prince George Citizen*, October 12, 2010. http://www.princegeorgecitizen.com/article/20101012/PRINCE GEORGE0101/310089938/-1/PRINCEGEORGE/a-behind-the-scenes-look-at-development-that-could-change-pg-39-s.

Hogg, P.W. *Constitutional Law of Canada*. Toronto: Thomson Carswell, 2005.

Horn, M. *Academic Freedom in Canada: A History*. Toronto: University of Toronto Press, 1999.

Human Resources and Skills Development Canada. "Canada Student Grants Program." Accessed July 31, 2013. http://www.hrsdc.gc.ca/eng/learning/canada_student_loan/cgsp.html.

Indian and Northern Affairs Canada. "Canada's Statement of Support on the United Nations Declaration on the Rights of Indigenous Peoples." Media release, November 12, 2010. http://www.ainc-inac.gc.ca/ap/ia/dcl/stmt-eng.asp.

Irvine, T. "The Queen's Bench Act, 1998: Old Wine in New Bottles." *Saskatchewan Law Review* 66 (2003): 63–126.

Janisch, H.N. "Educational Malpractice: Legal Liability for Failure to Educate." *Advocate* 38 (1980): 491–501.

Jones, C. "Immunizing Universities from Charter Review: Are We 'Contracting Out' Censorship?" *University of New Brunswick Law Journal* 52 (2003): 261–76.

Jones, D.P., and A.S. de Villars. *Principles of Administrative Law*. 2nd ed. Toronto: Carswell, 1994.

—. *Principles of Administrative Law*. 5th ed. Toronto: Carswell, 2009.

Jones, G.A. "A Brief Introduction to Higher Education in Canada." In *Higher Education in Canada: Different Systems, Different Perspectives*, edited by G.A. Jones, 1–8. New York: Garland, 1997.

—. "Canada." In *International Handbook of Higher Education*, edited by J.K. Forest and P.G. Altbach. Dondrecht, The Netherlands: Kluwer Academic Publishers, 2004.

—. "Canada." In *International Handbook of Higher Education*. Vol. 18. Edited by J. Forest and P. Altbach. Netherlands: Springer, 2011.

—. "Governments, Governance, and Canadian Universities." In *Higher Education Handbook of Theory and Research*. Vol. 11. Edited by J.C. Smart, 337–71. New York: Agathon Press, 1996.

—, ed. *Higher Education in Canada: Different Systems, Different Perspectives*. New York and London: Garland Publishing, 1997.

—. "Sectors, Institutional Types and the Challenges of Shifting Categories: A Canadian Commentary." *Higher Education Quarterly* 63, no. 4 (2009): 371–83.

—. "The Structure of University Governance in Canada: A Policy Network Approach." In *Governing Higher Education: National Perspectives on Institutional Governance*, edited by A. Amaral, G.A. Jones, and B. Karseth, 213–34. Dordrecht, The Netherlands: Kluwer Academic Publishers, 2002.

Jones, G.A., T. Shanahan, and P. Goyan. "Traditional Governance Structures – Current Policy Pressures: The Academic Senate and Canadian Universities." *Tertiary Education and Management* 8, no. 1 (2002): 29–45.

—. "University Governance in Canadian Higher Education." *Tertiary Education and Management* 7, no. 7 (2001): 135–48.

Jones, G.A., and M. Skolnik. "Governing Boards in Canadian Universities." *The Review of Higher Education* 20, no. 3 (1997): 277–95.

Kaplin, W.A., and B.A. Lee. *The Law of Higher Education*. 4th ed. San Francisco: John Wiley & Sons, 2007.

Kaplin, W.A. "Law on the Campus 1960–1985: Years of Growth and Challenge." *Journal of College and University Law* 12 (1985): 269–99.

Khan, A. "British Universities: Visitor's Jurisdiction." *Journal of Law and Education* 22 (1993): 197-208.

Klassen, T. "Quality Assurance in Ontario's Postsecondary Education Sector." *College Quarterly* 15, no. 3 (2012). http://collegequarterly.ca/2012-vol15-num03-summer/klassen.html.

Kulkarni, S.R. "All Professors Create Equally: Why Faculty Should Have Complete Control over the Intellectual Property Rights in Their Creations." *Hastings Law Journal* 47 (November 1995): 221–56.

La Forest, A.W. *Anger & Honsberger Law of Real Property*. 3rd ed. Aurora, ON: Canada Law Book, 2010.

—. "Domestic Application on International Law in Charter Cases: Are We There Yet?" *UBC Law Review* 37 (2004): 157–218.

Lai, A. "Grades Matter: Toward a Holistic Proposal for Academic Evaluations of Students in Public and Private Higher Educational Institutions." *Education and Law Journal* 21 (2001): 21–47.

Lape, L. "Ownership of Copyrightable Works of University Professors: The Interplay between the Copyright Act and University Copyright Policies." *Villanova Law Review* 37 (1992): 223–72.

LaRoche, K., C. Collard, and J. Chernys. "Appropriating Innovation: The Enforceability of University Intellectual Property Policies." *Intellectual Property Journal* 20 (May 2007): 135–175.

Law Society of British Columbia. "Bencher Meeting Consideration of TWU, April 11, 2014." https://www.lawsociety.bc.ca/page.cfm?cid=3891.

—. "Highlights." https://www.lawsociety.bc.ca/newsroom/highlights.cfm.

—. "Treasurer's Statement regarding Vote on TWU Law School." News archives, 2014. http://www.lsuc.on.ca/newsarchives.aspx?id=2147485737&cid=2147498273.

—. "Trinity Western University: Proposed Law School." Updated July 21, 2015. https://www.lawsociety.bc.ca/page.cfm?cid=3912&t=Special-General-Meeting-June-10,-2014&loc=banner.

Lazar, H. "The Social Union Framework Agreement and Canadian Fiscal Federalism." In *Canada: The State of the Federation, 1999–2000: In Search of a New Mission Statement for Canadian Fiscal Federalism*, edited by H. Lazar. Kingston: Institute for Intergovernmental Relations, 2000.

Leas, T. "Higher Education, the Courts and the 'Doctrine' of Academic Abstention." *Journal of Law and Education* 20, no. 2 (1991): 135–5.

Leskovac, H. "Academic Freedom and the Quality of Sponsored Research on Campus." *Review of Litigation* 13 (Summer 1994): 401–424.

Lewis, C.B. "The Legal Nature of a University and the Student-University Relationship." *Ottawa Law Review* 15 (1983): 249–73.

Likins, J.M. "Six Factors in the Changing Relationship between Institutions of Higher Education and the Courts." *Journal of the National Association for Women Deans, Administrators, and Counselors* 42, no. 2 (1979): 17–23.

MacFee Rogers, I. *Canadian Law of Planning and Zoning*. 2nd ed. Toronto: Carswell, 2005.

—. *The Law of Canadian Municipal Corporations*. 2nd ed. Toronto: Carswell, 2009.

MacKay, W. "Canadian Charter of Rights and Freedoms: A Springboard to Students Rights." *Windsor Yearbook Access to Justice* 4 (1984): 174–228.

MacKay, W. *Education Law in Canada*. Toronto: Edmond-Montgomery, 1984.

MacKinnon, P. "What Do We Mean When We Talk about Academic Freedom?" *University Affairs*, September 12, 2011. http://www.universityaffairs.ca/what-do-we-mean-when-we-talk-about-academic-freedom.aspx.

Magnusson, R. *A Brief History of Québec Education: From New France to Parti Quebecois*. Montreal: Harvest House, 1980.

Major, M.-F. "American Campus Speech Codes: Models for Canadian Universities?" *Education and Law Journal* 7 (1995–1996): 13–47.

Maritime Provinces Higher Education Commission. "Maritime Degree Level Qualifications Framework." http://www.mphec.ca/resources/DegreeLevelFrameworkEn.pdf.

—. "The Maritime Provinces Higher Education Commission Mandate." http://www.mphec.ca/about/mandateandact.aspx.

Marshall, D. "Degree Accreditation in Canada." Paper presented at the annual conference of the International Consortium for Education and Economic Development, Cancún, Mexico, February 18–21, 2004. http://www.mtroyal.ca/cs/groups/public/documents/pdf/degreeaccredincanada.pdf.

—. "Differentiation by Degree: System Design and the Changing Undergraduate Environment in Canada." *Canadian Journal of Higher Education* 38, no. 3 (2008): 1–20.

McCormack, N., and M. Bueckert. *Introduction to the Law and Legal System of Canada*. Toronto: Carswell, 2013.

McGill University Health Centre. "A Public-Private Partnership (PPP)." http://muhc.ca/new-muhc/page/winning-partnership-ppp.

McMullen, K. "Tuition Fee Deregulation: Who Pays?" *Education Matters* 3, no. 1 (2006). http://wwwstatscan.gc.ca/pub/81-004-x/2006001/9183-eng.htm.

McRoberts, K. "Federal Structures and the Policy Process." In *Governing Canada: Institutions and Public Policy*, edited by M.M. Atkinson, 140–79. Toronto: Harcourt Brace Jovanovich, 1993.

Mendelson, M. *Aboriginal Peoples and Postsecondary Education in Canada*. Ottawa: Caledon Institute of Social Policy, 2006.

Metcalfe, A. "Academic Capitalism in Canada: No Longer the Exception." *Journal of Higher Education* 81, no. 5 (July/August 2010): 489–514.

Milan, R., and M. Hicks. *Ontario Private Career Colleges: An Exploratory Analysis*. Toronto: Higher Education Quality Council of Ontario, 2014. http://www.heqco.ca/SiteCollectionDocuments/PCC%20ENG.pdf.

Mix-Ross, D.B. "Exploring the Charter's Horizons: Universities, Free Speech, and the Role of Constitutional Rights in Private Legal Relations." Master's thesis, University of Toronto, 2009.

Monotti, A.L. "The Legal Issues: Patenting and Technology Transfer." Presentation at the Intellectual Property Forum 2003 on the theme The Commercial Exploitation of Academic Science: A Contradiction? Oxford Intellectual Property Research Centre, Oxford, April, 25, 2003.

Monotti, A.L., and S. Ricketson. *Universities and Intellectual Property, Ownership and Exploitation*. Oxford: Oxford University Press, 2003.

Mullen, D.J. "The Universities and the Principles and Remedies of Public Law Case Comment: Vonogradov v. Univ. of Calgary." *Administrative Law Reports* 25, 1st Series (1991): 212.

Mullens, A. "When Students Sue." *University Affairs* 49, no. 5 (May 2008): 23–26.

National Association of Career Colleges. Home page. http://www.nacc.ca.

Networks of Centres of Excellence of Canada. Home page. http://www.nce-rce.gc.ca/Index_eng.asp.

Newson, J. "The Decline of Faculty Influence: Confronting the Effects of the Corporate Agenda." In *Fragile Truths: Twenty-Five Years of Sociology and Anthropology in Canada*, edited by W. Carroll, L. Christianson Ruffman, R. Currie, and D. Harrison, 227–46. Ottawa: Carleton University Press, 1992.

Nova Scotia Barrister's Society. "Council Votes for Option C in Trinity Western University Law School Decision." 2014. http://nsbs.org/news/2014/04/council-votes-option-c-trinity-western-university-law-school-decision.

Ontario. Ministry of Research and Innovation. "Strategic Plan." November 2006. Government of Ontario, Toronto.

Ontario. Ministry of the Environment. "Environmental Assessments." Government of Ontario. http://www.ontario.ca/environment-and-energy/environmental-assessments.

Organisation for Economic Co-operation and Development (OECD). *Education at a Glance: OECD Indicators, 2012*. Paris: OECD, 2012.

—. *Education at a Glance: OECD Indicators, 2012. Country Note: Canada*. Paris: OECD, 2012.

Ouellette, Y. "Le Contrôle Judiciaire sur l'Université." *Canadian Bar Review* 48 (1970): 631–50.

Papillon, M. "Canadian Federalism and the Emerging Mosaic of Aboriginal Multilevel Governance." In *Canadian Federalism: Performance, Effectiveness and Legitimacy*. 2nd ed. Edited by H. Bakvis and G. Skogstad, 291–313. Toronto: Oxford University Press, 2008.

Paquette, J., and G. Fallon. *First Nations Education Policy in Canada: Progress or Gridlock?* Toronto: University of Toronto Press, 2010.

Pettigrew, T. "Why Universities Should Just Say No to Expensive Varsity Athletics." *University Affairs*, March 26, 2014.

Petraglia, P. "The University Visitor." *Administrative Law Journal* 4, no. 2 (1988): 25–31.

Pochini, K. "Managing Risk of Violence in the Post-Secondary Educational Environment." *Education Law Journal* 18 (2008): 146–73.

Potts, D.J. "Universities and Housing: Applying Lessons Learned." Paper presented at the Canadian Institute's 5th National Summit on Creating and Enforcing Municipal By-laws, September 23–24, 2010.

Reidhaar, D.L. "The Assault on the Citadel: Reflections on a Quarter Century of Change in the Relationships between the Student and the University." *Journal of College and University Law* 12, no. 3 (1985): 343–61.

Répertoire du patrimoine culturel du Québec. "About Répertoire du patrimoine culturel du Québec." Ministère de la Culture, des Communications et de la Condition féminine. http://www.mcccf.gouv.qc.ca/index.php?id=2160#c20738.

Rhoades, G. "Whose Property Is It? Negotiating with the University." *Academe* 87, no. 5 (2001): 38–43.

Rigakos, G.S., and D.R. Greener. "Bubbles of Governance: Private Policing and the Law in Canada." *Canadian Journal of Law and Society* 15, no. 1 (2000): 145–85.

Robinson, B.M. "University of Pin-Stripes, Test Tubes, and Patents: Is the Commercialization of University Research Consistent with the Fundamental Tenets of the Patent Act?" *University of Ottawa Law and Technology Journal* 3 (2006): 385–420.

Robinson, D. *The Status of Higher Education Teaching Personnel in Australia, Canada, New Zealand, the United Kingdom, and the United States.* Report prepared for Education International, 2006.

Ross, M.G. *The University: The Anatomy of Academe.* New York: McGraw-Hill, 1976.

Ross, P. "University Technology Transfer: Public Dissemination or Commercial Exploitation – A Statutory Perspective." Unpublished LL.M. research paper, Osgoode Hall Law School, 2005.

Rowinski, J. "Municipal Consultation with First Nations: Evolving Law and Prudent Policy." In *Navigating a Rapidly Changing Municipal and Planning Law Landscape.* Toronto: Ontario Bar Association, 2008.

Royal Commission of Inquiry on Education in the Province of Quebec (Parent Comission). *Report of the Royal Commission of Inquiry on Education in the Province of Quebec.* Vol. 2. Quebec City: Government Press, 1963.

Royal Commission on the University of Toronto. *Report of the Royal Commission on the University of Toronto.* Chair, J.W. Flavelle. Toronto: King's Printer, 1906.

Russo, C.J. "Reflections on Education as a Fundamental Human Right." *Education Law Journal.* 20, no. 2 (2010): 87–105.

Savage, D.C. "Higher Education Organizations." In *Higher Education in Canada*, edited by A.D. Gregor and G. Jasmin, 27–35. Ottawa: Minister of Supply and Services, 1992.

Schrank, B. "Academic Freedom and University Speech Codes." *University of New Brunswick Law Journal* 44 (1995): 67–75.

Science, Technology and Innovation Council. *State of the Nation.* Ottawa: Government of Canada, 2013.

Shanahan, T., and G. Jones. "Shifting Roles and Approaches: Government Coordination of Post-secondary Education in Canada 1995–2006." *Higher Education Research and Development* 26, no.1 (2007): 31–34.

Shanahan, T., D. Fisher, K. Rubenson, and G. Jones. "Ontario." In *The Development of Postsecondary Education Systems in Canada: A Comparison between British Columbia, Ontario and Quebec, 1980-2010,* edited by D. Fisher, K. Rubenson, T. Shanahan, and C. Trottier, 121–200. Montreal: McGill-Queen's University Press, 2014.

Skolnik, M. "The Community College Baccalaureate: Its Meaning and Implications for the Organization of Postsecondary Education, the Mission and Character of the Community College, and the Bachelor's Degree." Paper presented at the annual Community College Baccalaureate Association conference, Florida, February 2001.

—. *Postsecondary Education in Canada: Thinking Ten Years into the Future.* Ottawa: Human Resources Development Canada, 2003.

—. "State Control of Degree Granting: The Establishment of a Public Monopoly in Canada." In *Governments and Higher Education: The Legitimacy of Intervention,* edited by C. Watson, 56–83. Toronto: Canada Higher Education Group, OISE, 1987.

Skolnik, M., and G. Jones. "Arrangements for Coordination between University and College Sectors in Canadian Provinces." *Canadian Journal of Higher Education* 23 (1993): 56–73.

Smith, D. "The Erosion of University Autonomy in Manitoba." *Canadian Journal of Educational Administration and Policy,* no. 154 (March 24, 2014). http://www.umanitoba.ca/publications/cjeap/pdf_files/smith.pdf.

Smith, P.M. "The Exclusive Jurisdiction of the University Visitor." *Law Quarterly Review* 97 (1981): 610–47.

Snowdon, K. *Without a Road Map: Government Funding and Regulation of Canada's Universities and Colleges.* Research Report W/31 Work Network. Ottawa: Canadian Policy Research Networks, 2005.

Snyder, R.M., ed. *Palmer & Snyder – Collective Agreement Arbitration in Canada.* 5th ed. Markham, ON: LexisNexis Canada, 2013.

Standing Senate Committee on Aboriginal Peoples. *Reforming First Nations Education: From Crisis to Hope.* Ottawa: Parliament of Canada. 2011.

Standing Senate Committee on Social Affairs, Science and Technology. *Opening the Door: Reducing Barriers to Post-secondary Education in Canada.* Ottawa: Parliament of Canada, 2011.

Standler, R.B. (1999, 2000). *Academic Freedom in the USA.* 1999, 2000. http://www.rbs2.com/afree.htm.

Statistics Canada. "Postsecondary Enrolments, by Registration Status, Pan-Canadian Standard Classification of Education (PCSCE), Classification of Instructional Programs, Primary Grouping (CIP_PG), Sex and Immigration Status." Table 477-0019. Accessed June 10, 2015. http://www5.statcan.gc.ca/cansim/a05?lang=eng&id=4770019.

—. *2008 Survey of IP Commercialization in the Higher Education Sector.* Ottawa: Statistics Canada, 2010. http://www.statcan.gc.ca/pub/88-222-x/88-222-x2010000-eng.pdf.

—. *University Tuition Fees, 2012/2013.* Statistics Canada catalogue no.11-001-X. Ottawa: Statistics Canada, 2012.

Stevenson, G. "Fiscal Federalism and the Burden of History." In *Fiscal Federalism and the Future of Canada: Selected Proceedings from the Conference.* Ottawa: Institute of Intergovernmental Relations, 2006.

Stonechild, B. "Pursuing the New Buffalo: First Nations Higher Education Policy in Canada." PhD diss., University of Regina, 2004.

Tamburri, R. "New Kid on the Block." *University Affairs* 52, no. 4 (2011): 22–25.

Thistle, W. "Major Legal Issues Facing Canadian Universities in the 90's." Paper presented at the 1994 annual conference of the Canadian Association of College and University Student Services, St. John's, New Brunswick, June 1994.

Thomson, M.M. *Law and Ethics in Biomedical Research: Regulation, Conflict of Interest, and Liability.* Edited by T. Lemmens and D.R. Waring. Toronto: University of Toronto Press, 2006.

Trinity Western University. "Community in Covenant." https://twu.ca/studenthandbook/university-policies/community-covenant-agreement.html#community-covenant.

Trottier, C., J. Bernatchez, D. Fisher, and K. Rubenson. "Quebec." In *The Development of Postsecondary Education Systems in Canada: A Comparison between British Columbia, Ontario and Quebec, 1980–2010,* edited by D. Fisher, K. Rubenson, T. Shanahan, and C. Trottier, 200–290. Montreal: McGill-Queen's University Press, 2014.

Tupper, A. "The Chrétien Government and Higher Education: A Quiet Revolution in Canadian Public Policy." In *How Ottawa Spends, 2003–2004,* edited by G.B. Doern, 105–17. Toronto: Oxford University Press, 2003.

Universities Canada. "Canada's Universities Adopt New Statement on Academic Freedom." Media release, October 25, 2011. http://www.univcan.ca/media-room/news-and-commentary/canadas-universities-adopt-new-statement-on-academic-freedom/.

Usher, A. *The Postsecondary Student Support Program: An Examination of Alternative Delivery Mechanisms: A Report to the Indian and Northern Affairs Canada.* Education Policy Institute, 2009.

University of Winnipeg Students' Association. Home page. 2014. http://theuwsa.ca/advocacy/canadian-federation-of-students/.

Van Slyke, P., and M. Friedman. "Employers Rights to Inventions and Patents of Its Officers, Directors and Employees." *American Intellectual Property Law Association Quarterly Journal* 18 (1990): 127–55.

Veitch, E. "Case Comment: Forestell v University of New Brunswick. Guess Who's Coming to Visit?" *New Brunswick Reports* 89, no. 2 (1988): 89–104.

Victoria R Proclamation, 1841. Reprinted in *Consolidated Royal Charter of Queen's University.* Kingston: Queen's University, 2011. http://www.queensu.ca/secretariat/index/RoyalCharter2011.pdf.

Weinrib, J., and G. Jones. "Largely a Matter of Degrees: Quality Assurance and Canadian Universities." *Policy and Society* 33, no. 3 (2014): 225–36.

Wellen, R., P. Axelrod, T. Shanahan, and R. Deasi Trilokekar. "The Making of a Policy Regime: Canada's Postsecondary Student Finance System since 1994." *Canadian Journal for Higher Education* 43, no. 3 (2012): 1–23.

Whyte, J. "Dispute Adjudication in the University." In *Universities and the Law,* edited by P. Thomas, 95–105. Winnipeg: Legal Research Institute of the University of Manitoba, 1975.

Winchester, I. "The Concept of University Autonomy an Anachronism?" In *The Professoriate – Occupation in Crisis,* edited by C. Watson, 29–42. Toronto: Higher Education Group, 1985.

Yang, S.Y. "University v. Student: Challenging the Contractual Understanding of Higher Education in Canada." *Lex Electronica* 14, no. 3 (2009): 1–30.
York University Development Corporation. *Success Stories: Archives of Ontario.* http://yudc.ca/successstories/.
Zinn, R. *The Law of Human Rights in Canada.* Looseleaf. Toronto: Canada Law Book, 2013.

Legislation

Accessibility for Ontarians with Disabilities Act, 2005, SO 2005, c 11
Adult Education and Training Act, RSNB 2011, c 101
Adult Learning Act, SNS 2010, c 31
Alberta Human Rights Act, RSA 2000, c A-25.5
Alberta Land Stewardship Act, SA 2009, c A-26.8, s 20(1)
Alberta Public Agencies Governance Act, SA 2009, c A-31.5
An Act respecting Duties on Transfers of Immovables, RSQ c D-15.1, s 2
An Act respecting Energy Conservation in Buildings, RSQ 2006, c E-1.1
An Act respecting Lakehead University, SO 1965 c 54, s 19
An Act respecting Land Use Planning and Development, RSQ, c A-19.1 s 145.14
An Act respecting Municipal Taxation, RSQ, c F-2.1, c 28
An act respecting the commission d'évaluation de l'enseignement collégial, CQLR c C-32.2
An Act respecting the conseil supérieur de l'éducation, CQLR c C-60
An Act respecting the Memorial University of Newfoundland, RSNL 1990, c M-7
An Act respecting the ministère de l'éducation, du loisir et du sport, CQLR c M-15
An Act respecting the Royal Institution for the Advancement of Learning, SQ 1861, c 17
An Act respecting the Université du Québec, CQLR c U-1
An Act respecting Trinity Western University [Title amended, 1972-65-2, 1985-63-3], SBC 1969, c 44
An Act respecting Université d'Ottawa, SO 1965, c 137, s 20
An Act to Grant Certain Powers to the Royal Institution for the Advancement of Learning, SQ 1962, c 101
An Act to Incorporate Laurentian University of Sudbury, SO 1960, c 151
An Act to Incorporate the University of Windsor, SO 1962, 1962 as amended in 1968, s 9
Apprenticeship and Certification Act, SNL 1999, c A-12.1
Apprenticeship and Industry Training Act, RSA 2000, c A-42
Apprenticeship and Occupational Certification Act, SNB 2012, c 19
Apprenticeship and Trades Qualifications Act, SNS 2003, c 1, s 1, amended 2006, c 23
Apprenticeship and Trades Qualifications Act, 2012 RSPEI 1988, c A-15.2
Apprenticeship, Trade and Occupation Certification Act, SNWT 2010, c 13
Apprenticeship, Trade and Occupations Certification Act and Regulations, RRNWT 1990, c A-8, as amended by R-024-98, R-039-98, R-077-98
Apprentice Training Act, RSY 2002, c 7
Assessment Act, RSBC 1996, c 20, s 27
Assessment Act, RSNS 1989, c 23, s 5(1)
Assessment Act, RSO 1990, c A.31, s 3(1) 4
Aurora College Act, RSNWT 1988, c A-7
Bankruptcy and Insolvency Act, RS 1985, c B-3, s 1; 1992, c 27, s 2

Bayh-Dole Act, PL 96-517, s 6(a), Dec 12, 1980, 94 Stat. 3018, (also known as the *University and Small Business Patent Procedures Act* of 1980)

British North America Act, 1867, SS 1867, c 3

Building Act, CQLR 2015 c E-1.1

Business Corporations Act, SBC 2002, c 57

Canada Act 1982 (UK), 1982, c 11

Canada Council for the Arts Act, RSC 1985, c C-2

Canada Education Savings Act, SC 2004, c 26

Canada Education Savings Regulations, SOR/2005-151

Canada Labour Code, RSC 1985, c L-2

Canada Savings Act, 2004, SC 2004, c 26

Canada Student Financial Assistance Act, SC 1994, c 28

Canada Student Financial Assistance Regulations, 1994, SOR/95-329

Canadian Charter of Rights and Freedoms, Part I of the *Constitution Act, 1982*, being Schedule B to the *Canada Act 1982* (UK), 1982, c 11

Canadian Environmental Assessment Act, SC 1992, c 37

Canadian Environmental Assessment Act, SC 2012, c 19, s 52

Cape Breton University Act, RSNS 1989, c 484

Charities Accounting Act, RSO 1990, c C.10, s 1(2)

Charter of Human Rights and Freedoms (Charte des Droits et Libertés de la Personne) SQ 1990, c 4

City of Toronto Municipal Code, 2010, c 415, s 415-6B

College Act, 1996, SNL 1996, c C-22.1

College and Institute Act, RSBC 1996, c 52

Community Colleges Act, SNS 1995-96, c 4

Concordia University Act, SQ 1948, c 91, s 7

Consolidation of Nunavut Arctic College Act, RSNWT 1988, c A-7 as amended

Consolidation of Occupational Training Agreements Act, RSNWT 1988, c16 (Supp)

Consolidation of Universities and Degree-Granting Institutions Act, SNu 2008, c 15

Corporations Act, RSO 1970, c 89

Copyright Act, RSC 1985, c C-42

Council on Higher Education Act, PSNL 2006, c C-37.001

Council on Post-secondary Education Act, 1997, SM 1996, c 38

Degree Authorization Act, SBC 2002, c 24

Degree Granting Act, RSNB 2011, c 140

Degree Granting Act, RSNL 1990, c D-5

Degree Granting Act, RSNS 1989, c 123, amended 2006, c 26

Degree-Granting Institution Authorizing Regulations, NS Reg 388/2008

Endangered Species Act, 2007, SO 2007, c 6 s 10(1)

Environmental Assessment Act, RSO 1990, c E.18

Environmental Assessment Act, SBC 2002, c 43

Environmental Management Act, SBC 2003, c 53 s 93

Financial Administration Act, RSA 2000, c F-12

First Nations University of Canada Act 2008

Freedom of Information and Protection of Privacy Act, RSBC 1996, c 165

Freedom of Information and Protection of Privacy Act, RSO 1990, c F.31

General and Vocational Colleges Act, CQLR c C-29

Higher Education Foundation Act, RSNB 2011, c 169

Higher Education Quality Council of Ontario Act, 2005, SO 2005, c 28, Sch G

Historic Resources Act, RSA 2000, c H-9 s 20

Holland College Act, RSPEI 1988, c H-6

Human Rights Act, amended SN 1991, c 12

Human Rights Act, RSNB 1973, c H-11

Human Rights Act, RSPEI 1988, c H-12

Human Rights Act, RSY 2002, c 116

Human Rights Act, SNu 2003, c 12

Human Rights Act, SNWT 2002, c 18

Human Rights Code, RSBC 1996, c 210

Human Rights Code, RSN 1990, c H-14

Human Rights Code, RSO 1990, c H-19

Human Rights Code, SM 1987-88, c 45

Income Tax Act, RSC 1985, c 1, s 118.6(1)

Income Tax Regulations, CRC c 945, s 3500, 3501(1)

Industrial Relations Act, RSNB 1973, c 1-4

Industry Training Authority Act, SBC 2003, c 34

Interpretation Act, RSBC 1996, c 238

Judicial Review Procedure Act, RSO 1990, c J.1

Labour Act, RSPEI 1988, c L-1

Labour Code, CQLR c C-27

Labour Relations Act, CCSM c L10

Labour Relations Act, RSNL 1990, c L-1

Labour Relations Act, SO 1995, c 1

Labour Relations Code, RSA 2000, c L-1

Labour Relations Code, RSBC 1996, c 244

Land Transfer Tax Act, RSO 1990, c L.6

Lobbying Act, RSC 1985, c 44 (4th Supp)

Local Government Act, RSBC 1996, c 323

Loi sur la Commission d'évaluation de l'enseignement collegial, CQLR c C-32.2

Loi sur la formation et la qualification professionnelle de la main-d'oeuvre (An Act respecting Workforce Vocational Training and Qualification), CQLR c F-5

Loi sur le conseil supérieur de l'éducation, CQLR c C-60

Loi sur le ministère de l'éducation, du loisir et du sport, CQLR c M-15

Loi sur l'enseignement privé (An Act respecting Private Education), CQLR c E-9.1

Loi sur les collèges d'enseignement général et professionnel (General and Vocational Colleges Act), CQLR c C-29

Loi sur les établissements d'enseignement universitaire (An Act respecting Educational Institutions at the University Level), CQLR c E-14.1

Maritime Provinces Higher Education Commission Act, CAP 1988, M-2

Maritime Provinces Higher Education Commission Act, RSNB 2011, c 187

Maritime Provinces Higher Education Commission Act, RSPEI 1988, c M-2.01

Maritime Provinces Higher Education Commission Act, 2004, SNS 2004, c 30

Memorial University Act, RSNL1990, c M-7

Ministry of Government Services Act, RSO 1990, c M.25

Ministry of Training Colleges and University Act, RSO 1990, c M.19, amended 2010

Municipal Code of Quebec, RSQ, c C-27.1

Municipal Government Act, RSA 2000, c M-26, s 362(1)

Municipal Government Act, SNS 1998, c 18

Municipalities Act, RSNB 1973, c M-22

Municipalities Act, RSPEI 1988, c M-13

Municipalities Act, 1999, SNL 1999, c M-24

New Brunswick Community Colleges Act, SNB 2010, c N-4.05, s 37

Nova Scotia Agricultural College Act, SNS 2008, c 7, s 27(4)

Occupational Training Act, RSY 2002, c 160

Ontario Assessment Act, RSO 1997, c 27 s 3(1)(4)

Ontario Colleges of Applied Arts and Technology Act, 2002, SO 2002, c 8, Sch F

Ontario College of Art and Design Act, 2002, SO 2002, c 8, Sch E

Ontario College of Trades and Apprenticeship Act, 2009, SO 2009, c 22

Ontario Development Charges Act, 1997, SO 1997, c 27, s 2(1)

Ontario Heritage Act, RSO 1990, c O-18, s 27(3)

Ontario Municipal Board Act, RSO 1990, c O-28, s 91

Not-for-Profit Corporations Act, 2010, SO 2010, c 15

Partnership Act, RMS 1987, c P30, CCSM c P30

Partnership Act, RSA 2000, c P-3

Partnership Act, RSBC 1996, c 348

Partnership Act, RSNB 1973, c P-4

Partnership Act, RSNL 1990, c P-3

Partnership Act, RSNS 1989, c 334

Partnership Act, RSNWT (Nu) 1988, c P-1; RSNWT 1998, c P-1

Partnership Act, RSO 1990, c P.5

Partnership Act, RSPEI 1988, c P-1

Partnership Act, RSS 1978, c P-3

Patent Act, RSC 1985, c P-4

Perpetuities Act, RSA 2000, c P-5, s 2

Perpetuities Act, RSO 1990, c P 9, ss 3 and 4

Perpetuities Act, RSPEI 1988, c P-3

Perpetuities and Accumulations Act, RSM 1987, c P33, CCSM c P33

Personal Information Protection and Electronic Documents Act, SC 2000, c 5

Planning Act, RSO 1990, c P-13 s 16(1)

Planning and Development Act, 2007, SS 2007 c P-13.2, s 214

Postsecondary Education Choice and Excellence Act, 2000, SO, c 36

Post-secondary Learning Act, SA 2003, c P-19.5

Private Career Colleges Act, SO 2005, c 28

Private Career Colleges Regulation Act, SNS 1998, c 23

Private Career Training Institutions Act, SBC 2003, c 79

Private Occupational Training Act, RSNB 1973, c P-16.1

Private Training Institutions Act, RSNL1990, c P-25

Private Training Schools Act, RSPEI 1988, c P-20.1

Private Vocational Schools Regulation Act, SS 1995, c P-26.2

Private Vocational Training Act, RSA 2000, c P-24

Property Transfer Tax Act, RSBC 1996, c 378, s 14(4)

Queen's University at Kingston Act, SC 1912, c 138, as amended by SC 2011, c 27

Real Property Tax Act, RSPEI 1988, c R-5 s 3(1)(f)

Royal Roads University Act, RSBC 1996, c 409

Ryerson University Act, 1977, SO 1977, c 47, s 16(1)

Sea to Sky University Act, SBC 2002, c 54

Society Act, RSBC 1979, c 390

The Advanced Education Administration Act, SM 2010, c 27, sch A

The Apprenticeship and Certification Act, CCSM c A110

The Apprenticeship and Trade Certification Act, SS 1999 A-22.2 REG 3

The Apprenticeship and Trade Certification (Designated Trades) Regulations, RRS c A-22.2 Reg 1

The Brandon University Act, SM 1998, c 48, CCSM c B90

The Colleges Act, SM 1991-92, c 26, CCSM c C150.1, s 18; amended in 2014

The Constitution Act, 1867, (30 & 31 Victoria), c 3

The Constitution Act, 1982, Schedule B to the Canada Act 1982 (UK), 1982, c 11

The Degree Authorization Act, SS 2012, c D-2.1

The Degree Granting Act, CCSM c D25

The Education Act, RSO 1990, c E.2

The Endangered Species Act, SM 1989-90, c 39, CCSM c E111, s 10(1)

The Environmental Assessment Act, SS 1979–80, c E-10.1

The Indian Act, RSC 1985, c I-5

The Local Freedom of Information and Protection of Privacy Act, SS 1990-91, c L-27.1

The Manitoba Institute of Trades and Technology Act, CCSM c T130

The Mennonite College Federation Act, CCSM c M105

The Municipal Act, SM 2005, c 40

The Municipal Act, SM 1996, c 58, CCSM c M225

The Municipalities Act, SS 2005, c M-36.1

The Private Vocational Institutions Act, CCSM c P137

The Providence University College and Theological Seminary Incorporation Act, RSM 1990, c 217

The Queen's Bench Act, 1998, SS 1998, c Q-1.01

The Regional Colleges Act, SS 1986-87-88, c R-8.1

The Saskatchewan Employment Act, SS 2013, c S15-1

The Saskatchewan Human Rights Code, SS1979, c S-24.1

The Saskatchewan Indian Institute of Technologies Act, SS 2000, c S-25

The Saskatchewan Polytechnic Act, SS 2014, c S-32.21

The Tax Administration and Miscellaneous Taxes Act, RSM 1987, c R150, CCSM c T2

The Université de Saint-Boniface Act, SM 2011, c 16

The University College of the North Act, SM 2004, c 16

The University of Manitoba Act, CCSM c U60

The University of Regina Act, RSS 1978 c U-5

The University of Saskatchewan Act, 1995, SS 1995, c U-6.1

The University of Winnipeg Act, SM 1998, c 50, CCSM c U70

The York University Act, 1965, SO 1965, c 143

Thompson Rivers University Act, SBC 2005, c 17

Trade Union Act, RSNS 1989, c 475

Trades Schools Regulation Act, RSY 2002, c 221

Transparency and Accountability Act, SNL 2004 c T-8.1

Trent University Act, SO 1962-63, c 192

Trustee Act, RSNS 1989, c 479, s 66(1)

Trustee Act, SS 2009, c T-23.01, s 58

Universities Act, RSA 2000, c U-3

University Act, RSBC 1996, c 468, s 54(1)

University Act, 2009 BCSC 425, rev'd 2010 BCCA 63, [2010] BCJ No 219, leave to appeal to SCC ref'd June 24, 2010, [2010] SCCA No 135

University Act, RSPEI 1974, c U-4
University College of the North Act, SM 2004, c 16
University Foundations Act, SNS 1991, c 8,
University of New Brunswick Act, SNB 1984, c 40
University of Ottawa Act, SO 1965, c 137, s 21
University of Toronto Act, SO 1971, c 56, as amended SO 1978, c 88, s 2(14)(l)
University of Western Ontario Act, SO 1988, c Pr 26
Yukon College Act, RSY 2002, c 234; amended by SY 2009, c 12

Cases

Aba-Alkhail v University of Ottawa, 2013 ONCA 633, 363 DLR (4d) 470
Abernethy v Hutchinson, (1825) 3 LJ (Ch) 209
Acadia University v Wolfville (Town) (1971), 29 DLR (3d) 441; 2 NSR (2d) 630 (CA)
Acadia University v Wolfville (Town) (1971), 2 NSR (2d) 630, 29 DLR (3d) 441 (CA)
Agduma-Silongan v University of British Columbia, 2003 BCHRT 22
Al-Bakkal v De Vries, 2003 MBQB 198, 176 Man R (2d) 127
AlGhaithy v University of Ottawa, 2012 ONSC 142
Algonquin College (College Employer Council for the Colleges of Applied Arts and Technology), and Ontario Public Service Employees Union (Full-time Appointments Grievance), [2012] OLAA No 5 (Knopf)
Al-Nowais v McGill University (Faculty of Medicine), 2013 QCCS 4559
Alsaigh v University of Ottawa, 2012 ONSC 2313
Anderson v University of Alberta, [1996] AJ No 1337(QL)(Alta QB)
Andrews v Law Society of British Columbia, [1989] SCJ No 6
Archer v Université de Moncton (1992), 129 NBR (2d) 289 (QB)
Assessors of Areas #1 and #10 v University of Victoria, 2010 BCSC 133
Assiniboine Community College v Manitoba Government and General Employees' Union, [2006] MGAD No 43 (Werier)
Assoc. des professeurs de l'Université Concordia c Université Concordia (grief de Petkov), 2014 LNSARTQ 42
Association of Professors of the University of Ottawa v University of Ottawa, [1999] OLAA No 945
Athabasca University Governing Council, and Canadian Union of Public Employees Local 3911 with respect to a Grievance concerning the Employee Status of Academic Coaches and Graduate Sessional Instructors (2012), 224 LAC (4th) 1 (Sims, QC)
Attaran v University of British Columbia, [1998] BCJ No 115 (QL)(BCSC)
Attorney General of Canada v Fiona Ann Johnstone and Canadian Human Rights Commission, 2013 FC 113
A.U.P.E. v University of Calgary, [2008] Alta LRBR 129
Aylward v McMaster University (1991), 79 DLR (4d) 119 (Ont Ct K (Gen Div))
B and W et al, 52 OR (2d) 738, 23 DLR (4d) 248
Baharloo v University of British Columbia, 2014 BCSC 762
Baker v Canada (Ministry of Citizenship and Immigration), [1999] 2 SCR 817
Balcilek v Kwantlen Polytechnic University, 2009 BCHRT 366
Bancroft v University of Toronto (1986), 53 OR (2d) 460, 24 DLR (4d) 620 (H Ct J)
Barbour v University of British Columbia, 310 DLR (4d) 130, [2009] 10 WWR 323; rev'd [2010] 316 DLR (4d) 354

Bareau v University of Alberta (1995), 35 Alta LR (3d) 403 (QB), aff'd 1999 ABCA
    202, leave to appeal refused (2000), 252 NR 400 (SCC)
Bason v American University, 414 A (2d) 522 (DC 1980)
Baxter v Memorial University of Newfoundland, 166 Nfld & PEIR 183, [1998] NJ
    No 222 (QL) (SC(TD))
Bell v St Thomas University (1992), 97 DLR (4d) 370, 130 NBR (2d) 31(NBQB)[*Bell*];
    Wong v University of Toronto (1989), 79 DLR (4d) 652, 45 Admin LR 113(Ont Dist
    Ct), aff'd (1992), 4 Admin LR (2d) 95 (Ont CA)
Bicknell v Air Canada (1984), 5 CHRR D/1992 (Can Trib)
Biggs v Hudson (1988), 9 CHRR D/5391 (BCHRC)
Bikey v University of Saskatchewan, 2009 SKQB 340
Bisaillon v Concordia University, 2006 SCC 19
Bitonti v British Columbia (Ministry of Health No. 3) (1999), 36 CHRR D/263 (BCHRT)
Blaber v University of Victoria (1995), 123 DLR (4d) 255 (BCSC)
Blass v University of Regina, 2012 SKQB 247, 400 Sask R 169
Blasser v Royal Institute for the Advancement of Learning et al (1985), 24 DLR (4d)
    507 (Qc CA)
Bloxam v Elsee, (1825) 1 Car & P 558
Boudreau v Lin, 150 DLR (4d) 324, [1997] OJ No 3397(QL) (Ont Ct J Gen Div)
Boyce v Westminster (City) (1994), 24 CHRR D/441 (BCCHR)
Brady v Interior Health Authority, [2007] BCHRTD No 231
Brewer v Fraser Milner Casgrain LLP, 2006 ABQB 258; appeal by Commission
    quashed 2008 ABCA 160; rev'd on other grounds 2008 ABCA 435; leave to ap-
    peal to SCC ref'd [2008] SCCA No 290
Brillinger v Brockie, [1999] OHRBID No 12
Brimacombe v Northland Road Services Ltd (1998), 33 CHRR D/53 (BCHRC)
British Columbia, Campbell River and North Island Transition Society, 2004 BCCA 260
British Columbia Civil Liberties Association v University of Victoria, 2015 BCSC 39
*British Columbia (Public Service Employee Relations Commission) v British Columbia
    Government Service Employees' Union*, [1999] 3 SCR 3, 66 BCLR (3d) 253
Brock University and Canadian Union of Public Employees, Local 4207, [2012] OLAA
    No 2 (Swan)
Brodie et al v Governors of Dalhousie College and University (8 March 1989), Halifax
    Claims 16743, 16744, 16745 (NS Sm Claims Ct)
Brown v Trebas Institute Ontario Inc, 2008 HRTO 10
Bubb-Clarke v Toronto Transit Commission (2002), 42 CHRR D/326 (Ont Bd Inq)
Burton v Chalifour Bros Construction Ltd (1994), 21 CHRR D/501 (BCCHR)
Canada (Labour Relations Board) v Yellowknife (City), [1977] 2 SCR 729
Capilano University Faculty Association v Capilano University, 2014 BCSC 712
Canpar v I.U.O.E., Local 115, 2003 BCCA 609
Carr v Atlantic Business College Ltd, 2007 NBQB 77
Carson v University of Saskatchewan, 2000 SKQB 322, 196 Sask R
Cash Converters Canada Inc v Oshawa (City), 2007 ONCA 502
C(D) (Litigation Guardian of) v Ridley College, 138 DLR (4d) 176, 1996 CarswellOnt
    2932 (WL Can) (Ont Ct J (Gen Div))
Central Alberta Dairy Pool v Alberta (Human Rights Commission), [1990] 2 SCR 489
Central Okanagan School District No 23 v Renaud, [1992] 2 SCR 970
Chamberlain v Surrey School District No. 36, [2002] 4 SCR 710

Charles I. Stastny v Board of Trustees of Central Washington (1982), Wash App LEXIS 2962

Chicoine v Ryerson Polytechnical Institute (1985), 15 Admin LR 261, 1985 CarswellOnt 901 (WL Can) (Ont Prov Ct (Civ Div Sm Cl Ct))

Ching v University of Windsor (1984), 3 OAC 228 (Div Ct)

C.I. Covington Fund Inc v White, [2000] 10 CPR (4th) 49 (SC)

Ciano v York University, [2000] OJ No 681(QL), 2000 CarswellOnt 633 (WL Can)(Sup Ct J), Winkler J; additional reasons, [2000] OTC 37, [2000] OJ No 183 (QL)(Sup Ct J), Winkler J; aff'd on other grounds, [2000] OJ No 3482 (QL), 2000 CarswellOnt 3248 (WL Can)(Ont CA), Feldman JA, Goudge JA, Laskin JA

City of Vancouver v Canadian Pacific Railway Co (1894), 23 SCR 1

College Institute Educators' Assn v British Columbia, 2002 BCSC 1480

Cominco Ltd v U.S.W.A., Local 9705, [2000] BCCAAA No 62 at para 181 (BC Arb)

Committee for Justice and Liberty v Canada (National Energy Board), [1978] 1 SCR 369 at 394–95, 68 DLR (3d) 716

Communications, Energy and Paperworkers Union, Local 707 v SMS Equipment Inc (Cahill-Saunders Grievance), [2013] AGAA No 41

Comstock Canada v Electec Ltd (1991), 45 FTR 241, 38 CPR (3d) 29 (FCTD)

Connell v University of British Columbia (1988), 21 BCLR (2d) 145 (CA)

Corporation de l'Ecole Polytechnique de Montreal v Fardad, 2010 QCCA 992

C.P.R. v A.G. for Saskatchewan, [1952] 2 SCR 231, 1952 CanLII 39 (SCC) 1952-06-30

Crerar v Grande Prairie Regional College, [2004] AJ No 905 (QL)(Prov Ct), rev'd [2004] AJ No 905 (QL)(QB)

Cruickshank v University of Lethbridge, 2010 ABQB 186

Dalhousie University v Dalhousie Faculty Assn, 2002 NSCA 1

Dandell v Thompson Rivers University, 2013 BCCA 490

Datt v McDonald's Restaurants of Canada Ltd, 2007 BCHRT 324

Dawson v The University of Ottawa (1994), 72 OAC 232 (Ont Div Ct)

Dean v University of Victoria and another, 2012 BCHRT 71

De Jong v Horlacher Holdings Ltd (1989), 10 CHRR D/6283 (BCHRC)

Delgamuukw v The Queen in Right of B.C., [1997] 3 SCL 1010

Deng v University of Toronto, 2011 ONSC 835 (CanLII)

Design Services Ltd v Canada, [2008] 1 SCR 737

Devoe-Holbein Inc. v. Yam (1984), 2 CIPR 229 (Que SC)

Dhillon v University of Alberta (General Facilities Council Academic Appeals Committee), 2000 ABQB 77, 81 Alta LR (3d) 65

Dickson v Canadore College, 287 DLR (4d) 570, [2007] OJ No 4125 (QL) (Ont Sup Ct J (Div Ct))

Dixon v Cabot College of Applied Arts, Technology and Continuing Education (1999), 177 Nfld & PEIR 162 (SC(TD))

Dolmage v Erskine, 23 CPR (4d) 495, [2003] OJ No 161 (QL) (Ont Sup Ct J)

Donaldo Pianezza Beauty Salon et al v Borough of North York et al, [1978] OJ No 3315, 19 OR (2d) 343

Double N Earthmovers Ltd v Edmonton, [2007] 1 SCR 116

Douglas/Kwantlen Faculty Assn v Douglas College, [1990] 3 SCR 570, 52 BCLR (2d) 68

Driver v Sault College of Applied Arts & Technology (2008), 165 ACWS (3d) 91, 2008 CarswellOnt 1374 (WL Can) (Ont Sup Ct J (Div Ct))

Dunne v Memorial University of Newfoundland, 2012 NLTD(G) 41; 321 Nfld & PEIR 342

Dunsmir v New Brunswick, [2008] 1 SCR 190

Dupuis v British Columbia (Ministry of Forests) (1993), 20 CHRR D/87 (BCCHR)

Dutton v British Colombia (Human Rights Tribunal), 2001 BCSC 1256

E v An Institution, [2010] BCHRTD No 212 (QL)

Eldridge v British Columbia (Attorney General), [1997] 3 SCR 624, 1997 CanLII 327

Entrop v Imperial Oil Ltd, [1996] OHRBID No 30 (Ont Bd Inq), affd [1998] OJ No 422 (Ont Div Ct), affd on this point [2000] OJ No 2689 (ONCA)

Faculty Assn of the University of British Columbia v University of British Columbia, 2010 BCCA 189, leave to appeal refused [2010] SCCA No 232

Faculty Assn of the University of Windsor v University of Windsor (1998), 59 OTC 216 (Ct J (Gen Div))

Fardad v Ecole Polytechnique, 2010 QCCA 992, [2010] QJ No 4729

Fenn v Yale University, 283 F Supp 2d 615 (2003 D Conn)

Ferrari v University of British Columbia, 2014 BCCA 18

Fiset v Gamble (1992), 18 CHRR D/81 (BCHRC)

Fisher v York University, 2011 HRTO 1229

Fornwald v Astrographic Industries Ltd (1996), 27 CHRR D/317 (BCCHR)

Frederick Zhang v University of Western Ontario, 2010 ONSC 6489 (CanLII)

Freeman-Maloy v York University (2006), 79 OR (3d) 401

Fufa v University of Alberta, 2012 ABQB 594, 543 AR 119

Gauthier v Saint-Germain, 2010 ONCA 309, 325 DLR (4d) 558

Gendron v Supply and Services Union of the Public Service Alliance of Canada, Local 50057, [1990] 1 SCR 1298

General Motors Acceptance Corp of Canada v Saskatchewan Government Insurance, 116 Sask R 36, [1994] 2 WWR 320 (CA)

Ghafourian v The Governing Council of the University of Toronto, 2010 HRTO 675

Giroux v Ontario (1984), 46 OR (2d) 276 (CA)

Gleason v Lethbridge Community College (1995), 36 Alta LR (3d) 103 (QB)

Goldberg v UBC, 2001 BCPC 0035

Gray v University of British Columbia-Okanagan Students' Union, 2007 BCHRT 424

Greater Glasgow Health Board's Application, [1996] RPC 207, (PatC)

Grochowich v Okanagan University College, 2004 BCCA 325

Grosz v University of British Columbia, 2005 BCHRT 70

Hague v University of British Columbia (1988), 21 BCLR (2d) 245, 47 DLR (4d) 150 (BCSC)

Hadjor v Homes First Society, [2010] OJ No 4079

Hafeez c Université McGill, [1996] JQ No 884

Hajee v York University (1985), 11 OAC 72, [1985] OJ No 1308 (QL) (Ont Div Ct)

Hancock v Algonquin College of Applied Arts and Technology (1981), 33 OR (2d) 257

Handa v University of Ottawa, [2008] OJ No 2589 (Ont Sup Ct)

Hannaford v Douglas College, 2000 BCHRT 25

Harelkin v University of Regina, [1979] 2 SCR 561, [1979] 3 WWR 676 [Harelkin], aff'g [1979] 3 WWR 673 (Sask CA), rev'g [1977] 3 WWR 754, 74 DLR (3d) 537 (Sask QB)

Harris v Camosun College (2000), 39 CHRR D/36

Harrison v British Columbia, [1990] 3 SCR 451

Harvey v Woodford Training Centre Inc, [2009] NLHRBID No 1

Hayat v University of Toronto, 181 DLR (4d) 496, [1999] OJ No 4238 (QL) (ONCA)

Hays v Sony Corp of America, 847 F 2d 412 (7th Cir 1988)

Hazanavicius v McGill University, 2008 QCCS 1617, 2008 CarswellQue 3458 (WL Can), Delorme JCS

Healey v Memorial University of Newfoundland (1993), 106 Nfld & PEIR 304, 14 Admin LR (2d) 259 (Nfld SC(TD))

Hickey v Everest Colleges Canada, 2009 HRTO 796

Hickey-Button v Loyalist College of Applied Arts & Technology, [2006] OJ No 2393 (QL)(CA)

Houston v University of Saskatchewan (Joint Senate-Council Board of Student Appeals), 1994 CanLII 4898 (SK QB)

Howard v University of British Columbia (1993), 18 CHRR D/353 (BCCHR)

Hurd v Hewitt (1994), 20 OR (3d) 639 (CA)

Ibrahim v Lakehead University, 2000 CarswellOnt 167 (WL Can)(Sup Ct J)

Innisfil (Township) v Shakell (1982), 19 MPLR 117, 37 DLR (3d) 117 (Ont CA)

Jaffer v York University, 2010 ONCA 654

Jalan v. Institute of Indigenous Government, 2005 BCSC 590

James v Northern Lakes College, 2012 ABQB 6

Janzen v Platy Enterprises Ltd., [1989] 1 SCR 1252

Jazairi v Ontario (Human Rights Commission), [1997] OJ No 1526 (Ct Jus Gen Div)

Jubran v North Vancouver School District No. 44, 2002 BCHRT 10

Justice Institute of British Columbia v British Columbia (1999), 17 Admin LR (3d) 267 (BCSC)

Kane v University of British Columbia, [1980] 1 SCR 1105, [1980] 3 WWR 125, 31 NR 214, 110 DLR (3d) 311

Kelly v University of British Columbia, 2013 BCHRT 302

Ketabchi v Future Shop Ltd, 2002 BCHRT 39

Khan v University of Ottawa (1997), 34 OR (3d) 535, 148 DLR (4d) 577

King v University of Saskatchewan (1968), 67 WWR 126, 1 DLR (3d) 721

Kobilke v Phillips, 2004 CanLII 7914 (Ont Sup Ct J)

Koh-Adelman v University of Saskatchewan, 2000 SKQB 303, 197 Sask R 103

Konieczna v Owners Strata Plan NW 2489 (No 2) (2003), 47 CHRR D/144 (BCHRT)

Kovacs v John's Bedrooms Barn and Foam Warehouse and Others, 2013 BCHRT 31

Kulchyski v Trent University, 2001 CarswellOnt 2759

Kwantlen College v Douglas and Kwantlen College Faculty Assn (Pawson Grievance), [1984] BCCAAA No 302 (MacDonald)

Lakehead University Board of Governors v Lakehead University Faculty Assn (Right to Privacy Grievance) (2009), 184 LAC (4th) 338 (Carrier)

Lakehead University (Board of Governors) v Lakehead University Faculty Assn (Shutdown Grievance), [2010] OLAA No 612 (Devlin)

Lakeland College Faculty Assn v Lakeland College, 1998 ABCA 221

Lalani v University of Toronto, 2014 ONSC 644

Lana v University of Alberta, 2013 ABCA 327, 91 Alta LR (5d) 250

Langara College v Langara Faculty Assn (Mirza Grievance), [2000] BCCAAA No 27 (Hall)

Laurentian University v Laurentian University Faculty Assn (Sessional Appointments Grievance), [2013] OLAA No 416 (Sheehan)

Lavigne v Canada (Office of the Commissioner of Official Languages), 2002 SCC 53, [2002] 2 SCR 773

Lavoie v University of Ottawa (1986), 55 OR (2d) 28, 27 DLR (4d) 763 (H Ct J)

Legge v Princess Auto and Machinery Ltd (1983), 4 CHRR D/1339 (Man Bd Adj)

Lerew v The St. Lawrence College of Applied Arts and Technology, 196 OAC 363, [2005] OJ No 1436 (QL) (Sup Ct J(Div Ct))

Lethbridge College v Lethbridge College Faculty Assn (Bird Grievance) (2007), 166 LAC (4th) 289 (Ponack, Chair)

Lisyikh v Canadian Law Enforcement Training College, [2007] OJ No 3621 (QL) (Ont SCJ)

Lobo v Carleton University, 2012 ONSC 254; aff'd 2012 ONCA 498

MacDonald v Acadia University, [1987] NSJ No 203 (QL) (NSSC(AD))

MacDonald v University of British Columbia, 2003 BCSC 1103, 18 BCLR (4d) 184

Machado v Vancouver College of Counsellor Training, [2007] BCHRTD No 430 (QL)

Mager v Louisiana-Pacific Canada Ltd (1998), 33 CHRR D/457 (BCHRT)

Mahe et al v Alberta (1990), 105 NR 321 (SCC)

Mahmoodi v University of British Columbia, [1999] BCHRTD No 52

Malaspina University-College v College Institute of Educators' Assn (Chen Grievance), [1999] BCCAAA No 419 (Blasina)

Martel Building Ltd v Canada, [2000] 2 SCR 860

Matoni v C.B.S. Interactive Multimedia Inc., 2008 CarswellOnt 7185 (WL Can) (Sup Ct J)

Matheson v School District No 53 (Okanagan Similkameen) and Collis, 2009 BCHRT 112

Matthews v Memorial University of Newfoundland (1991), 15 CHRR D/399, 1991 CarswellNfld 359 (WL Can)(Nfld Bd of Inquiry)

Maughan v University of British Columbia, 2009 BCCA 447

McBeth v Dalhousie College and University, 26 DLR (4d) 321, [1986] NSJ No 159(QL) (NSSC(AD))

McDonald v Mid-Huron Roofing, 2009 HRTO 1306

McGill University Health Centre v Syndicat des employes de l'Hopital General de Montreal, 2007 SCC 4

McKay v CDI Career Development Institutes Ltd (1999), 64 BCLR (3d) 386 (SC)

McKinney v University of Guelph (1986), 57 OR (2d) 1, 32 DLR (4d) 65, (H Ct J), aff'd (1987), 63 OR (2d) 1, 46 DLR (4d) 193, aff'd [1990] 3 SCR 229 at 52, 53

McNulty v G.N.F. Holdings Ltd (1992), 16 CHRR D/418 (BCCHR)

Memorial University of Newfoundland v Memorial University of Newfoundland Faculty Assn (Snook Grievance), [2007] NLLAA No 3 (Knopf, Chair)

Mikkelsen v University of Saskatchewan, 2000 SKQB 45, 191 Sask R 53

Miller v Thompson Rivers University, 2013 BCSC 2138

Miller v 409205 Alberta Ltd (2001), 42 CHRR D/311 (Alta HRP)

Miraglia v University of Waterloo, 2010 HRTO 1459

MJB Enterprises Ltd v Defence Construction (1951) Limited, [1999] 1 SCR 619

Mohamed v University of Saskatchewan, 2006 SKQB 23, 276 Sask R 87

Mohl v University of British Columbia, 2000 BCSC 1849, [2000] BCJ No 2572 (QL)

Montreal (City) v Montreal Locomotive Works Ltd (1946), [1947] 1 DLR 161 (Canada PC)

Moore v British Columbia (Education), 2012 SCC 61

Moore v British Columbia (Ministry of Education), 2005 BCHRT 580

Morgan v Acadia University, 69 NSR (2d) 109, [1985] NSJ No 74 (QL)(NSSC(TD))

Morgogh v Ottawa (City) (1980), 11 CHRR D/80 (Ont Bd Inq)

Mortazavi v University of Toronto, 2013 ONCA 655

Mpega v University of Moncton, 2001 NBCA 78, 240 NBR (2d) 349

Mulligan v Laurentian University, 2008 ONCA 523

Nadella v Kingston Education Group, Inc, 2009 BCSC 1143

Nazik Amdiss and University of Ottawa, Ltd., 2010 ONSC 4738

Neilson v Sandman Four Limited (1986), 7 CHRR D-3329 (BCCHR)

Nicola Valley Institute of Technology v Nicola Valley Institute of Technology Employees Assn, [2006] BCCAAA No 22 (Ready)

NLRB v Yeshiva University, 444 US 672 (USSC 1980)

Noah v Shuba, [1990] Ch D 14

Noble v York University, 2010 HRTO 878

Noël v Société d'énergie de la Baie James, 2001 SCC 39

Nunavut Teachers' Assn v Nunavut, 2010 NUCJ 13

Oak Bay Marina Ltd v British Columbia (Human Rights Commission) (2002), 217 DLR (4th) 747 (BCCA)

Ogden v Simon Fraser University, 1998 CarswellBC 3260 (WL Can), [1998] BCJ No 2288 (QL)(BC Prov Ct)

Okanagan College Board v Okanagan College Faculty Assn, [1982] BCCAAA No 250, citing *Faculty Assn of Vancouver City College (Langara) and Vancouver City College*, BCLRB No 60/74

Okanagan College Faculty Assn v Okanagan College, 2013 BCCA 561

Olar v Laurentian University (2007), 2007 Carswell Ont 3595, 49 CCLT (3d) 257, [2007] OJ No 2211, RC Gates J (Ont SCJ), 2008 ONCA 699 (CanLII)

Olar v Laurentian University, 2007 CanLII 20787 (Ont Sup Ct J), aff'd 2008 ONCA 699, 2008 CarswellOnt 10147 (WL Can)

Ontario Home Builders' Association v York Region Board of Education, [1996] 2 SCR 929, 1996 CanLII 164 (SCC) 1996-08-22

Ontario Human Rights Commission v Etobicoke, [1982] 1 SCR 202, 132 DLR (3d) 14

Ontario (Human Rights Commission) v Simpsons Sears Ltd, [1985] 2 SCR 536

O'Reilly v Memorial University of Newfoundland, 166 Nfld & PEIR 327, 1998 CarswellNfld 200 (WL Can) (SC(TD))

Ouimette v Lily Cups Ltd (1990), 12 CHRR D/19 (Ont Bd Inq)

Pacheco v Dalhousie University, 2005 NSSC 222, 238 NSR (2d) 1

Paine v University of Toronto (1981), 34 OR (2d) 770 (CA), leave to appeal to SCC refused (1982), 35 OR (2d) 528n

Palik v Lloydminster Public School Div No 99 (2006), 58 CHRR D/149

Parry Sound (District) Social Services Administration Board v OPSEU, Local 34, [2003] SCJ No 42

Pearlman v University of Saskatchewan, 2006 SKCA 105

Plews v Pausch, 2006 ABQB 607

Politzer v Metropolitan Homes Ltd, [1976] 1 SCR 363

Powlett and Powlett v University of Alberta et al, [1934] 2 WWR 209, 1934 CarswellAlta 25 (WL Can)(Alta SC (AD)); aff'g [1933] 3 WWR 322, 1933 CarswellAlta 39 (WL Can)(Alta SC)

Pratt v University of Lethbridge, 2001 ABCA 134, [2001] SCCA No 388

Pridgen v University of Calgary, [2012] ABCA 139 Can LII

Pridgen v University of Calgary, 2010 ABQB 644 (CanLII)

Québec (Commission des droits de la personne) v Habachi (1992), 18 CHRR D/485 (Que Trib)

R v Calder, [1996] 1 SCR 660

R v Dunsheath; Ex parte Meredith, [1950] 2 All ER 741 (KB)

R v Fegan (1993), 80 CCC (3d) 356

R v Keegstra, [1990] 3 SCR 697, 77 Alta LR (2d) 193

R v M (MR), [1998] 3 SCR 393

R. v. Sparrow, [1990] 1 SCR 1075

R v University of Saskatchewan, Ex parte King (1968), 1 DLR (3d) 721

R v Whatcott, 2012 ABQB 231

R v Whatcott, 2002 SKQB 399

Ramlall v Ontario Family Medicine Programs, 2012 ONSC 7260

Re B and W et al (1985), 52 OR (2d) 738 (sub nom B (Y) v W (R) 16 Admin LR 99
    23 DLR (4th) 248 (Ont HCJ)

Re Bruce and Toronto, [1971] 3 OR 62, 19 DLR (3d) 386 (Ont CA)

Re Edith Cavell Private Hospital v Hospital Employees' Union, Local 180 (1982), 6 LAC
    (3d) 229 (Hope, Chair)

Re Jamieson and Victoria Native Friendship Centre (1994), 22 CHRR D/250 (BCCHR)

Re Keyano College v Keyano College Faculty Association (1993), 34 LAC (4th) 182
    (Beattie, Chair)

Re McInnes and Simon Fraser University (1983), 52 BCLR 26, 3 DLR (4d) 708 (CA)

Re Okanagan College and Okanagan College Faculty Assn (Fu) (2007), 171 LAC (4d)
    310 (BC Arb Bd)

Re Polten and Governing Council of University of Toronto (1975), 8 OR (2d) 749, 59
    DLR (3d) 197 (Ont H Ct J)

Re University of Ottawa v Association of Professors of the University of Ottawa (1978),
    20 LAC (2d) 132 (Frankel, Chair)

Re William Scott & Co, BCLRB Decision No 46/76

Retail, Wholesale and Department Store Union v Canada Safeway Ltd (1999), 82 LAC
    (4th) 1 (Sask Arb Bd; aff'd 1999 SKQB 81; rev'd on other grounds 2000 SKCA 119

Richardson v University of St Michael's College (1995), 87 OAC 302 (CJ (Gen Div))

Rittenhouse-Carlson v Portage College, 2009 ABQB 342, [2009] 11 WWR 277, Gill J

Roback v University of British Columbia, 2007 BCSC 334

Robichaud v Canada (Treasury Board), [1987] 2 SCR 84

Robinson (Trustee of) v The Queen, [1998] 2 FC 569 (FCA)

Rothery v Grinnell (2000), 262 AR 182 (QB)

Royal Bank of Canada v Workmen's Compensation Board of Nova Scotia, [1936] SCR
    560, 1936 CanLII 39 (SCC) 1936-06-17

Ruiperez v Board of Governors of Lakehead University (1983), 41 OR (2d) 552 (CA)

R.W.D.S.U. v Dolphin Delivery Ltd, [1986] 2 SCR 573

Ryder v Cooper Market Ltd (1990), 13 CHRR D/38 (BCCHR)

Ryerson University v Municipal Property Assessment Corp, 2005 MPLR (4th) 4 (SCJ)

Ryerson University v Ryerson Faculty Assn (Norrie Grievance), [2012] OLAA No 608

Said v University of Ottawa, 2011 ONSC 6179

Scallen v Regents of University of New Mexico, 321 F (3d) 1111 (Fed Cir)

Schnurr v Douglas College, [2007] BCHRTD No 40

SDL v University of Alberta, 2012 ABQB 244, 531 AR 218

Shank v University of Toronto, 57 OR (3d) 559, [2002] OJ No 50 (QL)(Sup Ct J (Div Ct))

Shaw v Levac Supply Ltd (1990), 14 CHRR D/36 (Ont Bd Inq)

Shaw v Regents of the University of California (1997), 58 Cal App 4th 44

Simon Fraser University v Burnaby (District) (1968), 67 DLR (2d) 638 (BCSC), aff'd
    1 DLR (3d) 427 (BCCA)

Simpson v University of Guelph, 1982 CarswellOnt 2792 (Ont H Ct J)

Singer v Regents of the University of California, 1996 WL 775106 (Cal App Super, 1996)

Singer et al v Regents of University of California, 1997 WL 34594173 (California Court of Appeal)

Singh v University of British Columbia, 2010 BCCA 485

Sotiropoulos v York University, 2009 HRTO 2278 (CanLII)

Speck v North Carolina Dairy Foundation, 391 SE (2d) 139 (NC 1984)

Spiroll Corp v Putti (1976), 77 DLR (3d) 761, [1976] BCJ No 788 (SC)

Stephenson Jordan & Harrison Ltd v MacDonald and Evans, (1951) 69 RPC 10 CA

Stoffman v Vancouver General Hospital, [1991] 1WWR 577 (SCR)

Strofolino v Helmstadter (2001), 55 OR (3d) 138 (Sup Ct J)

Students' Union, University of Alberta v University of Alberta (1990), 67 DLR (4d) 593

Sutcliffe v Governors of Acadia University (1978), 95 DLR (3d) 95 (NSSC); aff'g (1978), 85 DLR (3d) 115 (NS Co Ct)

Sylvester v British Columbia Society of Male Survivors of Sexual Abuse, 2002 BCHRT 14

Senyck v WFG Agency Network (No 2), 2008 BCHRT 376

Syndicat des professeurs et professeures de l'Université Laval c Université Laval, [1998] JQ No 450 (CA)

Tanchak v Locke Property Management Ltd, [1997] BCHRTD No 27

Tang v McMaster University, 2014 HRTO 92

Techform Products Ltd v Wolda, [2000] 5 CPR (4th) 25 (SC), rev'd on other grounds [2001] 15 CPR (4th) 44 (CA), leave to SCC denied [2001] SCCA No 603

Technical University of Nova Scotia v Collins (1990), 97 NSR (2d) 76 (SCTD)

Tercon Contractors Ltd v British Columbia (Ministry of Transportation and Highways), 2010 SCC 4

Tervit v Canadian College of English Language, 2014 BCHRT 53

The Neighbourhoods of Winfields Limited Partnership v Death, 2009 ONCA 277

The Queen (Ontario) v Ron Engineering, [1981] 1 SCR 111

Thorne v University of London, [1966] 2 All ER 338 (CA), cited with approval in Houston v University of Saskatchewan (Joint Senate-Council Board of Student Appeals), 117 Sask R 291, [1994] 4 WWR 387 (QB)

Trend College (Kelowna) Ltd v British Columbia (Private Post-Secondary Education Commission), 2001 BCSC 905, [2001] BCJ No 1280 (QL)

Trent University Faculty Association v Trent University (Yee Grievance) (2009), 188 LAC (4th) 254 (Cummings)

Trident Holdings Limited v Danand Investments Limited (1988), 64 OR (2d) 65, 49 DLR (4th) 1; 39 BLR 296; 25 OAC 378

Trinity College v Levinter (1923), 54 OR 290 (Ont CA)

Turner v York University, 2012 ONSC 4272, 298 OAC 174

UFCW, Local 401 v Alberta Human Rights and Citizenship Commission, 2003 ABCA 246

Universite de Sherbrooke v Beaudoin, 2010 QCCA 28

University of Alberta v Edmonton (City), [2005] AJ No 421

University of Alberta (Re), [2001] AIPCD No 18 (QL)

University of British Columbia v Berg, [1993] 2 SCR 353, 79 BCLR (2d) 273

University of British Columbia v Faculty Assn of the University of British Columbia (Lund Grievance), [2012] BCCAAA No 26 (Hall)

University of British Columbia v Faculty Assn of the University of British Columbia (Tenure Policy Grievance), [2007] BCCAAA No 175 (Taylor, QC) at para 10, citing St Michael's College v Richardson, 1994, unreported

University of British Columbia v Magolan, 2008 BCPC 299, 2008 CarswellBC 2267(WL Can)(BC Prov Ct), Armstrong J.

University of British Columbia v University of British Columbia Faculty Assn, 2007 BCCA 201, leave to appeal refused [2010] SCCA No 232

University of British Columbia Faculty Assn v University of British Columbia (2004), 125 LAC (4d) 1

University of British Columbia Faculty Association v University of British Columbia, 2010, BCCA 189 (Canlii)

University of British Columbia (Re), [2007] BCIPCD No 30 (QL)

University of Calgary Faculty Assn v University of Calgary, [1999] AGAA No 104 (Sims, Chair)

University of Guelph v Canadian Union of Public Employees, Local 3913 (Bell Grievance), [2005] OLAA No 440

University of Manitoba and University of Manitoba Faculty Assn (Re), [1993] MGAD No 116 (Bowman)

University of Manitoba Faculty Association v University of Manitoba, [1991] MGAD No 19 (Schulman)

University of New Brunswick v New Brunswick (Human Rights Commission), 2013 NBQB 148

University of Ottawa v Assn of Professors of the University of Ottawa (Rancourt Grievance), [2008] OLAA No 356 (Picher)

University of Ottawa and Association of Professors of the University of Ottawa (Rancourt Grievance), unreported January 27, 2014 (Foisy, QC)

University of Saskatchewan v Professional Association of Interns and Residents of Saskatchewan, 2002 SKCA 75, 219 Sask R 244

University of Saskatchewan v Women 2000, 2005 SKQB 342, 267 Sask R 33

University of Sherbrooke v Beaudoin, 2010 QCCA 28, [2010] RJQ 89

University of Victoria v University of Victoria Faculty Assn, BCLRB No B190/99

University of Waterloo v Faculty Assn of University of Waterloo (Pan Grievance) (2007), 168 LAC (4th) 1 (Shime)

University of Waterloo v Ontario (Minister of Finance), [2002] 166 OAC 262 (CA)

University of Western Australia v Gray, [2008] FCA 498

University of Western Ontario v University of Western Ontario Faculty Assn (Rao Grievance), [2010] OLAA No 14 (Brent)

University of Windsor v Faculty Assn of the University of Windsor (Taboun) (Re) (2002), 112 LAC (4th) 1 (Adell, Chair)

University of Windsor v Windsor (City) Assessment Commissioner, 1965 CarswellOnt 131, [1965] 2 OR 455

Vancouver Community College v Vancouver Community College Faculty Assn (Grimman Grievance) (1994), 46 LAC (4th) 72 (Thompson)

Van der Peet v the Queen, [1996] 2 SCR 507

Vanek v University of Alberta, [1974] 3 WWR 167 (Alta SC), aff'd 57 DLR (3d) 595 (Alta CA)

Vatamanu v Baird, [2009] OJ No 5481 (QL)(Ont Sup Ct J)

Victoria (City) v University of Victoria, [1972] SCR 160

Wade v Strangway (1996), 132 DLR (4th) 406 (BCCA)

Waichenberg v University of British Columbia, 2006 CarswellOnt 4526 (WL Can), [2006] OJ No 3066 (QL) (Ont Sup Ct J)

Walia v University of Manitoba, 2013 MBCA 61

Wang v Humber Institute of Technology and Advanced Learning, 2011 HRTO 29 (CanLII)

Wanke v University of Calgary, 2011 ABCA 235

Webb v Simon Fraser University (1978), 83 DLR (3d) 244 (BCSC)

Weber v Ontario Hydro, [1995] 2 SCR 929

Weinstein v University of Illinois, 811 F (2d) 1091 (7th Cir 1987)

Whistler Village Land Co v North Shore-Squamish Valley Area Assessor, 1981 15 MPLR 192, 121 DLR (3d) 284 (BCSC)

Wiebe v Saskatchewan Institute of Applied Science & Technology, 2007 SKQB 60

Wilfrid Laurier University Faculty Assn v Wilfrid Laurier University (Harvey Grievance), [1997] OLAA No 568 (Adell)

Williams v University of British Columbia, 2007 BCSC 996, 2007 CarswellBC 1587 (WL Can)

Wilson v Douglas Care Manor Ltd (1992), 21 CHRR D/74 (BCCHR)

Wilson v Transparent Glazing Systems Ltd, 2008 BCHRT 50

Wilson v University of Calgary (Board of Governors), 2014 ABQB 190

Windsor University Faculty Assn v University of Windsor (Beaudrie Grievance), [2013] OLAA No 398 (Watters)

Wong v Lakehead University, [1991] OJ No 1901 (QL)(Ont Ct J)

Wong v University of Toronto (1989), 79 DLR (4d) 652 (Ont Dis Ct);

Woodward Stores (British Columbia) Ltd v McCartney, (1982) 3 CHRR D/1113

Yee v Trent University, 2010 ONSC 3307

Yen v Alberta (Advanced Education), 2010 ABQB 380

Yeshiva University v Greenberg, 681 NYS 2d 71 (App Div 1998)

York University General Accountant v Bloxam (1984), 15 Admin LR 51, 1984 CarswellOnt 779 (WL Can) (Ont Sm Cl Ct)

York University v Strazds et al, (10 October, 1985), (Ont SM Claims) [unreported]: apartment leases

York University v Strazds, 1985 CarswellOnt 3299 (WL Can) (Prov Ct (Sm Cl Div))

York University v York University Faculty Assn (Contract Grievance), [2002] OLAA No 945

York University v York University Faculty Assn (FES Workload Grievance), [2013] OLAA No 389 (Kaplan)

York University v York University Faculty Assn (Noble Grievance) (2007), 167 LAC (4th) 39 (Goodfellow)

York University Faculty Assn v York University (Policy Grievance) (2013), 231 LAC (4th) 288 (Larry)

Young v Bella, 2006 SCC 3, [2006] 1 SCR 108

Zaryski v Loftsgard (1995), 22 CHRR D/256, 1995 CarswellSask 946 (WL Can) (Sask Bd Inq)

Zeliony v Red River College, 2007 MBQB 308

CONTRIBUTORS

Li-Jeen Broshko, general counsel, Simon Fraser University, Burnaby, British Columbia

Brent Davis, manager and legal counsel, Research Contracts and Legal Affairs, McMaster University, Hamilton, Ontario

Patrick Gilligan-Hackett, lawyer, Gilligan-Hackett & Company, Barristers and Solicitors, Vancouver, British Columbia

David Hannah, director of student services at James Cook University in Queensland, Australia; former associate vice-president, Student Affairs, University of Saskatchewan

Wendy L. Kraglund-Gauthier, faculty member, Faculty of Education, St. Francis Xavier University, Antigonish, Nova Scotia

Christopher M. Lennon, lawyer, Richards Buell Sutton, LLP, Barristers and Solicitors, Vancouver, British Columbia

Jeffrey J. Lowe, lawyer, Richards Buell Sutton, LLP, Barristers and Solicitors, Vancouver, British Columbia

Peter Mercer, president of Ramapo College of New Jersey; former dean, Faculty of Law, University of Western Ontario and former vice-president, Administration, University of Western Ontario, London

Pamela Murray, lawyer, Gilligan-Hackett & Company, Barristers and Solicitors, Vancouver, British Columbia

Michelle Nilson, associate professor, Faculty of Education, Simon Fraser University, Burnaby, British Columbia

Lou Poskitt, lawyer, Harris & Company LLP, Barristers and Solicitors, Vancouver, British Columbia

Theresa Shanahan, lawyer and associate professor, York University; former associate dean of the Faculty of Education, York University, Toronto, Ontario

David Stack, QC, McKercher LLP, Barristers and Solicitors, Saskatoon, Saskatchewan

McCarthy Tétrault, LLP, Barristers and Solicitors, Vancouver, British Columbia

Magdalena Wojda, lawyer, currently engaged in graduate studies at the University of British Columbia,Vancouver, British Columbia

David C. Young, associate professor, Faculty of Education, St. Francis Xavier University, Antigonish, Nova Scotia

INDEX

Queen's Policy Studies
Recent Publications

The Queen's Policy Studies Series is dedicated to the exploration of major public policy issues that confront governments and society in Canada and other nations.

Manuscript submission. We are pleased to consider new book proposals and manuscripts. Preliminary inquiries are welcome. A subvention is normally required for the publication of an academic book. Please direct questions or proposals to the Publications Unit by email at spspress@queensu.ca, or visit our website at: www.queensu.ca/sps/books, or contact us by phone at (613) 533-2192.

Our books are available from good bookstores everywhere, including the Queen's University bookstore (http://www.campusbookstore.com/). McGill-Queen's University Press is the exclusive world representative and distributor of books in the series. A full catalogue and ordering information may be found on their website (**http://mqup.mcgill.ca/**).

For more information about new and backlist titles from Queen's Policy Studies, visit http://www.queensu.ca/sps/books.

School of Policy Studies

The Politics of Canadian Foreign Policy, 4th edition, Kim Richard Nossal, Stéphane Roussel, and Stéphane Paquin (eds.) 2015. ISBN 978-1-55339-443-3

Thinking Outside the Box: Innovation in Policy Ideas, Essays in Honour of Thomas J. Courchene, Keith G. Banting, Richard P. Chaykowski, and Steven F. Lehrer (eds.) 2015. ISBN 978-1-55339-429-7

Toward a Healthcare Strategy for Canadians, A. Scott Carson, Jeffrey Dixon, and Kim Richard Nossal (eds.) 2015. ISBN 978-1-55339-439-6

Work in a Warming World, Carla Lipsig-Mummé and Stephen McBride (eds.) 2015. ISBN 978-1-55339-432-7

Lord Beaconsfield and Sir John A. Macdonald: A Political and Personal Parallel, Michel W. Pharand (ed.) 2015. ISBN 978-1-55339-438-9

Canadian Public-Sector Financial Management, Second Edition, Andrew Graham 2014. ISBN 978-1-55339-426-6

The Multiculturalism Question: Debating Identity in 21st-Century Canada, Jack Jedwab (ed.) 2014. ISBN 978-1-55339-422-8

Government-Nonprofit Relations in Times of Recession, Rachel Laforest (ed.) 2013. ISBN 978-1-55339-327-6

Intellectual Disabilities and Dual Diagnosis: An Interprofessional Clinical Guide for Healthcare Providers, Bruce D. McCreary and Jessica Jones (eds.) 2013. ISBN 978-1-55339-331-3

Rethinking Higher Education: Participation, Research, and Differentiation, George Fallis 2013. ISBN 978-1-55339-333-7

Making Policy in Turbulent Times: Challenges and Prospects for Higher Education, Paul Axelrod, Roopa Desai Trilokekar, Theresa Shanahan, and Richard Wellen (eds.) 2013. ISBN 978-1-55339-332-0

Building More Effective Labour-Management Relationships, Richard P. Chaykowski and Robert S. Hickey (eds.) 2013. ISBN 978-1-55339-306-1

Navigationg on the Titanic: Economic Growth, Energy, and the Failure of Governance, Bryne Purchase 2013. ISBN 978-1-55339-330-6

Measuring the Value of a Postsecondary Education, Ken Norrie and Mary Catharine Lennon (eds.) 2013. ISBN 978-1-55339-325-2

Immigration, Integration, and Inclusion in Ontario Cities, Caroline Andrew, John Biles, Meyer Burstein, Victoria M. Esses, and Erin Tolley (eds.) 2012. ISBN 978-1-55339-292-7

Diverse Nations, Diverse Responses: Approaches to Social Cohesion in Immigrant Societies, Paul Spoonley and Erin Tolley (eds.) 2012. ISBN 978-1-55339-309-2

Making EI Work: Research from the Mowat Centre Employment Insurance Task Force, Keith Banting and Jon Medow (eds.) 2012. ISBN 978-1-55339-323-8

Managing Immigration and Diversity in Canada: A Transatlantic Dialogue in the New Age of Migration, Dan Rodríguez-García (ed.) 2012. ISBN 978-1-55339-289-7

International Perspectives: Integration and Inclusion, James Frideres and John Biles (eds.) 2012. ISBN 978-1-55339-317-7

Dynamic Negotiations: Teacher Labour Relations in Canadian Elementary and Secondary Education, Sara Slinn and Arthur Sweetman (eds.) 2012. ISBN 978-1-55339-304-7

Where to from Here? Keeping Medicare Sustainable, Stephen Duckett 2012. ISBN 978-1-55339-318-4

International Migration in Uncertain Times, John Nieuwenhuysen, Howard Duncan, and Stine Neerup (eds.) 2012. ISBN 978-1-55339-308-5

Centre for International and Defence Policy

Afghanistan in the Balance: Counterinsurgency, Comprehensive Approach, and Political Order, Hans-Georg Ehrhart, Sven Bernhard Gareis, and Charles Pentland (eds.), 2012. ISBN 978-1-55339-353-5

Institute of Intergovernmental Relations

Canada: The State of the Federation 2012, Loleen Berdahl, André Juneau, and Carolyn Hughes Tuohy (eds.), 2015. ISBN 978-1-55339-210-1

Canada: The State of the Federation 2011, Nadia Verrelli (ed.), 2014. ISBN 978-1-55339-207-1

Canada and the Crown: Essays on Constitutional Monarchy, D. Michael Jackson and Philippe Lagassé (eds.), 2013. ISBN 978-1-55339-204-0

Paradigm Freeze: Why It Is So Hard to Reform Health-Care Policy in Canada, Harvey Lazar, John N. Lavis, Pierre-Gerlier Forest, and John Church (eds.), 2013. ISBN 978-1-55339-324-5

Canada: The State of the Federation 2010, Matthew Mendelsohn, Joshua Hjartarson, and James Pearce (eds.), 2013. ISBN 978-1-55339-200-2

The Democratic Dilemma: Reforming Canada's Supreme Court, Nadia Verrelli (ed.), 2013. ISBN 978-1-55339-203-3